JOURNEYS TO HEAVEN AND HELL

Tours of the Afterlife in the
Early Christian Tradition

BART D. EHRMAN

Yale
UNIVERSITY PRESS
New Haven and London

Yale University Press books may be purchased in quantity for educational, business, or promotional use. For information, please e-mail sales.press@yale.edu (U.S. office) or sales@yaleup.co.uk (U.K. office).

Set in Janson type by Newgen North America.
Printed in the United States of America.

Library of Congress Control Number: 2021942673
ISBN 978-0-300-25700-7 (hardcover : alk. paper)

A catalogue record for this book is available from the British Library.

This paper meets the requirements of ANSI/NISO Z39.48-1992 (Permanence of Paper).

10 9 8 7 6 5 4 3 2 1

To Radd
Who shares my name, my birthday, and my love of antiquity

Contents

Acknowledgments

I HAVE SPENT A good deal of my life thinking about heaven and hell; these past four years have been especially intense. I thank the institutions and individuals who have helped me reach the happy end of this particular literary adventure, a virtual katabasis. As the Sibyl says, going into the underworld is easy—no effort required. "But to retrace your step and escape to the air above, this is the toil, this the labor" (*hoc opus, hic labor est; Aen.* 6.128–29).

At an early stage of my work, I applied for funding and am highly grateful to have received it. In 2018–2019 I was awarded a fellowship at the National Humanities Center. This is one of the great institutions supporting the humanities not just in the country but in the world. My thanks to Robert Newman, President and Director of the NHC; to all the staff, who were helpful beyond words; and to my fellow fellows for the year, with whom I enjoyed hours of food, drink, and dialogue, intellectual and otherwise, intercalated among long periods of research solitude.

That same year I was also awarded a Guggenheim Fellowship, and the administration of the foundation kindly allowed me to defer it for twelve months so that I could accept the offer from the NHC as well. The Guggenheim, obviously, is one of the truly great fellowships available to academics in an enormous range of fields. I know of none better. I am deeply thankful for having received it.

Finally, the University of North Carolina at Chapel Hill, my beloved home institution, generously allowed me to accept both fellowships, giving me two solid years of relief from teaching and administrative duties to devote to research. In particular, I thank Terry Rhodes, Dean of the College of Arts and Sciences; Elizabeth Engelhardt, Senior Associate Dean of Fine Arts and Humanities; Barbara Ambrose, our long-suffering chair of the Department of Religious Studies; and all of my colleagues in the department, an impressive array of scholars and teachers with whom I am proud to be associated.

Special thanks go to individuals who helped me with the research and writing of the book. Because of the wide range of texts and traditions involved I asked well-established experts in various fields to read appropriate sections for suggestions and comments. They did so with enthusiasm, both improving the book and saving me from numerous faux pas. Some of these I've known for a long time; all of them, now, are friends for life:

- Janet Downie, Associate Professor of Classics, University of North Carolina at Chapel Hill
- Mark Goodacre, Frances Hill Fox Professor of Religious Studies, Duke University
- Zbigniew Izydorczyk, Professor of English, University of Winnipeg
- Sarah Isles Johnston, College of Arts and Sciences Distinguished Professor of Religion, The Ohio State University
- James O'Hara, George L. Paddison Professor of Latin, University of North Carolina at Chapel Hill
- David Reeve, Delta Kappa Epsilon Distinguished Professor of Classics, University of North Carolina at Chapel Hill
- Loren T. Stuckenbruck, Professor, Evangelisch-theologische Fakultät, Ludwig-Maximilians-Universität München

Two of my oldest and dearest friends who have broad expertise in New Testament studies but have never (till now) been heavily invested in ancient katabasis performed a work of supererogation by reading the entire manuscript with the eyes of highly trained professionals in a cognate field. This was a significant labor of love. On the other hand, they owe me, since I introduced them over two decades ago:

- Jeffrey Siker, Professor of Biblical Studies, emeritus, Loyola Marymount University
- Judy Siker, Vice President and Professor of New Testament, emerita, San Francisco Theological Seminary

In addition, five seasoned scholars with deep expertise in the broad range of this material generously read and shared their knowledge in comments on the entire manuscript, making numerous suggestions to improve the work and help me save face.

- Harry Attridge, Sterling Professor of New Testament, emeritus, Yale Divinity School
- Jan Bremmer, Professor of Religious Studies and Theology, emeritus, University of Groningen
- Tobias Nicklas, Professor of New Testament Studies at the Faculty of Catholic Theology and—of particular importance for this project—Director of the Beyond Canon Centre, University of Regensburg, Germany
- Pierluigi Piovanelli, Professor of Classics and Religious Studies, Faculty of Arts, University of Ottawa
- Zlatko Plese, my colleague and friend, Professor of Religious Studies, University of North Carolina at Chapel Hill

I also thank my current PhD student and research assistant, Michelle Freeman, who undertook a number of investigative projects connected with the work and made helpful comments on the chapters. Michelle is industrious and insightful; you will be hearing more from her.

In addition I thank the members of a reading group I have been running for lo these many years. The group is named Christianity in Antiquity and so, of course, we call it the CIA. It comprises graduate students and faculty from both UNC and Duke working in (or around) New Testament studies and early Christianity. Once a month we spend an often intense evening over assorted beverages to discuss a paper one of us has produced. On two occasions over the past year the group has engaged with selections from my book; each time I survived the onslaught, and the book emerged better for it.

I am especially grateful to Jennifer Banks, my editor at Yale University Press, whom I've known for years but now, at last, I have had a chance to work with. It has been a very pleasant experience indeed. Jennifer was excited about the book when she first heard of it, she enthusiastically pursued the possibility of publishing it, and throughout the process she has been inordinately helpful. May her editorial tribe increase.

Finally, two of my readers have long been part of my life. First is Sarah T. Beckwith, Katherine Everett Gilbert Distinguished Professor of English at Duke University, not only my beloved partner but also an inordinately passionate intellectual and the best reader of texts I know. Sarah has yet again made unusually insightful comments on my work and helped me see things I never would have seen on my own.

Second is my brother, Radd K. Ehrman, Professor of Classics at Kent State University, who has been reading Homer and Virgil since I was playing Little League and has never refused a plea for help on philological obscurities. Radd has thought about katabasis since taking a graduate seminar on the topic back in the 1970s, and he has a personal interest in visionary experience in general, as the translator of three volumes of Hildegard of Bingen (Oxford University Press). I dedicate the book to him.

JOURNEYS TO HEAVEN
AND HELL

Introduction

The Well-Trodden Paths

SCHOLARS HAVE PAID surprisingly little attention to the "journeys to the afterlife" in the early Christian tradition.[1] The oldest surviving account is the *Apocalypse of Peter*, first circulated in the early part of the second century CE; the most famous is the late-fourth-century *Apocalypse of Paul*, probably known to Dante. Important as well are two near death experiences narrated in the *Acts of Thomas* and Christ's descent to hell in the *Gospel of Nicodemus*, one of the most theologically influential narratives from outside the biblical canon. All these visits of the living to the realms of the dead informed Christian imagination and played significant roles in Christian theology, ethics, and evangelism. It is difficult to explain their relatively sparse treatment.

This book engages in a series of comparative analyses of these texts, situating them in relation to otherworldly journeys in select Greek, Roman, and Jewish traditions as well as to one another. Many other comparanda could be considered, but my goal is not to provide an exhaustive analysis. I also explore the transmission histories of two of the Christian accounts, showing how their texts were changed over time by editors and scribes who apparently did not fully appreciate their original claims. In every case I work to show how each account's historical, cultural, religious, and intellectual contexts affect and illuminate its meaning. Most important, I assess how each journey, Christian and non-Christian, uses the realities of death to explore the meaning of life, promoting distinctive

perspectives, attitudes, behaviors, and, at least for Christian iterations, beliefs for those who have not yet reached the end of their mortal existence.

These have not been the typical goals of research in this field. Modern
scholarship on early Christian otherworldly journeys began almost immediately after the publication of the *editio princeps* of the *Apocalypse of Peter*
by U. Bouriant in 1892, five years after a Greek version had been discovered by a French archaeological team in a cemetery in Akhmim, Egypt.[2]
The text was part of a sixty-six-page manuscript, Codex Panopolitanus,
which also contained portions of three other texts: the *Gospel of Peter, 1
Enoch*, and the *Martyrdom of Julian of Anazarbus*. The *Apocalypse*, oddly, was
sewn into the codex upside down. It was a text that had been mentioned by
early Christian writers, some of whom considered and quoted it as sacred
Scripture, but it had fallen into disrepute and disappeared from sight for
well over a millennium.

The publication raised a number of important questions pursued in
scholarly publications that appeared with unusual rapidity: Was this "the"
Apocalypse of Peter mentioned in the Muratorian Fragment and by Clement of Alexandria? How did it relate to the other work ascribed to Peter in
the codex? What were its connections with other Petrine pseudepigrapha,
and, most especially, with the canonical 2 Peter? Among the various puz-
zles, it was the issue of origins that rose quickly to prominence. The account described a guided tour of the realms of the dead, a description that
celebrated the blessed eternity enjoyed by saints in heaven, and, in far
greater detail, the horrific torments endured by sinners in hell. This was
the earliest Christian forerunner of Dante's *Commedia*, the first known instance of a Christian *katabasis*—a journey to the afterlife. Scholars of classics, biblical studies, and early Christian apocrypha immediately became
intrigued with where such a notion came from.

All the participants in the debate were naturally familiar with a range
of katabaseis in other ancient writings: Homer's *Odyssey* 11; Virgil's *Aeneid*
6; Aristophanes' *The Frogs*; Plato's eschatological myths; accounts in Plutarch, Lucian of Samosata, and others; not to mention Jewish examples
known from apocalyptic texts such as *1 Enoch*. The best-known Christian
account was the *Apocalypse of Paul*. But now its predecessor and (evidently)
major source had appeared, a work assigned to Peter but almost certainly
produced in the early second century. That raised questions: How are all
these works related to one another, and where did the idea of a human observation of the realms of the dead originally come from? What, in short,
was the ultimate source for this account in the *Apocalypse of Peter*?[3]

German scholars in particular were absorbed by such questions. Soon after the text's initial publication, still in 1892, Adolf von Harnack produced an edition and largely philological commentary, and—as one might expect from the great Harnack—made the quick observation that came to dominate the scholarship: the picture of hell did not derive from Jewish tradition "but Greek-Orphic."[4] Early the following year Eduard Norden advanced the view significantly in an article whose title reveals its ultimate concern, "Die Petrus-Apokalypse und ihre antiken Vorbilder" ("The *Apocalypse of Peter* and Its Ancient Models"): the original, now lost, *Vorbild*, appeared in Orphic-Pythagorean circles, and it is possible to trace its subsequent development over the centuries. As impressive as these, and other, learned discussions were—written nearly as fast as the authors could think and appearing as fast as they could write—the most remarkable achievement came in the full and learned monograph that appeared already in 1893, Albrecht Dieterich's influential *Nekyia: Beiträge zur Erklärung der neuentdeckten Petrusapokalypse*. Here was a full analysis, produced before Dieterich even had a chance to lay his eyes on Norden's shorter but comparable study. Again, the driving concerns are to the fore, announced already on the opening page: Dieterich seeks to solve "this question of the origin and sources of the *Apocalypse of Peter*."[5] After three preliminary chapters devoted to common Greek understandings of the realms of the dead, and then the teachings of the mystery cults, Dieterich draws his conclusions, based on hints provided in a range of texts, starting with Plato (*Republic* 363c and *Phaedo* 69c), that the idea of rewards for the righteous and punishment for the unrighteous derives from the "Orphic mysteries," especially as these became known and embraced in the religious ferment of Athens in the sixth century BCE. This Orphic tradition later came to influence the katabatic ideas advanced by such figures as Empedocles, Pindar, Lucian, Plutarch, and, of course, the newly discovered *Apocalypse of Peter*. Dieterich devotes a brief penultimate chapter to arguing that the rewards and punishments embraced in this tradition bear almost no relation to Jewish apocalyptic thought. The genealogical line of Christian journeys descended from Orphic circles.

Our various *Forschungsgeschichten* show that once this question of origins had been resolved to the satisfaction of most concerned, scholarly interest in the *Apocalypse of Peter* more or less disappeared, almost as if there were nothing more to say—a rather astounding and perplexing development in the history of scholarship.[6] Could one imagine such a thing in, say, the study of Dante? That once scholars determined that

Dante's idea of a journey to the realms of the dead in the *Commedia* could ultimately be traced back to the *Apocalypse of Paul*, from there to the *Apocalypse of Peter*, and ultimately all the way back to a lost Orphic-Pythagorean myth, there would be little more to say about the work?

It was not until the 1980s that interest revived, starting with the published Princeton dissertation of Martha Himmelfarb, *Tours of Hell: An Apocalyptic Form in Jewish and Christian Literature* (1983). Here was a fresh examination of the issues connected with early Jewish and Christian katabasis traditions, groundbreaking because it reached a different conclusion from its predecessors. Even so, the driving questions—origins and genealogies—were the same. Himmelfarb examines seventeen Jewish and Christian katabaseis in five languages from over a period of a thousand years in order to establish patterns of similarity, some of which suggest genealogical relations and dependence. Her overarching thesis is that Dieterich and those in his camp were wrong to posit a lost Orphic-Pythagorean myth as the "origin" of the Christian tradition. On the contrary, the Christian tradition arose out of the Jewish, which can be traced back to the "Book of the Watchers" (*1 En.* 1–36). A key to Himmelfarb's argument is that the texts in this Jewish and Christian line of tradition characteristically depict an angelic guide who uses demonstrative pronouns to explain what the seer observes. In response to a query about sinners suffering one torment or another in hell, the angel replies, "These are those who. . . ." This then leads to an explanation of what sin had been committed, warranting this particular punishment. Though not found in Greek and Roman accounts (Homer, Plato, Virgil, Lucian, and so on), such demonstratives can be seen relatively early in the Jewish exempla, such as the *Apocalypse of Zephaniah*. From there they moved into the Christian texts. In short, the Christian otherworldly journeys emerged out of a Jewish milieu.

The centrality of this question of origins and genealogies can be seen in the important history of research on the *Apocalypse of Peter* produced by Richard Bauckham in 1988.[7] In his detailed seven-page section on scholarship devoted to the "Descriptions of Hell and Paradise" from 1892 to his own day, the one and only issue concerns their point of derivation: Orphism? Egyptian religion? Other "oriental" religions? Zoroastrianism? Judaism? Nothing else appears to matter.

Somewhat remarkably, the same question still lives on. Probably the general consensus now is a compromise position, as expressed clearly by Pierluigi Piovanelli in a 2015 article with an unusually informative title,

"Katabáseis orphico-pythagoriciennes ou *Tours of Hell* apocalyptiques juifs?: la fausse alternative posée par la typologie des péchés et des châtiments dans l'Apocalypse de Pierre" ("Orphic-Pythagorean Katabaseis or Jewish Apocalyptic Tours of Hell? The False Alternative Posed for the Typology of Sins and Punishments in the *Apocalypse of Peter*").[8]

This question of origins and genealogies is obviously important for anyone interested in the social and religious contexts of the katabatic literature and the history of its development as a whole, which of course involves a large number of texts from Greek, Roman, Jewish, and Christian antiquity. The difficulty comes only when it is treated as the ultimate question, the answer to which somehow resolves the difficulties and mysteries posed by these texts. Such a focus may have made sense in the 1890s, given the ongoing passion for "origins" inherited by Continental, British, and American heirs of the Enlightenment, and especially the obsession with genealogy across a swath of intellectual discourse at the time—not just biology but fields as diverse as comparative linguistics, anthropology, classics, and, of course, biblical studies. One naturally thinks of the nineteenth-century focus on the oldest layers of the Pentateuch and the sources of the Synoptic Gospels, the determination to find the "original" text of the New Testament through genealogical reconstructions of manuscripts, the "quest of the historical Jesus" behind the legendary Gospel narratives, and then the preoccupations of the *religionsgeschichtliche Schule*, some of whose prominent members rubbed elbows with precisely such classicists as the aforementioned E. Norden and A. Dieterich.[9]

For many of the investigators in these various fields, "origins" in one sense or another clearly had explanatory force or was even determinative of meaning. Even so, the significance of genealogical derivation varied from one field of investigation to the next. For some, it marked positive development and evolutionary improvement. In religious studies one sees this in several commonplace Darwinian schemas, such as supersessionist claims that religion "advanced" from pantheism to pagan polytheism to Jewish monotheism to the (supreme) Christian trinitarianism. But in other fields derivation marked decline and degeneration. Thus, again in religious studies, we have the "corruption" of the text of the New Testament over the course of its transmission, the move to get back to "original" doctrines and even polity of earliest Christianity, and, of course, the push to return to the original teachings of Jesus, unmarred by the bizarre atonement theory of the apostle Paul. One might be tempted to see this stress on Christian origins simply as an intellectual by-product of the

Reformation, worked out over time; but as I have been arguing, its intellectual history is much broader than that.[10]

As interesting as matters of origins and genealogies may to be, they
are obviously not the only questions to be asked of literary texts—whether
canonical Gospels, eighteenth-century novels, or fan fiction. Although it
was a "slow train coming" with respect to the literary tours of the afterlife,
different foci have appeared in more recent times, sparked in large part by
the pioneering work of Richard Bauckham and seen in a range of publications by scholars working on disparate texts and with different goals, approaches, and agendas, including Rémi Gounelle, Thomas Kraus, Tobias
Nicklas, Meghan Henning, Emiliano Fiori, and others, who are interested
in such matters as historical settings and interpretation, use and function,
and theological and cultural significance.[11] But in some ways the work has
only begun.

In this book I am not principally interested in questions of origins,
sources, and genealogies but in historical analysis and interpretation. Social history, broadly defined, will be essential. None of the texts I discuss
is or can be contextually detached. It is not possible to understand the
climax of Aeneas's visit to Hades in *Aeneid* 6, celebrating the eschatological
significance of the civilizing power of Rome, without situating it in Virgil's
sociohistorical context and the occasion of his writing. So too the shifting
emphases of hellish torments between persecuting pagans in the *Apocalypse of Peter* and sinful leaders of the church in the *Apocalypse of Paul* make
no sense apart from the relative positions of the accounts in the history of
the Christianization of the Roman Empire.

In addition to sociohistorical analysis, though, it is also useful to consider intellectual history, the concomitant development of ideas in different times and places—in this case, most obviously (but not only) developing views of the afterlife itself. Understandings of postmortem realities
differed quite significantly from eighth-century Ionia to fourth-century
Athens; from Judaism in the second century BCE to Christianity four
hundred years later; from the embattled Christian church of the early second century to the thriving church of the late fourth. To be sure, these
changes are intimately related to social and cultural realia, but human
thought and literary texts are more than reflections of context. They need
to be explored as significant objects and producers of meaning. As part
of the literary analysis, it is helpful, in this case, to provide a comparative
assessment, not to the end of producing stemmata to demonstrate origins and genealogical development but to understand more fully the close
interworkings of text, context, and meaning.

In the chapters that follow I engage in comparison on two levels. Roughly speaking, the first three chapters consider a range of Greek, Roman, Jewish, and Christian texts in light of the literary and social worlds in which they appeared and in relation to each other. The final three chapters explore textual traditions of two of the Christian accounts to consider how later scribes and editors chose to alter the texts in the course of their transmission in order to make them more relevant, acceptable, or appealing to other readers, or even to encourage their acceptance as part of canonical Scripture.

A casual glimpse at my choice of texts and topics will show that I have no intention of presenting a comprehensive analysis of the Christian tours of the afterlife, and certainly not of literary katabasis as a whole throughout antiquity and late antiquity. I have chosen my spots, fully cognizant that there are other spots to choose. Some readers will find my choices uncomfortably limiting. Within the Greek and Roman traditions, I have more or less restricted myself to Homer, Virgil, two of Plato's eschatological myths, and one of Lucian's dialogues. A complete analysis could not be done even in a single volume but in any event would certainly require a sustained analysis of the Orphic Golden Tables, Aristophanes' *The Frogs*, the other Platonic myths, the Dream of Scipio, other Lucianic dialogues, Plutarch's three eschatological myths, and so on. My goal in examining the texts I do is to note their striking similarities and distinctions to illustrate what each katabasis means and to consider the work it does, but also to set the stage for an analysis of texts deriving from Jewish and Christian traditions. For the latter, my interests lie with the *Apocalypse of Peter*, the *Acts of Thomas*, the *Apocalypse of Paul*, and the *Gospel of Nicodemus*.

Other texts and topics could easily have been chosen, and one hopes they will be. Through the valiant labors of others, the study of early Christian katabasis has begun to escape the dank prison below into the fresh air of the world above. I hope this book will contribute something to its full emergence.

The various assessments I examine are all governed by an overarching perspective. In no case, obviously, do literary portrayals of an otherworldly journey merely serve to provide factual information about what lies beyond to readers who might understandably be curious. They consistently work even more to other ends, in broadest terms, parenetic, that is, delivering advice, exhortation, or instruction. They encourage certain ways of living in the world in light of the realities of what lies ahead. That is, by showing what happens after death, the texts emphasize what matters in life, providing insight into the purpose, meaning, and goals of human existence so as to encourage certain ways of being and living in the world: attitudes, dispositions, priorities, commitments, life choices, beliefs, practices, public activities, relationships—in fact, almost everything involved with being a sentient and conscious human being. In one way or another, in theory at least, readers who realize what life will be after death are driven to live, think, act, and be in certain ways before then.

CHAPTER ONE

The Realities of Death
and the Meaning of Life I

Journeys to Hades in Homer and Virgil

J OURNEYS TO THE REALMS of the dead constitute an important corpus of Greek and Roman texts of ranging genre and date. I do not provide here full coverage or even a generalized overview. Instead, I focus on the well-known accounts of Homer and Virgil, both to understand them on their own terms and to provide instructive comparanda for the Christian exempla that appeared in their wake. These are the two longest and most culturally significant katabaseis to survive from classical antiquity. Their similarities strike even first-time readers; their differences reveal widely disparate conceptions of the afterlife and, as a corollary, profoundly different understandings of the relevance of the intransigent realities of death for life in the present. The Virgilian account provides particularly instructive contrasts with the later Christian versions and therefore occupies more of our attention.

Odysseus's Journey to Hades

The oldest journey to Hades in the Western tradition comes to us in Homer's *Odyssey*, Book 11,[1] where Odysseus travels to consult the blind but far-sighted prophet Tiresias.[2] To understand the account, we need to set it in its broader literary context.

The *Odyssey* narrates the ten-year journey of Odysseus following the sack of Troy to his home island and kingdom, Ithaca, to reunite with his faithful wife, Penelope; their now-grown son, Telemachus; and his aged father, Laertes. The epic is all about the "return home," *nostos* (νόστος), the first half dealing, roughly, with Odysseus's ill-fated adventures en route and the second with his adventures once he arrives, as he confronts and eventually disposes of the suitors trying to woo his wife and take over his rule.

The journey to Hades occurs as a flashback at the midpoint of the epic, narrated by Odysseus himself near the end of his travels. At this stage of the narrative Odysseus has lost all of his ships and companions and ended up alone, shipwrecked, without a stitch on his back, on the Island of Phaeacia, where he is welcomed and then entertained by the local king and queen (Books 6–8). In the course of a long dinner, he is asked to recount his adventures, and the following four books (9–12), the *Apologoi* (= Tales) are told in the first person as Odysseus describes his various traumas and narrow escapes from such figures as the Lotus-Eaters, the Cyclops, Circe, and Scylla and Charybdis.

All of Book 11 is devoted to the journey, but it is set up in the preceding book by an episode with the bewitching goddess Circe. Circe has used her magical powers to turn half of Odysseus's men into pigs, but when she tries the trick on him, he survives unscathed because of a prophylactic provided by the god Hermes. Recognizing Odysseus to be someone unusually special, Circe, in a somewhat unexpected move, immediately takes him to bed. For the next year she entertains both him and his (now restored) troops with wining, dining, and, for Odysseus at least, sundry other pleasures. Odysseus eventually persuades Circe to release them for their homeward journey, but she instructs him that his first order of business is to go "to the house of Hades and the fearful Persephone" (*Od.* 10.491) in order to consult with the blind prophet Tiresias of Thebes about what lies ahead.

The goddess indicates that Tiresias is unusual. Unlike everyone else in the realms beyond, he has a full mental capacity—"his mind is steadfast" (τοῦ τε φρένες ἔμπεδοί εἰσι; 10.493). This is because "to him alone among the dead" Persephone has "granted reason" (νόον); "he alone has understanding/has his faculties" (νόον οἴῳ . . . πεπνῦσθαι). None of the others in the realms below has a satisfying existence: "They are shadows, flitting around" (τοὶ δὲ σκιαὶ ἀίσσουσιν; 10.495).

Odysseus is not eager to make the trip—no one has ever yet done such a thing (10.502)—but Circe gives him clear directions. He and his men are to sail away to the other side of the river Oceanus and then go on foot "to the moldy house of Hades" (10.512), where the rivers Pyriphlegethon and Cocytus flow into the Acheron. Once there, he is to dig a pit, pour a libation to the dead, and petition them with promises of additional sacrifices when he later arrives home in Ithaca, along with a special sacrifice to Tiresias himself; he is to sacrifice a ram and a black ewe, apparently (we learn later) letting them bleed into the pit. Many souls of the dead will then come. When they do, Odysseus is to draw his sword to keep them away from the blood until he has been able to consult with Tiresias, who will tell him about his path ahead and his eventual *nostos* (10.516–40).

Odysseus and his men immediately sail away, lamenting what they must do, and bringing Book 10 to a close. The next book narrates Odysseus's journey to Hades, the so-called *nekuia*.

Nekuia *and* Katabasis

From antiquity *Odyssey* 11 has been called the *nekuia* (Diodorus Siculus, *Library of History* 4.39.2), a term that is not altogether apt, especially when taken to suggest that the account, or a portion of it, involves an act of necromancy.[3] As Sarah Isles Johnston has pointed out, Odysseus does not conjure the spirits up to the land of the living (contrary to how the account is often read) but goes to the place of the dead. Moreover, unlike a necromancer he does not compel the shades to speak; they do so of their own accord, or even refuse to speak altogether.[4] Even if *nekuia* is taken in the looser sense to refer simply to "a magical rite by which ghosts were called up and questioned about the future," it scarcely applies here.[5] To be sure, Odysseus does perform sacrifices that attract several disparate groups of shades out of Erebus: brides, unmarried young men, long-suffering old men; "tender" young women who are recently mourning; and men slain in battle (11.36–41).[6] But these fade from the story as quickly as they appear. In addition, only the brief conversation with Tiresias concerns the future. Odysseus's other encounters focus on the terrible events on earth in the past and the arguably more terrible realities of Hades in the present.

Nekuia is certainly an inappropriate moniker for later underworld tours that follow in Homer's wake, including the *Apocalypse of Peter*, despite the title of the first full-length study devoted to it, the German classicist Albert Dieterich's *Nekyia* (1893). The vast majority of these Greek, Roman, Jewish, and Christian journeys do not involve consultation at all, let alone with souls called up to predict the future; typically the accounts involve journeys of living persons to the realms of the dead, not of the dead to the living; and the travelers are almost always interested observers, not anxious interrogators. As a matter of tradition and convenience I will continue to refer to *Odyssey* 11 with the traditional term, *nekuia*, but for the broader phenomenon I will speak of *katabasis* (a "going down"—that is, to the realms of the dead), a term that admittedly has its own problems.[7]

The Narrative Function of the Nekuia

The *nekuia* stands out among the narratives of the *Odyssey*. On one hand, coming at the center of the epic, it is both the focal and the turning point, as the protagonist, after random and hopeless wandering from one ill-timed disaster to another, receives some direction for his return home and a much-welcome prophecy about what will happen once he arrives.[8] Moreover, and yet more obvious, it is completely unlike any of Odysseus's other adventures: here he travels beyond the normal world of human existence to the realm of the deceased, a place of complete darkness, where, apart from Hades and Persephone, not even the gods themselves go. It is a place of ultimate reality in a rather terminal sense—the final destiny for everyone who lives.

One would therefore expect the adventure to be centrally important, encapsulating in some sense the message of the entire epic, and the narrative does not disappoint.[9] Some readers have considered the episode symbolic: Odysseus, in a sense, dies and rises again, reborn into a new outlook and given courage for his ongoing mission, allowing him to move from his heroic past of glory in war to a future life in Ithaca. There may be something to this reading, but it is not the whole story. The desperate desire for *nostos* has been very much alive from the outset of the narrative and has already been set in sharp contrast with *kleos* (κλέος), the passion for "fame" and "glory" at all costs, especially as it can be attained through valiant effort on the battlefield, even to the point of death. What matters for the entire *Odyssey* is instead coming home—place, property, position, and the beloved people in life: wife, son, father. The *nekuia* does not alter that emphasis or create it through a rebirth into a new life or a new perspective. It does, however, confirm it in a radical way, showing that the desire for home and longevity is not merely a personal or idiosyncratic predilection of Odysseus but is the only sensible approach to life, given the realities of death.

This may come as a startling claim to anyone steeped in the world of epic in general, and the world of the *Iliad* in particular. No longer are τιμή (*tîmé;* honor) and *kleos* the ultimate desiderata. Of course, honor and renown remain important to the living; but their importance is relative, especially in comparison with values associated with home and family. Odysseus does not first acquire this understanding in his encounters with the dead, but he is strongly confirmed in it, with insights beyond what is available to earthbound mortals.

Odysseus's First Encounters

Book 11 begins with the voyage across the river Oceanus to a place where there is no light. An obvious narrative tension occurs immediately, just one of the account's many incongruities: everyone in that land, including the newcomers, appears to see clearly in pitch blackness.[10]

Once he arrives, Odysseus performs the prescribed rites, and after the blood has flowed into the pit, a number of "souls of the dead" arise "up out of Erebus" (ὑπὲξ Ἐρέβεος; 11.36–37). Partly because of this statement, commentators often claim that Odysseus does not actually go "into" Hades but only to its entrance, except possibly toward the end of his journey.[11] This is almost certainly a misreading, however: the text repeatedly places him in Hades.[12]

Since the shades that rise up from the pit disappear from the narrative as soon as they arrive, they are not of major importance for our interests.[13] But it is worth noting that they are aptly called "powerless heads of the dead" (νεκύων ἀμενηνὰ κάρηνα; 11.29, 49). These are pathetic shadows of what had been full-bodied humans. Odysseus has to ward them off because they are eager to drink the blood in the pit. Later we learn why: the blood will temporarily restore their powers of recollection and speech. In their "normal" state not only are the shades void of all strength, but they lack all memory. And so the grim description of afterlife existence begins: the dead dwell in complete darkness with no strength, memory, intelligence, or speech—mere shadows of life. Much of the book serves to reinforce these points.[14]

Odysseus first encounters his recently deceased but as yet unburied colleague Elpenor, who desperately pleads for burial rites but without indicating why. In the comparable case of Patroclus in the *Iliad*, burial was a requirement for the deceased to enter Hades (*Il.* 23.65–92). That may be the case here as well, but it is not clear: Elpenor has already crossed the river Oceanus and appears to be in Hades (*Od.* 11.65, 69), in the same location as, say, Anticleia and Tiresias.[15] Still, a reader might at least imagine a decent burial will somehow improve Elpenor's lot in the underworld. Given what Odysseus is to learn later in this account, however, it is hard to see how: the eternal state of those already buried could scarcely get any worse.[16] It may be that Elpenor simply wants a funeral to celebrate him as the valiant hero he never was.[17]

One further narrative oddity is that whereas other shades need to drink the sacrificial blood to regain their memory and power of speech, Elpenor speaks coherently with full memory without having done so. One could interpret this to mean that the unburied still have their memories. Then again, later in the book Achilles also engages with Odysseus without drinking the blood, as, to a lesser extent, does Tiresias, although as a divinely inspired prophet he may have been an exception to the rule. It is not clear whether Agamemnon drinks the blood or not—it depends on the textual decision at 11.390.[18] However one resolves this issue, the internal discrepancies remain, and the most frequently suggested options are also the most obvious: maybe Homer simply wanted to avoid needless repetition—although that would be an odd explanation for the first omission (Elpenor). More likely, the account is simply inconsistent.

Odysseus next meets the prophet Tiresias, the raison d'être of the journey. As Circe had indicated, Tiresias does have a functioning memory, and he immediately recognizes Odysseus, asking him why he has left the light of the sun in order to "see the dead and the place where there is no joy" (ἀτερπέα χῶρον; 11.94), a description that heightens the foreboding of what is to come. Even though Tiresias apparently does not require the blood to speak, he wants a draught anyway, possibly to allow him better to make his predictions, or possibly simply because he sometimes enjoyed a nice drink. In any event, the conversation that follows strikes most readers as anticlimactic.[19] The prophet does tell Odysseus what will happen to him during his return home, but he gives him only one piece of advice: on no account should he and his men harm the cattle and sheep of Helios when they land on Thrinacia, or all but he alone will perish. In the event, the men ignore the warning and are indeed all killed. Thus neither the description of the home journey nor the advice has any effect on the wider plot or on Odysseus's trip. As to what will happen on the journey itself, Circe later provides the same information, at least insofar as it unfolds in the *Odyssey*.

So what was the point of the trip to Hades? Surely it is a simple narrative ploy, allowing the prophet not so much to see Tiresias as to meet others and learn from them not just how they arrived in the world below but, even more, what existence is like there.[20] For our purposes the three most important of these meetings are with his mother, Anticleia, and his erstwhile colleagues in war, Agamemnon and Achilles.

The Reality of Death: Anticleia

Anticleia had arrived at the pit before Odysseus encountered Tiresias but had been kept from the blood by Odysseus's sword. It is not that she has been patiently biding her time; she is witless, unable to recognize her son or to speak. Odysseus asks the prophet how her memory can be restored, and Tiresias explains the function of the blood: any of the shades who drinks it will speak truthfully (νημερτὲς ἐνίψει; 11.148). Odysseus allows her to drink, she recognizes him immediately, and they have their famous heartbreaking reunion.

She cannot understand how he could be there, a living man in the land of the dead; he, on the other hand, does not know how, when, or why she has arrived.[21] Their initial discussion is all about the recent past: he explains why he has come, and she gives him information about family life back in Ithaca, his wife, son, and father. Part of what makes her report interesting for the reader is that she reveals only what she knew up to the time of her death, for example, that Telemachus was not having any problems but was being treated with due respect by all ("Telemachus is peacefully managing the estate"; 11.185). Odysseus has already learned from Tiresias that all is not well on the home front, and the reader knows from Books 1–4 that Telemachus in particular is not in a good state.[22]

More grievous to Odysseus, though, is his mother's revelation of her own demise. She was not taken off by illness or the arrows of Artemis, but out of unbearable grief for Odysseus himself: "It was my desire for you and your counsels, glorious Odysseus, and for your gentle disposition, that stole away my honey-sweet life" (11.203–4). Odysseus responds to these gut-wrenching words with deep compassion and rushes to fold his mother in his embrace. But to no avail. She is a shade of no substance, and his arms pass through her: "Three times I rushed to her and my heart ordered me to clasp her; but three times she flew from my hands like a shadow (σκιῆ) or even a dream (ὀνείρῳ)" (11.206–8). His failed embraces deepen his grief, and he makes a pathetic plea: "My mother, why do you not stay when I want to clasp you, so that even in Hades the two of us can throw our arms around each other and at least take pleasure in our cold mourning?" (κρυεροῖο τεταρπώμεσθα γόοιο; 11.210–12). The wording of that final clause is important. Tiresias had already announced that Hades was "the land of no joy" (ἀτερπέα χῶρον). Here we see it in its most pathetic and pronounced form: Odysseus cannot even find a sliver of consolatory joy (τεταρπώμεσθα) with his mother.

Out of frustration he wonders whether "dread Persephone" is pulling a trick on him by showing him only an "image" (εἴδωλον) of his mother rather than her real self. But Anticleia tells him the hard truth, which, unbeknownst to him, he has come to Hades to find. Everyone shares the same fate. After death there is no life; the body is gone with all its strength. All that is left is a shadow of existence. And so we have some of the key lines of the book: "My son . . . Persephone, daughter of Zeus, is not deceiving you. This is what happens to mortals (αὕτη δίκη ἐστὶ βροτῶν) when they die. The sinews no longer hold flesh and bones together, but when life leaves the white bones the blazing fire's overwhelming force destroys the body, and the soul (ψύχη) flies off, fluttering like a dream (ἠΰτ ὄνειρος ἀποπταμένη πεπότηται)" (11.216–22). The shades really are shades, shadows of life. They are not physical entities; they can feel no physical pain, pleasure, or joy; they have no more substance than a passing dream. They are "powerless" and "witless," epithets common in the narrative.

Anticleia's sad truth is confirmed by Odysseus's subsequent encounters with two of the mightiest men of his age who are now without strength, power, honor, or status. Like everyone else, they are simply dead.

The Once Mighty Agamemnon

After other episodes of less moment for our concerns (the Catalogue of Heroines, 11.225–332, and the Interlude in Odysseus's storytelling, 11.333–84), we come to his meeting with Agamemnon, the leader of the Greek armies in their ten-year war. Homer's audience, of course, would have been well aware of Agamemnon's horrible fate after the war, later immortalized by the fifth-century tragedians. Once home from his heroic exploits on the battlefield, the Greek armies' commander-in-chief was mercilessly slaughtered in his own home through the machinations of his wife, Clytemnestra, and her lover, Aegisthus.

Most of Agamemnon's conversation with Odysseus involves a harrowing description of his betrayal and death (11.404–34), leading to his hortatory conclusion: you cannot trust women (11.456). In particular Odysseus himself needs to be wary when he reaches the shores of Ithaca. Homer, of course, is using the tale as a study in contrasts. Ever-faithful and persevering Penelope is no Clytemnestra, and the stark differences serve to highlight the glories of Odysseus's own, joyful *nostos*.[23] On the other hand, to be fair, unlike Agamemnon, Odysseus had not slaughtered one of his own children to propitiate a god who was frustrating his passion for a war of revenge and honor. But that too is part of the point.[24] Some passions (war, vengeance) are not worth pursuing at any price, in particular the sacrifice of home and (literally) family; failing to grasp the point can bring utter disaster.

In any event, more germane for our purposes is the contrast Homer draws between the power and renown of the once-mighty Agamemnon and the pathetic state he is in now and forever. The reader is not only struck by the contrast between his glorious life and disastrous death, but also by the reversals brought by the realities of death, which serve to in-stantiate Anticleia's claims about the "way of mortals" (δίκη . . . βροτῶν; 11.218). Agamemnon meets Odysseus not as the intrepid, fearless, power-ful commander of the greatest army Greece had ever mustered, but as a pathetic, enervated shade. He approaches Odysseus grieving and weeping loudly and tries to touch him, reaching out his hands to grasp him in sorrow and affection (11.385–91). But as happened earlier with Odysseus himself, the attempt at physical contact comes to naught. In this instance Homer does not stress the anatomical issue (sinews, flesh, and bones) but its corollary: utter powerlessness: "He no longer had the firm strength or vitality (ἲς ἔμπεδος οὐδέ τι κῖκυς) he formerly enjoyed in his supple limbs" (11.393–94). Agamemnon can no longer clasp hands, let alone bear arms, and Odysseus weeps at the pathetic sight.

If that is what happens to the mightiest warriors of powerful armies, what will happen to the rest of us? As it turns out, it will be no worse; but the terrifying news is that it will be the same—the same for everyone, ruler or peasant, valiant or cowardly, rich or impoverished, powerful or decrepit, upright and godly or wicked and godless. There are no rewards and punishments and no levels of happiness and despair.[25] It is all the same. That becomes yet more clear in Odysseus's next encounter, with the mightiest of the Greek heroes, Achilles.

Choosing Life on Any Terms: Achilles

In Odysseus's meeting with Achilles we find the clearest expression of the wrenching and pathetic state of the dead and, thus, the ultimate lesson of the account. The goals of life are not *tîmé* and *kleos* at any price. The cost may be too high. Death shows that the summum bonum of life is to continue living it.

As readers of Homer know full well, that is not the view of Achilles in the *Iliad*. It is especially striking that the hero directly reflects on the relative importance of renown and life in the earlier epic; moreover, the reflection comes precisely in a conversation with Odysseus. In Book 9 of the *Iliad*, the war is not going well, and Odysseus has been sent to Achilles' tent to persuade him to forgo his wrath and return to battle before it is too late (*Il.* 9.179–306). Characteristically, Achilles holds firmly to his grudge against Agamemnon and refuses to yield. Near the end of his long reply (9.307–429), Achilles says he has long known he must choose between two paths—a glorious death in battle or a return to his beloved homeland for a long life: "For my mother, the silver-footed goddess Thetis, has told me that two kinds of fate are carrying me to the end in death. If I remain here to do battle before the city of the Trojans, my return home (νόστος) will perish, but my renown (κλέος) will never die; but if I return home to my beloved homeland, my noble renown (κλέος) will perish, but I will have a long life and my end in death will not come to me soon" (9.410–16).

It is striking that in the *immediate* context of his deliberations in *Iliad* 9 Achilles claims to prefer long life to renown, and he urges his companions to pack up and return home with him. That changes, though, with the death of Patroclus. At that point Achilles firmly rejects a peaceful return home and chooses *kleos* (18.78–137). Eventually (outside the epic) he will go down fighting.

Whatever Odysseus may have thought of the matter in *Iliad* 9, his view is clear throughout the entire narrative of the *Odyssey*. He seeks home above all else. On one hand, then, his encounter with the shade of Achilles contrasts the paths taken by the two great heroes. In the narrative world of Homer, however, the conflict is much larger. It is the *Iliad* versus the *Odyssey*. On an even larger scale, it is a conflict that threatens the entire epic tradition. Does the reality of death undermine the traditional epic ideal *ne plus ultra*, "renown" above all else?[26]

The conflict very much shapes the tone of the conversation between the two heroes (*Od.* 11.473–537). Unlike Odysseus's other encounters in Hades, this one involves hard words, sarcasm, disagreement, and reproof. It seems to start well enough. Achilles recognizes Odysseus and weeps, addressing him with the well-worn epithet "Born of Zeus" (διογενές). But then he maligns and suspects him, addressing him as σχέτλιε—something like "you savage" or "you wretched man"—and asks how he could come up with a more audacious plan than to visit the dead while still living. It is so like the "man of many devices" (πολυμήχανος), to "dare" to come down to Hades (πῶς ἔτλης Ἀϊδόσδε κατελθέμεν; 11.473–75).

Odysseus does not rise to the bait. Or at least he seems not to. He greets Achilles with words of praise, calling him the "mightiest of the Achaeans," and informs him that he has come to consult Tiresias for help to return home. But he then launches into a lament over his own misfortune: he has not yet reached Achaea and has done nothing but suffer hardship (αἰὲν ἔχω κακά; 11.482). It may seem a little insensitive to complain about the difficulties of life to someone who has already died, but Odysseus clearly does not see it this way. "But you, Achilles," he says, "no man was ever more blessed than you, or ever will be" (11.482–83). He then explains why; Achilles was the greatest mortal ever to have lived and is now the greatest among those who have died: "For before, when you were living, we Argives gave you honor equal to the gods (ἐτίομεν ἶσα θεοῖσιν), and now that you are here, you rule the dead mightily (μέγα κρατέεις νεκύεσσιν ἐνθάδ' ἐών). So do not grieve at all about having died, Achilles" (11.484–86).

To this point in the narrative Odysseus has shown that he knew almost precisely nothing about the dead before he arrived in Hades. And so his claim that Achilles is ruler of the dead appears to be empty flattery, a *captatio benevolentiae* based on nothing. But more than that it is a sarcastic vaunt. Odysseus knows full well that he himself is a strong, vibrant, living warrior making a temporary stop in a place that is not his own; Achilles is a pathetic shadow of a man with no hope of ever becoming anything different. Even so, he has retained his wit, and he annihilates Odysseus's mock admiration and self-pity with a withering response, the most memorable words of the book: "Do not console me about death, O shining Odysseus" (φαίδιμ' Ὀδυσσεῦ, an epithet returning the sarcasm; 11.488). "I would prefer to be a low-class serf attached to the soil, serving someone else, a man with no property of his own who has barely enough to live on, than to rule over all the dead who have perished" (βουλοίμην κ' ἐπάρουρος ἐὼν θητευέμεν ἄλλῳ, ἀνδρὶ παρ' ἀκλήρῳ, ᾧ μὴ βίοτος πολὺς εἴη, ἢ πᾶσιν νεκύεσσι καταφθιμένοισιν ἀνάσσειν; 11.489–91).[27]

This passage has often been interpreted to indicate that Achilles, the greatest of all shades, does indeed rule the dead but that, even so, he would prefer life in the world above as an impoverished day laborer slaving away in service of a peasant. But in fact that may not be right. Achilles does not concede that he rules below; he simply ignores the comment. Robert Schmiel has argued that he actually denies the claim.[28] There are serious problems with Schmiel's argument at this point,[29] and even more with the unwarranted conclusions that he draws, that in fact Achilles retains the same view of *kleos* he had in the *Iliad*, does not regret his decision for it, and given the choice would do it all again. This interpretation flies completely in the face of Achilles' forceful claim: he would rather be alive as a man without any *kleos* whatsoever, a low-class field hand with no power, authority, or reputation, working his fingers to the bone in service of a low-life peasant, another man with no *kleos*, than to lord it over all the dead. He made the wrong choice. It is better to be alive with no *kleos* than dead with all the *kleos* in the (under)world. This is a stark reversal of the *Iliad*. Death does not merely put the ideals of life in perspective, by, say, relativizing them. It completely alters them. Nothing is worth death, not even eternal renown. Life can mean ongoing existence, vitality, strength, mental acuity. Death robs a person of all that. It means going to the "joyless kingdom," as a mere image of oneself, a powerless and mindless shadow flitting around the realms of the dead forever. Odysseus has taken the better path—not glory in battle but life in his native land, at home with wife, son, and father. *Nostos* triumphs over *kleos*.

Even so, the end of the encounter with Achilles has been read by other interpreters as calling that view into question, and for understandable reasons. After the dead Achilles has schooled Odysseus on the brutalities of underworld reality, he asks for news of his son, Neoptolemus. On this Odysseus has first-hand knowledge. Neoptolemus is one of the most handsome men on earth, wise in counsel of war, brave and mighty in battle, and well-rewarded for his feats. The news of his son's renown brings Achilles joy, and he departs by striding away through a "field of asphodel" (ἀσφοδελὸν λειμῶνα; 11.539). Does this not show that *kleos* is in fact the dominant virtue, that it is what really matters to Achilles, even in the world below?

Several points need to be made. For one thing, Achilles is proud of Neoptolemus precisely because he is *living* with *kleos*. He did not have to sacrifice his life to receive it. What if he had done so? He would be yet another empty shade longing to live the life of a starving field hand. There is no telling how proud Achilles would be of him then, or for how long. Moreover, the happiness that Achilles temporarily feels is unrelated to his own situation in Hades, whether he is ruling or not. He is still down there, forever, a powerless shade. What has made him happy is news from the world of the *living*. Of course it is better to be alive with *kleos* than without it, and Achilles is proud that his son has it in spades. But that would not mean he would want him to die on the battlefield to advance his renown yet further. As he himself says, life on any terms is far more valuable than renown in death.

Finally, the rosy picture most readers have of Achilles striding off joyously through a field of freshly blooming flowers ("asphodel") as if in a summer meadow on a pleasant sunny day may not be the image Homer was trying to create. Yes, Achilles is glad to hear the news. But one recent study has argued that contrary to popular imagination "asphodel" is not a bright, blooming flower. The word may instead refer to dull grey ashes, such as the remains from cremation. It was a dusty, gloomy meadow.[30]

Final Encounters

Odysseus encounters seven other individuals before leaving Hades, six of whom do not say a word to him. First he sees one other former colleague from the war, Ajax, who had committed suicide in anger when Odysseus was awarded Achilles' arms after the great warrior's death. Ajax harbors his resentment and refuses to answer Odysseus when addressed (11.541–67). Also silent is Orion, seen a bit later, herding a group of wild beasts he had killed in life (11.572–75). Odysseus then sees Minos, who, in a role that became traditional, was "rendering judgments for the dead" (θεμιστεύοντα νέκυσσιν; 11.569) as they came to him pleading their cases (δίκας εἴροντο; 11.570). It is hard to know exactly what this means, but it appears to suggest that not all shades are treated equally, at least when it comes to justice. Still, justice for what? Conceivably for what had happened while they were still living, but more likely for slights they received once dead. However one construes the matter, the idea of differentiated treatment does not seem consistent with the rest of the account.

A more obvious incongruity, frequently noted, comes next: Odysseus sees three people being tortured. The giant Tityos is stretched over nine plethora (about three hundred yards), helpless to defend himself from two vultures devouring his liver. His sin is specified: he had tried to rape Leto, the lover of Zeus. Tantalus stands in a pool up to his chin, perpetually taunted, in thirst and hunger. Whenever he stoops to drink, the water recedes from his reach; above him are trees with luscious fruits within his grasp, but whenever he stretches out his hand, the wind blows them away. Sisyphus is perpetually rolling a huge stone up a hill to move it over the crest; but as soon as he reaches the top, its weight turns it back and it rolls to the bottom. So he begins again (11.576–600).[31]

Why these three sinners, in particular? Numerous interpretations have appeared over the years, principally based on later myths describing their heinous activities and respective punishments. Often it is said that these three were especially vile offenders against the gods. That may be so (the text gives no indication), but it bears emphasizing that nothing suggests they represent *types* of humans to be perpetually tormented. They are three exceptions.[32] They do show, however, that Homer knew of traditions involving differentiated afterlives in which some have it much worse than others, as also suggested in other places in his epics.[33]

Odysseus's final encounter involves one other exception to the rules of eternity—the demigod Heracles. Either because of his divine lineage as the offspring of Zeus or in reward for his heroic deeds, Heracles has a double life, or at least a simultaneous existence in both life and death. Odysseus explains that when he encountered Heracles, he actually saw his image (εἴδωλον). Heracles "himself" (αὐτός) was enjoying (τέρπεται, again) a feast among the immortal gods, married to Hebe, daughter of Zeus and Hera (11.601–4). And so Heracles' shade is with the other mortals in Hades while his real self is reveling up in heaven, able to enjoy himself outside the realms Tiresias had called "joyless."

Yet even just Heracles' image is a mighty presence in the world below: the other shades flee that presence in terror of his menacing arrow. When he addresses Odysseus, it is only to comment on the similarities between them, pointing out that they both suffered immeasurably in the world above and, while living, came down to Hades. After recounting his own heroic deeds in the world below, Heracles breaks off without expecting a reply.[34]

Odysseus ends his tale by indicating he had hoped to see some others in the world below, but he fled in terror at the thought that worse could come, that Persephone might send out the head of the Gorgon. He escaped to his ship and with his crew embarked across the river Oceanus to return to the world of the living.

Conclusion

The broader lessons of Homer's katabasis are clear. Most important: the nature of death puts into perspective the value of life. The world of mortals may be hard and full of suffering; but whether it is the constant dangers confronted by heroes desperately trying to return home or the daily grind of field hands enduring a life of poverty, the suffering of the present cannot be compared to the perpetual banality of what lies ahead. The miserable existence of the living, on any terms, is better than anything on offer in the realms of the dead, where there is literally nothing to live for, since no one is alive. Existence there is a mere shadow. There are no pleasures to appreciate, no goals to achieve, no strength to enjoy, no memories to relish, and no future to anticipate. It is a life of flitting shadows. In the moving words of Erwin Rohde from more than a century ago, in the Homeric picture, "Nothing is so hateful to man as death and the gates of Hades: for when death comes it is certain that life—this sweet life of ours in the sunlight—is done with."[35]

Within the broader narrative of the epic, Odysseus's journey to Hades thoroughly validates his single-minded desire to return home. Glory and renown are indeed worth striving for, but they pale in comparison with the fact of life itself. Homer does not overly sentimentalize the view. Not every homecoming goes well, as Agamemnon so pathetically explains. But on balance, the greatest good is life at home among property and loved ones. Even if that is not a reality everyone can enjoy, no one should abandon life before absolutely necessary, since after life is only death.

The Katabasis of Aeneas

To shift from Homer to Virgil is to move to a vastly different world: separated by seven centuries; living in different parts of the Mediterranean with correspondingly different social, cultural, and political contexts; working in different languages; composing their works for altogether different reasons and with vastly different assumptions, commitments, ideologies, perspectives, and beliefs about the world and the world to come.[36] They do share a great deal as well, of course, including similar inherited mythologies and understandings of cultic practices. Most important they share a genre, with Virgil quite deliberately modeling his epic on those of his predecessor. Among other things, he places a katabasis of his traveling hero, Aeneas, also at the center of a divinely guided but fraught journey.

Since we do not know the actual circumstances of Homer's composition and his motivations—or even his identity—they provide no hermeneutical purchase for reading his work.[37] Not so, Virgil. Scholars have come to doubt the claim of Servius that Virgil had been commissioned by Augustus to produce an epic of the founding of Rome to rival the greatest epics of Greece.[38] But at the very least Virgil did so on his own initiative.

The *Aeneid* was neither conceived nor designed as a disinterested history of the Roman past. It was unapologetically an encomium on the glories of the world's greatest city and, in particular, a tribute to its greatest ruler.

But the encomium is not, in the end, unadulterated sycophantic praise. As scholars such as Wendell Clausen and Adam Parry recognized more than a half century ago, the *Aeneid* has a dark and ominous side that casts the Roman achievement seriously into doubt with some regularity, most stunningly in the katabasis of Book 6. As Clausen put it, "It is the paradox of the *Aeneid*, the surprise of its greatness, that a poem which celebrates the achievement of a national hero and the founding of Rome itself should be such a long history of defeat and loss."[39]

The epic as a whole describes the toils of Aeneas, heroic warrior of Troy up to its tragic end, who, with divine instructions, fled the burning city with family, colleagues, and city gods to found the Roman people who were later to build the city, and then the empire, of Rome. The Homeric model is evident even on the level of narrative structure: the first six books recount Aeneas's journeys with their gut-wrenching struggles and setbacks, closely related to those of the *Odyssey*; the final six books describe his arrival in Italy and the battles that ensued as he sought a permanent home for his people, a new Troy, a war narrative comparable, in broad terms, to the *Iliad*.

At the center stands the katabasis, whose parallels with Homer's *nekuia* are obvious even to a first-time reader. A hero's interminable, danger-filled, but divinely guided journey is interrupted by a trip to the realms of the dead where he is to receive guidance for what lies ahead. While there, he encounters numerous people from his past, beginning with a traveling companion who had unexpectedly died but had not yet been buried; he sees fallen soldiers from the recent Trojan War; he joyfully meets a parent, whom he three times tries to embrace but to no effect. And on and on. The self-conscious modeling of *Aeneid* 6 on *Odyssey* 11 gives us an interpretive advantage over its predecessor, a comparative leverage unavailable to the reader of Homer. In the broadest terms, as we will see, the lesson to be drawn from the world below is no longer the same except in the remotest sense. To be sure, on a very basic level, Virgil's portrayal is equally, if not even more, pessimistic about the possibilities of existence after death, even though it has not usually been read this way. Still, the fact is that for all except a very few special and chosen individuals, the life to come is truly awful: not because those who have died continue to exist as mere shadows of their former selves, as in the *nekuia*, but because they are very much alive and are subject to mental and physical pain, either for a long period of purgation or forever.

Corresponding to this very different conception of the world to come is the parenetic point derived from it: The goal of life is not to enjoy the beauties of the world in the comforts of home and the presence of family for as long as possible before meeting one's inevitable fate. Virgil's account does stress the importance of life in the world above rather than in the world below, but now it is not the long life of the satisfied individual. Instead, ultimate earthly good lies in national achievement. The realities of what comes after death reveal that the most important feature of human existence is the civilizing influence of the greatest empire the world has ever seen. The significant "end" or "goal" of all things is the rule of Rome. This is a presentist, realized eschatology.

Traditional Influences on Aeneid 6

Before proceeding with an analysis, it is important to stress that traditions outside of Homer also significantly influenced Virgil. Much of his account draws on subsequent Greek thought, most obviously Platonic, concerning the nature of reality, the soul, and the life to come.[40] There is no need to summarize the major elements of Plato's philosophy here, except to say that his lengthy disquisitions on the immortality of the soul function, in part, to establish its innate superiority to the body, with the parenetic emphasis that true philosophy, and so the best way of being, entails nurturing the soul rather than yielding to the more natural inclinations/pleasures of the body. The soul is the "real" person; the body is a prison. Yielding to bodily desires both taints the soul and secures its trapping. Thus the goal of life is to escape the body. That comes completely at death, when the body ceases to function, decays, and is no more; but the soul survives, tainted as little as possible, it is hoped, by its lifelong material associations. That is why the business of philosophy is to practice death in life, to "die daily"—that is, to separate the soul from the body.

Most of Plato's instruction comes through dialectical exchange, but on several occasions he resorts to myth to provide a different grounding and justification for his views.[41] Plato's myths of the afterlife describe the postmortem existence of the soul, most famously at the end of the *Republic* in the Myth of Er, a near death experience of a soldier who awakes on his funeral pyre and describes what he has seen in the world beyond (see Chapter 3). Er's vision of the realms of the dead confirms Plato's dialectical teaching that the soul lives on beyond the grave, but in a more-or-less tainted state. Souls that have become hopelessly defiled will experience dire punishments in the world to come; souls that have remained pure will be rewarded. All except the worst of sinners will have a chance to improve through a cycle of reincarnations. Souls are returned to the body in hopes they will choose to live the philosophical life that allows them to achieve the greatest good. Virgil is deeply indebted to these views.

Even so, it is remarkable and often noted that Virgil's heavily Platonized account employs numerous Stoic and Epicurean ideas and terms as well—the latter being the most remarkable, given the famous Epicurean denial of individual life after death in any sense.[42] Partly as a result of Virgil's use of such traditional materials, *Aeneid* 6, much like the *nekuia*, is chock-full of incongruities. Eduard Norden, the book's most famous commentator, stated the matter succinctly: Virgil's underworld has "no unified conception."[43]

Many of the inconsistencies arise in blocks of material, one section of the katabasis to the other, especially in the final sections, where the internal problems proliferate. As one might expect, the patchwork of material led earlier generations of interpreters to obsess over source theories that completely obscured the meaning of the book's final form. Today the Virgilian redaction is more widely respected as a unit, a literary product that constructs a sensible if sometimes incongruent narrative. The earlier fixation was already recognized as a problem in 1954 by Frances Norwood: "This energetic *Quellenforschung* has revealed that Virgil richly deserves his epithet of *doctus*, but the poem itself has been submerged in a sea of notes the majority of which, so far from assisting the reader to appreciate Virgil's work, leave him with the impression that its chief characteristic was a plagiarism which lacked even the merit of consistency."[44] In broad terms, *Sourcekritik* did make tenable arguments that the account comprises three major but disparate blocks of material with varying understandings of the afterlife: an opening section that embodies a kind of mythical, almost Homeric, view; a second that accepts a moral (originally "Orphic-Pythagorean"?) understanding of future rewards and punishments; and a third that advances a philosophical (Pythagorean? Platonic?) understanding of the soul polluted by the body and needing purification. To these Virgil has added his own contribution: the ultimate eschatological significance of Roman rule.[45] I have no objection to this kind of analysis per se, and at the least it serves to highlight some rather striking incongruities in the overall perception of the afterlife. But I also agree with James O'Hara that internal inconsistencies do not necessarily indicate sloppy editing and it is useful to interpret the text as it has come down to us.[46]

Aeneas's Katabasis in Narrative Context

As with his Homeric predecessor, Aeneas seeks the underworld on the instruction of another, in this case his father, Anchises, dead now for a year, sent in a vision by Jupiter to instruct his son to go to "the houses of Dis" to seek a meeting with him, Anchises, who now dwells not in the awful realms of Tartarus but in Elysium with the "pleasant assemblies of the pious." Aeneas will be led there by the divine prophetess, the Sibyl, to learn about the future of his race and the city they will be given (*Aen.* 5.722–37).[47]

When Aeneas and his men land on Italian soil at Cumae, he immediately ascends the heights to seek the Sibyl in the awesome citadel of Apollo. When he finds her in her vast cavern, she is seized by the god, thrown into an unwilling state of possession, and prophesies Aeneas's future. It will not be filled with peace and joy. When he arrives at his destined end after a disastrous sea voyage, Aeneas will encounter even greater hardships on land (*terrae graviora manent;* 6.84). There will be horrible wars and the Tiber will flow with blood. A goddess has borne a new Achilles—Turnus, Aeneas's rival and archenemy in the second half of the book—who will hound the Trojans with the support of Juno herself. As was the case of the Trojan War, the conflict will arise because of a "foreign marriage" (i.e., Aeneas's union with Lavinia, who had earlier been committed to Turnus; cf. Helen). But Aeneas is to go forward and face his perils bravely, as "fortune allows" (6.83–97). To this point of the narrative, the Sibyl functions like Homer's Circe, a divine prophetess who indicates a future with ordained results but complicated by real twists and difficult struggles.

Once Aeneas learns what is to come, he addresses the Sibyl about his other ultimate concern: he wants to see his father Anchises in the underworld. A trip to the realms of the dead, he reminds the prophetess, had been made before him by Orpheus, Theseus, and Hercules (he does not know about Odysseus, of course, since they are contemporaries); and he, like all of them, comes from divine blood, born of Anchises and Venus, daughter of Jupiter.

The Sibyl replies to his request with some of the most memorable and sobering lines of the book: "Oh you, born from the blood of the gods, son of Anchises the Trojan, the descent to Avernus is easy (*facilis descensus Averno*). Night and day the door of dark Dis stands open. But to retrace your step and escape to the air above, this is the toil, this the labor (*hoc opus, hic labor est*)" (6.125–29). Yes indeed. Everyone goes to the realms of the dead, no effort required. The trouble is getting back.

But if Aeneas is determined to make the attempt, the Sibyl instructs him, first he must find and pluck the mysterious "golden bough" hidden away in a shadowy grove, if Fate allows. This will provide passage to the world below. Moreover, before going to the underworld, he must provide proper burial rites to one of his own companions who has unexpectedly made the journey himself.

Aeneas follows the Sibyl's instructions. Divinely guided to the spot, he retrieves the golden bough and then arranges for the burial of his companion, Misenus, found dead on the beach. After that the underworld adventure begins.

En Route to the Underworld

The journey to the realms of the dead is vastly different from that in Homer, and far more terrifying. In this case it really does involve a descent. The halls of Dis are not located in the far west, reachable by ship across the river Oceanus. They are down below, and Aeneas, guided by the Sibyl, must make the harrowing trip on foot.

The entrance itself does not inspire hope for what lies beyond. It is a vast, rocky cave guarded by dark woods and a black lake emitting a vapor so foul that no bird can fly above it. As in the *Odyssey*, animal sacrifices must be made, in this case first by the Sibyl, then by Aeneas. Here the rites do not draw shades up from below but allow the living to descend from above. The woods quiver, dogs seem to howl, and the Sibyl screeches a warning, urging Aeneas to draw his sword before they madly plunge through the open gate (6.260–63).

They pass through the dark halls and empty realms of Dis until they come to the gates of the underworld. Here there is yet more foreboding. The doors are surrounded by the incarnate banes of mortal existence: Grief, Avenging Cares, Pale Diseases, Sad Old Age, Fear, Hunger, Poverty, Death, Fatigue, Sleep the Brother of Death, Guilty Joys of the Mind, Deadly War, the Iron Chambers of the Furies, and Demented Strife (6.273–81). These are not the pearly gates of later Christian imagination. In their midst stands a mysterious, giant elm tree with spreading branches, on which "empty dreams reside en masse (*quam sedem somnia vulgo vana tenere*), clinging under every leaf" (6.283–84). What are these profuse empty/false/groundless/vain dreams? Are they futile hopes checked at the door of death? Hopes of what one might have attained in life, decisively denied? Of what might be enjoyed in the life to come, hopes that will soon be radically disconfirmed? The clue will come only at the end of the account.

Along with the tree are yet other disheartening sights, monsters of ancient myth: Centaurs, Scyllas, the sea monster Briareus, the Hydra, the Chimaera, Gorgons, Harpies, and Geryon. The terrified Aeneas wields his sword and is set to attack, but the Sibyl holds him back. There is no point: these are immaterial forms, without actual bodies (*sine corpore vitas*; 6.292). One wonders why she told him to draw his sword in the first place (6.260).[48]

Crossing the River Styx

Passing through the entrance they come to the river Styx, the boundary that must be crossed to enter the realms of the dead. One can't swim across; they have to be conveyed by the divine ferryman, Charon.

Aeneas is astounded by the sight: an enormous throng of the dead is rushing to the banks, "mothers, husbands, the deceased bodies of great-souled heroes, young boys, unmarried girls, young men placed on their funeral pyres before the eyes of their parents"—a crowd as thick as the leaves in a forest, falling in autumn (6.305–10). These appear to be the counterparts of the shades who first arrived at Odysseus's bloody pit, made up principally of those who died before their time (*Od.* 11.36–41). But the immediate focus, again, will be on those who have not been buried.

Aeneas is surprised to see that many of the souls pleading to be taken aboard Charon's skiff are not granted passage. The Sibyl explains these others are the crowds of "helpless and unburied" (*inops inhumataque*; *Aen.* 6.325). Charon is not allowed to ferry them "until their bones are laid to rest" (6.328). If not buried properly, they must "flit around these shores" for a hundred years; only then will they be allowed to return to "these greatly desired pools" (6.330). When he learns their plight, Aeneas becomes reflective, "feeling pity in his heart for their unjust lot" (*sortemque animo miseratus iniquam*; 6.332). These poor souls have done nothing to deserve their fate, and he recognizes the inequity. It won't be the last time.

Aeneas then has his first encounter with a dead soul, a travel mate who had just recently died but had not been buried (cf. Homer's Elpenor). Palinurus had been the helmsman of Aeneas's ship but had been swept overboard before reaching land, a tale related at the end of the previous book (5.827–71). Aeneas asks the soul of his former companion how it had happened. Palinurus's account differs in significant ways from the earlier version—whether he is altering the story to put a better face on it (not wanting his commander to know he had fallen asleep at the wheel?), or because reality seen from the world below differs from that seen above (if so, which one is "true"?), or just because the account is incoherent.[49]

In any event, like the others, Palinurus desperately wants to cross the Styx to arrive at his final resting place. He begs Aeneas to find his corpse after returning to the world above and throw dirt on it for burial. If that is not possible, then to use his divine connections—his mother is a goddess, after all—to allow his erstwhile companion to join him on his onward journey across the river, "that at least in death I might rest in a peaceful abode" (6.371). This is a desperate plea but based on the false assumption that he will eventually find "rest" and a "peaceful abode." If only he knew what was waiting for him on the other side. In any event, a premature transport is not possible. The Sibyl upbraids Palinurus for thinking he can cross without burial. But she provides at least some solace by assuring him that he will indeed receive an honorable, even magnificent burial, and his name will live on.

Aeneas and the Sibyl continue on their way. The grizzled and cantankerous old Charon requires some convincing before agreeing to ferry them across: whenever he has provided crossing to mortals before, it has not gone well (one thinks of Orpheus, Hercules, and Theseus and Pirithoüs). But the Sibyl assures him their mission is harmless, and when that has little effect, she shows him the golden bough. He relents and his leaky vessel groans under the weight of living mortals—it is accustomed to weightless shades—and finally they cross.

Once there, Aeneas and his prophetic companion find themselves faced with the dread three-headed hound of hell, Cerberus. He can apparently do them real harm, even though the earlier monsters were all bark and no bite. But the Sibyl quickly quiets him with a drugged morsel brought for the purpose, and the two continue on. Then we begin to see the real agonies of the deceased.

The First Three Regions

Aeneas's initial encounters in the realms of the buried dead are not heartening. He and the Sibyl first come to a region that houses various kinds of "untimely dead."[50] Immediately on arriving Aeneas hears the loud wailing of newborns. These are victims of infant mortality, who, just on "the threshold of sweet life" (*in limine primo quos dulcis vitae;* 6.427–28), were snatched away from their mothers' breasts by "the dark day," which plunged them into bitter death (*funere mersit acerbo;* 6.429). Is this a happy ending for a short life? No, they are incessantly squalling.

Then there are souls who had been condemned to death on false charges. These at least appear to have a chance at some kind of redemption. In a reflection of the ambiguous passage near the end of the *nekuia*, Minos is judging their cases (*Od.* 11.568–71). In neither text is it clear what a favorable judgment might bring other than the satisfaction of knowing that one has been recognized as having been mistreated.

Most pathetic are the suicides, who, though innocent, despised the light of the world above and flung away their lives. Presumably they thought they would be better off, but they could not have been more wrong: "How they now wish they were putting up with poverty and hard toil in the ethereal world above" (*Aen.* 6.436–37; cf. Achilles in *Od.* 11.489). Any of these expecting postmortem justice or peace is living, or dying, a dream.

The image of the agonized suicide is encapsulated in one of the most celebrated and wrenching scenes of the underworld: Aeneas's encounter with his former lover Dido, queen of Carthage, his one-time protectress and then besotted partner, who took her life in despair when he abandoned her. The powerful story of their passionate alliance takes up all of Book 4, and to make sense of what Aeneas learns of her in the underworld, it is important to recall why she had chosen to go there before her time. In the earlier narrative, when Aeneas is given divine orders that he cannot refuse, he sails from Carthage, unannounced, to fulfill his destiny. On land, Dido, in anguish, raves like a Maenad, vows ultimate revenge, and realizes she simply cannot live with such heart-rending pain. She decides she must "turn aside her sorrow with the sword" (*ferroque averte dolorem;* 4.547). After extended agonizing, she does the deed: climbing the pyre she had ordered built, she speaks her last words, asking Fate and God to "receive my spirit and release me from these sorrows" (*accipite hanc animam meque his exsolvite curis;* 4.652) . . . "I will die unavenged, but let me die . . . So, so I am glad to go under the shadows" (*sic, sic iuvat ire sub umbras;* 4.659–60).

Like the other suicides, Dido has supposed death will put an end to her woes. But as we discover in her postmortem encounter with Aeneas, nothing could be farther from the truth. Aeneas comes to the *Lugentes Campi*, the Mourning Fields. Here are hidden those who had died of broken hearts from unrequited love. Among these pathetic souls Aeneas grieves to find his beloved Dido. He speaks to her, asking first whether the

tale was true that she ended her own life and then, somewhat disingenu-
ously, if he was to blame. Interpreters debate whether what he says next
is similarly disingenuous or rather reflects sincerity and a broken heart:
Aeneas swears he had no choice but to leave her. He was compelled by the
gods themselves.

Dido answers him not a word. He pleads with her: this will be their
last chance ever to speak. But she fixes her eyes on the ground with a face
as hard as flint. Finally she tears herself away as his enemy (*tandem corripuit
sese atque inimica refugit*; 6.472) and returns to the shady wood, back to her
first husband, Sychaeus, who is waiting for her and trying to comfort her
with a loving response. It is hard not to see him as a consolation prize.
Aeneas leaves in tears, "devastated by her unjust misfortune" (*casu percussus
iniquo*; cf. 6. 332) and pitying her as she goes (*miseratur euntem*; 6.475–76).

To this point of his journey everything seems unjust, with everyone to
be pitied: the unburied who can't cross, the innocent babies, the wrongly
executed, the suicides, and the broken-hearted. Unfortunately, it does not
get better. Aeneas and his companion move to "the farthest fields" (6.477–
78), presumably the "farthest" of that particular region of the underworld
(since they go yet farther afterward). This is where the "renowned in war"
reside, those who fell on the battlefield, including Trojan warriors Aeneas
had known, who are delighted to see him, and the battalions of Agamemnon, who are terrified by the armed enemy warrior who has suddenly appeared with his vibrant mortality. They turn tail to flee. Again, as in the
Odyssey, it is not clear what they fear, since a sword cannot harm them.

Among those Aeneas encounters is his former colleague Deiphobus,
son of the Trojan king Priam, husband of the beautiful Greek Helen after
the death of Paris. Deiphobus had died on Troy's final night at the hand of
savage Greeks. In his postmortem state, Deiphobus is not a pretty sight.
He had been brutally mutilated and still bears the scars: face and hands
cruelly lacerated, ears and nostrils lopped off, and apparently doomed to
live like this forever (6.498–99). Astonished at his appearance, Aeneas asks
for an explanation, and Deiphobus pours out his tale of woe (6.509–30): a
betrayal by Helen herself, who in the end had sided with the Greeks and
had made the signal for them to return to the city. Once the attack had
begun, but while Deiphobus lay sleeping in their bedchamber, unarmed,
Helen flung open the doors of their home to the troops headed by Menelaus. She wanted to return to her former lover's good graces now that she
was to go back to him, after having caused the catastrophic ten-year war in
the first place. Once the Greek soldiers found the defenseless Deiphobus,

they did their dirty work with some apparent delight. As a result, he now lives on with the wounds of betrayal and malicious revenge, in realms that he calls "sad houses without sun, lands of disorder" (*tristis sine sole domos, loca turbida*; 6.534). There are no happy times here or reward for heroism and bravery, only a massively unpleasant ever-after of anger, bitterness, regret, and grotesque mutilation.

When the Sibyl realizes the two Trojan warriors are settling in to converse for hours, she hurries Aeneas and the plot along.

Tartarus

They come to a place where the road splits, the path to the right leading to their ultimate destination, Elysium, and the one to the left to "accursed Tartarus" (*impia Tartara*; 6.543), the place of eternal punishment. But Aeneas is not allowed a side trip to the latter: no one can enter, the Sibyl informs him, except those who will never emerge again. She herself had been granted a personal exception: when Hecate had appointed her over the groves of Avernus, she gave the Sibyl a one-time-only guided tour. The Sibyl assures Aeneas he would not want to see the place; he can only look on from a distance (6.548–61). Under a cliff stands an extensive city, surrounded by a triple wall and bound by a river of fire—not a place of torment but a fiery moat to keep inhabitants in and spectators out. A giant gate fronts the city, with adamant pillars no one can uproot, not even the gods. Above the gate rises an iron tower where one of the fearsome Furies, Tisiphone, sits, sleepless, watching the entrance day and night. Aeneas cannot see over the walls, but he can hear the horrifying sounds: "groans, savage whips, the grating of iron, and the dragging of chains" (6.557–58). He stops dead in his tracks and asks what kinds of crimes are being punished, and with what torments.

The Sibyl provides some of the details (6.566–627). Rhadamanthus serves as judge over this "incredibly hard kingdom," chastising and hearing the guilty pleas of those he makes to confess. These are the dead who had delayed atoning for their sins in the world above until it was too late. Once they make their belated confession, Tisiphone pounces on them, armed with a lash and holding grim snakes in her left hand, calling her fierce sisters to join in. Then the gates of hell open up, leading down to Tartarus itself, twice as far beneath the surface as the heaven is above. There the wicked writhe in eternal torment: both divine beings (the Titans and the giant sons of Aloeus, who tried to tear down heaven with their bare hands and to drive Jupiter from his realm) and human (e.g., Salmoneus, who sought to emulate the king of the gods). Tityos is there too, and two Lapiths who are tantalized—allusions to the sinners of Homer.[51]

But in contrast to the *nekuia*, everlasting torture is not reserved only for those who directly affronted the gods (assuming that is the crime in Homer). On the contrary, sinners of all sorts suffer for ethical infractions, including some that are surprisingly commonplace (6.608–14): those who hated brothers, struck parents, implicated clients in fraud, jealously guarded acquired wealth without sharing with families (we are told this is a particularly large group; 6.611), and adulterers who were murdered (but apparently not adulterers who were not). Other sinners had committed crimes against the state: treason or revolt against masters in times of war (6.612–14). All these suffer horrible punishments—perpetually forced to roll a boulder, or being attached to the spokes of a wheel or compelled to sit in place forever. But there are also more specific sins. One sinner had sold his homeland for gold and placed it under a tyrant; another raped his daughter and "obtained a forbidden marriage" (6.621–23). The Sibyl explains these are just a sampling: she could name far more heinous sins and innumerable horrible torments. No longer is eternal punishment reserved for isolated individuals, let alone the "three sinners" of Homer. As the Sibyl sums up in ominous words: "Not if I had a hundred tongues and a hundred mouths, a voice of iron, would I be able to add up the kinds of sins or recount all the punishments" (6.625–28). Understandably, Aeneas and the Sibyl hurry on.

Elysium

At last they arrive at Elysium (6.637–44). This, unlike the other realms (apart from Tartarus), is a gated community, but Aeneas and his companion are granted access when he plants his golden bough at the entrance. After finding such incessant misery on virtually every other front, Aeneas, and we, finally arrive at a peaceful and joyful world. Or so it seems at first. For now we learn that these are the "delightful places, pleasant green fields and splendid grounds of the Blissful Groves" (*locos laetos et amoena virecta fortunatorum nemorum sedesque beatas;* 6.638–39). It is a place of ample, luxuriant light, with its own sun and stars—quite the opposite of the impenetrable darkness of Homer's Hades. And it is a place whose inhabitants are allowed to pursue what they love best: some exercise on the green swards, others play sports, others wrestle on the sand, yet others dance and sing songs. Orpheus is there, playing his lyre. There too are the great names of the Trojan past, including the founder of the race, Dardanus. Some of the men take pride in their horses and empty chariots. Others are enjoying banquets and chanting paeans in chorus in the midst of pleasant-smelling laurel trees near a river.

Aeneas learns these are the dwelling places of the "ancient race of Teucer" (a remote ancestor of the Trojan people; *genus antiquum Teucri*), big-spirited heroes born in better times (*magnanimi heroes, nati melioribus annis*; 6.648–49);[52] here are those who died valiantly in battle for their country, pure priests, poets who recited lines fit for Apollo, those who enriched the lives of others through the arts they discovered, and others deservedly remembered for their great accomplishments (6.660–64). This is a highly select group, a point not often noticed by interpreters. The inhabitants of this realm are not basically good and well-meaning hoi polloi; they are the crème de la crème among the social and cultural elites. This will become an important issue as we proceed.

The Reunion with Anchises

After surveying the wonders of the place, the two earthly travelers become eager for their audience with Anchises, the raison d'être of their trip. Among the crowd they see the great bard Museaus, standing head and shoulders above the rest. When they ask him for directions to Anchises' dwelling, Museaus informs them that no one in Elysium has a fixed residence. Everyone lives among the shady groves, on the cushions of the riverbanks, and in the meadows freshened by streams. But he can show them Anchises, over the ridge ahead and along an easy path.

Aeneas and the Sibyl leave the high summit and descend to find Anchises in a green valley, contemplatively observing the "souls who were imprisoned and about to go to the light (in the world) above" (*inclusas animas superumque ad lumen ituras*; 6.680). This comment on Anchises' ruminations must surely make readers catch their breath in wonder and confusion. It certainly has that effect on Aeneas, once he realizes the situation. Who are these people? If they are in Elysium, how are they "imprisoned"? And why would anyone living in a world like *this* want to return to the world above?

It is at this point in particular that the narrative of Book 6 becomes hopelessly entangled, as perspectives change and the understanding of the underworld shifts. Anyone who works hard at mental gymnastics can probably reconcile the account, but surely it is better to concede that we are dealing with major incongruities. We have seen a number of others throughout the account, and just within this final section are two different perspectives that Virgil has placed in tandem. It has long been recognized that in what follows, he is combining a kind of mythical-philosophical exposition of the afterlife, given in highly Platonic terms (whether or not these were derived from Orphic or Pythagorean sources), with his own contribution that glorifies the accomplishments of Roman rule, a kind of realized eschatology that celebrates the ultimate meaning of life not in a world to come but in the empire of Rome. Even so, as stressed before, the question of sources gives us only so much hermeneutical purchase, and it is helpful to understand how the entire passage, in the end, fits together, without attempting to make a seamless reconciliation of inconsistencies.[53]

The opening line about imprisoned souls returning to the light sets the stage. As we will see, most of the dead who are not either eternally miserable (e.g., suicides, the deceased broken-hearted, and Deiphobus) or eternally tormented (in Tartarus) are destined to be sent back to the world above, in what appears to be a never-ending cycle. But before that happens, even outside of Tartarus, there will be terrible suffering, a point not sufficiently appreciated in most readings. In this account, human imperfections have to be purged, and purging is painful.

Aeneas, of course, does not know yet what his father is contemplating as he peruses the souls preparing to return to life, and so he deals with what he sees. He comes to Anchises and they enjoy a happy reunion with tears and expressions of love. His father inquires about Aeneas's adventures and the dangers he has overcome. While they weep, Aeneas tries to hug his father three times. As in the Homeric model, he fails miserably. The "image" (*imago*) of his father slips through his hands, like "light winds, most like a dream on wings" (*par levibus ventis volucrique simillima somno*; 6.702).

Rather than rant and rail at his rotten luck, Aeneas immediately becomes distracted. Off in the distance he sees a valley in a secluded forest through which flows the river Lethe, past the peaceful homes. Around the river wander "innumerable clans and peoples" (6.703–6).[54] In his surprise Aeneas asks who these multitudes are, and Anchises tells him they are "souls owed other bodies by fate" (*animae, quibus altera fato corpora debentur*; 6.713–14), who are to drink the water of Lethe, "tranquil (or tranquilizing/taking-away-cares/forgetfulness-producing) fluids and long oblivion" (*securos latices et longa oblivia*; 6.715). They will forget all about their experiences in the world below before ascending above. Anchises indicates he has long been eager to tell Aeneas about these souls so he could feel greater joy when he finds Italy by knowing something more about their own descendants.[55] Aeneas, though, is incredulous. "But father," he says, "how can anyone think that any souls go above from here to return again to sluggish bodies (*ad tarda reverti corpora*)?[56] Why do these miserable creatures have such a dreadful passion to see the light (*quae lucis miseris tam dira cupido*)?" (6.719–21). It is a question everyone has when reading the text. Anchises has a clear, decided, and unexpected answer that puts Virgil's understanding of life after death into a radically different perspective. It comes in the form of a myth that shows the hopeless plight of nearly all humans in their material existence.

The Myth of Anchises

The myth is dense and its interpretation widely disputed (6.724–51).[57] Even so, parts of it are clear. It involves the human spirit and the body that defiles it.

Anchises begins by pointing out that an "inner spirit sustains" (*spiritus intus alit*) the entire physical world—heaven, earth, sea, moon, and sun. This spirit, also called "mind" (*mens*), is infused in all parts ("limbs," *artus*) of the material order and sets the whole mass in motion (*totam . . . agitat molem*), mixing itself into the great body of the world (*magno se corpore miscet*; 6.724–27). This infusion or mixing brings forth living beings: humans and animals of land, sky, and sea. The "seeds" that generate life have a "fiery vigor" and a "celestial origin," as long as "harmful bodies" do not "impede" them (*quantum non noxia corpora tardant*; 6.731) or, synonymously, as long as the earthly limbs or mortal body parts do not "blunt" or "weaken" them (*terrenique hebetant artus moribundaque membra*; 6.732). This damaging effect, the corporeal dulling of the divine and vigorous seeds, leads to human emotions and longings: fear, desire, grief, and joy. Moreover, because humans are trapped in the gloom and dark prison of the body (*clausae tenebris et carcere caeco*), they cannot see the light of heaven (*neque auras dispiciunt*; 6.734).

Here we have the view of body and soul best known from Plato, but heavily Stoicized.[58] The divine spirit is trapped in the dark prison of the body, which hinders and damages it. After death, the spiritual evils and plagues generated by the body do not disappear. On the contrary, *necessarily* (emphatically: "it is deeply necessary," *penitusque necesse est*) the evils have become solidly ingrained in the soul because of its long association with the body (*multa diu concreta modis inolescere miris*; 6.736–38). They can be removed only through painful purging in the afterlife.

Anchises portrays this purging alternatively as "retribution" and "cleansing." Souls do have to pay for their sins with torments and punishments (*poenis . . . supplicia*; 6.739–40), but the torments also cleanse the soul of its material taints. To that end, some souls are hanged, empty to the winds; others have their dyed-in guilt (*infectum . . . scelus*) washed away under a whirlpool; yet others have it burned away with fire (6.740–42). The purgation does not take just a few minutes. It is only after the "orb of time is completed" (*perfecto temporis orbe*) that the "long day has removed the stain ingrained on the soul" (*longa dies . . . concretram exemit labem*), so that what remains is "pure ethereal/heavenly sense and the fire of the un-compounded air" (*purumque relinquit aetherium sensum atque aurai simplicis ignem*; 6.745–47). And how long is that day? It lasts until the souls have rolled the wheel—of time or of torture—for a thousand years (*ubi mille rotam volvere per annos*; 6.748).[59]

Who then is required to experience this thousand-year purgation through wind, water, or fire? That is the very bad news indeed: it is everyone whose soul has been seriously tainted by the body. And since "it is deeply necessary" that anyone with a corporeal existence stains their souls through a material association, it appears that virtually every human on the planet requires purgation. Maybe Elysium is not such a happy place after all.

Anchises does name an exception in two lines that have created interpretive headaches roughly forever. After listing the possible means of purgation—wind, whirlpool, or fire—he makes an enigmatic statement: even though "each of us" has to suffer from her or his own "Manes" (*quisque suos patimur manis*), meaning, in this case, something like "divine spirit," afterward "we [first person] are sent to broad Elysium and a few of us possess the happy fields" (*exinde per amplum mittimur Elysium et pauci laeta arva tenemus*; 6.743–44).

The lines appear unusually obtrusive in their context. Stylistically, they shift from third-person to first-person description and from feminine (referring to souls) to masculine (referring to humans). The third-person feminine resumes in 6.748 (*has omnis*).[60] In terms of content, the lines interrupt the flow of thought: the lines before and after both deal with purgation, either its means (before) or its duration (after). Thus the stylistically distinct lines interrupt the discussion to describe a trip to Elysium for a "few" of us, for a happily ever after. The point cannot be emphasized enough: Elysian bliss is not for everyone, but for the few (*pauci*).

Rather than supposing the lines have been interpolated,[61] scholars have generally either argued they were transposed in the textual tradition from a location where they more readily seem to fit (e.g., after 6.745) or explained them as a parenthetic aside by Anchises that interrupts his thought with an important exception. Advocates for textual transposition go back to the eighteenth century, but there is no hard evidence for it and, equally important, no convincing grounds to explain it, apart from interpreters' inability to make sense of the text as it stands—obviously not the best guide for suggesting a textual corruption.[62] It is better simply to take the lines as they come and—because of the shift in both style and content—see them as an important "aside," in which Anchises indicates there are indeed a few (*pauci*) exceptions to the purgatorial rule.

We will consider who those few were in a moment, but first we should inquire about all the others—the vast majority of humanity. Anchises' next comment reveals the stunning truth, a little detail whose horror has not registered among most interpreters. Once souls are cleansed, the god summons them—the "innumerable mass" of humanity (*has omnis . . . agmine magno*) that is, all but the *pauci* who stay in Elysium—to the river Lethe to prepare them for their reincarnation. They return to the world above without their memories. Indeed, they actually now begin to "want" to return to bodies (*et incipiant in corpora velle reverti*; 6.751).

But the careful reader might well ponder: What good will *that* do? Within Anchises' own perspective, it surely is about the worst thing that could happen. If after being cleansed, souls return to bodies, especially without their memories of what that will entail, the logic of the myth requires them to be stained again by their new bodies (it is "deeply necessary"). They will then die again and need to be painfully purged for yet another thousand years—and then they will repeat the cycle ad infinitum. Leaving aside Tartarus, it's the soul's worst nightmare.

But does everyone suffer equally? On any arrangement of the text, everyone suffers *some*. That is to say, even the *pauci* have to suffer for a time—including Anchises himself: note "each of us suffers from his or her own Manes" (*quisque suos patimur manis*; 6.743). But obviously not for "the long day," the interminable millennium of hurricane, whirlpool, or conflagration: within the narrative, Anchises has been dead for a year. Whatever suffering he had to endure did not require many centuries, but months at worst. From *there* (*exinde*), that is, from the suffering required, he and the

other exceptions ("we") go to Elysium, and then these few (*pauci*) retain/
possess/stay (*tenemus*) in the happy fields. The *other* souls (*has omnis*), however, revolve the wheel of purgation for up to a thousand years. Then it is
back to a body to start all over again.

Still, given the fact that a (very) few escape with only a brief purgation, it may make sense to consider whether *all* the punishments are to be
understood as calibrated.[63] Possibly different souls are purged for different amounts of time, depending on the extent and depth of the stain that
requires scrubbing. If so, then some souls may take the entire millennium,
but others less. That would make sense if indeed this mythical conception
of future purgation is even more fully rooted in the Platonic dialectic.[64]
Some people in life abandon themselves completely to the pleasures of the
flesh; others more moderately so. Yet other people—philosophers—focus
almost entirely on their souls and renounce bodily passions and longings.
Presumably, then, the stains "dyed into" souls are widely variant, and one
might assume that the requirements for cleansing are as well. If the period
allotted to the procedure is a thousand years, then possibly once the requisite purgation has been accomplished (for however many months, years,
or centuries), the soul is allowed into Elysium for the balance of time that
remains, until lining up at Lethe to return to a body again. The text, of
course, is not explicit on the point.

Who then are Anchises' exceptions, the *pauci* who go virtually straight
to Elysium for eternal happiness with just a minimum of purging? He
includes himself in the lot, presumably in part (the most part?) because
of his divine connection through his inamorata, Aeneas's mother, Venus.
This would be in keeping with the Homeric model, where Menelaus escapes eternal witlessness in Hades, transported to the Blessed Fields because of his connection to Zeus through marriage to his daughter Helen
(*Od.* 4.561–69). The cases are not identical, of course: Menelaus, for example, does not come to Elysium after death; he is whisked off while still
alive. For Homer, all *deceased* mortals go to Hades.[65]

But who are among Anchises' *pauci* besides a tiny group of divinely
connected humans? The best guess would be that they encompass the
happy souls Aeneas saw immediately on his arrival: the heroes of the Trojan past, the "pure priests," bards with songs fit for Apollo; artists who
made a significant impact on culture; and those who were long remembered for the good they did for the human race (*Aen.* 6.650–67). This is
indeed a highly elite corps: not the favored 1 percent but far fewer. If so,
then the other 99-plus percent are either eternally miserable (such as the
infants, suicides, and heart-broken lovers of an earlier region) or merci-

lessly tortured forever in Tartarus or (the majority, one might assume) subject to painful purgation for up to a thousand years before being reincarnated to do it all again.

This myth of Anchises clearly does not cohere with the rest of Virgil's portrayal of the underworld.[66] Nothing in the discussions of the suicides Dido and Deiophobus, for example, suggests they will ever have any fate other than what they are now experiencing: they are not being purged, released to Elysium, or lined up for reincarnation—a circumstance long noticed by critics. As James Zetzel baldly states about Anchises' myth: "Nothing in the previous sections of the underworld either anticipates this or is consistent with it. . . . The Virgilian underworld, therefore, embodies radically different and mutually incompatible accounts of the afterlife and the nature of the soul, and it is hard to see how they can be reconciled."[67]

Norden and many others blamed the incoherence on Virgil's decision to incorporate a variety of irreconcilable sources. That may well be right. At the same time, as more recent interpreters have insisted, Virgil did choose to link these sources together into a narrative, and he certainly had something in mind. For hermeneutical purposes, it would seem best, therefore, to accept the actual climax of the account, coming in Anchises' myth, along with the episode that follows that it is designed to set it up— the Parade of Heroes—as the controlling perspective and understand the earlier portions of the journey, even if purely traditional, as subservient to this larger view, even if they cannot be fully reconciled with it.[68]

In one major way—indeed, the most important way—the account, all parts considered, is coherent. Virgil's afterlife is not a happy prospect. True, his readers do not have to anticipate the eternal powerless and witless boredom of Homer's Hades. There will indeed be rewards and punishments in the world to come. Even so, this eschatological vision is, when carefully examined, almost entirely void of hope for the vast majority of people on the planet. And that is no accident. On the contrary, it provides the point driving the entire epic, even if it is not developed until its end. If the life to come provides no hope, what does? Virgil's answer comes in the final scene. Hope lies in life in the world above, a world that has reached its glorious apex, the civilized, peaceful, and just world that Virgil's contemporaries now enjoy. The world created by Rome.

Virgil presents a realized eschatology where the hope of the future depends on the Roman achievement. And so he ends his account not with a look ahead for individuals destined for the realms of the dead but with a projection, from the time of Aeneas, of life in his own authorial world, life under Roman rule. Aeneas's encounter with Anchises has all along been leading up to the Parade of Heroes, the final major section of the kataba-sis, where the souls of their important descendants pass before their eyes and Anchises explains who they are and what they will accomplish in the glorious empire of Rome. What is most striking is that this is not a trium-phalist ending. To the reader's surprise, even the ultimate eschatological goal is deeply flawed. Virgil's eschatology is realized and Roman, but it is not utopian.

The Parade of Heroes

Anchises' myth sets the Parade of Heroes in a narrative context: once the reader realizes that souls will be reincarnated, it makes sense for Aeneas to see the most important ones, those destined to become the greats of Roman history. This section, however, creates yet more incongruities with the rest of the underworld journey and the myth in particular. The most obvious must surely have occurred to the first hearers of the tale: If the souls who pass under Aeneas's review are to be imagined as some of the greatest ever to have lived (Augustus, for example), why would they not be included among the *pauci* who inherit Elysium for all time without being reincarnated? The reason is obviously less related to afterlife logic than to the requirements of the narrative. Virgil wants Aeneas to see his most noteworthy descendants of centuries yet to come, and for that to happen, he has to observe them in their preembodied state, even if it makes little sense in the overall perspective.

An even more fundamental incongruity goes to the heart of Anchises' myth in relationship to the parade, as D. C. Feeney in particular has rec-ognized in a justly celebrated article.[69] The parade's espousal of a pres-entist eschatology that focuses ultimate meaning on social and political matters comes on the heels of a myth that rejects the importance, let alone the paramount eschatological significance, of life in this world. The Pla-tonic myth, in Feeney's words, stresses that life on earth is "in its essence antipathetic to the soul." Yet the reincarnation of the Roman heroes "is a catalogue of earthly achievement, of kings and statesmen, the very cat-egory against which Plato warns so strenuously." For Feeney, "It is not the mere fact of inconsistency which should arrest us, for Vergil's eclecticism is by no means always synthetic. At issue here is a fundamental paradox, an eschatology which is expressed and presented within a recognized philo-sophical tradition, but which appears to champion mundane values dispar-aged by that tradition, turning our eyes insistently toward this corporeal world, away from the concerns of the soul." Even more, "The paradox is not inert . . . but operative; it is not one which the poet glosses over, or leaves tactfully unstressed, but one to which he regularly directs our attention."[70]

Anchises takes Aeneas to a hill in the midst of the throngs waiting to be reincarnated and shows him his major "descendants from the Italian people" (*Itala de gente nepotes;* 6.757)—that is, those who will be descended from Aeneas and his future Italian wife, Lavinia. He begins with Aeneas's eventually last-to-be-born child, Silvius, future king of the city of Alba Longa, from which Rome will be established. He goes from there, pointing out one person after another, some of them even still household names—Romulus, Caesar, and Augustus himself; others, household names in Virgil's time—Brutus (the first, not the assassin of Caesar) and Cato; and yet others who were vital for the ongoing conquests and internal vitality of the Roman people.

In this parade, Augustus takes center stage, though not in a way one might expect. He is indeed the ultimate star of the field, the last and greatest in Virgil's time, the pinnacle of all that went before. But he does not come last in the list. Instead, he appears almost exactly in the middle.[71] He is therefore structurally central to the account and historically the goal toward which it moves.

The end of the list is its own climax and provides the interpretive key to the whole, with two of Rome's most important conquering heroes and, finally, at the very last, with its most heart-wrenching disappointment. In 6.845 Anchises identifies the soul of Quintus Fabius Maximus, the famed opponent of Hannibal, affirming that he is indeed "the mightiest" (*maximus*). He then uses him to summarize, glorify, and, especially, enjoin the great Roman achievement in a direct address to an ideal, constructed Roman, set in contrast to other producers of civilization: "Others, I indeed believe it, will more gently form bronze that breathes, bring living faces out of marble, better argue legal cases, and trace the motions of the heavenly bodies with a pointer or describe the rising stars. You, Roman, remember (*tu . . . Romane, memento*): these are your arts: rule the peoples with power (*imperium*), establish peaceful customs, spare the conquered, and crush the proud" (6.847–53). The Greeks will indeed have superior artists, orators, and scientists, and these endeavors are important. But the Roman accomplishment will be superior. Rome is to assert its imperium over the world and so bring peace and justice. High culture in the arts and sciences is of no avail in a world filled with anarchy, senseless violence, and tyranny. Rome alone will spread culture, civilization, and the rule of law to the world. It is the pinnacle of human striving, the eschatological goal.[72]

Anchises then points to one other Roman great, Marcus Claudius Marcellus, only the third ever to win the *spolia opima*—spoils taken by a Roman general from the opposing general in the field of battle (6.854–59). The reference to Marcellus is laudatory, but brief and seemingly anticlimactic, again for reason of the narrative. He has been mentioned in order to introduce his namesake of two centuries later, Virgil's own contemporary, Marcellus the younger, with whom the Parade of Heroes will end. At first glance it seems an extremely odd choice.

Aeneas sees a young and beautiful soul with a noble mien and an impressive entourage passing before him, and he asks his father who it is (6.860–65). Anchises' proud delineation of Roman greatness immediately shifts to gut-wrenching despair. He tells Aeneas not to seek out the agony of his future people. This youth is one whom the gods could not allow to live long; otherwise, the Roman people would have become too powerful. His death has brought universal grief. This is one on whom all the hopes of state had been placed, an invincible warrior, but fated to die before his time. He then names him: "You will be Marcellus" (6.883).

Marcellus was Augustus's nephew, son of his sister Octavia, married to his daughter Julia, and widely considered his chosen heir to the throne. He was indeed the hope of Rome's future. But he contracted a fatal illness when only nineteen years old (23 BCE), shattering the dreams of the imperial family and, presumably, the Roman aristocracy. Anchises expresses his longing to scatter lilies on the grave of this last great hope of the future.

And that is how Virgil ends his Parade of Heroes—not in triumph but in tragedy, with the untimely death of the presumed imperial successor who would have made the empire greater still. This is not what a reader might expect from an epic designed to celebrate the divinely fated glory of empire. Surely the parade of future Roman greats would end with Augustus himself and the mention of one of his most glorious achievements, say, the Battle of Actium, or with the climactic injunction for the Roman to assert power over the earth ("You, O Roman, remember . . ."; 6.851–53). But no, Virgil chooses to end it with heartbreaking loss, the senseless death of the heir of the sonless emperor, the now-lost hope.[73]

If nothing else has done so to this point, this ending should put a prominent question mark over Virgil's entire endeavor and his ostensible goal, both in Book 6 and in the epic itself. Is this the great future of Rome, the eschatological goal toward which all else is heading—untimely death and dashed hopes?[74]

As I already pointed out, scholars for more than half a century have recognized that the *Aeneid* is no panegyric on the Roman state. Making the death of Marcellus the "climax" of Roman history is in fact not anomalous in the broader narrative but is oddly characteristic, even though more subtle indications of future pain and misery have often been passed over by readers. Still, they are there for all to see, and have been seen with some regularity over the past decades. Just within the Parade of Heroes itself we encounter not only unambiguous and unproblematic glorious figures but also Romulus, who killed his own brother at the laying of the foundations of the city; Lucius Junius Brutus, yes, "founder" of the Republic but also famous for supporting the execution of his own sons for an attempted rebellion; even Caesar, enveloped in a civil war that nearly destroyed the state before he was himself assassinated. It is not an unblemished history.[75]

The underlying pessimism of the Parade of Heroes in fact pervades the epic from beginning to end. The destruction of Troy, the disastrous journey to Italy, the bloody wars that ensue, the executions, civil strife, lost battles, meaningless deaths that follow: Virgil is not interested in hiding the ugly and painful realities of Roman history or fabricating an unproblematic triumphalist account of the glories that were achieved. At every stage, at every turn, it is hardship, struggle, pain, misery, and suffering, world without end. Rome may be the greatest accomplishment of the long history of the human race. It may be the pinnacle of human achievement. It may be the eschatological reality ordained by the gods. But it is deeply flawed, and always will be.[76]

The Gates of Sleep

The most perplexing and controversial passage of the *Aeneid* comes at the end of Book 6 when Aeneas and the Sibyl leave the underworld. Virgil grants it only a terse narrative that both creates and belies its importance (6.893–98). We are told there are two gates of sleep (*sunt geminae somni portae*), one said to be made of horn (*cornea*), which provides an easy exit for true shades (*qua veris facilis datur exitus umbris*); the other, of white ivory (*candenti . . . elephanto*; 6.893–95), through which the "spirits of the dead" (*manes*) send false dreams (*falsa . . . insomnia*) into the world (*ad caelum*). Anchises takes his son and the Sibyl and sends them up through the ivory gate (*portaque emittit eburna*; 6.898). Aeneas then heads for his ship to join his colleagues and sets sail for the city harbor of Cajeta.

There are two significant conundrums here: What are these gates, and why does Anchises send his son and the Sibyl precisely through the gate of false dreams?

One aspect of the gates is unambiguous: they are an allusion to the *Odyssey* 19.559–67, where Penelope tells Odysseus, disguised still as a beggar, her dream of the eagle that had flown in to kill her twenty geese. When he explains that her husband has sent the dream to assure her that he is soon to return and destroy her wooers, she expresses her doubt. Could it be a false dream? For, she says, there are two gates of "powerless dreams" (ἀμενηνῶν . . . ὀνείρων), one of horn and one of ivory; the dreams that pass through the ivory (ἐλέφαντος) gate deceive (ἐλεφαίρονται) people, giving words that are not fulfilled; the dreams that come through the gate of horn bring true things to pass (ἔτυμα κραίνουσι). She does not think hers came that way.

In *Aeneid* 6 the gates are the exits from the underworld, one for true shades, and the other for false dreams. But why would Aeneas pass through the latter? Interpreters have had a field day with the passage, virtually everyone agreeing that earlier suggestions are problematic and some admitting that theirs is as well.[77] Our earliest commentator, Servius, suggested that the exit was meant to indicate that Virgil's entire narrative was false: "*vult autem intelligi falsa esse omnia quae dixit*" ("he wants everything he says to be understood as false").[78] But surely not—the point of the Parade of Heroes, for example, is that this really is going to happen. Norden went a completely different direction, pointing to an ancient tradition that true dreams appear only after midnight. The passage, then, means that Aeneas left the underworld before the stroke of twelve, an explanation widely seen as lying somewhere between anticlimactic and desperate. Clausen later objected: "I have a sense, which I cannot quite put into words, that Virgil was not merely telling the time of night."[79]

Brooks Otis embraced the suggestion that Aeneas had not actually gone below but that the visit itself was a dream.[80] That too is problematic: Otis admits that what Aeneas saw in this "dream" was actually true. So what would be the point of saying it was a "false" dream—or that it was even "just" a dream? R. G. Austin argued that Aeneas had no choice about the gate: he could not go through the exit for true shades because in fact he was not a shade.[81] This view seems to have made sense to other interpreters, but there is a very big problem. Aeneas also was not a "dream," let alone a false one. Moreover, no one should argue that Virgil had little option in the matter since there are only two gates. Nothing forced him to allude to Penelope's words and thus restrict the modes of egress—he chose two gates and sent Aeneas through one of them.

R. J. Tarrant had a more philosophically inclined view, based on the Platonic ideas endorsed by Anchises. Plato distinguished between dreams and reality, the former corporeal and the latter spiritual; and so, for Tarrant, the passage indicates that Aeneas is returning to the false dream world above by resuming his corporeal existence.[82] It is an intriguing suggestion, but it derives more from views set forth in Platonic dialogues other than those lying behind Anchises' myth; for the myth, corporeality is a problem not because it conveys a poor or false representation of spiritual reality (as, say, in the Allegory of the Cave in *Republic* 514a–20a), but because it is an all too real corrupting influence that pollutes the spiritual essence.

Numerous other suggestions have been made over the years, none of them winning a great deal of enthusiastic support. One overarching problem with most of them is that they have not considered the ending in light of the whole narrative of Book 6 and the ultimate point it drives home. With respect to the gate of horn for "true shades," in terms of Virgil's underworld, there is no such thing as a "real" shade in contrast to a "false" one: shades are shades; they are not bona fide or fake. And so Virgil is not indicating that the exit is only for actual shades. The shades that emerge from there must be "true" in another sense. A better option is that shades, by the very nature of their postmortem existence in a world of ultimate reality down below, reveal the "truth" when they occasionally emerge from there into the world above. It is important to note that when shades appear elsewhere in the epic, they are "true" in just this sense—that is, they invariably speak the truth: thus Hector (2.270–97), Creusa (2.771–94), and Anchises (5.722–40), all of whom reveal important and truthful information. So too on the flip side with the gate of ivory. The dreams are not "false" because they are not really dreams; they are dreams that convey false information, dreams that do not come true.

And so why would Virgil provide a pointed contrast between what emerges from the world below as being either "true shades" or "false dreams"? It may well be that one gate is for shades that return to the land of the living to provide true information to mortals and the other is the portal for mistaken ideas of no substance, "false dreams" sent from below to the realms above. It is worth noting that this way of construing the text maps well onto Virgil's intertext—Penelope's two gates, one conveying true information and the other false (*Od.* 19.559–67).

We saw already that newcomers to the underworld appear to check their dreams at the door: that would be why dreams are hanging on the giant elm tree at the entrance, where, it is said, "empty dreams reside en masse, clinging under every leaf" (*quam sedem somnia vulgo vana tenere, foliisque sub omnibus haerent;* 6.283). Note: these are "dreams," insubstantial notions, unreal mental constructs. People have wrong ideas about the afterlife, as Aeneas has learned at every stop on his route. Palinurus and the multitude of other unburied souls eagerly desire passage across the river Styx so, they imagine, they will finally enter their resting place. Little do they know what awaits them when they get there: up to a thousand years of agonizing purgation before being forced to return to the world above in bodies that will again defile their souls and so require centuries of yet more purging and then a return for more of the same, in a never-ending cycle. One might hope that infants who innocently die at their mothers' breasts will at least be treated kindly in the world to come. But no: they weep and wail, apparently with no end in sight. Suicides take their own lives expecting to end their troubles, but after they perform the deed, they desperately regret what they have done and long to return to earth even under the most miserable of circumstances rather than suffer forever with their grief below. Dido had explicitly declared she would end her pain with a sword, but she lives on in agonizing anger, along with other forlorn lovers. Other people thought they could get through life without atoning for their sins. These end up in the dungeons of Tartarus tormented for all time. So too do masses of ordinary sinners, including those who have merely hated their siblings or tricked their clients into bad business dealings.

Even those who escape any of these never-ending torments have a terrifying end, widespread hopes to the contrary notwithstanding. Apart from a very few who are either personally related to a god or who make huge improvements in the welfare of the human race in general, everyone undergoes horrifying purgation through wind, whirlpool, or fire for a "long day." For many (most?) it is a day of a thousand years, followed by enforced reincarnation and a return trip for more purging, a cycle to be repeated ad infinitum.

Despite hopes or even assumptions that the afterlife must be better than life in this world, for Virgil it is just not true. There are only rare exceptions: the *pauci.* For everyone else, life after death will entail massive suffering. Anyone who thinks otherwise has been deceived. Hopes based on a happy future in the world below are false dreams.[83]

For the *Aeneid* (whatever Virgil himself thought) the eschatological hope does not come in the afterlife. It comes instead in life here on earth. An improved life. A life lived in safety and peace; a life of justice, a life under the rule of law, administered by rulers who benefit the world at large and who crush those who oppose the empire that is humanity's best hope. Only in such a world of justice, law, and beneficent power can culture thrive. This is the progress to true civilization, and it is a world created and sustained by Rome, so that Rome is the eschatological goal of human existence. All dreams of utopian afterlife based on imagined realities of what is to come are false. It is no accident that in the remaining half of the epic Aeneas never mentions, let alone describes, his journey to the underworld. Meaning does not come from that realm. It comes in this life, in the civilized conditions brought by a mighty empire that promotes peace and enforces justice.

But even this hope is not truly utopian, in any real sense, any more than any other eschatological fantasy. Rome may be the climax of human eschatological destiny, but it too is a dream. Any sense that it involves eternal bliss is simply false. Virgil was too much of a historian to think that the sociopolitical climax of human existence would either come easily or achieve perfection when it arrived.[84] Establishing Roman rule will not merely prove moderately difficult or experience occasional setbacks. The entire *Aeneid* works to show that the Roman achievement will be fraught with pain and suffering—bloody wars, senseless killings, civil unrest, attempted rebellions, occasional tyranny, dashed hopes, moments of despair—from the outset and into perpetuity. The glory of Rome comes with a terrible price.[85] Both the glory and the price are pronounced and uncompromised, as W. R. Johnson stresses, never reaching any kind of equilibrium in the poem, any synthesis of reconciliation: "The pathos does not nullify the grandeur, but the grandeur does not redeem the pathos."[86]

Greek and Roman Katabaseis

These analyses of Homer and Virgil obviously do not constitute a synthetic overview of katabasis in the Greek and Roman traditions. My goal has been far more modest: to set forth the visions of the realms of the dead in the two most influential katabaseis from Greek and Roman antiquity. Virgil utilized Homer for his own ends, creating obvious points of comparison, but in many ways the differences are most revealing, including his emphasis on rewards and punishments, purgation, reincarnation, and the telos of human existence, the rule of Rome.

We should not overlook, however, one fundamental similarity. In their very different ways both accounts stress that life after death will be extremely unpleasant, if not for everyone (Homer), then for nearly everyone (Virgil). It is not the solution to life's problems. It is not a goal toward which one should strive. It is not a price one should be willing to pay. It is not a hope one should harbor, a dream one should trust. It will be awful. The ultimate point of life in this world is not determined by a world to come. Life is itself the goal, its own summum bonum.

I stress the point because the Christian katabaseis will move in the opposite direction. In the Christian vision, the afterlife is indeed the ultimate answer to all the difficulties in life. It alone is worth striving after. Paradise is waiting—not only for those with literal family ties to the gods, as in Homer, or just for a tiny sliver of the human population, the most highly accomplished people ever to have lived, as in Virgil. No, it can come to anybody, regardless of the accidents of birth, relations, or worldly accomplishments. That's the good news for the Christians: eternal bliss is available to all who want it and do what is necessary to obtain it.

The bad news is that anyone who refuses to do so will be subject to tortures far more graphic than anything portrayed in Homer's Hades or even Virgil's Tartarus. The postmortem punishments in the earliest Christian katabatic traditions do not involve purgations leading to other chances, and they will not be limited to the worst of sinners. They will be retributive punishments that never end, the fate of the vast majority of the human race, with only one way to avoid them. Christians preached both pearly gates and fiery pits, and, as we will see, their narratives of afterlife journeys helped fuel their imaginations, guide their lives, and drive their missionary efforts.

CHAPTER TWO

The Realities of Death
and the Meaning of Life II
Jewish and Christian Journeys

J EWISH AND CHRISTIAN GUIDED tours of heaven and hell have little
in common with the *nekuia* of Homer but a good deal with the
katabasis of Virgil: a specially chosen human is shown the various
realms of the dead by a divine being; the dead experience differentiated fates, with some gloriously rewarded and others horribly punished; these fates depend entirely on how they have lived. The accounts
differ a great deal from the *Aeneid* as well. None of them, obviously, glorifies Rome. Even more important, future punishments do not derive from
the necessities of natural existence—the polluting influences of human
bodies on souls that require painful purgation. On the contrary, punishments and rewards depend wholly on the will and justice of the Lord God
Almighty, sovereign of heaven, earth, and under the earth, who exacts his
judgment on all people, rewarding those who are faithful to him and punishing those who are not. The rewards are permanent for all rather than,
as in Virgil, mostly temporary, and the punishments are correspondingly
retributive, not purgative. In the earliest Jewish and Christian accounts,
any exceptions to eternal punishment for sinners derive not from individual merit but from a sovereign decision of the divine ruler of all.

As one would expect, each Jewish and Christian account has distinctive features, and despite broad similarities, Christian versions generally

differ in significant ways from the Jewish, largely, but not only, because of the determinative role of Christ and the nature of salvation he provides. None of the accounts, of course, presents a disinterested observation of heaven and hell. These are eschatological visions with hortatory intent, using the realities of the world beyond to influence behavior, attitudes, perspectives, and, in the Christian versions, beliefs.

Scholarly discussion of the Jewish versions has often focused on their influence on Christian successors.[1] This is indeed an important question but, as I have indicated, it is not the one I choose to pursue here. Rather, I am interested in seeing how the similarities and differences among the texts provide some purchase on their meaning and function—not simply with respect to their distinctive portrayals of afterlife realities *in se* but also, more broadly, in relation to their particular cultural and religious contexts.

No one will mistake the literary merits of the Jewish and Christian katabaseis for those of the great Greek and Roman classics. No longer do we soar into the poetic heights with Homer or plumb the narrative depths of Virgil. Still, what these texts lack in artistic sophistication they make up for in intrigue and historical significance. In this chapter I first focus on two of the most interesting early Jewish otherworldly journeys: the "Book of the Watchers," preserved in *1 Enoch*, and, by way of comparison, the fragmentary *Apocalypse of Zephaniah*. I then turn to the earliest full-fledged Christian account in the *Apocalypse of Peter* and finally to its most famous successor, the *Apocalypse of Paul*.

Katabasis in the Jewish Tradition

The Hebrew Bible never describes the realms of the dead. Samuel is temporarily summoned from death at Saul's request, but he does not describe what it was like (2 Sam 28); Elijah ascends to heaven, but we never learn what he sees there (2 Kgs 2); Ezekiel has a vision of the throne room of God, but not the dwelling places of the deceased (Ezek 1); Sheol appears a number of times, principally in poetic texts, but is never described (e.g., Pss 16:10, 49:10, 86:13). Our earliest Jewish description of postmortem existence, then, comes to us in the first major section of *1 Enoch*,[2] the "Book of the Watchers," and its description of Enoch's otherworldly journeys.[3]

The "Book of the Watchers"

The journeys are part of a mythological elaboration of the already mythical Genesis 6:1–6, the seduction of the beautiful "daughters of men" by the heavenly "sons of God," named "watchers." The "Book of the Watchers" was almost certainly composed in Aramaic; some Aramaic fragments survived at Qumran. The full text of the book is available only in Ethiopic translation. Most of the book, including the passage of particular interest to us here, also survives in Greek in Codex Panopolitanus, the same manuscript from Akhmim, Egypt, that provided scholars with their first look at the long-lost *Apocalypse of Peter*.[4] The Greek and Ethiopic versions come from the same textual tradition, as shown by their agreements in scribal error. The text was probably composed in the mid-third century BCE.[5]

The idea of divine beings coming from heaven to have sex with beautiful women recurs throughout antiquity, but in the Greek and Roman traditions such entanglements were not considered a fatal violation of the divinely ordained fabric of existence. The affair might lead to some bad spousal confrontations, but it was not the end of the world. In Genesis, it is. The sons of God perform an act strictly forbidden, and the result is worldwide destruction. For the biblical text all the created order—including the "sons of God"—are to be subservient to the one creator God who had envisioned a separate and not-equal difference between the inhabitants of heaven and earth. The breach of this order has enormous consequences. In this strand of the flood tradition, it, rather than disobedient humans, is what drives God to return the earth to its original chaotic state, with the waters above and below flooding in to destroy virtually all life.

We have no way of knowing how earlier readers understood the biblical passage, but by the time of the "Book of the Watchers," a full tradition had developed. After an introductory section of five chapters comes a much-expanded account of the rebellion of the watchers and its catastrophic results, for both them and the human race. Here God's judgment does not involve a worldwide destruction followed by an opportunity to start anew but the condemnation of both watchers and humans on an approaching Day of Judgment. The account describes Enoch's journeys to the realms beyond human habitation where, among other things, he observes the holding places of human souls, who are experiencing a foretaste of their ultimate destinations, whether eternal glory or endless misery.

THE ESCHATOLOGICAL JUDGMENT

Even though a major portion of the "Book of the Watchers" focuses on past sin and interim punishment, its ultimate orientation is future—a final judgment to come upon all angelic and human beings at the end of time. The book begins with a superscription that sets forth the theme of the narrative: "The words of the blessing with which Enoch blessed the righteous chosen who will be present on the day of tribulation, to remove all the enemies; and the righteous will be saved" (1.1).[6] This will be a revelation given to and through Enoch; it will focus on the coming Day of Judgment when God's enemies will be destroyed. The righteous, however, will experience a blessed salvation.

After a short proem the author launches directly into his account of the coming judgment by describing a future theophany to (literally) end all theophanies:

> The Great Holy One will come from his dwelling
> >and the eternal God will tread from thence upon Mount Sinai.
> He will appear with his army,
> >He will appear with his mighty host from the heaven of heavens.
> All the watchers will see and quake,
> >and those who are hiding in all the ends of the earth will sing;
> All the ends of the earth will be shaken,
> >and trembling and great fear will seize them (the watchers) unto
> >the ends of the earth.
> The high mountains will be shaken and fall and break apart,
> >and the high hills will be made low and melt like wax before the
> >fire.
> The earth will be wholly rent asunder,
> >and everything on earth will perish,
> >and there will be judgment on all. (1.3–7)

This is a thoroughly apocalyptic message of coming destruction, delivered with the poetic resonances of the Hebrew prophets of doom. The end will not involve a worldwide flood but something far more significant—the destruction of the entire created order. Even so, in good biblical fashion, the author stresses that some people will be saved:

> With the righteous he will make peace
> >and over the chosen there will be protection,
> >and upon them will be mercy.
> They will all be God's
> >and he will grant them his good pleasure.
> He will bless them all,
> >and he will help them all.

Light will shine upon them,
> and he will make peace with them. (1.8)

The next section (2.1–5.4) explains the harmony and obedience of the natural order that God has created—on earth and in the heavens above—as an indictment against those who have violated it, that is, the fallen angels. Their disobedience will lead to disastrous results. Then comes an extended account of the myth of the watchers, a full expansion that names names—Shemihazah, Asael, and other leaders—of the two hundred rebellious angels who defy God's law by taking human wives, who bear to them "great giants" who themselves then produce the heinous Nephilim (see Gen 6:1–4).[7] The Nephilim consume everything humans can produce. Still ravenous, they begin to devour the humans themselves, and then one another (7.2–5). Moreover, they introduce humans to the weapons of war and various divine arts—spells, astrology, magic—that lead to massive corruption.

Ultimately such acts lead to divine condemnation. At the direction of God, four archangels destroy the giants and bind their leaders for imprisonment and torture, along with humans who sided with them (ch. 10). Of particular importance for the fates of humans is the punishment of the angel Shemihazah and his companions, who are to be bound by the archangel Michael "for seventy generations in the valleys of the earth, until the day of their judgment and consummation, until the eternal judgment is consummated. Then they will be led away to the fiery abyss, and to the torture, and to the prison where they will be confined forever. And everyone who is condemned and destroyed henceforth will be bound together with them until the consummation of their generations" (10.12–14).[8] The binding is long term with no hope for later release but is only preparatory for a final judgment that will be "eternal"—torture by fire in an inescapable prison. Equally important, this fate is reserved not merely for the angels but for "everyone who is condemned"—that is, the humans as well—who have participated in the angelic wickedness. For this author, this includes virtually the entire human generation, imprisoned for the time being but awaiting the final judgment and its eternal tortures. As we will see, this view of undifferentiated judgment of the damned stands at odds with what we will find later in Enoch's second journey (22.9–13).[9]

Just as important is the following assurance to the righteous, that they will escape the divine wrath to come and lead extraordinarily long and, literally, fruitful lives: "They will live until they beget thousands" (10.17).

The earth itself, relieved of the presence of evil, will become again a paradise of great fecundity:

> Then all the earth will be tilled in righteousness. . . .
> They will plant vines on it,
> And every vine that will be planted on it will yield a thousand jugs of wine;
> And of every seed that is sown on it, each measure will yield a thousand measures,
> And each measure of olives will yield ten baths of oil. (10.18–19)

Later apocalyptic accounts will multiply this paradisal bounty many times over, in both Jewish and Christian traditions (2 *Bar.* 29.5; Jesus apud Papias apud Irenaeus, *Haer.* 5.33.3).

Enoch eventually undertakes two journeys to see the places of torment and reward. During the first he observes the punishments of the watchers before their final judgment (chs. 17–19); on the second he sees the interim state of humans and, then, their ultimate places of glory and horror, currently uninhabited (chs. 21–36).[10]

ENOCH'S JOURNEYS TO THE INTERIM STATE

The first journey focuses largely on the contents and geography of the heavenly realm, including the luminaries, fire, great rivers, mountains, storerooms of winds, foundation of the earth, pillars of heaven, and paths of angels. He also sees a horrific, immeasurably deep chasm with "pillars of fire" descending into it—the interim place of punishment for the watchers for cohabiting with women and leading the human race astray to worship false gods.[11]

Moving past the chasm Enoch comes to a place outside the realms of heaven and earth, "a prison for the stars and the hosts of heaven." These had "transgressed the command of the Lord in the beginning of their arising, for they did not come out in their appointed times" (18.15). Apparently these are other angelic creatures who, like the watchers, violated the divinely ordained order of the cosmos by not appearing at the appropriate times (see 18.1–5); that is, they were willful and stubborn luminaries. Their punishment: they roll around in the fire because God "was angry with them." Still, even though the punishment is severe and lengthy, it is not eternal. It is a purgation to last ten thousand years (18.16). Evidently at that point the stars will be allowed to shine once again. In what is to come, nothing suggests mortals too will be allowed a second chance.

Enoch's second journey (chs. 21–36) is much longer, covering several geographical areas in a rather confusing sequence that involves both duplications of sights from the first journey and internal doublets.[12] Of greatest importance for us is the first stop—the interim holding places for human souls. The passage is relatively terse and, in key verses, perplexing.[13] After again seeing the place of punishment for the watchers (ch. 21), with an accompanying angel or more, Enoch travels to the east to see a high mountain, with four deep pits, or "hollow places." Three of them are dark; one is illuminated and contains a fountain of flowing water (implying the others are dry).[14] Enoch learns from the angel Raphael that the pits are for human souls who are confined there "until the day on which they will be judged" (22.4).[15] Clearly then this is an interim state for the deceased, in four distinct groups—not just saints and sinners.

Enoch asks his angelic guide for an explanation. Modern interpreters might wish the response were fuller; the passage is obtuse in places and internally inconsistent in others: Are there four pits (22.2) or, as later stated, three (22.9)? Are three dark but one illuminated (22.2b), or are all of them dark (22.2c)? Such problems have led to some intriguing, complex, and, of course, speculative composition theories about original texts and later expansive redactions (e.g., vv. 1–4 are the older form; vv. 8–13 a later exposition), most comprehensively by Marie-Theres Wacker.[16] But inconsistencies remain despite all efforts, and the complexities of the theories themselves make any certainty difficult. In any event, for our assessment we are interested in the narrative as it has come down to us, not its (theoretically) earlier formulations.[17]

Raphael explains that the four pits house different kinds of human souls. The description of the first pit is straightforward: it is reserved for the righteous in anticipation, as we learn later, of glories to be revealed. This, obviously, is the pit that is bright and watered. The descriptions of the other three pits are anything but straightforward.

The second houses souls of those who were not punished for their sins while living. They are clearly separated from the righteous for punishment, but it is not clear how badly they are suffering in the pit. Raphael indicates they are spirits separated "here" for "this great torment, of scourges and tortures of the cursed forever" in anticipation of "that great day he [God, presumably; or one of his servants] will bind them forever" (22.11). It is hard to construe the sense, but it may be that the souls are suffering scourges and tortures in the pit while awaiting a judgment in which they will be removed from it (unlike those in Pit 4?) for an even worse fate: being scourged and tortured while bound and therefore unable to move.[18]

The eschatological logic of the third pit is even more mysterious.[19] It contains spirits "that make suit, who make disclosure about the destruction, when they were murdered in the days of the sinners" (22.12). At the very least these appear to be spirits who were innocent victims of murder, calling out for justice. These may, then, be successors of Abel (described in vv. 5–7), but nothing indicates they were comparably righteous. For one thing, their pit is dark and waterless and they are there awaiting punishment. That would make no sense if they were righteous, since then they would be in Pit 1. Are they, instead, innocent victims who are neither truly righteous nor truly sinful, as those in Pit 2? Possibly they are spirits whose cases are yet to be decided given the circumstances of their lives and deaths, somewhat like those discussed later in Virgil, who were unjustly killed and waited on Minos to render a verdict (*Aen.* 6.432–33).

The fourth pit provides an interesting variant in the sequence. This is no intermediate stopping place, but a permanent abode for sinners "who were godless, and . . . companions with the lawless" (22.13). Unlike the more obviously wretched sinners of Pit 2, "they will not be punished on the Day of Judgment, nor will they be raised from there."[20] That is, they will never be taken out of the pit but will stay there in a dark, waterless place forever. It seems likely these souls committed fewer sins than those destined for an eternity of scourging and sundry other tortures, although it is also possible that they are sinners who had already been punished in life. That would be suggested by 22.10 (Pit 2 holds those who were *not* earlier punished). On the other hand, it scarcely makes sense that punishments aboveground for, say, a few years (for those in Pit 4), could be seen as equivalent to the tortures destined for others for all eternity (Pit 2). Then again, we have yet to see a vision of the afterlife that makes consistent good sense, morally or theologically. The same equivocation applies to the suggestion sometimes made that the souls of Pit 4 were the sinners destroyed in the flood:[21] surely being drowned for a few minutes is not equivalent to being mercilessly flogged for all eternity.

In any event, this fourth pit appears to embody the traditional understanding of Sheol: a dark place for souls who have nothing to do for all eternity. Are we to imagine it as the largest of the pits? Surely there would be fewer absolutely vile sinners who deserve eternal torment (Pit 2, comparable to Virgil's Tartarus), and innocent victims of murder whose cases are yet to be decided (Pit 3, like the charges of Minos), and even truly righteous people who will be provided ecstatically satisfying eternal bliss (Pit 1: thus Virgil's *pauci* in the Elysian Fields).

However one parses the character of the pits and their inhabitants, in some ways the most important perspective of the account is that after death comes a waiting period. Spirits still exist because the soul survives the body. Yet the soul has clear bodily features: it can see and therefore requires light; it has physical needs and so desires water; it has physical limitations and so can be bound; it can feel pain and so can be tortured; it can feel pleasure and so can be rewarded. That is happening now, to all souls, postmortem. Even so, this intermediate state on a heavenly mountain with four enormous holding places is only preparatory, at least for souls in three of the four pits: the righteous, the wicked, and the cases that cannot be decided will all face a *final* judgment to determine their fate for eternity.

It is interesting that this Jewish text makes no connection between cultic and/or cultural practices and the interim or future destination of human souls and God. Judgment focuses on righteous and wicked behavior. Nothing indicates a differentiation between the chosen ones and gentiles. But what the requisite behavior entails is left unspecified. Is it purely an ethical code, implicitly involving a simple criterion of doing good to others as opposed to harming them? It is striking that unlike Virgil and later Christian accounts, no specific sins are mentioned, just "sinners." We are left wondering whether some (or most?) of their transgressive behavior also involved improper actions toward God (as already in Homer). If so, are cultic acts, rituals, worship in view? Does the author in fact imagine a difference between the Jews and the nations? We are left in the dark, like most of the other souls in the story.[22]

ENOCH'S VISION OF THE ULTIMATE DESTINATIONS

After Enoch sees the interim state of souls, he goes on to observe the ultimate places of reward and punishment, destined to be populated after the Day of Judgment. These do not correlate directly with Virgil's Tartarus and Elysium, let alone with later Christian notions of heaven and hell, but with the Jews' most sacred and defiled spots—a "heavenly" Jerusalem and a horrifying Gehenna.

When Enoch continues on his way, he sees "seven glorious mountains." The seventh is the highest and has the appearance of the seat of a throne. Around it are fragrant trees, one in particular more fragrant than the others, with beautiful fruit and leaves that never wither (24.2–4). As Enoch marvels at the sight, the archangel Michael explains that the great mountain "is the seat where the Great Holy One, the Lord of glory, the King of eternity, will sit, when he descends to visit the earth in goodness" (25.3). This then is the throne of God at the final judgment. In 25.4 we are told that the judgment will involve vengeance on some (though the text says "on all") and great reward for "the chosen." The fragrant tree, which is beyond human touch now, will then be given to "the righteous and the pious." At that point it will be "transplanted to the holy place, by the house of God," and will serve as food for the chosen while its fragrance enters their bones (that is, into their inner beings). These saints will "rejoice greatly and be glad, and they will enter into the sanctuary." Somewhat surprisingly, however, they will not live forevermore but instead only "a long life upon the earth, such as your fathers lived in their days, and torments and plagues and suffering will not touch them" (25.6).

In this vision we have a mingling of traditional images: the "tree of life" in paradise, the theophany of God on the Day of Judgment, the sacred city Jerusalem as a dwelling place of the saints, and the temple as the dwelling place of God and site of worship. Unlike those experiencing God's vengeance, the chosen ones will experience no pain. The tree of life will sustain them in the holy place. All this will be "upon the earth," not in heaven above but in the world that was originally meant to be their habitation, a place of no sin and no suffering, a place of joy and innocent pleasure, in the presence of God, his sanctuary, his city, and his people, a literal return to paradise with the tree of life given freely to all who are there.

It is difficult to know what to make of the long lives of the elect. If the punishments of the wicked are eternal, why aren't the rewards of the righteous? Instead, they will be granted longevity unusual for mortals; they will live as long as Enoch's ancestors ("such as your fathers lived"). The oldest of these was his father Jared, who clocked in at 962 years before passing off his mortal coil (Gen 5:20), seven years shy of Enoch's own son Methuselah (Gen 5:27). Is the text suggesting the saints will enjoy the blessings of paradise for a thousand years, a millennium? It's a traditional number, but why not forever?[23]

Enoch then travels to "the center of the earth" and sees a place that is "blessed" but with a dark side. There are three glorious mountains and a deep valley, which is desolate and barren. Enoch immediately recognizes the valley as a desecrated place. It is not named, but as the cursed valley next to the holy mountain (Zion), just outside the holy city, it is almost certainly Gehenna.

Now it is the angel Sariel who explains: this "cursed valley is for those who are cursed forever" (27.2). These are those who "utter with their mouth an improper word against the Lord and speak hard things against his glory." These sinners will be gathered there "in the days of righteous judgment," and remarkably they will "be in the presence of the righteous for all time." It is hard to make sense of the passage in relation to the differentiated treatments of souls in the three pits described earlier.[24]

On its own terms, the idea of Gehenna is no problem in particular. From early times this valley outside Jerusalem suffered from a wicked reputation, as seen, for example, in the Deuteronomic History, which condemns the spot as a place of child sacrifice to the Canaanite enemy-god Molech (2 Kgs 23:10). In many ways the desecrated spot represented the polar opposite of the site immediately above it: the temple of Yahweh where true sacrifices were offered to the God of Israel. Much earlier Jeremiah did not fail to see the contrast, when he declared that God would destroy his people because Judeans had put up an altar in "the valley of the son of Hinnom" in order to "burn their sons and their daughters in the fire" (Jer 7:31).[25] Jeremiah announces that now the name will be changed. It will be called "the valley of Slaughter: for they will bury [there] until there is no more room. The corpses of this people will be food for the birds of the air, and for the animals of the earth; and no one will frighten them away" (Jer 7:32–33). This most unholy of all places will be where God will slay those who are disobedient among his own people, after which the scavengers will come.

The angel Sariel does not explain to Enoch what the "cursed" sinners gathered in this place would be experiencing. Possibly he expects his readers to think of Jeremiah. But now the sinners are not the unburied dead, food for carrion. They are very much alive. The fact that the "righteous" are present, presumably looking on, suggests that sinners will be subject to both physical punishment and humiliating ridicule. Most remarkable of all, those being tortured not only acknowledge that their punishment is just, but they spend their time "blessing" God because of it. This is a motif we will see again in Christian versions of katabasis. Behind the idea is the conviction that God is not like other judges who make mistakes. He is completely righteous and correct, and in the end, everyone will admit it—even those in eternal anguish. Whatever their earlier beliefs, perspectives, inclinations, motivations, desires, and sensibilities, they will agree they were wrong, they are getting what they deserve, and God is to be blessed for it.

Enoch then travels from Gehenna to its (other) antithesis, the "paradise of righteousness" (chs. 28–32). En route he sees more great mountains, valleys filled with water, glorious trees, fragrant spices—a description striking some readers as fulfilling no obvious narrative function since no one resides there. Possibly the same can be said about paradise itself, since it too will be vacant for all time: Enoch has already described the future dwelling place of the righteous in chapters 24–25.[26] What he sees now is not the future paradise but the original one, the garden of Eden and its environs, devoid of humans but filled with amazing trees, including, of greatest note, the "tree of wisdom," from which "your father of old and your mother of old . . . ate" before they "were driven from the garden" (32.6). It is difficult to know why the narrative takes him to this place, since it has no bearing on future realities. Possibly it concludes Enoch's journey to show why the realms of the dead he had seen came into existence in the first place. The parents of the human race were driven from paradise, and their descendants will remain outside.

THE AFTERLIFE IN THE "BOOK OF THE WATCHERS"

The distinctively Jewish perspectives on life after death in the "Book of the Watchers" can be quickly summarized. Earlier than Virgil, but much like him, *1 Enoch* insists there will be a differentiated afterlife of rewards and punishments, based on how one lives. But here it is not a matter of nature—the stains on a soul that need to be cleansed—but of justice: the true, invariable, and implacable justice of the one creator God. As a result, punishments are not purgative, designed to improve souls by bringing them bring back to the desired state; they are purely retributive. The ways of God have been violated, so there must be punishment. And these punishments are not temporary. We are never told why they are never-ending; possibly it is because for this author, like his pagan contemporaries (but unlike traditional Jews), the soul is eternal and so, therefore, will be its fate. Or possibly because if God himself is eternal, so too must be his justice. But neither explanation would explain why the rewards are to be enjoyed for only a millennium.

The ultimate judge, of course, is the God of Israel, but there is nothing nationalistic about the account—again in sharp contrast with Virgil's eschatology, where the goal of existence is not eternal life but the rule of

Rome. Nothing could be farther removed from *1 Enoch:* realities of life to come are not about worldly empire. They are about one divine Sovereign, whose rule will indeed be eternal, *imperium sine fine* in a very different sense. But the rule will not happen on earth, at least as it now exists. Even the original paradise is emptied of its human inhabitants, never to be re-populated. God's ultimate rule will be manifest after a final judgment in what appears to be a "new Jerusalem."

In some ways this is the most striking difference from the Greek and Roman perspectives we have seen. Homer, of course, portrays the postmortem state as permanent: Anticleia, Achilles, and Agamemnon will remain pathetic, witless, powerless shades for all time, with no changes to come. Virgil imagines a very different cycle, involving life-death-purgation-rebirth. *First Enoch* presents a third alternative: death is fol-lowed by a temporary differentiated state, based on how one had lived, to be followed by a final Day of Judgment when the verdict will be eternal with no possibility of appeal. This in effect is a combination of originally diverse traditions of future divine judgment and ongoing postmortem ex-istence; that is to say, here the Jewish apocalyptic Day of Judgment has been elided with the notion of the existence of the soul after the death of the body, presupposed in earlier Greek traditions but virtually absent from the Hebrew Bible.[27] This amalgam later became part of Christian tradition as well, stressed in a paradox that was never satisfactorily re-solved in either tradition, that is, why the body would be resurrected if the soul were already immortal.[28]

The Apocalypse of Zephaniah

In further assessing the account of *1 Enoch* we can turn to a helpful set of comparanda from the much shorter and fragmentarily preserved *Apoca-lypse of Zephaniah.*[29] The account shares numerous features with Enoch's visions in the "Book of the Watchers" but presents important and striking differences as well. Our attestation of the text is sparse: a quotation by Clement of Alexandria and two fragmentary Coptic manuscripts discov-ered near the end of the nineteenth century.[30] One of the manuscripts is a very small Sahidic fragment; the other is our principal source, a much longer Akhmimic piece.[31] The work was probably composed in Greek and is usually dated to 100–175 CE, but questions of origins and composi-tional history have proved elusive. Is it a strictly Jewish text? A Christian one? A Jewish text edited/interpolated by a Christian scribe? A Jewish text translated with prejudice by a Coptic (Christian) scribe? Various options are embraced, sometimes with fervor, by one scholar or another.[32]

Whatever its origins, in its present state the account is notable for indicating that rewards and punishments are meted out immediately at death, not only after a future Day of Judgment. Moreover, these are for deeds and nothing else. In this case, however, unlike *1 Enoch*, specific transgressions are named. At least in the surviving portion, far greater attention is paid to divine punishment than reward, even in passages that are allegedly about the future blessed state.

THE JUDGMENT OF THE DEAD

The brief, nine-verse Sahidic fragment is entirely about punishment. The seer, who identifies himself as Zephaniah (v. 7), begins by saying he had a vision of a soul being punished by five thousand(!) angels, who are beating it with numerous lashes, somewhere in the "West." An accompanying angel assures Zephaniah he can escape such treatment: the offending soul has been "taken out of its body" and is being punished for "lawlessness" committed "before it attained to repenting." The point is clear: people need to repent while they can.

The prophet then sees "myriads of myriads" of angels, but the text breaks off right after describing their long hair and hideous teeth—not, obviously, comforting signs.[33] The Akhmimic fragment provides much more information, some of it hopeful for those who are saintly—but here again, retributive suffering prevails. It begins in the middle of a sentence describing a burial rite and then launches into the prophet's vision, as he is taken "up (over) all my city." From his heightened vantage point he sees "the whole inhabited world hanging like a drop of water, which is suspended from a bucket when it comes up from a well." That is, he has a comprehensive view of the world of mortals. He is struck by the brightness of his observatory: the accompanying angel assures him there is no darkness there, since he is in the realm of "the righteous and the saints" (2.7). Somewhat oddly, he does not see any of the saints—or at least does not mention them—only "all the souls . . . as they exist in punishment" (2.8).

The angel suggests a change of scenery, offering to show Zephaniah the place of righteousness. Or so he says. What Zephaniah sees instead are three sons of the priest Joatham, who have obeyed neither their father nor God (3.4). He then sees angels weeping over the three; his interpreter tells him these are the angelic secretaries who record all the good deeds of the righteous in a manuscript to be carried to the Lord Almighty, who will then write their names in the "Book of the Living." But they also record the sins of the wicked and inform the angelic "accuser," who re-records the information to present to the divine tribunal before taking the sinners out of the world to go "down there."[34] With this explanation, it is not difficult to see where the sons of Joatham are heading.

It is interesting that righteous deeds are recorded along with unrighteous ones. Righteousness is not simply a matter of avoiding sin but of active engagement, and the specificity of the actions matters. Moreover, in this model of eternity, the blessed go to the realm above and the doomed to the one below on the basis of the reports of good angels and the "accuser." These are clear differences from *1 Enoch*, where there are no records, no dichotomy of up and down, and no angelic accuser. The account would fit as comfortably in a Christian as in a Jewish context.[35]

Zephaniah then comes upon many myriads of angels with long hair, tusks, scourges, and other frightening features. These spend three days among the souls of the ungodly before ultimate judgment is pronounced, presumably afflicting them before taking them "into their eternal punishment" (4.7). Then Zephaniah does have a happier vision of a "beautiful city" that he walks around. The description is very brief, however, focusing mainly on the fact that the city has bronze gates (mentioned four times in six verses; 5.1–6). The prophet circumnavigates the place but does not mention other features or say a word about its inhabitants, or indeed whether it even has any. What he does see is that "fire was being cast forth for about fifty stadia" from the bronze gates. It is not clear whether these are the gates of hell and whether the city is an entryway to it or instead the blessed city of the saved, protected from external influences by all those gates.[36]

The author then skips quickly from paradise to Hades. Zephaniah comes to a sea that he assumes is water but learns instead is a "sea of flame" burning with "sulfur and bitumen" (6.1). Terrified, he prays to be saved. He then sees two angels, one a frightful accuser and the other the great Eremiel, who has charge of Hades, where "all of the souls are imprisoned from the end of the flood . . . until this day" (6.15). Eremiel is holding a manuscript that records all of Zephaniah's deeds, including his moral shortcomings: failing to visit the sick, the widows, and orphans; not fasting and praying; and so on. Nonetheless, his righteous deeds outweigh his sins, and he is allowed to the place of salvation, where he is praised by many myriads of angels and robed with an "angelic garment" (8.3). Thus, salvation depends on the balance of good deeds and bad (both omission and commission), and at death humans can become angels—both themes attested elsewhere in afterlife texts of the period.[37]

Zephaniah receives praise for "having triumphed over the accuser" (9.1) and is welcomed to the "crossing place" to join the righteous, because his name is "written in the Book of the Living." But immediately we return to more punishment: an angel blows a golden trumpet, and the prophet once again sees the frightful sight of Hades, the sea of liquid fire whose "waves came up the clouds." Now he realizes what the sea actually is—the place of torment for "all the souls sinking in it" (10.1).

THE SEA OF TORMENT

Zephaniah sees four groups of sinners in torment, suffering specific punishments for their characteristic sins (10.1–14). First are souls with hands bound to their necks and both hands and feet fettered (while, of course, they are sinking). He asks who they are and receives a confusing reply. O. S. Wintermute translates: "These are the ones who were bribed and they were given gold and silver until the souls of men were led astray" (10.5). The sin makes sense, but only because the key word "bribed" is a textual emendation. The Coptic actually uses the Greek loanword φορεῖν ("to bear/carry"). Bernd Diebner makes a stab at its meaning by suggesting the word is derived from φέρω and rendering it, "These are those who used to own" ("Diese sind die, die sie zu besitzen pflegen").[38] But what does that mean? Slave trading? Bribery? Illicit commerce?

In any event, these sinners have been involved in some kind of shady financial dealings and are being punished for it. So too the sinners of the second group, who are "covered with mats of fire." The punishment may be difficult to conceive regardless of whether the sea is an immense body of water or of fire, but at this point in our study we are not expecting coherence. These are people who have given out loans for interest, an obvious allusion to Mosaic laws (Exod 22:25, 25:35–37; Deut 23:19–20), even though the scriptural injunctions refer to Israelites taking interest from fellow Israelites and close kin, not from people in general.

Group three are people who are blind. Presumably, this is their punishment, but we are not told that this is the case. Their transgression is very interesting indeed: "These are catechumens who heard the word of God, but they were not perfected in the work which they heard" (10.9).[39] It is difficult to read the verse and not think of the Christian catechumenate, though some commentators go out of their way to direct their thoughts elsewhere, insisting that the entire text and this verse in particular are Jewish. Thus, Wintermute argues that κατηχέω occurs in Philo and Josephus to refer to giving instruction. This should come as no surprise, however, since that is, after all, more or less what the verb means.[40] Moreover, it should be noted that the "instruction" concerns the "Word of God" that leads to "perfection." Where are the Jewish parallels for this? On the contrary, precedents for the usage are entirely Christian, as already found in the New Testament (Acts 16:25, Rom 2:18, Gal 6:6). It is significant that the word is used as a technical term for religious instruction specifically to new believers, seemingly the idea here, in the roughly contemporary 2 *Clement* 17.1.[41] Surely the verse comes from a Christian hand. Whether it is an interpolation or part of the original composition is difficult to gauge.[42]

Zephaniah is particularly bothered by the punishment of these catechumens and wonders whether there is any chance for them to repent. The angel replies that they have up until the Day of Judgment. This is the only indication in the text that postmortem punishments are, theoretically at least, temporary and that what we are seeing is an interim state, as in the "Book of the Watchers." On the other hand, it is a bit difficult to make sense of the idea that even now sinners can repent. Surely that must mean they will escape *eternal* judgment by repenting, not the current torment. Otherwise, they would surely not hesitate but leave the sea of fire on the spot simply by admitting they were wrong.

The fourth group of sinners is stranger still. No sins and no punishments are specified. The distinctive feature of these sinners is that they have "hair on them" (10.12). Zephaniah is surprised: "Then there is hair and body (σῶμα) in this place?" The angel's reply is equally odd: God "gives body and hair to them as he desires" (10.14). Apparently, souls in Hades do not automatically retain their bodily features, but God provides them at his own discretion—so that some poor souls have bodies and hair and others do not. Since these sinners are not charged with a specific transgression, and yet are almost certainly mentioned for a reason, presumably it is to stress the physical nature of the punishment. But why hair? And if Zephaniah's question is about hair, why did the angel bring "bodies" into it? Is hair simply the somatic feature that makes the prophet realize these souls are *embodied?* Or is he surprised that the hair has not burned off in the fire? The reader may be surprised as well, but then again, bodies without hair are also normally consumed by fire.[43]

Taken as a whole it is a rather strange grouping of sinners: two involving harmful financial transactions, one a failure to take religious instruction to heart, and one that is hairy. One wonders why the author chose these sinners in particular. Surely one would expect murderers, adulterers, or tyrants, not, say, bankers and imperfect catechumens. Two of the three punishments may be connected to the sins in question: the hands of those exchanging money are bound to the neck and fettered, possibly because they sinned in their handling of resources to the detriment of others; the unfaithful catechumens are blind, apparently because they did not see the truth and follow it. Why usurers are clothed in mats of fire is a mystery.[44]

The account quickly shifts from horrible punishments to pleas for mercy. Every day, in heaven and on earth, an angel blows a trumpet to summon the "multitudes" of the righteous who along with the patriarchs come forth to pray for God to bring the torments to an end. The idea of a plea for mercy would make no sense in Virgil, let alone Homer, since in neither case is punishment a retribution by a higher authority against one who had transgressed. But it is in Jewish and Christian texts, and God has the power to reverse the judgment. This, then, is a distinctively Jewish and Christian view of postmortem retribution, based on a judicial model and a penal code. Oddly enough, here God does not appear to listen to any of the pleas for mercy. This will become an issue in our Christian texts: Are believers more merciful than God himself? And does mercy necessarily compromise true justice (see Chapter 5)?

The Akhmimic fragment ends with the prophet complaining that he has not seen all the sinners being punished. Yet again the author appears far more interested in torment than bliss. But we do not know what was described in the manuscript's final four pages, now missing. What we have of the account does end on an appropriate note, however, with a reference to the final judgment yet to come. We learn that no one can see the ultimate fate of sinners until "the Lord Almighty rises up in his wrath to destroy the earth and the heaven" (12.8). It will be a worldwide cataclysm, affecting all plant life and birds and . . . and there the text ends.

Jewish Katabaseis in Comparison

In broadly comparative terms, the Jewish katabaseis we have examined share far more with Virgil than with Homer, and even more with each other. As with the *Aeneid* 6, the "Book of the Watchers" and the *Apoca-*

lypse of Zephaniah portray differentiated afterlives, with horrific torments for some and tactile pleasures for others, all dependent on how one has lived. Unlike Virgil, both portray the current interim state before a final judgment when eternal destinies will be determined. In these, however, the judgment comes from the one sovereign God, Lord of heaven and earth, who rewards the righteous but punishes sinners. The punishment is purely retributive; there is no purgation. Both accounts are far more invested in describing the torments of the condemned than the bliss of the saved.

Zephaniah departs from the earlier "Book of the Watchers" in allowing postmortem repentance, and even more important it specifies sins worthy of punishment. It is a strange list, but the differentiation of sins and punishment will be found in Christian versions as well. Whether a Jewish tradition affected the Christian or vice versa is not our major concern, but there are other aspects of the *Apocalypse of Zephaniah* account that appear to reflect Christian notions—especially those blind catechumens.

Neither of the two Jewish accounts concedes anything to nature. Sin is a wicked deed or the refusal to do a good one; some people behave in a righteous way, others opt for a life of sin, and both choices have eternal consequences. That in itself is not all that different from Virgil, but nothing in these Jewish traditions suggests that the problem resides in the troubled relationship between a polluting body and an originally pure soul. Condemnation is not the natural course of things; it comes from the sovereign God whose laws are to be obeyed. This ultimate sovereignty may have been modeled on earthly analogues, but the Jewish God is no mere Caesar Augustus. He is the creator and judge of the world, and as such he determines what happens to souls after death.

As with the Greek and Roman accounts, here too the future fate of souls demonstrates with exquisite clarity what matters in life. The most striking contrast is with Virgil, for whom there is no ultimate hope at all for the vast majority of humans, since they are necessarily polluted by virtue of their bodily existence. Only a few enjoy eternal happiness, based either on the accident of personal relations with the gods or on remarkable success in life—for example, in transforming human civilization. All other souls are either tortured forever in Tartarus or subject to periods of up to a thousand years of painful purgation before being returned to the body, to have their souls stained once more, leading to another purging and reincarnation, in an endless cycle. Thus the eschatological hope for Virgil lies in this world, in the imperial power that has made life livable and civilized. But not these Jewish versions. Life here is prologue, and the prologue determines the course of the rest of the narrative. It is life after death that matters—a life of torment or bliss that will last forever for those who do not repent; no other chance in life will be provided.

Also important: the bliss is not reserved only for special cases. It apparently can come to anyone, independent of chance or incredible ability. Those who are poor, outcast, uneducated, unimportant, powerless, and unknown can be rewarded forever. They simply need to be obedient to God. If they are sinners, they can instead expect excruciating torment.[45]

Katabasis in the Christian Tradition

Even though the rest of this book focuses on katabasis in the Christian tradition, with some close attention to comparanda, even here I do not provide comprehensive coverage or exhaustive analysis. In terms of both topics and texts my goal is to be illustrative rather than encyclopedic. In the rest of this chapter, we examine the two most famous accounts from Christian antiquity: the apocalypses of Peter and of Paul, with the specific object of comparison in mind, both to the Greek, Roman, and Jewish versions we have seen already and to one another. Like the others, these Christian versions are also not purely didactic, written to inform interested readers about what Reinhold Niebuhr once termed "the furniture of heaven or the temperature of hell."[46] One of our driving concerns is with the parenetic emphases of the Christian katabaseis for life in the here and now, in relation to the non-Christian iterations we have already seen.

All these texts, of course, are multivalent at the level of both meaning and function. Even so, it is no surprise that the Christian versions resemble most closely the Jewish—to the extent, as we have already seen, that in some instances it is difficult to determine whether a particular account, or part of an account, is one or the other. At the same time, one obviously expects distinctive features in Christian portrayals of the realms beyond, and one finds these in spades. Moreover, as the Christian church grew over the early centuries, devised more complex internal structures of organization, developed more sophisticated theological views, moved into the world of the cultural elites, became the religion of empire, and increased its opposition to some outside groups (Jews) even as tensions relaxed with others (pagans)—that is, as Christianity changed over time—one would expect that its views of the afterlife and its significance for life in this world would change as well. As we will see, the *Apocalypse of Paul* is not simply a second edition of its Petrine predecessor, but an entirely new vision.

The Apocalypse of Peter

As we saw in the Introduction, it was the discovery of the *Apocalypse of Peter* that propelled scholarship into ancient katabatic traditions in the first place. Here was the earliest Christian forerunner of Dante's *Commedia*. Whence did it come? How did it relate to its non-Christian predecessors? How did these relate to each other? Where did the tradition originate? As we have seen, when European savants resolved these questions to their satisfaction, they moved on to other things and the study lapsed into an interim state, only to be resurrected in relatively recent times.

Even now the *Apocalypse of Peter* is the most discussed otherworldly journey of early Christianity.[47] As is sometimes observed, it is not actually a tour of the realms of the dead, at least in its oldest surviving form, since it does not record a vision of what exists now but of what will happen later. That makes it different not only from the Greek and Roman versions but, in a different way, also from the Jewish ones we have considered. These do record the postmortem present, even if it is only as a waiting period up until the Day of Judgment; the *Apocalypse of Peter* has nothing to do with an interim state—it is a vision of what will happen when God has passed his verdicts.[48]

Even though this is the first surviving full-fledged katabasis in the Christian tradition, it would be a mistake to think the author of this account was the first follower of Jesus to envision an otherworld journey. Precedents of various kinds appear already in books that later became part of the New Testament. Most famously, our earliest biblical author, Paul, claims that he was taken up to the "third heaven" where he experienced "visions and revelations" that were of such divine significance they were to remain unspoken (2 Cor 12:1–5). He does not say these visions involved the realms of the dead, but they were certainly interpreted that way later.[49] Luke's parable of Lazarus and the rich man is clearly a vision of the postmortem fates of a person above and another below, not a journey by an outsider to either place, although it has been discussed in that way in recent years.[50] So too the book of Revelation does not exactly provide a katabasis, though it certainly is an apocalypse with a heavenly journey, generically similar to some Jewish antecedents. But the prophet does not journey to the current realms of the dead, with one partial exception: he observes the Christian martyrs under the altar who call out for divine vengeance before being placated with white robes and told to rest a while until the number of martyrs comes to completion (Rev 6:9–11). These martyrs are obviously exceptional among the world's deceased, and apart from their location, garb, and vengeful wishes, we do not learn anything about their condition, let alone the postmortem condition of anyone else who had ever lived.[51]

BACKGROUND TO THE *APOCALYPSE OF PETER*

The *Apocalypse of Peter* was originally composed in Greek, sometime toward the middle of the second century CE. Heated debates continue to rage over the precise date, fueled largely by Richard Bauckham's argument, developed out of suggestions of others, that the book was written at the time of the Bar Kokhba uprising, and so sometime around 135 CE.[52] A number of scholars have been convinced; others, including some of the most recent contributors, have found the evidence thin and have proposed interesting counterevidence.[53] The actual date does not matter a great deal for my analysis, which is not affected by a time of composition a couple of decades in either direction. In any event, the book must have been written before the end of the second century, since it is known to Clement of Alexandria, who, as we will see, considered it Scripture. After that it became relatively popular in proto-orthodox Christian circles and was accepted as canonical by other significant witnesses up to the fourth century, a matter to which we return in Chapter 5.[54]

Despite its early popularity, the *Apocalypse of Peter* was unknown to modern scholarship until it was discovered near Akhmim in 1886 or 1887, in the same sixth- or early-seventh-century codex as the *Gospel of Peter* and the Greek fragment of *1 Enoch*.[55] The complete Ethiopic version was inadvertently published in 1910 by S. Grébaut, in a manuscript containing a previously unknown Pseudo-Clementine work; it was M. R. James who realized that a section of the work contained the *Apocalypse of Peter*, in a complete form.[56] Later, two small Greek fragments came to light, the Bodleian (B) and Rainer (R). James immediately judged that the Ethiopic presented an older "more original" form of the text and that the Akhmim manuscript represented an edited version—a view supported by agreements of the Ethiopic (against the Akhmim) with the two older Greek fragments.[57]

At this stage it is enough to say that the superior antiquity of the Ethiopic text is now recognized on all sides.[58] The differences between the two are quite obvious from a parallel-column reading, such as provided by the standard editions of both Hennecke-Schneemelcher and J. K. Elliott.[59] The later Greek version is significantly shorter and, among other things, names fewer kinds of sinners and sometimes describes punishments in less detail (e.g., abortion). At the same time, despite its greater brevity overall, it devotes more attention to the realm of the blessed, reversing the order of the treatment to make the vision of heaven precede the descriptions of hell.

Just as significant, the wording of overlapping material is often altered. One immediately obvious alteration: whereas in the older Ethiopic version Peter observes the punishments that are yet to come, in the Akhmim version he sees what is *currently* happening to souls who have died. In other words, the Ethiopic details what will happen after the Day of Judgment, when glorious rewards and horrible punishments are doled out, but says no word about what souls are experiencing in the meantime. The relatively early Greek fragments B and R agree with the Ethiopic on the point. Almost certainly the Greek text was edited to make the future the present. And why? The author does not tell us, of course, but it seems likely that his community, or just he himself, no longer expected an imminent end of the age. He focused therefore on the immediate postmortem fate of the soul.

In Chapters 4 and 5 I engage in a more extensive comparison of these two major versions; but for now I deal principally with the older and more substantive Ethiopic as the best witness to the first Christian katabasis, focusing on passages of particular significance for our purposes.[60]

THE APOCALYPTIC FRAMEWORK

The opening title is highly descriptive of the book's driving concerns: "The Second Coming of Christ and the Resurrection of the Dead which he told to Peter, those who die on account of their sin for they did not keep the commandment of God, their creator" (*Apoc. Pet.* Prologue).[61] This is not a description of what happens to people once they die. It is about the future that everyone will undergo when Christ, the judge of all the living and the dead, comes to earth a second time. This Christological focus is important—it is specifically Christ who will be the judge of all. Katabasis has moved into a different world.

The account begins with a Gospel episode, reminiscent of the apocalyptic discourse of Mark 13 and its Synoptic parallels, with particularly close ties to Matthew 24–25. On the Mount of Olives, Christ is talking with his disciples, who want to know how and when the end will come. He explains by telling a version of the parable of the fig tree (cf. Matt 24:32–35), imagined now as a prediction of the imminent apocalypse to come in retribution for the Jews' rejection of their messiah.[62] Once Christ explains the parable, the "revelation" proper begins. He shows Peter his right hand, filled with the "souls of all people," along with the image of what is yet to happen at the end of time. It is Christ who holds and therefore controls the fate of the planet and the destiny of all, living and dead. The disciples see that "at the last day," righteous souls will be separated from the wicked, to the serious distress of the damned, who "will be rooted out forever and ever" (3.2). These weep in anguish and sorrow; those who look on—the righteous and the angels—respond with tears as well, as does Christ himself.

Peter in particular is moved by the scene and asks Christ the sensible question: Would it not have been better for those being punished "forever and ever" not to have been born? (3.4). Christ gives a surprisingly stern response: Peter is putting himself above God, who is far more merciful with sinners than Peter or anyone else. God is the one who brought them into existence out of nothing; they are the ones who have transgressed. And so he will judge them. As the reader will see, that will involve severe retributive punishment—torture in the pits of hell. It may be difficult to perceive any actual mercy in this execution of justice, but Christ insists that sinners will simply receive what they deserve (3.7–4.1).

Most of the rest of the account is devoted to this purpose, as Christ describes the future resurrection of the dead (ch. 4); the day of judgment (ch. 5); the coming of the Son of Man (ch. 6); then, at greatest length and most vivid detail, the future punishments of the wicked, followed with the rewards for the wicked and righteous (chs. 7–12). The descriptions of the "end times" on earth in chapters 4–6 are vital to the conception of the book. As with *1 Enoch*, not until then will the eternal destinies of souls be decided once and for all. But for the *Apocalypse of Peter*, the end of the waiting period appears to be imminent.[63] That may be why it provides no description of the interim state of souls, the precise interest of *1 Enoch*.

Also unlike *1 Enoch*, the events of the Day of Judgment are then detailed in an apocalyptic discourse, with cataracts of fire, the melting of creation, populations fleeing from east to west and south to north, and sinners abandoned to the "abysses of the darkness" (ch. 6). Most important, this judgment comes at the hands of Christ, the Son of Man, who will be crowned as Lord forever as he sits at the right hand of his Father with angels all around. "The nations," who have not recognized Christ or obeyed the dictates of his Father, will weep as they are forced to the river of fire. And that, for them, is only the beginning: "But the evildoers and the sinners and the hypocrites will stand among the abysses of the darkness which does not go out and their punishment (is) the fire. And the angels will bring their sins and prepare for them a place where they will be punished forever, each one according to his guilt" (6.5–6). We are a far cry from Virgil and not even in the same universe as Homer.

THE PUNISHMENT OF SINNERS

Without a doubt the heart and core of the *Apocalypse of Peter* is its famously lurid description of the punishment of individual sinners, most striking when contrasted with what we have observed in non-Christian katabatic traditions. As can be seen from the following summary, the text details twenty-one different types of sinners, each type with its own punishment. Some of the punishments bear an obvious connection with the sin, others a less than obvious one. Yet others seem to be rather arbitrarily assigned.[64]

1. Blasphemers are hanged by their tongues; their tongues are continuously shredded, but never destroyed, so they can be used for purposes of suspension in perpetuity (7.1–2).
2. Those who denied righteousness—we are not told what exactly that means—dwell in fire in a pit with angels tending to the fires (7.3–4).[65]
3. Women who plaited their hair to seduce men into adultery are hanged by their hair and cast into a pit (7.5–6).
4. The men with whom they committed adultery are hanged by their "thighs"—that is, their genitals—in the same place (7.7–8).
5. Murderers and their accomplices are cast into fire filled with poisonous, and presumably fire-resistant, animals (snakes?), and lots of worms, while their victims look on. (With Schadenfreude? A sense of righteous anger? Sorrow?) Those being punished admit they are getting what they deserve (7.9–11).
6. Women who underwent (or performed?) abortions are in pits of "discharge" (lochia?), up to their necks in pain. The children they aborted observe them from a distance and shoot

lightning into their eyes (8.1–4; in this case there is obviously no sorrow).

7. Married men and women who committed infanticide are gathered together in an awful place with the children they murdered opposite them in a place of delight, cursing them; the women have milk coming from their breasts that congeals and rots and out of which emerge flesh-devouring beasts that attack both the women and their husbands. The children looking on are handed over to the angel Temlakos, almost certainly for relief from their anguish (8.5–10).

8. Those who persecuted and betrayed the righteous (the Christians) have half their bodies set on fire, are placed in darkness, and are whipped by an angry spirit while worms devour their entrails (9.1–2).

9. Those who blasphemed Christ and turned against (or "betrayed") his righteousness gnaw their tongues and have red-hot irons thrust into their eyes (9.3).

10. Those who practiced fraud by telling lies that led to (Christian) martyrdoms have their lips cut off and fire thrust into their mouth and entrails (9.4).

11. The self-contented wealthy who have overlooked the plights of widows and orphans are dressed in rags and filthy garments and cast onto sword-sharp pillars of fire (9.5–7).

12. Those who lent money at interest stand in excrement up to their knees (10.1).

13. Those who worshiped idols (presumably the vast majority of the human race) cast themselves from heights and return to do it again, forever, being chased by demons. These people have also abandoned appropriate sex roles, men by cutting their flesh (becoming eunuchs?) and committing sodomy, and women by participating with them, along with men who engage in same-sex acts—a complicated passage, but obviously influenced by Romans 1:18–27[66] (10.2–4).

14. Idol makers are fettered with chains of fire and beat themselves in front of the idols they have made (10.5–6).

15. Apostates who abandoned God's commandments and followed demons are burned with fire (10.7).

16. Adults who did not honor their parents and kept away from them are constantly forced to tumble down from high

places, apparently into fire, and then ascend to do so again
(11.1–3).

17. Children and virgins (that is, unmarried women under paren-
tal care) who did not obey their parents and elders are chas-
tised with pains and hanged, while being attacked by meat-
eating birds (11.4–5).

18. Women (or girls) who did not preserve their virginity are
clothed in darkness while their flesh is torn to shreds (11.6–7).[67]

19. Disobedient slaves gnaw their tongues incessantly and are
tormented with fire (11.8–9).

20. Those who did good deeds (gave alms?) and claimed righteousness, without actually seeking it, are blind and deaf and
push one another onto fiery coals (12.1–3).

21. Sorcerers and sorceresses are in pits, attached to wheels of fire
(12.4–7).

It is quite a collection of sinners. One has the sense that the author could
have continued for a long time: it is not difficult to think of other hell-
worthy transgressions. Why these in particular are singled out is a bit difficult to say, especially since some of them overlap to a considerable degree (e.g., vague violations of "righteousness"—nos. 2 and 9, and possibly
no. 20; or honoring parents—nos. 16 and 17).

It is worth noting how many of the sinners come from outside the
Christian communities: certainly no. 8, persecutors; no. 10, those responsible for martyrdoms; no. 13, worshipers of idols; no. 14, idol makers;
possibly, as well, no. 1, blasphemers; no. 2, deniers of righteousness; no.
9 blasphemers of Christ; and no. 20 unrighteous do-gooders. But it is
equally striking that one group comprises one-time members of the Christian community—no. 15, apostates who have abandoned God's commands
(which assumes they had once followed them) and returned to idol worship. More intriguing, some of the sinners may well be ongoing members
of the Christian community who have not adhered to faith commitments
and practices this author considers essential for those who are truly elect:
possibly no. 9, those who turned against God's righteousness, and no. 20,
those who claim to be righteous but are not. If these are people within the
church, then professing faith in Christ, engaging in Christian practices,
and confessing Christian doctrines are not sufficient for eternal reward.
The deeds Christians perform matter—a view we will see significantly
developed when we come to the *Apocalypse of Paul.*

THE NATURE OF THE PUNISHMENTS

Scholarship has paid considerably more attention to the punishments of the *Apocalypse of Peter* than to the sins, often trying to make sense of each and every one of them as if rules of logic can be applied to the mysterious ways of divine justice, or even to the afterlife in general.[68] Most commonly it is asserted that all, or virtually all, of the punishments operate on the principle of the lex talionis or "law of retaliation" ("an eye for an eye").[69] It is true that a number of the punishments involve specifically body part for body part: those who blaspheme with their tongue are hanged by it; men who commit adultery, by their genitals. But this is not lex talionis, at least as enunciated in the Hebrew Bible. In Peter's hell there is no eye for an eye or tooth for a tooth—that is, sinners do not suffer what they have inflicted on others. Rather, the principle is (in some instances) bodily correspondence; that is, the body part that sins is the one that is punished, as found throughout legal and literary texts of antiquity, such as that expressed in the witty but gruesome statement of Aelius Theon in his *Progymnasmata:* "Didymon the flute-player, on being convicted of adultery, was hanged by his namesake" (the Greek word for "testicle" is *didymus*).[70]

In another sense even these occasional body-part-for-body-part punishments are not at all consistent with leges talionis. The very principle behind such laws is that punishment should be commensurate with the crime. In the biblical tradition, someone who knocked out a tooth was not to be punished by decapitation. Despite widespread misconception, often part of anti-Jewish polemic (even though it is found as well in other legal traditions), this was a law for judicial mercy rather than inordinate severity. And of which of the punishments of the *Apocalypse of Peter* can *that* be said? Someone who has made interest on bank loans for, say, ten years, is hideously tortured in muck for all eternity. Commensurability is the farthest thing from the author's mind.

Bauckham provides a more measured assessment. Four of the twenty-one punishments are definitely body part for body part (e.g., tongues and hair); six others could well be seen this way (e.g., haughty rich folk are clothed in filthy rags; women who committed infanticide—and thus deprived their children of milk—are tormented with congealing, rotting milk from their breasts that produces flesh-eating animals); others replicate common human punishments made eternal (burning, whips); others reflect what happens to corpses (consumed by scavengers); and yet others are traditional associations with Jewish Gehenna (darkness, fire).[71]

One interesting question is whether these torments are related to the tortures of Christian martyrs, a suggestion once made, mutatis mutandis, by Saul Lieberman for rabbinic imaginations of postmortem punishments.[72] Certainly fire, hot irons, chains, hangings, and flesh torn to shreds would fit the bill eventually. But at the time of composition? Suppose the *Apocalypse of Peter* really were produced in 135 CE. There were few known Christian martyrdoms at that point, especially public ones. None of the infamous punishments doled out in Nero's persecutions are replicated in the text, except the distant connection of fire ("human torches"). More likely the author has been inspired in part simply by *typical* forms of Roman torture and execution.

But even that is significant. The ultimate sovereign of heaven and earth is understood by analogy. He is like an earthly ruler. The more powerful the sovereign, the more brutal; the more brutal, the more severe in retribution. No governor, king, or emperor can allow rebellion: it needs to be quashed, publicly, emphatically, and ruthlessly; otherwise, his sovereignty will be at risk. So too, God. The image has to be modified, of course. In the earliest Christian tradition God did not usually judge people in the here and now by torturing or executing them while on earth as a warning to others. That will come at the end of time. Christians had little choice about shifting the focus of retribution onto postmortem justice and vengeance: it was not difficult for anyone to see that in this world, still, the wicked usually rule and the righteous often suffer. But that will be reversed when God reasserts his sovereignty over this world and everyone in it. When he does so, he will not merely flex his muscles as a cautionary note. He will assert the full power of his almighty Lordship; his judgments will be final and immensely painful.

In another sense God can and does teach people a lesson in the meantime, not by openly torturing offenders of his majesty in the public square but by warning people of what is to come, in gruesome terms. Romans may publicly crucify rebels and insurgents as a graphic disincentive, but the Christian God does it in different ways; and he depicts the inevitable fate coming to sinners in the written or spoken words of his servants, as a warning to all.

THE PRAYERS OF THE SAINTS

Once our text sets forth its twenty-one sins and punishments, it moves to an unusually significant passage that brings the issues of justice and mercy into close relation (chs. 13–14). The angels bring all the "elect and . . . righteous ones, perfect in every righteousness," and clothe them with a heavenly raiment (13.1). Apparently, however puzzling it may seem, the author imagines that all the saved are absolutely perfect or have been perfected. These righteous ones look down on the pains inflicted on the wicked as God "takes vengeance on them" (13.2). As one might expect, those below cry out for mercy: they did not believe it would all come to this, even though they had been warned. But they know now, in astoundingly tactile ways, and beg for relief. The angel Tatirokos responds, remarkably, by increasing their torment even more, telling them they had their chance—now it is too late. They react as probably anyone would just to make the torture stop: they agree with everything they see and hear, declaring that God is right and righteous in his punishments. For the author, of course, the ultimate point is that God really is just, and no one can deny it. Even those who have burning rods thrust into their eyes for all eternity admit—yes, this is absolutely what I deserve, world without end.

But then comes the most unexpected verse of the entire book. There are textual problems here, but the oldest form of the text of chapter 14 is fortuitously preserved for us in the early Rainer fragment:

> I will grant to my called and my elect whomever they ask of me from punishment, and I will give them a good baptism in (or for) salvation in the Acherusian Lake, which they call the Elysian Field, a share of righteousness with my saints. And I and my elect will go rejoicing with the patriarchs into my eternal kingdom. And I will fulfill my promises that I promised them, I and my Father in heaven. (14.1–3)

Despite Christ's earlier reluctance—or rather outright refusal (chs. 5–7)—he now not only hears the cries of the tormented and of the anguished saints looking on, but he responds with an act of mind-boggling mercy.[73] This is a passage that demands our full attention, and we turn to it again in Chapter 5 where, among other things, I argue that it means Christ empties hell of all sinners and that the text was later altered by scribes and translators who could not abide its claim that in the end all will be saved.[74]

REWARDS FOR THE SAINTS

Whereas the author devotes ten chapters to God's retributive torment of the wicked (chs. 3–13), he allows only a chapter and a half to a description of the blessings of the righteous. The brief passage is notably lacking in detail and creative spirit. Possibly heavenly glory was not the author's principal interest or concern, or possibly he thought one can say only so much about eternal bliss: saints have a fantastic eternity ahead of them. The account does not provide a lot of differentiation among the eternal pleasures, unlike the smorgasbord of torments on offer.

It begins in chapter 15 with Jesus taking his disciples to the holy mountain, presumably Mount Zion. There they see two men, later identified as Moses and Elijah, whose heavenly happiness is described in highly sensory terms. The face of the first is brighter than the sun; his garments radiate; he is stunningly beautiful. The other gleams like crystal; his body is colored like roses; his hair resembles a rainbow. The contrast with sinners in dirty rags, stuck in muck, or infested with gut-devouring worms is not overly subtle. Peter asks where the patriarchs and the "other righteous fathers" are, and Jesus shows them a large garden, filled with trees and amazing fruit, smelling of sweet perfume. And that is it. It is all we learn about paradise, home of the patriarchs and those "who pursued my righteousness" (ch. 16).

The account concludes with the rewritten transfiguration scene, unmistakably related to the Synoptic accounts (ch. 17; see Matt 17:1–9, Mark 9:2–10, Luke 9:28–36; cf. 2 Pet 1:16–18). Moses and Elijah are (already) present, Peter wishes to make three tabernacles for the divine beings, the voice comes from heaven affirming that Jesus is his Son and needs to be obeyed, and a cloud descends upon them (see Mark 9:1–9 and parallels). But now the episode has been reconceived as the "ascension" modeled in part on Acts 1:9–11 (a cloud; "two men" being taken up into heaven). Here, Jesus is welcomed into the heavenly realm specifically by "men in the flesh"—an interesting touch for a text so focused on souls but apparently meant to stress the tactile realities of what is to come. After greeting the three greats, these fleshly men go off to "another heaven" and the angels flock together. Then heaven is shut, the disciples praise God, and the book ends (17.6–7).

THE *APOCALYPSE OF PETER* AND ITS NON-CHRISTIAN COMPARANDA

It is instructive to consider the *Apocalypse of Peter* in relation to the Greek, Roman, and Jewish accounts we have already explored. Its vision of postmortem realities is markedly unlike Homer's; but like the Jewish versions, it has a good deal in common with Virgil, including differentiated fates for the wicked, who suffer horrible tortures, and the righteous, who enjoy an idyllic existence in gorgeous landscapes with fruit-bearing trees and lovely smells. On other key points, the account compares favorably with both *1 Enoch* and the *Apocalypse of Zephaniah:* all three, for example, stress the coming worldwide judgment of the almighty God of Israel.

In every version, the realities of life after death serve as parenesis, instructing readers how to live in the here and now. The pagan accounts, however, prioritize life before death: in Homer, a long life with loved ones at home; in Virgil, the civilizing power of Rome. For the Jewish and Christian versions it is just the reverse. Earthly life is a prolegomenon to what really matters in the life to come. For these accounts, the postmortem experience will not involve painful purgation leading to another chance, as in the *Aeneid.* Moreover, whereas only some of Virgil's deceased have entered their eternity—the wretched sinners in Tartarus and the lucky few who remain in the Elysian Fields—for the Jewish and Christian versions, an eternal fate is for everyone, even if, in the *Apocalypse of Peter* at least, that fate comes to be changed.[75]

In this account, perpetual bliss is open to everyone, not just to the superstars of human civilization, as in Virgil. Even so, there is still a kind of elitism here, not social or cultural, but spiritual, based not on family connections, status, rank, wealth, prestige, or fame but on spiritual will and discipline, in obedience to the one true God. Christ, of course, is the one who ultimately provides salvation. Also, unlike the Jewish versions, in the *Apocalypse of Peter* the sinners' verdict to condemnation will eventually be overturned. Thus here the final judgment is not final. In the end, mercy prevails.

In *1 Enoch* and the *Apocalypse of Zephaniah* we never learn whether rewards are meant only for members of the covenantal community: proper cultic practices and worship are never mentioned. If "righteous pagans" are allowed in, presumably it would be because they have done the kinds of things required by the law of God. In the *Apocalypse of Peter* there is no doubt: there will be no righteous pagans in heaven until God finally bows to the saints' requests for mercy for all. Before that, idolaters are subject to torment in hell, period.

What about Jews who also refuse to obey the dictates of the Christian God? One might think they too will be judged for their resistance, given the tenor of the narrative as a whole—especially the opening condemnation of Jews for refusing to acknowledge their messiah (ch. 2) and the overall prospect of torture for those who blaspheme or slander. For Christian audiences, "blasphemers" would almost certainly include anyone who resolutely rejected God's messiah. Still, it is striking that unlike idolaters, non-Christian Jews are never explicitly mentioned among the sinners in hell. Possibly already in this period of Christian history the condemnation of Jews went without saying.[76] On the other hand, possibly the author did say it. In his initial summary in chapter 6 of the coming judgment, he speaks of the "abysses of the darkness which does not go out" where "punishment is the fire" and specifies who will go there: "the evildoers and the sinners and the hypocrites." "Hypocrites," of course, became a code name for Jews in some early Christian texts, probably based on the polemic of the Gospel of Matthew (e.g., 23:13–15; cf. *Didache* 8.1).[77]

It may be worth considering whether some of the sinners experiencing torment were imagined to be less-than-stellar Christians. As suggested, one group does appear to have been Christian at one time: those who "abandoned the commandment of God and followed demons" are apparently apostates.[78] As to those who continued within the Christian community, it is striking that the author never indicates or even suggests that the sinners in torment are only non-Christians[79] and never differentiates between non-Christian and Christian adulterers, usurers, or disobedient slaves. Could the slaves who gnaw their tongues in fire, for example, have otherwise been obedient Christians? They are still gnawing away, nonetheless.

Clearly the overwhelming focus of the *Apocalypse of Peter* is on the coming judgment of God as it will strike the world in the apocalyptic crisis yet to come (chs. 4–6) and lead then to horrific physical torments for individual sinners (chs. 7–13). The parenetic emphasis is surely related to this focus. The only way to secure eternal bliss and avoid torture in hell is to follow the Christian path in both worship and behavior. Anyone engaged in idolatry, anyone who rejects God's messiah, and anyone who practices sin will be subject to the retributive judgment of the one God who created all things.[80] This message would obviously be of particular relevance to sinners outside the Christian community, but there is little reason and no evidence to suggest the text was written to be circulated among such readers. Like the Christian apologies that sprang up at about the same time (Quadratus, then Justin), the *Apocalypse of Peter* was more likely in-house literature meant to comfort Christians: they had the truth, they would be glorified, their enemies would pay a horrible price in the life to come, and they needed to remain faithful to their commitments by how they lived or they too would descend to the depths of hell.

The Apocalypse of Paul

By far the most culturally and historically significant katabasis of early Christianity is the *Apocalypse of Paul*.[81] Originally written in Greek, it is best attested in Latin translation, with numerous ancient versions and vernacular translations.[82]

There have been long and protracted debates about the date of the account. Its famous discovery narrative of chapters 1–2 claims the book was miraculously found through divine intervention, an angelic revelation that went unheeded until force was applied (on its third appearance, the angel beat the human recipient into submission) during the reign of Emperor Theodosius.[83] Normally that has been understood to refer to Theodosius I, suggesting the text appeared near the end of the fourth century CE. Some important studies have argued that the passage is instead referring to Theodosius II, and so date it to the early fifth century, but the arguments on the whole do not convince.[84] Whichever date is preferred, much of the debate has focused on the final product as attested in the manuscript tradition. Early in the modern scholarship on the text R. P. Casey argued that some form of the account was already known to Origen, so an "original" would date from 240–250 CE, with the discovery narrative and other episodes added nearly a century and a half later. The view continues to be accepted widely, though not universally.[85] For my analysis I focus on the late-fourth-century version, the only one we have; whether it was published around 390 or 410 will not matter a great deal for what I have to say. The text had to be available before 415 or so, since Augustine made a denigrating comment about it then.[86]

The author was obviously acquainted with and influenced by both the "Book of the Watchers" and the *Apocalypse of Zephaniah*, and, most especially, given the obvious similarities, by the *Apocalypse of Peter*.[87] It may be that the multiplicity of sources generated some of the glaring incongruities of the account involving the geography of heaven and its residents.[88] In any event, our concern here is not with origins, sources, and compositional histories, and I do not treat the differences from the *Apocalypse of Peter* as necessarily redactional changes, even if they are. My interest is in comparisons, which are intriguing on any theory of sources. Rather than a full analysis of the text, episode by episode, I focus on significant contrasts with the earlier Christian account, since, in my judgment, these are keys to unlocking both the emphasis of the narrative and its historical function in the community for which it was written, a function quite different, I argue, from that of its predecessor.[89]

The contrasts matter, of course, only because the two accounts are strikingly similar: both are thoroughly rooted in a Christian understanding of divine judgment based on obedience to the dictates of the God of Jesus; both narrate a renowned Christian apostle's journey to the world above to observe the sins and punishments of the wicked, described in lurid detail, as well as the glories of heaven, where they meet Old Testament saints; both include prayers for mercy for those being tormented; and in both Christ answers the prayers.[90]

Some of the many differences between the accounts involve simple narrative choices: since we now are reading a vision of Paul instead of one of Peter, the mise-en-scène shifts from a postresurrection appearance of Jesus on the Mount of Olives to the vision of the "man in Christ" mysteriously mentioned by Paul in 2 Corinthians 12:1–5. Other differences are significant for understanding the major reorientation of eschatological perspective: now there is no description of, let alone emphasis on, the coming apocalypse. It is true that the punishments described in the text appear to be interim before the Day of Judgment,[91] but there is no indication that the state of affairs will change in a future cataclysmic series of events on earth. Possibly the judgment already rendered and described in the text will be made permanent at the later point.[92] The apocalyptic eschatology has still left some traces in several passages that mention a Day of Judgment, but otherwise, the reader would not know that the glorious and the horrifying fates described were not the eternal state of things. Possibly as a result of the shift away from an apocalyptic perspective—or at least symbiotically related to it—it is now precisely the *souls* of the righteous and wicked who experience the rewards and punishments, even though these postmortem experiences continue to be entirely tactile.

The portrayal of sinners and their punishments clearly reflects a different historical context from that in the *Apocalypse of Peter*. No longer are we considering a revelation produced in the first half of the second century, when the Christian community was a tiny and occasionally opposed minority in a big and hostile world. Now we have an account firmly situated at the end of the fourth century or the beginning of the fifth, when Christianity was well on the way to establishing its dominance in the Roman world and was, for all practical purposes, the "official" religion of the empire. The new context understandably generated a different parenetic focus, evident in one of the most telling shifts in the portrayal: with the *Apocalypse of Peter* we had to ask whether any of those experiencing torment may be Christian; with the *Apocalypse of Paul* we have to ask whether any of them are not.[93]

CHRISTIANS LIVING IN SIN

The Christian emphasis is clear immediately after the discovery narrative (chs. 1–2), in God's opening injunction to the apostle: "Speak to this people: 'How long will you transgress and pile sin upon sin, and tempt the God who made you? You are the children of God, but you do the works of the Devil because of the impediments of the world, even though you believe in Christ'" (*opera diaboli facientes in fiducia Christi propter impedimenta mundi*; ch. 3). This revelation is meant to shock Christians (literally, those "in the faith of Christ") back into proper behavior. They pursue the pleasures of this world, and if they do not reform, they will be punished once they leave it. If they do return to God, eternal life will be very good indeed.

The account continues with the entire cosmos expressing anguish over the pervasive sin in the world—with complaints by the sun, moon, stars, sea, and earth itself, all requesting permission from the Almighty to blot the human race out of existence (chs. 3–7). It is especially important to consider which sins most upset the created order, as becomes evident when two groups of angels lend their voices to the rising chorus. One group rejoices over ascetics who have "renounced the world" (*qui abrenunciaverunt mundo*) for the sake of God's name, wandering like pilgrims through rock caves, weeping and mourning over others who inhabit the earth (ch. 9). The other group weeps because "those who call on your name" (*ab illis qui invocaverunt nomen tuum*) make themselves miserable because of the "impediments of the world" (ch. 10). The text focuses on Christians, not outsiders.

When Paul observes these cosmic and angelic responses to human activities, he wants to know the outcome of good and wicked behavior, and so he asks his angelic companion to be shown what happens at death, "when the souls of the just and sinners leave the world" (ch. 13).[94] He observes three exemplary instances. First is a righteous person whose soul leaves his body and is warmly welcomed by the holy angels, taken up to heaven before God himself and assured of a happy eternity at his future resurrection (ch. 14). Then there is a sinner who spent his life eating, drinking, and making merry in willful ignorance of the judgment he would face afterward, who, when the afterward comes, realizes much to his chagrin that it is too late for repentance; he is taken away for punishment until the time of the resurrection, when his horrible fate will be sealed for all eternity (ch. 16). It is possible that this sinner is simply a loose-living pagan, but there are good reasons for thinking he was someone who either knew about the Christian faith but chose not to accept it or was a nominal Christian. He is said to have excused his unrighteous, worldly behavior explicitly because he could not believe that anyone had risen from the dead as a proof of judgment to come. Even more, his guardian angel indicates that it had tried to minister to the person day and night and simply had not been heeded; moreover, the (good) spirit that lived within him from the moment of his birth also testifies that he had simply refused to do what he was enjoined (ch. 16). This then is someone with Christian knowledge and a ministering angel and a heavenly spirit—presumably a Christian sinner who learned too late the error of his ways. We will find many of them in the pits of hell.

Finally Paul sees a bodiless soul that appears before the heavenly court and is urged to confess its sins but insists it has done nothing wrong. The Lord asks an attendant angel for a list of transgressions—not for the soul's entire life but for just the past five years. They are substantial. Because this soul has refused to repent, it is condemned to torments until the final Day of Judgment, after which, again, the sentence will presumably be eternal. Once more there is no clear statement of whether the soul was a nominal Christian, but the fact that he refused to repent on earth suggests that he should have known he needed to do so—an easier assumption if he had been influenced by the Christian message despite (or because of?) his insistence on being a good (perfect!) person to the very end, an easily documented Christian "type."

THE PUNISHMENT OF SINNERS

However one evaluates the Christian commitments of these three souls on their own, the overarching concerns of the *Apocalypse* with specific Christian sinners become crystal clear in the fuller description of the punishments sinners will experience in the world to come.[95] To facilitate our comparisons with the *Apocalypse of Peter*, I start there—off in hell—rather than in the heavenly realms that the *Apocalypse of Paul* addresses first (as we will see, it deals with paradise both before and after the fiery pits). Like Peter, Paul observes in graphic detail the torments of the damned and is told by the accompanying angel the sins being punished; he cites a comparable number of sins and punishments (chs. 31–42), with some overlapping categories (adulterers, women who lost their virginity before marriage). But most of his sinners do not appear in the earlier account, and virtually all of these are specifically Christian, including, most remarkably, church leaders and theologians.

The first groups of sinners are standing in a river of boiling fire, some up to their knees, others to their navels, others to their lips, others to their hair. These are bad Christians, all of them: some who left church but then argued with one another; others who took the Eucharist but then fornicated; others who slandered fellow Christians when they were in church; and others who plotted against their neighbors (ch. 31). Another group of sinners ignored the word of God as it was read to them in church; these are confined in a narrow place, ringed by fire, and forced to gnaw their tongues (ch. 37). Others committed infanticide, ignoring what the Son of God had told them in the divine Scriptures they had heard read; they are forced to remain on pillars of fire while beasts tear them to shreds, and they are not allowed to call out for pity (ch. 40).

Three categories of tormented Christians are particularly intriguing and unimaginable in the earlier *Apocalypse of Peter:* church officers, failed ascetics, and bad theologians. None of these earns a slap on the wrist for making a good effort but coming up rather short. On the contrary, they are guilty of unpardonable sins and are hideously tortured for eternity.

And so Paul sees a presbyter who did not "perform his ministry well," or at least behaved inappropriately outside of it, "eating and drinking and committing fornication" when (or, presumably, before or after) offering the Eucharist. He is being tortured by angels piercing his bowels with "an iron instrument with three hooks" (*ferrum trium angulorum*; ch. 34). Next is a bishop forced by angels to run at top speed into a river of fire and being stoned in the face. His tormentors will not allow him even to pray for pity because he did not administer justice well or pity widows and orphans (ch. 35). Then comes a deacon up to his knees in a river of fire; his outstretched hands are bloody and worms pour out of his mouth and nostrils. This one ate the offerings (of the Eucharist?), committed fornication, and did not do what was right in the eyes of God (ch. 36).[96] Finally there is a "reader" (*lector*) thrown into the river of fire up to his knees, next to an angel who takes a razor to his lips and tongue; he had failed to follow the words of Scripture he had read (ch. 36).

Later copyists of this section of the account chose to elaborate on horrors to come for lifelong but flawed devotees of the Christian cause. One ninth-century Latin manuscript describes torments reserved for unholy nuns, one of whom is thrown into a fiery furnace to join the company of a bishop. Five others meet a similar fate but with a rather hideous twist: they are attended by demons and have snakes sucking their breasts, vipers eating their tongues, and fiery birds striking their eyes.[97] Clearly, anyone who embarks on the path of full-time commitment should consider the cost of failure. It may be better to remain unnoticed on the back pew.[98]

That much is clear even in the older and better attested form of the text. Two of hell's punishments come to failed ascetics. Those who stopped fasting before the "appointed time" (*constituta ora*) suffer the penalty of Tantalus, suspended dry-mouthed above water and with abundant fruit within their sight but beyond their grasp (ch. 39). Those who "appeared to renounce the world and put on our habit," but who succumbed to the "impediments of the world" and showed no charity[99] or pity for widows and orphans or refused to receive a pilgrim, make offerings (to charity?), or pity a neighbor—these are clothed with rags filled with pitch and sulfur, with serpents (*drachones*) wrapped around their necks, shoulders, and feet and fiery-horned angels beating them while holding their nostrils shut (ch. 40).

That may seem to be as bad as it can get, but as it turns out, it can get much worse—not for those who reject Christ, but for theologically deviant Christians. After seeing these sites of unspeakable torment, Paul asks the angel whether it would not have been better for them not to have been born (cf. *Apoc. Pet.* 3). The angel replies with a surprisingly calloused rebuke: Paul has no reason to feel sorry for these people; they are simply getting what they deserve (cf. *Apoc. Pet.* 3). When Paul grieves even more, the angel informs him that what these people are suffering is relatively light, and they have no claim on his pity: "Are you weeping when you have not yet seen even worse punishments? Follow me and you will see (punishments) seven times worse than these." The angel takes him to a well that is sealed off and tells the angel in charge to remove the top. When he does so an unbearable stench arises that is "worse than all other punishments" (*qui superaret omnes penas*). The well is so narrow that only one person can be dropped into it at a time, and its walls are covered with "fiery masses" (*massas igneas*). It is permanently sealed (except, apparently, for an occasional observation) so that whoever is sent into it for all eternity will not even be "remembered by the Father, Son, Holy Spirit, and holy angels." Paul naturally wants to know who these people are, the most awful sinners who deserve far greater torture than anyone on the planet. They are those who do not confess that Christ came specifically in the flesh (*in carne*) and that the "Virgin Mary" bore him, or that the bread and cup of the Eucharist are the body and blood of Christ (*corpus et sanguinem Christi*) (ch. 41). One might think these are nonbelievers. But no—just as the church officers we have already seen, they are people in the church, heretics who embrace a docetic Christology that denies the real, fleshly incarnation; embraces a wholly inadequate Eucharistic theology; and denies the fleshly resurrection of both Jesus (past) and humans (future).[100] Run-of-the-mill sinners have it much better.

Associated with them is a related group of sinners who are gnashing their teeth in a place that is eternally freezing, nothing but cold and snow, and surrounded by two-headed worms that never rest, doing God knows what to the frozen souls. These are sinners who say that "Christ was not raised from the dead and that this flesh is not raised" (ch. 42). These may again sound like non-Christians, but that is probably a mischaracterization: Christian authors who insisted on a fleshly resurrection of both Jesus and believers—going back to Paul in 1 Corinthians 15— regularly maintained that followers of Jesus who believed in a "spiritual" resurrection (understood, of course, in a variety of ways) rather than a "fleshly" one flat-out *denied* the resurrection—both of Jesus and, in the future, of his followers (see *3 Corinthians* and the *Epistula Apostolorum*). Why a late-fourth-century text would attack docetic views of earlier times is an intriguing question, but we certainly have other excellent instances of the same phenomenon from exactly the same period, most notably in the Pseudo-Ignatian epistles.[101]

Of the twenty kinds of sinners distinguished in this vision, at least half are almost certainly Christian. For others, there is no way to know. These would include the requisite usurers (ch. 36), practitioners of magical arts (ch. 38), adulterers (ch. 39), girls who lost their virginity before marriage without informing their parents (we are not told what happens to those who did inform them; ch. 38), and men and women (*viros ac mulieres*) who committed the sin of Sodom and Gomorrah, *masculi in masculos* (ch. 39). How women do that is a puzzle. It is also impossible to determine the religious affiliation of those suffering in a virtually bottomless pit because they "did not hope in the Lord" (ch. 32) or whose hands and feet have been cut off, forced to reside naked in a place of ice and snow being eaten by worms, who also "did not hope in the Lord" and harmed those who were in need (ch. 39).

One other possible exception to the Christian-populated hell is especially interesting. A group of people who are blind (or blinded, presumably) have been placed in a hellish pit (ch. 40). Paul asks who they are, and the accompanying angel replies: "These are people from the (pagan?) nations who have given alms but have not known the Lord God" (*hii sunt de gentibus qui fecerunt elemosinas et dominum deum non cognoverunt*). The comment may seem straightforward on the surface: surely these are pagans, the typical Christian designee of *gentes*. But if so, why are they practicing almsgiving (see my discussion in Chapter 3)? Are they possibly nominal Christians who are not, in the author's opinion, true devotees of Christ and so, in his view, "from the outsiders"/"among the nations"? Or are they polytheists, who include Christ among their objects of worship and engage in Christian practices but without an exclusive devotion (something like "partial" Christians)? Or are they simply pagan do-gooders? As with the other possible exceptions to Christian sinners, from the immediate context it is hard to say, but since, as we have seen, the account as a whole is primarily concerned for those within the Christian community, it seems more likely these are as well.

This view is confirmed immediately after the descriptions of torments, when Christ responds to the pleas for mercy from the sinners by (somewhat reluctantly) granting them a brief reprieve, for the sake of "your brothers (*fratres vestros*) who are in the world and offer oblations, and for the sake of your children, because my commandments are in them" (ch. 44). That is, the sinners in torment have "brothers" and "children" praying for them. It seems implausible that everyone in hell, pagan and Jew as well as Christian, is thought to have blood relatives who are devoted Christians. More likely they have concerned brothers, sisters, and children in Christ, members of the Christian community—of which, then, they were once a part. If so, the account is talking about Christians in hell.

Unfortunately, the account never expresses a view of non-Christians, those in every sense outside the church. It is interesting and often noted that unlike the *Apocalypse of Peter*, here no punishments are doled out to specifically "pagan" sinners: idol worshipers, makers of idols, or persecutors of Christians—prominent among the tortured in the earlier apocalypse— are nowhere to be seen in the *Apocalypse of Paul*. The reason may seem fairly obvious. We are now in a different period, the end of the fourth century at the earliest. Christians are no longer persecuted; Theodosius has made Christianity the religion of the state. Pagan cults are suffering; pagan numbers are shrinking; Christianity is strong, influential, and growing by leaps and bounds. The "pagan problem" is scarcely a problem at all, and so the author's attention has turned elsewhere—to the burgeoning but problem-ridden Christian community itself.

Equally elusive is the question of whether the author places any non-Christian Jews in his hell. There certainly do not seem to be any specific punishments for them. But one passage appears decisive on the matter—a clear instance of anti-Jewish polemic not found, again, in the *Apocalypse of Peter*. Near the end of his journey, Paul meets various Jewish saints in paradise (the Virgin Mary, the patriarchs, the prophets, and so on), and as a rule they heartily greet him on very friendly terms (chs. 46–51). But there is one exception. He finds Moses weeping because he is deeply upset about his own people, the "sons of Israel," among whom he toiled and suffered but who have not come to the truth by converting to faith in Christ. Moses's work among them was to no avail and "bore no fruit." Unlike pagans, the Jews rejected the one who died for them. As Moses laments:

> I am amazed that strangers and those who are uncircumcised and worship idols have converted and entered into the promises of God, but Israel has not entered. But I say to you brother Paul, that in that hour when the people hanged Jesus whom you preach, the Father, God of all, who gave me the law, and Michael and all the angels and archangels, and Abraham and Isaac and Jacob and all the righteous, wept over the Son of God as he hung on the cross. At that hour all the saints looking on attended to me and said, "See Moses, what those from your people have done to the Son of God." (ch. 48)

Jews crucified the Son of God and they have not entered into the promises. There are exceptions: Moses, the patriarchs, "righteous" Jews, and as we will see, of course, the prophets. But not the people as a whole, Israel. Moses weeps because his toil was in vain. Are those who have not entered the promises being tormented in hell? One would assume so.

It should be clear from what has already been said that the author endorses and supports a particular kind of Christian practice. He certainly advocates complete obedience to the law of God in general. But more than that he celebrates those who deny themselves the pleasures of the world to practice an ascetic life. He bestows some of his most pronounced laments and harshest torments on those who take up the ascetic life and then abandon it. This is not a milquetoast Christian text urging people simply to believe in Christ. It champions a complete removal from this world in dedication to the God above. Pain and hardship now will lead to exquisite glory later. Here then is one of the greatest ironies of the early Christian tradition, expressed in graphic narrative form: to enjoy bodily pleasure forever, one must punish the body now. Harsh bodily deprivation in this world leads to pronounced, tactile luxury in the world to come. Small wonder this katabasis in particular appealed to the most rigorous of late ancient Christian readers. The mid-fifth-century Sozomen comments in his *Ecclesiastical History* that despite its lack of ancient attestation, the *Apocalypse of Paul* was highly esteemed in monastic circles (7.19).

CALIBRATED REWARDS IN HEAVEN

This stress on afterlife ecstasy for those who make themselves suffer hardship in life helps explain why the *Apocalypse of Paul* provides a relatively full treatment of rewards to come, in contrast to the mere chapter and a half devoted to them in the *Apocalypse of Peter*. The later account provides descriptions of the realms of the blessed before the vision of hell (chs. 20–30) and after (chs. 45–51). Just as striking, there are different places and different fates for different people, even though all are saved forevermore. The heavenly realm comprises four main areas: "Paradise" in the third heaven, where Paul arrives first and meets Elijah and Enoch (chs. 20–21); the "Land of Promise," outside the heavens—the lush, glorious, and mind-bogglingly fecund interim home of the saints who have departed from their bodies and will reside during Christ's triumphant millennium (chs. 21–22); the "City of Christ," across the Acherusian Lake, the enormous multilayered place of eternal blessing for the saints once the promises have been fulfilled—apparently after the millennium—where Paul meets the biblical prophets, the patriarchs, Lot, Job, and other saints (chs. 23–30); and finally another (?) "Paradise" (of Adam and Eve), described after the intervening vision of hell, where he meets the Virgin Mary, the patriarchs, Moses, the twelve prophets, Lot, Job, Noah, Elijah, and Elisha, bringing the narrative to an end (chs. 45–51).

Even from this summary one cannot help being struck by perplexing confusions and contradictions, as observed already by Robert Casey in the first critical study of the text, and more recently in the full analysis by Claude Carozzi, who put the matter most succinctly, with respect to just one aspect of the problem: "This is all perfectly contradictory."[102] So, for example, Paul visits "Paradise" in chapters 20–21 but again in chapters 45–51. Is it the *same* paradise? If so, why is it described twice and why does Paul make two journeys there? If it is different, why, for example, is Elijah in both places (chs. 20 and 51)? Or how can the Land of Promise be the temporary residing place ("for a while") of the "souls of the just when they come out from their body" if it will not "be revealed" until the

earth is dissolved and "all the saints" are brought into it for Christ's mil-
lennial reign (ch. 21)? Moreover, if the Land of Promise is the temporary
residence of the just souls, why does Paul meet the souls of the patriarchs,
the prophets, Lot, and Job elsewhere, in the City of Christ, along with
both humble and proud ascetics, presumably of his own time (chs. 25–27)?
Moreover, if all the Old Testament saints are there, in the City of Christ,
why does Paul meet them again in Paradise later, as if for the first time
(chs. 47–51)? These problems may well have resulted from a rather casual
combination of sources, as the author attempted to explicate more fully
the heavenly bliss awaiting the saints, but the result is a glorious incoherence. It is interesting that the problems are not much resolved in other
text forms and versions.[103]

Apart from the internal tensions, the heavenly realms are striking for
one innovation in particular: differentiated levels of blessing, with far more
gradations of reward than of curse in the infernal realm, where everyone is
unimaginably miserable. The heavenly differentiations are stated already
in the description of the Land of Promise. When Paul marvels at the glories that virtually passeth all understanding—rivers of milk and honey,
trees bearing incredible fruit, tens of thousands of grapes on the vines, and
so on—he asks whether these are the only promises to come from God
(as if they weren't enough). The accompanying angel replies that in fact
there are "seven times more" (*Non, sunt enim his maiora septies*; ch. 22—
corresponding, of course, to the seven times worse torments for particular
heretics in hell).[104] The more one experiences self-imposed starvation in
this life, the more access to milk, honey, fruit, and wine in the life to come.

It is not just ascetic practice that counts; it is also the ascetics' disposition toward their rejection of the world and its pleasures. When Paul
eventually comes to the City of Christ—the future abode of the saints—he
is surprised to see outside the gate, among the trees, a small group of men
who weep every time anyone else enters the city. The apostle asks the
angel who these are and learns they are zealous ascetics who rigorously
fasted but were proud of it, exalting themselves over others.[105] Because of
their pride they are not allowed in the city, at least not yet. They will be
granted entrance only when Christ comes to rule the city. For now, they
lament their earthly lack of humility back when they were starving themselves for the sake of the kingdom. Even though the scene makes no sense
in terms of the broader narrative (since these ascetics and all the other just
should be in the Land of Promise for now), it makes perfect sense thematically. Some ascetics are better than others, and only the best receive

the highest reward. The goal may be to punish the body to the utmost, but people who are pleased about their success will have to camp outside for a few centuries.

The levels of reward become especially clear in the description of the City of Christ. It is not one undifferentiated abode of glory for all the righteous. It is to be sure an amazing place throughout—even more than the Land of Promise, one must infer, since here the promises are fully realized. But there is amazing and then there is amazing. The city is an enormous series of twelve concentric circles, containing twelve interior walls. The distance between each wall is greater than the distance between God in heaven and people on earth. That obviously makes the city massive, but size is not the main point. The farther toward the center one is allowed, the better it gets. Already in the outer circle the blessings defy belief, and that's the worst of the options. How good can it get? The next level is as much better than the first as the first is from the miserable existence of mortals below. And the next? It is a mind-boggling progression. Paul does not even try to describe the higher levels. A reader who may have been a shade disappointed by the rather vapid exposition of the glories of heaven in the *Apocalypse of Peter* will have the opposite reaction here. Granted, most would like to be told what could possibly be better than what Paul has already seen. To find out, they will need to renew their denial of physical pleasure with full humility. Paul provides them with real incentives.

MERCY ON THE SINNERS?

Not all sinners will suffer the full brunt of God's retributive justice: those who commit fornication and impiety can, while living, still repent, reform, and go on to live fruitful Christian lives. These will receive a baptism in the Acherusian Lake and presumably then reside somewhere on the outskirts of the first circle of the heavenly city (ch. 22). But those who have already died and gone to their torment have no chance to turn things around. Their torment is decidedly never-ending. There is, however, one surprisingly weak concession to mercy, described in one of the more peculiar passages of the book.

As with its predecessor, in the *Apocalypse of Paul* the touring apostle observes the gruesome torments of hell while the damned plead for mercy (chs. 43–44). In this case the archangel Michael and the whole army of angels also descend to hear their pleas, and Michael informs the tormented that he prays without ceasing for humans while they are living, but usually to no avail. Sin continues to abound despite his best efforts. And now it is too late. Still the archangel continues to weep for the sinners who have, in the end, discovered what it means to cross God Almighty. As one would expect, these continue to cry out to Christ himself for help. Paul begs for God to have mercy on them. The twenty-four elders around the throne and the four beasts who are eternally praising God (see Rev 4: 6–10) intercede for them.

Finally, in response, Christ descends from heaven to respond to their cries. At this point one might expect a show of divine magnanimity. Instead, Christ upbraids the sinners for not repenting when they had the chance, reminding them that he had to suffer himself in order to provide them with salvation.[106] But finally Christ relents. Because he has heard the pleas of Michael, the angels, Paul, and the Christians still on earth—and for his own sake—he will show the condemned an act of supreme kindness. He agrees to release them from torment. On occasion. They will no longer be punished on the day of his resurrection. This presumably means every Sunday, rather than every Easter.[107] That one day a week is the full extent of this somewhat less than boundless display of divine mercy. A Sabbath day off for sinners to escape their demonic and bestial torments and climb out from the river of fire where they otherwise scream twenty-four hours a day, six days a week, for all eternity. The damned respond with wild enthusiasm for this incredible show of mercy.[108]

The Functions of Christian Katabaseis

A full comparison of the apocalypses of Peter and Paul could occupy considerably more of our time and attention. Enough has already been said, however, to elicit some reflections on the purpose and function of the later and more influential one, separated from its predecessor by at least two and a half centuries and thus reflecting a vastly different historical and cultural context. If, as I argued, the *Apocalypse of Peter* was in-house literature that provided embattled Christians with the religious ammunition they needed to convert their pagan family, friends, and neighbors to the Christian faith, what might the *Apocalypse of Paul* have been designed to do?

Most of the differences do suggest an alternative purpose. Pagans are no longer a concern or a threat here. There are no dire warnings against idol makers, idol worshipers, or persecutors. Why should there be? At this stage the Roman Empire was rapidly becoming Christian, and unlike the early second century now it was the pagans who were on the defensive and occasionally on the run. Christians have less need for an instruction manual on how to scare the hell into outsiders. The Christian views were already widely known, and others could join the movement as they saw fit. They were already doing so hand over fist.[109]

Unlike its predecessor, this text does turn its eye to Jews, but it is not because they are a "problem" for the Christian message and community. On the contrary, for this author it is unfortunate that Jews have proved so recalcitrant and do not see the truth that even most pagans have found persuasive. They are a stiff-necked people who have never obeyed God and who actually killed his son. It is unlikely they will ever see the light. This too is a feature of the period. The defensive lashing out made in an earlier age by a beleaguered Christian minority filled with hateful invective has now become the assured confidence of the Christian majority, for whom Jews are not a threat but a small group of God's enemies. At just this time Jews were starting to lose more of their civic and cultic rights, beginning with edicts passed by the very emperor under whose reign the *Apocalypse of Paul* was allegedly written and who, by implication of the discovery narrative, sanctioned its divinely inspired opposition to the recalcitrant children of Israel. Their only defense from persecution would be to convert.[110]

Thus this is probably not a text meant to arm Christians for their interactions with those outside their community. It is directed to Christians and is meant to convert *them*—or at least to bring them under control. The goal is not to urge them to join the church; they are already in the church. That, however, is not enough. The church is no bulwark of salvation, and many Christians will roast in hell for eternity. Those who disobey the dictates of God need to change their ways or there will be no hope. Belief in Christ does not suffice, nor does participation in church activities, worship, prayer, fasting, communion. It is not enough to be a church leader—at the low level of lector, at the high level of bishop, or at any of the levels in between. It is not enough to adopt an ascetic style of life on occasion, to deny the body for a period, to wear the habit. All such people are liable to eternal fire, and worse.

To be sure, faith in Christ and active participation in his worship and church are sine qua non for salvation, but they are not sufficient. A person really does need to be a saint, avoid all the sins of the flesh, and obey the commands of God. Sexual immorality, failing to care for the needy, even lending money out at interest can lead to eternal torment. Without quoting the scriptural proof-text, the book fully embraces the hardest teaching of Jesus: "You must be perfect as your Father in heaven is perfect" (Matt 5:48).

Still, there are levels of perfection. Faithful Christians who abstain from sin and live good lives, obeying the commandments of God and helping others in need, can be saved and experience the glories of heaven, at least at the lower levels of glory. Those who practice the ascetic life will have greater rewards—far greater. If they do so without pride, better still. The more one denies oneself in humility, the more one will revel in glory later.

It is hard to make sense of the irony: followers of Christ must deprive themselves of all physical pleasure in this life—food, drink, sex, sleep—in order to enjoy the very tactile, physical pleasures of the world to come. The goal is not to live eternally starving. It is to live eternally sated, surrounded by magnificent bodily pleasures that are indulged in forever (though probably not sex!). To acquire the most unimaginable physical pleasures of life beyond requires complete abandonment of the pleasures of life here. Only those who lose their life will gain it; pain produces pleasure; destruction brings salvation; real life requires death. This is the Christian paradox promoted already in our earliest surviving Christian texts, driven here to the narrative extreme.[111] The greater the abandonment of the world and its pleasures, the more spectacular the pleasures of the world to come.

CHAPTER THREE

Incentives from the World Beyond

Christian Ethics and Evangelism

K ATABASEIS USE IMAGINED REALITIES of life after death to reflect on life in the here and now and to influence how it is lived.[1] Rarely does the parenesis involve a vapid appeal to "be a good person." Human behavior is always specific to historical, cultural, social, and religious circumstances, and the ethical demands of one context will not always replicate those of another.[2] Virgil's Roman katabasis condemns treason, for obvious reasons, but not the horrendous "crime" of usury, as found in the Jewish *Apocalypse of Zephaniah*. The *Apocalypse of Peter* agrees with Zephaniah about usury but also heartily condemns abortion, a matter absent from its Jewish counterpart. The later *Apocalypse of Paul* agrees with its Christian predecessor on abortion but adds an even more unusual twist to the ethical panoply: those who fail to keep their ascetic vows will pay an eternal price.

In this chapter I dig deeper into the guidance for life provided by various katabaseis that emerge out of different cultural and religious traditions. My approach here is shaped by an interesting but little noticed phenomenon: some katabaseis address the same issue but endorse radically different views. In this chapter we examine two sets of such parallel treatments. The first concerns a specific ethical matter, the "problem of wealth," as addressed widely in both pagan and Christian discourse. The second involves a broader issue, not merely one aspect of life but the entire orientation of life and the need for a complete transformation, a "conversion" to a totally different philosophical or religious set of beliefs, practices, and ways of living. Altogether, then, we examine four katabaseis: one from Lucian of Samosata (on wealth), another from Plato (on "conversion"), and two from the Christian *Acts of Thomas* (Acts 2 and 6).

From *Autarkeia* to Almsgiving: The Ethical Problem of Wealth

For most of those living in antiquity, wealth was not considered a "problem," let alone an ethical one. Wealth was good; people who did not have it wanted it, and those who did have it wanted to keep it. They often took extraordinary measures to do so. This is true today as well, of course, but with one very big difference: throughout antiquity, wealth—anything substantially above mere subsistence—was discomfortingly rare. In Roman society the wealthy elite formed a tiny sliver of society; more than that, there was no middle class to speak of, and the vast majority of people simply had no choice but to scrape by, with an astounding number not managing to so.

It is difficult to establish anything like a reliable demographic for ancient economies. Even so, recent analyses paint a dire picture.[3] Probably 80 percent or even 90 percent of the Roman Empire's population was rural, with simple farming by far the most common occupation.[4] This normally entailed a hand-to-mouth existence; the extent of the deprivation was almost certainly extremely high, though it is not possible to estimate it. We are better situated to discuss stratification in urban areas (say, cities of ten thousand or more), where wealth was in theory attainable, but even here the data are scarce. The best informed guestimates suggest that the top tiers of the population—those with abundant wealth—comprised no more than 2–3 percent of the urban population. Another 5–10 percent or so enjoyed a moderate surplus above subsistence levels (merchants, traders, artisans, and others who made more than they had to spend to survive). Probably another 20 percent or so were fairly stable, without daily fear of want. But another 40 percent or so appear to have existed very much on the edge, just at or below subsistence level, and something like 30 percent dragged along below that.[5]

Taking the entire population into account—rural and urban—a very small number of people enjoyed any kind of surplus, and far fewer than

1 percent could be considered elite, at the top of the scale. It is these elite, of course, who have left us most of our literary sources by which to gauge the views of "antiquity." But a few authors do come to us from the (somewhat) lower levels. In the first three centuries CE, for example, many Jewish and most Christian texts were almost certainly written by (economic) non-elites. These authors must have been educated, but that does not mean they had money in the bank. We have already looked at several such authors: we obviously do not know who the actual writers of the Jewish *Apocalypse of Zephaniah* or the Christian *Apocalypse of Peter* were, let alone the authors of any sources or prototypes they may have been following, but nothing suggests they came from within the top 1 percent of the economic scale. And we have seen they both condemned the wealthy—in particular those who used their wealth to acquire more wealth (e.g., usury), which, of course, is a principal way the rich multiply their riches.

But it is interesting to see that Virgil's katabasis also deals with the wealthy who abuse their affluence—in this case, those who hoard their riches rather than share them with their families (a particularly large group, he tells us). These, along with other egregious sinners, are damned to eternal torment behind the impassable gates of Tartarus (*Aen.* 6.610–11). The problem is not that the rich have money, but that they do not share it with their own kin—that is to say, relatives of comparable social class. Indeed, almost all the ethical discourse against wealth in Roman sources involves the rich speaking to the rich about how to interact with people of their own socioeconomic class. So far as we can tell from our surviving sources, and somewhat shocking to modern sensibilities, Roman moral philosophers were not particularly concerned about the run-of-the-mill poor or, even less, about the multitudes who were starving. They were concerned about the rich—sometimes in relationship to others who were well off (e.g., their own families and friends) and almost always in relation to themselves. Being fabulously wealthy was not always seen as a great good, even by those who had the wealth. The problem, however, was not that others had to do without. The problem was that wealth might badly affect character. Rich authors were the only ones who understood the problem from the inside.

This perspective and the rhetoric it engendered was radically changed by an early Christian discourse that stressed the well-being not of the rich but of the destitute. God was on the side of the poor, and his followers needed to be as well. Both these discourses, the pagan and the Christian, were driven by a concern for superabundant riches; but one focused on the personal character of the wealthy and the other on the needs of the poor. The contrast is seen with particular clarity through a comparison of two nearly contemporaneous katabaseis, the *Downward Journey* of Lucian and a section of the *Acts of Thomas*.[6]

Lucian of Samosata

The modern study of Lucian (115–180 CE) began in the 1870s, and usually not to the benefit of the satirist, especially among prominent German philologists such as Ulrich von Wilamowitz-Moellendorff, Eduard Norden, and Rudolf Helm.[7] These classical assessments treated Lucian's displays of polemical wit as the work of a shallow "Oriental" with no serious interests or abilities. Luckily for the rest of us, his genius became more apparent with the passing of time. Born in Samosata on the Euphrates, outside the centers of intellectual power and not known for its cultural icons, Lucian originally would have spoken Aramaic, but he came to be trained in Greek rhetoric. He eventually abandoned law for a literary career.[8] Some eighty of his prose pieces survive, many of them attacks on charlatans and hucksters (Alexander of Abonuteichos, Peregrinus), mockery of philosophers (*Philosophies for Sale, Fisherman*), and satirical dialogues with sundry purposes, one of which was to ridicule the affluent by revealing the devastating harm of wealth (e.g., *Dialogues of the Dead, Mennipus, Charon, Dream of the Cock*, and *Timon*).

Lucian had a complicated relationship with philosophy.[9] A good deal of his work parodies it, not from a specific philosophical perspective of his own but in general and on principle. He never undercuts philosophical positions by espousing a better one; on the contrary, even in antiquity he was notorious for never espousing any view at all. This was recognized as far back as Photios and reiterated in modern times: "Photios expresses a great truth about Lucian; one never knows where he himself stands";[10] or "Lucian had no philosophy, and that is all there is to it."[11]

As a rule, Lucian maligns the philosophers rather than their views per se: they contradict each other, propose all kinds of nonsense, and engage in endless and rather pointless debates. Moreover, they are hypocrites who cannot be trusted, urging actions they do not take and propounding views of no use to anyone else simply to line their own pockets. Nearly the only philosopher who comes in for serious praise is Lucian's own teacher, Demonax, who appears to have been a prominent Cynic.[12] Notably, in his short *bios* of Demonax, Lucian never calls him such, possibly because he did not want to align himself with the movement. Indeed, in *Philosophies for Sale* Cynics come off as badly as all the others—Academics, Stoics, Pythagoreans, Skeptics, and so on: the Cynic is annoying, loud, insulting, and confrontational (*Philosophies* 11). After publishing the work, Lucian received considerable flack that compelled him to write a defensive follow-up, *The Fisherman*, in the name of Parrhesiast ("Outspoken One"), claiming not to have slandered the great philosophers themselves but only philosophical impostors. Notably, in the account his views are defended by two of the famous Cynics, Diogenes and Menippus.

THE CYNIC VIEW OF WEALTH

These connections are worth noting because throughout his works Lucian endorses a characteristically Cynic perspective on wealth. Some background on the Cynics is therefore useful for my analysis.[13] But it is not a simple task: the Cynic movement extended over two discrete periods of antiquity; the bulk of the Cynics' own writings have not survived, and as a result most of the ancient discussions of Cynic views are filtered through non-Cynic perspectives, either vituperative or assimilating.[14]

Unlike other philosophies, especially in its Roman phase, Cynicism cannot appropriately be considered a "school." There were no classes or lectures and no doctrines or detailed philosophical justifications for them, for example, in a well-thought-out physics. On one level, of course, a good deal of philosophy in the period was moving toward the "practical," with advice about how one should live in order to maximize happiness and satisfaction. For Cynics, however, that was virtually all that mattered. It was all about practice. As such, being a Cynic required no education or, indeed, mental labor. The later Stoic Apollodorus famously called it "a shortcut to virtue" (Diogenes Laertius, *Lives of Eminent Philosophers* 7.22). It was a way of life, one that denied the values and worth of virtually everyone else. The Cynic life entailed abandoning all the trappings of life to live without possessions and therefore without needs that could be frustrated. Cynics did not pursue or even abide human comforts or conform to traditional human social standards.[15] And so they lived like κύνες, "dogs."

In the Cynic view, most people are miserable precisely because they locate their ostensible happiness in matters outside themselves: their possessions, status, reputation, position, influence, health, even families. But these things do not provide true happiness. Look at those who have such things in spades: the wealthy and powerful, the major athletes and social elite—are they happy? No, most of them are miserable, always wanting more, endlessly complaining about their investments, enemies, workloads, struggles, losses, and occasional failures. Possessions and social position are not keys to happiness; it does not reside in anything outside of ourselves that we can "acquire."

Moreover, anything acquired can be lost: you may go bankrupt; your house may burn to the ground; someone may steal your possessions; your status and reputation may be ruined; you may lose your job; your strong body may grow ill; if you survive, you will certainly grow old and decrepit; your children may die. If these are the things you live for in pursuit of happiness, you will be miserable once they are taken away. So do not cling to them. Get rid of them. If you hold on to them, they will take ahold of you. Instead, value those things you can never lose, things no one can take away. No one, for example, can take away your judgments about what is right and wrong, about what is good and bad. No one can compel you to agree that something is true when you know it is false; or to call what is evil, good. No one can force you to be rich, and no one can force you to abandon poverty. If such choices are within your sole power to make, they are what can make you happy, free from restraint from others. They, then, are what you should live for. If they are all you desire, you will always get exactly what you want. Dispose of everything else.

In the summary overview of (the Stoic) Epictetus:[16]

> This is the way of the Cynic who has become worthy of Zeus's scepter and diadem, who says, "Look people: you are searching for happiness and serenity (τὴν εὐδαιμονίαν καὶ ἀταραξίαν) not where they are but where they are not. See, I have been sent to you by God as a model. I have no possessions, house, wife, or children, not even a bed, cloak, or furniture. And see how healthy I am! Put me to the test and see my serenity (ἀτάραχον): hear about my medications and what things have healed me. (*Discourses* 4.8.30–31)

He then explains that he has been healed because he "does not desire or seek after anything, not another person, a position, or a way of life." He instead is "equipped all around with self-respect (αἰδοῖ)," just as other people are equipped with walls, doors, and doorkeepers (*Discourses* 4.8.33).

For Cynics, this praxis had obvious relevance to wealth. It was Diogenes who called "the love of money . . . the mother-city of all evils" (τὴν φιλαγυρίαν . . . μητρόπολιν πάντων τῶν κακῶν; adopted in 1 Tim 6:10). And so in Cynic discourse, it was the wealthy who were subject to the harshest criticisms.[17] Wealth leads naturally to vices: greed, avarice, rank materialism, injustice, hubris, and profligacy. But more than that, obsession with wealth interferes with what really matters, such as time for reflective thought, self-sufficiency, and freedom from worry. And so, in many senses, it was precisely the renunciation of possessions—especially in their extreme form of wealth—that, as William Desmond says, marked the life of a Cynic, virtually being a "rite of passage."[18] Happiness required complete independence from the trappings of life, that is, *autarkeia* (αὐτάρκεια) or "self-sufficiency."

Almost everywhere this was acknowledged as a radical view, at odds with moral philosophy as endorsed, for example, by traditional Stoics and Platonists. It nonetheless seems to be the view endorsed by Lucian—not in his own life, but in his writings, where he maligns wealth as a great evil that leads to misery, a view that stands precisely counter to the one endorsed, whether explicitly or implicitly, by most of the rest of his world. So much becomes clear in a number of his dialogues that could yield to fruitful analysis along this line, especially *Menippus* and *Timon*. But here I focus on *Cataplus*—the *Downward Journey*.

In some ways it is not quite right to call the work a katabasis. It is less a guided tour of the realm of the dead than an account of people journeying to it as a permanent residence. It is the reader who is given the tour, to see the wealthy go there in abject misery, having lost all they cherished in life, their possessions in particular; whereas others—including a Cynic and an impoverished cobbler—go down rather merrily, finding that an afterlife with no poverty, hunger, and injustice provides a pleasant prospect indeed.

THE *DOWNWARD JOURNEY*

The account begins with a discussion between one of the Fates, Clotho, and Charon, ferryman of the dead. Charon is upset that the god Hermes, "conductor of the dead" (νεκροπομπός), who guides the recently deceased down to Hades, has not yet arrived with his first batch of souls for the day, and Charon has so far not earned a single obol. He suspects that since the underworld is not exactly a place of high entertainment, Hermes has found more interesting things to do. But eventually the god shows up with 1,004 of the deceased in tow and in a very bad mood. One of his charges has repeatedly been trying to escape back to the land of the living, and

Hermes has been having to constantly make chase. The deceased miscreant is set in contrast with one other, a fellow with a pack over his shoulder and a club in his hand—equipment traditionally associated with Cynics—who not only is happily coming to the river Styx but has also proved helpful in securing the runaway. We later learn this person is called Cyniscus.

And the runaway? He is a fabulously wealthy tyrant, aptly named Megapenthes ("Great Grief"), out of his wits with anger and frustration for having just lost his fabulous wealth, power, and pleasure; he is desperate to get it all back. When he arrives at the river, he begs Clotho: surely she could reverse her decision, if just for a day. He needs to complete the palace he has been building, instruct his wife about the treasure he has buried, finish his municipal building projects, subdue his warring enemies, learn how his death has been received, and take vengeance on his manservant who abused his corpse. He offers significant bribes, pleads the injustice of it all, and argues that as a tyrant he should be above the law of the dead. It is all to no avail. His life is over, his fate has been decided, and the judge Rhadamanthus will soon render his verdict. Having everything he desired in the world above, Megapenthes will now be perpetually miserable, having lost it all simply by experiencing the fate common to all mortal flesh.

The dialogue shifts then to another of the deceased, an impoverished cobbler, Micyllus. He too is upset—not for being removed from the world of the living, but for being delayed from crossing the Styx. He cannot get to the underworld fast enough and is perturbed that Charon's boat has filled up without him and he has to wait on shore. Clotho is surprised that Micyllus does not welcome the delay, but he replies by referencing Homer: unlike Odysseus in the cave of the Cyclops, he is not at all pleased by the promise that "I will devour 'Noman' last" (πύματον ἐγὼ τὸν Οὖτιν κατέδομαι; *Od.* 9.369, quoted in *Cat.* 14). That is, Micyllus sees no advantage to being the final one to cross, and he says so with a striking witticism: ἄν τε γοῦν πρῶτον, ἄν τε πύματον, οἱ αὐτοὶ ὀδόντες περιμένουσιν ("Whether [I am] first or last, the same teeth are waiting"). Yes indeed.

He then explains why he has no qualms about going on to his destiny. People like him are not "like the rich"; on the contrary, their lives are "poles apart." He explains: this tyrant, Megapenthes, seemed happy his entire life, feared and respected by all, having everything a person could desire—gold, silver, wardrobes, horses, feasts, beautiful servants, and gorgeous women. It is no wonder he was distressed and vexed when dragged away from it all. People like that get attached to such things like "birdlime" (ἰξός), and it is very difficult for them to break away. It is as if they are bound by an unbreakable chain (ἄρρηκτός . . . ὁ δεσμός) but are taken away by force, wailing and begging. Bold about everything in life, "they are found to be cowards on the path that leads to Hades." The rich simply cannot help clinging to their possessions and pleasures: material birdlime and chains (*Cat.* 14).

He himself stands in sharp contrast: a cobbler who never had anything in life—no field, no living quarters, no gold, no equipment, no reputation. When it came his time to go, he gladly tossed aside his knife and leather and hurried to his new destiny, leading the pack. For him, this was a major advance over life: "And by Zeus, I already see that everything here is splendid with you." Everyone is equal, no one is better than their neighbor. There are no creditors to fear, no taxes to pay, no fear of freezing to death or taking sick or being beaten by social superiors. There is no violence, and "all of us who were impoverished laugh" while the wealthy lament in their distress (*Cat.* 15).

Lucian makes it plain that Megapenthes is not the only one in despair. As they move across the Styx in Charon's ferry, the rich all lament: "Alas, my possessions! Alas, my fields! Woe, such a house I have left beyond. Such wealth my heir will receive and carry away. Ah, my newborn children. Who then will harvest the vines I planted last year?" (*Cat.* 20). Hermes, on board as well, notices that Micyllus alone is not lamenting his losses, and the god objects: grief is mandatory. Micyllus complies the best he can, not so subtly mocking his distressed companions with the best lines of the account: "If you want me to, Hermes, I'll grieve then. Alas, the soles of my shoes! Alas, my old boots! Ah, my rotting sandals! Miserable wretch that I am, no longer will I go about without food from dawn to dusk, or go around without shoes and half naked, grinding my teeth because of the cold. And who will inherit my knife and awl?" (*Cat.* 20).

When they reach the shore, the deceased are shuffled off to appear before Rhadamanthus, who can see who is "marked" for judgment based on the "stigmata" on their backs. The Cynic Cyniscus goes first, and he has only a few faint scars. He explains that he had once, early in life, been wicked through ignorance and earned some marks that way; but he later turned to philosophy, and the scars were washed from his soul. Rhadamanthus appoints him to the Isles of the Blessed. For his part, Micyllus is completely clean and unmarked; he is to join Cyniscus.

But then comes Megapenthes, and now we have the semblance of a trial, the defendant a tyrant who murdered ten thousand people and confiscated their property to make himself fantastically rich. From there he obtained everything he desired and practiced every form of profligacy, sexual assault, savagery, and torture. The tyrant pleads his innocence, but in a strange narrative twist, his lamp and bed are called to the witness stand, and as silent observers of the innermost parts of his life, they confirm the reports of his outlandish behavior. When Megapenthes shows Rhadamanthus his back, it is a patchwork of black and blue marks.

The judge has difficulty deciding on a suitable torment, but Cyniscus has a suggestion. Everyone in Hades is required to drink the water of "Lethe," forgetfulness. They no longer remember their lives. And so the most extreme, horrible punishment for Megapenthes? Do not allow him the drink. He will go through all eternity remembering what he possessed and experienced during his life of luxury (τρυφῆς) and remain in abject despair over what he has lost forever. It will be never-ending torment. Rhadamanthus agrees, and the tyrant is taken off in fetters.

This is the Cynic view of wealth, captured in a witty and imaginative journey to the world below. Wealth corrupts character and destroys the soul. It clings to a person like birdlime. Those who are attached to it in the end suffer horrible miseries. Lucian situates the horror in the life to come, but as a satirist he is not explicating eschatological realities. He is using a portrayal of the afterlife to a parenetic end: wealth should be avoided. It will ruin your life and only make you miserable. Yes, Megapenthes' material passions drove him to commit unutterable crimes against others, but this dialogue is not about his victims. It is about him and his personal well-being, which he sacrificed when he began living for what he could possess. He would have been far happier had he embraced *autarkeia*. This dialogue is thus not about the plight of the poor and oppressed but about the plight of the wealthy; it is directed to the rich and those who want to become rich.

CYNIC VIEWS IN THEIR PHILOSOPHICAL CONTEXT

The Cynic view of wealth was an extreme version of a widely held perspective throughout Greek and Roman antiquity, differing from the dominant (elite) moral discourse not in character but in degree. Unlike the Cynics, most moral philosophers typically insisted that the problem was not wealth per se, but attachment to wealth. For that reason, it was perfectly fine, even good, to be abundantly affluent. The (potential) problem was being obsessively attached to possessions and allowing wealth to control the course of life. You could be rich if you did not feel a need to be. This may sound like a bourgeois justification for inequality, injustice, and all the side effects of lucre, and in some sense it is. But it was the dominant discourse about wealth whenever there was any discourse about it at all, on those relatively rare occasions when the elite decided to reflect on the matter, the rich speaking to the rich.

These two perspectives—the radical Cynic insistence on poverty and the more common injunction not to be possessed by one's possessions— go far back in Greek ethical reasoning, set in contrast already in the *Symposium* of Xenophon (4.29–44), in an alleged conversation among the friends of Socrates. As with Lucian later, the dialogue shows no concern for the poor—the unseen masses of humanity. It is focused on the dire situation of the wealthy. Does the rich person become happy by giving away all the wealth or simply by becoming emotionally detached from it? In the discussion, one of the characters, Charmides, celebrates the fact that having lost everything, he is the happiest he has ever been. When he was rich, he was constantly afraid of being robbed or blackmailed and was forced by the government to spend his money for municipal purposes. Now that he is poor, he sleeps like a baby, fears no threats, and receives no civic demands. People leave him to his own devices to do whatever he wants. Most important, "Now I don't lose anything because I don't have anything"—and so he is perfectly content (4.32). The lesson is extreme: the best approach to wealth is to give it up.

His companions, as one might expect, find this view far too radical. One of them, Antisthenes, replies that the problem is not having wealth but having the wrong relation to it. If two brothers split a large inheritance, one may be happy because he uses his share wisely and takes care never to spend more than he has; the other is miserable because he never thinks he has enough of anything and so is always in debt. Even worse are the despots who are desperate to get more and more, committing far more heinous crimes than the destitute who need to steal just to survive. Tyrants on the other hand destroy whole families, order mass killings, and enslave entire cities for money. They are like gluttons who cannot get enough to eat: no matter how much they consume, they never feel full (4.37). And so Antisthenes advises that it is best to live frugally and within one's means, to be honest and pursue virtue, and not to covet what belongs to others. This was the view that became more or less de rigueur, at least among philosophers who saw that wealth could be a problem. Complete divestiture was too extreme. It was better to adjust one's perspective. Have money, but don't long for it; use wealth, but don't abuse it; give to others, but do so prudently.

Such views are expressed, for example, throughout the writings of Seneca, who preaches against greed and high living (*Epistles* 108.12), claiming that "having wealth is more torture than seeking it" (*maiore tormento pecuna possidetur quam quaeretur;* 115.16) and wishing that anyone wanting to get rich would consult with a wealthy person to see what it is really like (115.17). And yet, an incredibly wealthy man himself, Seneca does not argue that the problem is money itself but the bad attitudes and actions it stirs up in people, making them self-important and haughty and unsettling their minds (87.31–32). This problem can be mitigated by cultivating wealthy virtue. Elsewhere, he argues that as long as you own possessions without allowing them to own you, riches are actually desirable (*De beata vita* 20–24). The reason: wealth enables virtue. This may seem like a rich man's argument (again, it is), but Seneca points out that the poor literally cannot be obsessed with their wealth or unnecessarily worried about it. They don't have any. Only the rich can *choose* not to be obsessed or worried. And so wealth is a pathway to virtue. So too the poor cannot give their money away to those who deserve it; only the rich can. More virtue. For that reason, those who are wise may not crave wealth, but they would be insane not to accept it: "No one has condemned wisdom to poverty" (*nemo sapientiam paupertate damnavit;* 23.1). To be sure, riches are not themselves "good." If they were, they would make their owners good. But it is nonetheless good and useful to have them since they do, after all, "add great comforts to life" (24.5).[19] Similar expressions of deep concern for the well-being of the affluent can be found throughout the moral discourse of the period.[20]

In light of this overarching concern to help rich people find happiness despite their burdens of overabundance, one might wonder whether anyone had incentive to give resources away at all. In fact, giving was a standard feature of municipal life, both because the wealthy were expected, and even required, to supply the needs of their cities and because magnanimity was celebrated as a virtue. But almost never was the giving meant to help the poor. Outside of civic expenditures such as building projects and public entertainments, giving in Greek and Roman moral discourse was almost always about helping oneself in one way or another—for example, by developing a character of virtue, establishing a good reputation, helping family members and others on the same socioeconomic plane, or, well, buying up votes for office. There are, of course, numerous instances of pity and concern for those who are in need, but normally those "in need" belong to one's own social class who have fallen on hard times, not the destitute.

This is a theme of Paul Veyne's justly celebrated discussion of ancient giving practices in *Bread and Circuses*. Consider, for example, his summary of motivations for gift giving in the Roman (pagan) world: "careerism, paternalism, kingly style, corruption, conspicuous consumption, local patriotism, desire to emulate, concern to uphold one's rank, obedience to public opinion, fear of hostile demonstrations, generosity, belief in ideals."[21] Among these, only "generosity" might suggest to readers a concern for the poor, but not in the Roman context. Generosity was celebrated as a personal virtue to be cultivated for the sake of one's standing in the upper class. Veyne himself is a bit generous when it comes to the charitable effects of municipal giving: "Every class of the population benefited from the gifts."[22] But that was true only on a certain level. To be sure, it was a good thing for a poor person to be allowed entrance to see entertainments paid for by the local elite—even if the benefit was restricted to fellow citizens (noncitizens don't count)—and it was very nice indeed to receive a meal at a periodic public sacrifice funded by a higher-up. But what does one eat the next day? So too, the occasional distributions of grain to the indigent did feed the hungry for a time; but the driving concern was to prevent riots, not to fill empty bellies. There was no systematic or sustained motivation to help the poor, only an interest in keeping society functioning smoothly for those who were paying for it.

As frequently noted, the broader ideology of giving in Greco-Roman antiquity involved what André Boulanger termed "euergetism."[23] This kind of financial "good work" came in two forms, either *ob honorem*, that is, "because of an honor," in connection, for example, with election to an office that required outlays of resources to ensure the welfare of the community, or voluntary, with no legal or civic requirement and meant to promote the welfare of the upper classes.[24] Occasional exceptions involved little more than tossing a copper or a piece of bread to a beggar, an act that Seneca casually mentions in order to explain why such acts are not to be considered an actual "benefit" to be valued: the act itself is too petty and insignificant, and the recipients are not "worthy" (*De beneficiis* 4.29.2). Elsewhere Seneca points out that he would never give money to the poor, since they would be poor even if he gave them money, so what would be the point (*De beata vita* 24.1). He indeed stresses that a wise person should give liberally, but never to those who are "unsightly and unworthy" (*turpes indignosque; De beata vita* 24.3). The only exception is to give to such people if they might provide support for a coming election to public office.

A character in Plautus's little-read work on luxury and want, *Trinummus*, sums up the view nicely.[25] Lysiteles, a young man from a wealthy family, tells his father, Philto, that he would like to make a sizeable loan to help out a friend who has fallen on hard times. Even though the friend is his social equal from a good family, he has lost his money because he has been obliging to others and interested in pursuing his own pleasures. Philto is dead-set against the loan, despite the social equalities: "The one who gives a beggar something to eat or drink does him a disservice, because he loses what he gives and hands the beggar's life over to (more) misery" (*Trin.* 339). Here we have the ancient version of "They'll just spend it on beer and cigarettes."

There is some debate among scholars about the relationship of these elite discourses to actual practice: Were all Roman elites oblivious to the plight of the poor? Didn't foundations and public donations help? Isn't it true that some welfare practices of the state could ease the pain? Often these discussions read as sophisticated attempts by modern elites to reflect and promote the agendas of the ancient elites about whom they write. Protesting that food donations were given even to poor citizens may make sense on one level, even if the donations were few and far between. But they would not have done much good for the noncitizens. And what about the millions of rural destitute who were never even in the picture?[26]

Be that as it may, my analysis is less concerned with what was happening on the ground than with the discourse surrounding wealth, poverty, and giving. In sum so far: most Greeks and Romans had no difficulty whatever with wealth but saw it as an amazing if unattainable good. Those few who had it strove to keep it, and those who did not have it would have been ecstatic to receive a share. Moral philosophers who saw the problems with wealth focused almost entirely on the happiness of the wealthy: How can a rich person enjoy a satisfied life? Most of that discourse focused on attitude and personal character, stressing that it was important not to be attached to wealth but to maintain high standards of virtue, not to be corrupted, and to have a detached attitude of *autarkeia* (self-sufficiency). The Cynic perspective as found in Lucian's *Downward Journey* was an outlier. Here the way for the rich to achieve happiness was to give it all away—a radical view, rarely adopted.

Christian Attitudes Toward Wealth

It is interesting that both perspectives are found as well in our Christian sources, and in about the same proportion. As Peter Brown in particular has emphasized, the dichotomies drawn between early "pagans" and "Christians" are usually sharper in scholarship than they were in reality.[27] Brown is principally interested in social experience, but even within the world of literary discourse—the focus of our attention here—the similarities are striking. Among Christian writers, some authors urge the wealthy to give away their material possessions for a greater good and then to assume the mantle of rigorous asceticism. The "good" in this case will be very different indeed from what was promoted in the broader Roman world since it involves helping the indigent, but the personal motivation is roughly the same: it is a matter of "working out your salvation." That is, it is largely about one's own well-being. Other writers, however, argue that wealth is not itself evil or necessarily a trap, an obstacle to the good and holy life. Righteous people can continue to enjoy their wealth while using it to good ends, bringing even better results for both others and themselves. Wealthy beneficence was a cherished Christian virtue. As in the pagan world, this became the dominant Christian view.

What is most different about the early Christian view is the value placed on the poor—the seriously destitute in particular—and on the reasons for giving to them. This is one way in which Christianity transformed the ancient world. In this emerging tradition, God is concerned with those who lack basic resources, and he expects his chosen people to place a very high priority on helping them. Those who give their money to the poor will receive treasure in heaven. The stress on *autarkeia* in Greek and Roman discourse has been transformed into an emphasis on almsgiving. It is true there is still a self-centered focus; it is still about what will most benefit the giver. But that benefit differs as well, and in a significant way. No longer does it principally come in life. It is about rewards in heaven. All this we will see in our next katabasis, from the *Acts of Thomas*.

The Acts of Thomas

The *Acts of Thomas* is one of the five major surviving noncanonical "Acts of the Apostles," each of which describes the missionary endeavors of an individual apostle: Peter, John, Paul, Andrew, and Thomas. These are all historical figures, of course, but the accounts are almost entirely legendary.

The *Acts of Thomas* in particular comes with a delightful twist: Thomas is not merely one of the twelve disciples (see John 20:24), he is also the brother of Jesus, Jude (see Mark 6:3), and, in fact, is Jesus's identical twin.[28] Thomas the twin is known from other traditions normally associated with Syria, which was almost certainly the place of composition of the *Acts* as well, sometime in the early third century CE, a half century or so after Lucian's work.[29]

The broader narrative comes to us in thirteen Acts that describe the missionary adventures of Thomas en route to and then in India, ending with a separate account of his martyrdom. As with the other apocryphal *Acts*, it is never clear whether the anonymous author meant his account to be a dead-serious elaboration of the apostolic mission or (also?) an amusingly entertaining narrative. Modern readers certainly find some of the anecdotes humorous, including the deceptive ploy used by the heavenly Jesus after his resurrection to sell his brother into slavery to an Indian merchant who was seeking a skilled carpenter (Act 1). This is what compels the reluctant Thomas to travel from Jerusalem to India in the first place. Equally amusing is the play on the "twin" theme in the next episode, which narrates Thomas's adventure at a wedding feast during his trip (still in Act 1). After the ceremony, Jesus appears in the bridal chamber of the royal newlyweds, to their great confusion, as they had just seen him (or at least someone who looked exactly like him) already leave the palace.

These two episodes in a sense set the stage for the rest of the narrative. Thomas has one apostolic function: to take the Gospel message to the royal family and peoples of India, and his message will mirror Jesus's words to the wedded couple: to inherit the kingdom and obtain true happiness, they must deny the desires of the flesh. It is a particularly pressing matter in this early scene, since obviously the bride and groom have entered the chamber eager to consummate their marriage. But they listen attentively to Jesus's unsolicited advice to "refrain from this filthy intercourse" (ἀπαλλαγῆτε τῆς ῥυπαρᾶς κοινωνίας ταύτης): sex is only to produce offspring, and children can become demon-possessed, insane, crippled, or paralyzed. Even if they are healthy, they may grow up to be lazy and good for nothing or adulterers, murderers, or robbers. It is better to avoid them altogether and keep oneself pure and free from grief and anxiety (*Acts of Thomas* 12). Somewhat to the surprise of readers not accustomed to these Christian Acts, the married couple—in their bridal chamber—instantly accept Jesus's ascetic Gospel and devote themselves to lives of chastity. And so the tale begins.

Thomas picks up Jesus's ascetic mantle and carries it a very long way. Throughout his missionary proclamation he insists that it is indeed necessary to repent, turn to Christ, and await him as the judge of the world (ch. 28). But that is far from the overarching point of this missionary journey. True followers of Christ must avoid the sins of the flesh to inherit an eternal reward. Thus we have Thomas's first public evangelistic appeal once in India:

> Men and women, boys and girls, young men and virgins, you in your prime and elderly, slave and free! Abstain from sexual immorality, and greed, and gluttony (ἀπέχεσθε τῆς πορνείας καὶ τῆς πλεονεξίας καὶ τῆς ἐργαίας τῆς γαστρός). . . . Repent and believe the proclamation . . . so that you may live and not die. Come to the one who is truly good, so that you may receive his grace, and place his sign on your souls. (ch. 28)

For the analysis of early Christian perspectives on wealth, it is interesting to see the incommensurate treatment of two of the main moral concerns in the rest of the narrative—sex and greed. Followers of Jesus are never to enjoy physical intimacy. But they can certainly enjoy wealth as long as they aren't greedy about it (or covet it). One wonders why that doesn't apply to sex.

Within the context of Thomas's mission we find two katabatic episodes, both of them recounting near death experiences—one of them involving heaven (Act 2), and the other, hell (Act 6). We consider the first one here, as it is directly connected to Thomas's understanding of wealth.

GUNDAPHORUS, GAD, AND THE VALUE OF WEALTH

Act 2 begins with Thomas's arrival in India and his introduction to King Gundaphorus, his new master, who has acquired him for his carpentry skills, which obviously run in the holy family. Gundaphorus wants a new palace in a remote site, and Thomas is perfect for the job: he works in wood and stone and has experience constructing regal dwellings. This Act is all about the distinctive kind of building he can make.

The apostle draws a design for the structure, and the king approves it, bestows a hefty sum on him for the work, and leaves him to get on with construction. But Thomas gives all the money to the poor and the afflicted (τοῖς πένησιν καὶ τεθλιμμένοις). The king later sends a messenger to check on the progress, and Thomas informs him that the building is complete, needing just the roof. The king supplies him with additional funds, and Thomas again gives it away to those in need (ch. 19).

When the king arrives to inspect the apostle's work, he is more than a little incensed to find no palace and a depleted building fund. His friends inform him that Thomas has given the money to the poor and that he spends his time preaching a "new god," healing the sick, casting out demons, and doing other miracles—all for no charge. Moreover, he leads a remarkably austere life: always fasting and praying, eating only bread and salt, drinking only water, and wearing a single cloak, whatever the weather. What little surplus he has he gives to others and keeps nothing for himself (ch. 20). Thomas here certainly sounds like a Christian Cynic, but the distinction is all-important: this is rigorous asceticism driven by religious devotion demanded of him by God, not by a personal interest in securing his own happiness in this life apart from the trappings of the world.

In any event, the king is not impressed. When he confronts the apostle, Thomas tells him he has indeed built a palace, but it is one the king will not see until he enters the afterlife. Gundaphorus summarily throws him in jail (along with the merchant who had purchased him in the first place) and spends the evening considering how best to torture him to death. Then comes the divine intervention expected in such texts.

In the course of the night, the king's brother, Gad, dies and is taken up to heaven by angels. They show him the options for his eternal dwelling and ask for his preference. One of the places is so spectacular that he wants to spend eternity in just one of its lower chambers. But the angels inform him that that won't be possible: this is the palace "that Christian" has built for his brother. Gad, not quite grasping the point of giving one's possessions to the poor, begs the angels to be allowed to return to life to persuade his brother to sell him the house. They give him leave, his soul reenters his body while it is being prepared for burial, and he calls for his brother, who comes terror-stricken and unable even to speak.

But Gad has no such trouble and tries to maneuver his brother into selling the heavenly domicile. His request brings Gundaphorus to an abrupt realization. By giving the king's money to the poor, Thomas really *had* built him a fantastic palace, not to last the rest of his natural life but for all eternity. On the spot Gundaphorus commits to changing his life so that he can be found worthy of his newly constructed residence. He suggests his brother follow suit by having the apostle build one for him as well. The apostle is released from his chains and brought in, and both brothers express their change of heart and purpose, committing themselves now to serve the God that Thomas proclaims. From then on they are followers of the apostle, "helping those in need, giving to all, and providing relief to all" (αὐτοὶ ἐπαρκοῦντες τοῖς δεομένοις, πᾶσιν διδόντες καὶ ἀναπαύοντες πάντας; ch. 26). The Christian emphases of this account are stark and unlike anything we have encountered in the pagan tradition. The wealthy should direct their focus away from pleasure in this world to prosperity in the world to come, and their principal objects of concern in this transient existence should be the poor.

Clearly the "problem" of wealth for the *Acts of Thomas* is not that it can interfere with the personal happiness of daily life, as in Hellenistic philosophy. The problem is that it can interfere with a blessed eternity. But those with material abundance can use it to secure a glorious afterlife.[30] In its most crass form, the lesson is that glory in the world beyond can be purchased: the rich can buy treasure in heaven. They do so by giving their money away, not to municipal building projects, public entertainments, desperate family members, "deserving" peers of high-placed society, or even those of lower classes who might help them achieve personal or political objectives. The money is to be given to the desperately poor, with no hope of earthly benefit or return. The reward for this sacrifice in life comes after death, and it is worth giving everything for.

But not exactly. Remarkably, even though Judas Thomas himself practices strict asceticism, he does not enjoin it on his two regal converts. He does not tell them to sell everything and give all their money away, to eat only bread and salt, drink only water, and live like paupers. On the contrary, while they spend the rest of their lives engaging in acts of charity, they themselves continue to live with superabundance. Their palaces in heaven come not in exchange for a total, painful, irreversible divestment, but by giving some of their surplus to those in need.

Just as this was a tension in pagan circles, say between a penniless Cynic like Diogenes and a rich Stoic like Seneca, so too within the Christian tradition. There were, of course, advocates for the extreme view, of welcoming complete poverty for the sake of the kingdom; there were others who opted for the more bourgeois ethic of keeping a good deal while giving some away. And there were numerous levels between these two views. But, predictably, what happened earlier in the Hellenistic tradition came to be reflected in the Christian as well. In a battle between a Cynic injunction to give everything away and a Stoic insistence on staying rich but (allegedly) unattached, the Stoic will win nearly every time.

THE DISTINCTIVELY CHRISTIAN "PROBLEM OF WEALTH"

Probably the most significant difference between Gundaphorus's relatively modest decision to give away some of his riches and the ethos promoted in pagan moral philosophy can be summed up in the terse formulation of Paul Veyne: "Almsgiving . . . succeeded euergetism."[31] Unlike Christian charity, pagan euergetism had no particular connection with cult or worship of the gods. Also, as we have seen, it was not at all directed to the impoverished masses, who were of no concern to the well-placed elites— at least the elites who have provided us with any writings. Moreover, it both focused on and was driven by civic responsibility and social standing, not by obedience to divine instruction, concern for personal salvation, or compassion for the needy. Again, from Veyne: "Euergetism and pious and charitable works differ in ideology, in beneficiaries, and in agents, in the motivations of agents and their behavior." And what a change it was, Veyne continues: "Paganism had abandoned without much remorse the starving, the old and the sick. Old people's homes, orphanages, hospitals, and so on are institutions that appear only with the Christian era, the very names of them being neologisms in Latin and Greek."[32]

No one with any historical sense would claim that Christians as a whole embraced, let alone fully implemented, this "new ethic." Moreover, since the ethic was directed to individual Christians or, at most, their collective worshiping communities, it did not translate into sweeping social policy. Rich people gave as they saw fit, more or less on an ad hoc basis. There never was a move to eradicate poverty by altering the economic system or the sociopolitical structure that sustained it. On the other hand, the new ideology did provide an incentive for giving for those on all levels of society, even the very poor. Nearly every Christian could give *something* to another, even if they had almost nothing to give. And for that they would receive treasures in the world to come.

How do we account for this major transformation in the idea of giving?[33] About this there can be little doubt. It has to do with the Jewish roots of the Christian tradition in general and the teachings of Jesus in particular.[34] Unlike the pagan tradition, the Hebrew Bible consistently pronounces God's concern for the poor and repeatedly instructs those who have means to assist them.[35] Thus in the Torah: "Give liberally and be ungrudging [. . .], for on this account the LORD your God will bless you in all your work and in all that you undertake. Since there will never cease to be some in need on the earth, I therefore command you, 'Open your hand to the poor and needy neighbor in your land'" (Deut 15:10–

11). Many of the most emphatic passages occur, as one might expect, in the prophets:

> The LORD enters into judgment
>> with the elders and princes of his people:
> It is you who have devoured the vineyard;
>> the spoil of the poor is in your houses.
> What do you mean by crushing my people,
>> by grinding the face of the poor? says the Lord GOD of hosts.
>> (Isa 3:14–15)

> Is not this the fast that I choose . . .
> Is it not to share your bread with the hungry,
>> and bring the homeless poor into your house;
> when you see the naked, to cover them,
>> and not to hide yourself from your own kin? (Isa 58:6–7)

> Thus says the LORD:
> For three transgressions of Israel,
>> and for four, I will not revoke the punishment;
> because they sell the righteous for silver,
>> and the needy for a pair of sandals—
> they who trample the head of the poor into the dust of the earth,
>> and push the afflicted out of the way. (Amos 2:6–7)

Some of the most pithy statements can be found in Proverbs.

> Whoever is kind to the poor lends to the LORD,
>> and will be repaid in full. (19:17)

And then there is the flip side:

> If you close your ear to the cry of the poor,
>> you will cry out and not be heard. (21:13)

The tradition continues on in later writings, for example, in the book of Tobit:

> Give alms from your possessions, and do not let your eye begrudge the gift when you make it. Do not turn your face away

from anyone who is poor, and the face of God will not be turned away from you. If you have many possessions, make your gift from them in proportion; if few, do not be afraid to give according to the little you have. So you will be laying up a good treasure for yourself against the day of necessity. For almsgiving delivers from death and keeps you from going into the Darkness. Indeed, almsgiving, for all who practice it, is an excellent offering in the presence of the Most High. (4:7–11)[36]

As would be expected, the later Christian discourse appealed to such traditions, but it found yet greater impetus in the recorded teachings of Jesus. In our earliest Gospel, Mark, we find the story of the earnest query from a rich man of how to obtain eternal life. When Jesus tells him to keep the law, the man replies he has done so; to which Jesus gives a remarkably simple but discomforting response: "You are lacking one thing. Go and sell everything you have and give to the poor, and you will have treasure in heaven; and come, follow me" (Mark 10:21). The teaching is surprisingly uncomplicated: treasure in heaven comes from divesting completely and giving it all to the poor. It does not come, for example, by belief, Torah observance, or even unusual but limited generosity. Note: the man is enjoined to follow Jesus only after he gives *everything* away.

In this story he simply cannot do so and so walks away in sorrow. Jesus explains to his incredulous disciples: "It is easier for a camel to go through the eye of a needle than for a rich person to enter God's kingdom" (Mark 10:25)—a passage that mystified not only the Twelve but large numbers of other Christians ever since, leading, as we will see, to remarkable exegetical footwork designed to show that Jesus didn't really mean what he said. Jesus's claim that a person will obtain treasure in heaven by forsaking treasure on earth reappears in Matthew's Sermon on the Mount (Matt 6:19–21) and lies at the heart of Luke's form of the Beatitudes, where the (literally) poor and hungry are blessed and the rich and sated are condemned (Luke 6:20–25). There is some question about whether the same lesson is expressed, in narrative form, in Luke's parable of Lazarus and the rich man (16:19–31). Readers have not always noticed, or appreciated, that the story's anonymous lover of lucre is not said to have entered to the torment of fire for any other reason, for example, heartlessness. He simply held on to all his riches and lived an exorbitant life while a poor beggar suffered at his door. Some interpreters have therefore argued the story teaches that riches in and of themselves will damn the soul. But others have claimed that the problem is not wealth but with what the rich man has done, and not done, with it.[37] However the problem is interpreted, it soon becomes clear that Luke's Gospel as a whole embraces a different view of wealth from that attested in the earlier traditions about Jesus, which called for complete divestment. Three chapters later, Jesus declares that the exceedingly wealthy Zacchaeus has earned the kingdom of heaven because he gave half his money to the poor (19:1–10). He did not need to give away everything; like the later Gundaphorus, he was still filthy rich. If the point of the parable of Luke 16 is the same, then at most it shows that Lazarus's affluent neighbor made some very bad investment decisions. Giving a bit of it away for an eternal day would have put him in very good stead: he could have stayed rich and still had treasures in heaven.

So too in later New Testament materials such as 1 Timothy: those who "want" to be rich are warned, but there are no condemnations for those who are already rich or orders for them to divest. Instead, they are instructed to have the right *relationship* to their wealth: not to devote their entire lives to it and to give some of it away generously (1 Tim 6:9–10, 17–19).[38] By now the radical injunctions of Jesus have fallen away: a bit of charity will bring eternal treasure. But there is one clear virtue of this alternative position: it makes almsgiving more democratic and even socially reasonable. Just about anyone can give something, which means that more people will.

In the records of earliest Christianity, giving was indeed enjoined on all. According to the book of Acts, the members of the first community in Jerusalem sold everything and shared all things in common so that no one was in need (Acts 2:43–45, 4:32–37). This sounds like Jesus's own vision, though whether Acts can be trusted to describe social reality soon after Jesus's death is another question. It is clear, however, that years later the churches of Paul, populated predominantly by those without substantial resources, were willing to share with those who had even less, as seen in Paul's famous collection for the "poor" in Jerusalem (e.g., Rom 15:25–27; 1 Cor 16:1–4). This Christian tradition of the relatively poor giving to the very poor continues to be attested over time (e.g., Tertullian, *Apol.* 39.7). Quite extreme versions of charity for the sake of others are attested as well, including, at the end of the first century, *1 Clement*'s remarkable claim that some Christians had sold themselves into slavery to pay for the manumission for others (*1 Clem.* 55.2).

Why would anyone do that? Treasures in heaven. The redemptive value of giving in the Hebrew Bible (Prov 19:17; Tob 4:7–10, 12:9) and in the teachings of Jesus (Mark 10:21) became a standard feature of early Christian discourse: almsgiving is considered a form of "sacrifice" in Hebrews 13:16, a "redemption" or "ransom" (λύτρωσις) for sins in the *Didache* (4.6), and a "lightening" or "alleviation" (κούφισμα) of sins in *2 Clement* (16.4).[39]

Almost always, though, giving involved generous sharing as urged by the Gospel of Luke and 1 Timothy, not the complete divestment as enjoined by the Markan Jesus and the early apostolic band in Acts. Over time the resolutely positive endorsement of Christian wealth moved to an extreme that would surely have astounded the historical Jesus. And so we have the peculiar second parable of the *Shepherd of Hermas* (ch. 51), which celebrates the intertwined relationship of an elm tree and a vine that grows up it. Only by being lifted above the ground can the vine produce fruit that will not rot. Thus, in unison, the strong but fruitless tree and the weak but fruit-bearing vine produce fruit that would be impossible for either of them separately. For Hermas, that is like rich and poor Christians. The rich may be deeply impoverished in spiritual matters: their prayer and confession bear almost no fruit. But they give some of their money to the poor, who in turn pray for them; and these prayers of the poor are efficacious in covering over the sins of the rich. Here then is a new way to obtain salvation without engaging in fanatical acts such as divestment. Everyone benefits: the rich are right with God despite how they live and how badly they pray; the poor don't starve to death; and God receives more people into his kingdom.

The most famous early move to justify wealth comes in Clement of Alexandria, writing not long before King Gundaphorus was to make his literary appearance. Clement's treatise "Who Is the Rich Person Who Will Be Saved?" surely warmed the cockles of every reasonably affluent heart in his congregation. The piece is written for them in particular and works hard to assure them that they do not need to abandon their material goods. Clement wants to "remove their groundless despair" (ch. 3). No one should think that Jesus meant those words about camels and eyes of needles "carnally" (σαρκινῶς, ch. 5). No, one must find "the meaning hidden in them" (ch. 5), namely, that everyone needs "to know the eternal God . . . and to possess him by knowledge and apprehension" (ch. 7). And so when the rich man of the Gospel story approaches Jesus to learn about eternal life, what does the Lord want him to do? Clement argues that Jesus urges the man to cleave to God. If the man had been fool enough to act on Jesus's words literally, he would have had nothing left. But abject poverty is not the way of salvation. Otherwise, the destitute would inherit the kingdom, and surely that cannot be right.

For Clement, Jesus does not order the man to engage in the "outward act" of divestment but to do something "greater, more godlike, more perfect, to strip the soul itself and its disposition of its underlying passions" (ch. 12). Those who are rich can stay rich, as long as they are not passionate about it. In fact, they should stay rich; that way they can help the poor. Clement is emphatic on the point: "Riches that also benefit our neighbors are not, then, to be renounced" (ch. 14). The wealthy should stand assured: God saves the rich and the poor alike; otherwise, it would not be fair. God would wrong people who, through no fault of their own, were born into a comfortable situation. And so Clement's ultimate point: the rich should not rid themselves of their possessions but of their passions.

At the same time, giving is very important for Clement, in no small measure because those who give can expect to receive, in abundance, in a kind of divine reciprocity. *Do ut des.* In Clement's words, there is a "great reward for our sharing, an eternal dwelling! Oh, what a great business! What a divine market-place (ὦ καλῆς ἐμπορίας, ὦ θείας ἀγορᾶς)! A person buys immortality with money, giving away worldly things that are perishing to receive in exchange an eternal mansion in heaven" (ch. 32). Here is an unusually fitting epigraph for the story of Gundaphorus.

Lucian and Thomas in Sums

Despite their many differences, the stories of Megapenthes and Gundaphorus share numerous similarities in overall conception and design. Both focus on the plight of a fabulously wealthy ruler who is tied to his wealth. In both, a glimpse of the realities of the afterlife reveals and clarifies the problem of affluence. Both provide a counterintuitive solution to deal with the problem. Neither tale is interested in broad social policy, governmental intervention, or economic revolution. They are concerned with the personal welfare of individuals who have money to burn. This may not be a widespread problem throughout human society, but the solutions advanced can indeed bear upon the problems of the 99 percent, at least those who are the beneficiaries.

At the same time, the tales are a study in contrasts. Few readers have ever taken Lucian's katabasis as a serious attempt to portray eschatological reality. It is precisely the humor of the account that provides its satirical delights. Lucian is concerned to explore the way to happiness in this life, embracing a Cynic view that great wealth can lead to great loss and therefore real anguish; it is better to be poor with nothing to lose. Cynics were not focused on postmortem realities. Many Christians of the second and third centuries, however, were, as shown by the numerous discussions of the contrasting afterlives of those who followed Christ and those who did not. These come to us in nearly every Christian genre available: theological discourses; ethical treatises; apologies; martyrologies; polemical tractates; heresiological reports; homilies; apocryphal Gospels, Acts, and apocalypses; personal correspondence. In the Christian world at the time, afterlife did not serve simply as a kind of metaphor, but also as a future reality. And so, Thomas's tale of Gundaphorus is imaginative, but at least in part it is probably meant to be taken seriously as a statement about postmortem salvation. The quality of one's life for eternity hinges on the character of one's life now. When Jesus instructed the rich to give what they had to the poor in order to have "treasures in heaven," he apparently really meant it.

Another key difference between Lucian and Thomas has far greater social implications. Lucian's account focuses on the needs and well-being of the wealthy person with no concern for the recipients of divestment. But for Thomas, the recipient is everything. Gifts out of one's abundance are not to go to the municipality, family, friends on the same social level, or even fellow citizens having a bit of a hard time. The money is to go to the poor and destitute. This may be a watered-down version of Jesus's radical message. It does not maintain that the wealthy have almost zero chance to enter the kingdom, and it does not require total divestment here to have treasures above. But it does share Jesus's concern for those in need. The destitute are no longer out of sight and out of mind. They are front and center in the Christian imagination. Eventually, long after Thomas's day, when wealthy elite began to enter the church in droves, this shift in focus would make a very big difference indeed to the social welfare of those in dire straits. At least it should have done.

Heaven, Hell, and Incentives for Conversion

Katabatic parenesis is sometimes extremely broad: life is short and nothing will follow, so live as long and well as you can (Homer). Or, this is as good as it gets, so appreciate the civilizing power of Rome (Virgil). Other times it is extremely specific, involving just one malfeasance or another: practice usury now and stand in muck for all eternity; commit adultery and hang by your genitals over the fires of hell (*Apocalypse of Peter*). Sometimes these specific injunctions affect major aspects of life: divest completely and be perennially happy (*Downward Journey*).

The very specificity of some of these injunctions must surely give the reader pause. Will a person's fate for all eternity be determined by one life practice? What if Gundaphorus gave vast sums to the poor but continued to engage in tyrannical murder, lechery, and deceit? Would he still earn that incredible mansion in the sky? Presumably not, but the text does not say: it is concerned with the distribution of wealth.[40] Other katabaseis, however, are much broader in their implications, urging a radical transformation of life on every level and in every way—a life-changing "conversion" experience.

Conversion in Antiquity

The term "conversion" has long been fraught within religious studies, but as with many complicated terms in the field (think "pagan," "Christian," or, one scarcely need mention, "religion"), there is no particularly good substitute, and it may be best simply to define the term and use it consistently.[41] In the present context I use "conversion" to refer to a life-changing shift from one set of beliefs, understandings, and practices to another—a major reorientation of one's mind and actions.[42] Normally one thinks of conversion as a religious experience; but as widely recognized, it did not figure as such in traditional Greek and Roman religions or the literary traditions associated with them.[43] To find something analogous to Christian "religious" conversion in antiquity, one needs to look to philosophy. And so we need to cross a disciplinary divide if we want to contrast pagan and Christian katabaseis urging a complete transformation of life, but doing so can be highly instructive. Here I consider a Greek katabasis urging conversion to philosophy, Plato's Myth of Er, and a Christian katabasis urging conversion to (a particular) religious faith from the *Acts of Thomas*.

First some brief background. As argued long ago by Arthur Darby Nock, in admittedly dated and problematic terms, pagan cults and related discourses and practices had nothing—or almost nothing—comparable to what Christians later insisted on as a total change of direction, a radical reorientation of life that involved dissolving all ties with former cultic practices, beliefs about the gods, acceptance on some level or other of stories told about them, and concomitant understandings and perspectives about the divine, all in exchange for new ones.[44] I need to stress, emphatically, that I am not saying (contra Nock) that those who came to accept and worship the Christian God always or even typically had a Damascus-road, blinding-light, earth-shattering experience subject to psychological analysis, or even that something we might imagine as a "complete" conversion is what normally happened. It seems improbable that polytheists typically turned into fully committed, practicing, orthodox Christians overnight and never turned back. In any event, even if they sometimes did, the issue is not relevant to my purposes here. I am not engaging in a sociohistorical analysis of what happened on the ground. For the purposes of this analysis, I am interested in the literary tradition, that is, rhetoric about conversion rather than social reality.

The reasons religious conversion was not found in Greek and Roman cultures, let alone their texts, have long been known and discussed and do not require a sustained analysis here.[45] In simple terms, traditional Greek and Roman religions (actual and textual) recognized a vast multitude of gods that deserved to be worshiped, and none of these religions insisted on exclusive devotion, even when they centered on *Theos Hypsistos* ("the highest God"), whether as a distinct divinity or as the one god all others represented or comprised.[46] Moreover, among these religions, the only real "competition" arose among gods when a particular divine being did not receive proper cult, not instead of other divinities but in addition to them. There were of course incentives and inducements for a person in Greek and Roman antiquity to begin worshiping a god that was not already in their pantheon: for example, the benefits this particular god could supply, the tragedies this god could avert, shifts in family practices (e.g., through marriage), or changes in physical location from one town to another. The new god would naturally be worshiped in somewhat distinctive ways, but not in radically different ones. Similar kinds of prayers and sacrifices, in broad terms, would still be in order. Even if someone urged a neighbor, cousin, or fellow worker to begin worshiping his or her own favorite god, it did not require the rejection of other forms of worship or a significant "religious transformation." Cultic practices were nearly always cumulative, not exclusive.[47]

The one exception that Nock cites continues to intrigue: the seemingly complete change that comes over Lucius in Book 11 of Apuleius's *Metamorphosis*, as he "converts" to become a rather fanatical devotee of Isis, whom he comes to see as the supreme divinity and the one ultimate manifestation of all the gods and goddesses. Lucius's initiation into the cult of Isis and his highly intense devotion to her is indeed extreme in the pagan literary tradition, but even here the alteration is not what we find in concurrent Christian texts. Lucius does not stop worshiping the gods alongside Isis; in fact, he comes to see that Osiris is even greater and then goes through another initiation. Within the world of the narrative, it is hard to say whether he is open to discovering yet other gods who are greater still. He certainly has grown tired of paying for the expensive initiations, so he appears to stop there. In any event, even though the mysteries of Isis were in many ways unlike anything Lucius had experienced before, and even though he became intensely devoted to her, he did not experience a fundamental change in his basic orientation or modes of worship. At least not in the ways Paul, Justin, or Constantine did—all complicated cases themselves, except to say that their views, understandings, beliefs, and cultic practices drastically changed, in fundamental ways. Again, in simple terms, Lucius became focused on and obsessed with a particular deity within his own "system"; the focus and obsession of these other converts required a new system.

Conversion in the Philosophical Tradition

Since Greek and Roman religions lacked conversion in the sense I'm using it here, there obviously would be no literary encouragements for it, in a katabasis or anywhere else. But, again as Nock observed, one other area of Greek and Roman culture allowed and promoted something comparable to religious conversion: philosophy.[48] It is certainly true that throughout the imperial period a good deal of philosophy was eclectic and syncretistic, with most serious thinkers picking and choosing as they preferred rather than associating exclusively with one school or another. At the same time, there were also serious devotees of the established philosophical traditions, with elements of exclusivism. To focus on two of the extremes, it was widely understood that an Epicurean who chose to become a Cynic would necessarily abandon the simple pleasures of life that had previously been a focus of attention. That would be a life-transforming decision.

Moreover, in terms of exclusivism, unlike devotees of one cult or another, most serious philosophers, by the nature of things, tended to defend the correctness of their views and the problems of others, including how, as a consequence, they behaved.[49] In broad terms, this marked a major difference between religion and philosophy: no one insisted that since the worship of Jupiter was "right," the worship of Venus was "wrong"; but anyone who wholeheartedly endorsed Stoic physics could not at the same time fully embrace Platonic or Epicurean (even if many people did amalgamate them, and others). Moreover, people who think they are right, and know that it matters, not just to themselves but to everyone else, are naturally inclined to want to persuade others. Many philosophers did. The issues were not just cognitive: arguably more significant, they affected how people lived their lives.

The most famous example is an early one, Plato's Socrates. The Dialogues are meant to persuade people to change their views and transform their lives accordingly. These changes are not understood as minor shifts in thinking; they are major overhauls of understanding and perspective that meaningfully change how people live. In this case, for Plato, this overhaul did not involve abandoning one philosophical position for another (his own) but the more fundamental decision to leave behind an "unexamined life" for the sake of philosophy itself.

Plato famously used afterlife myths to establish and promote his views. For a long time it was scholarly de rigueur to denigrate these myths, with many modern philosophers simply not seeing why they are there.[50] It is easy to understand the problem: the entire point of the Platonic system is to establish and demonstrate a position through dialectic logic and thus to establish its superiority to alternatives held not just among hoi polloi but also among rhetorically trained sophists and weak-thinking philosophers. A particular object of attack is any opinion acquired through shallow, popular means, such as the myths and tales told by Homer and Hesiod. And that is precisely what raises a key question: Given Plato's sharp contrast between logos and mythos, why would he stoop to using the latter in the context of hard dialectical reasoning? There may be reasons, of course, and some readers have recently become more forgiving or even appreciative of Plato's myths within their broader dialectical context, not as superfluous add-ons but as providing a different dimension to their overall purpose of transforming the reader's understanding and, correspondingly, life.[51]

The Myth of Er

The most famous of Plato's myths is also the most debated, the Myth of Er at the end of Book 10 of the *Republic*.[52] The theme of the *Republic* appears at the outset of Book 1: "justice" or "righteousness" (δικαιοσύνη) and the importance of pursuing it (331c).[53] Already here at the beginning the theme is linked to widespread "myths of those in Hades" (μῦθοι περὶ τῶν ἐν Ἅιδου; 330d–e). The dialogue's particular thesis about righteousness is clearly set out in Book 2, a thesis seemingly simple yet so complex that it requires the following nine books to demonstrate it: the best life is one that is lived justly, no matter the cost (357a–b). For this dialogue, as Ronald Johnson summarizes, one who lives a just life "pursues the Good in all its forms and always tries to choose what will aid him in this pursuit."[54] Since almost no one does that, Plato works to persuade his readers they should. Plato here is proselytizing, trying to make converts. For him, a person's soul depends on it. As M. Vorwerk has put it, "According to the final word of Socrates (621b8–d3), the function of the myth [of Er] is to save its hearers by affirming the immortality of the soul and thus to encourage a righteous life so the soul will fare well in the afterlife."[55]

The bulk of the *Republic* provides the dialectic logic, but Plato sets a high challenge for himself: he contends that a person should strive to be just even if there are no material benefits for it. On the contrary, even if living a just life leads to poverty, pain, death, "or anything else that seems to be evil, these things will all turn out to be good, in both life and death" (613a). It is only after providing all the dialectic needed to establish the point that Plato turns to argue, toward the end of Book 10, that even though one should live justly without expectation of reward, righteousness in fact will bring rewards. He claims that the just are rewarded in this life as a rule, whereas most of those who are unjust, in the end, are miserable and unhappy. And even more so in death.

This reversal in reasoning—are there ultimate benefits to being just or not?—is in part what has led the ending of Book 10 into disrepute among some readers.[56] The Myth of Er advances precisely the view that Plato refused to concede throughout the long dialogue: a just life leading to suffering will be rewarded in the end. But as others have pointed out, the criticism is unwarranted.[57] Plato's view is that one should not seek to live the just life because it will bring benefits; but in fact, nonetheless, it will indeed do so. What better way to illustrate the point than by discussing ultimate benefits? The Myth of Er is obviously not meant as a literal description of what happens after death, any more than is the *Downward Journey* of Lucian or the *Aeneid* Book 6. It is an imaginative vision of life to come that stresses what preeminently matters in life here and now: not glory, fame, wealth, or position, but living justly.[58]

Er is said to have been a Pamphylian soldier who died on the battlefield. When the slain were finally gathered for burial, ten days later, his body, oddly enough, had not at all decayed. Two days later, on his funeral pyre, Er returned to life and told what he had seen and heard in the world beyond (614b). This is the most famous near death experience of antiquity. When Er's soul left his body, he traveled with a large group of people to a "divine place" (τόπον τινὰ δαιμόνιον; 614c) where he saw two openings in the earth and two in the sky, with judges sitting between them. The people recognized to have been "just" (or "righteous": τοὺς δικαίους) were sent through one of the openings up to heaven; the unjust (or "unrighteous"; τοὺς ἀδικαίους) were sent the other direction, through one of the openings down below (614c). Er was dispatched to neither place but was told that he was to be a messenger back to the living to inform them what was in store for them in the world to come. In other words, he was to explain how the realities of life after death should affect life in the present.

The other two openings were exits from the worlds beyond: souls emerging from below were squalid and dusty; those from above, clean. All the discharged souls gathered together and went off to a meadow, with Er in tow. There they spent a week sharing stories about their experiences over the previous thousand years. Those from below moaned and wept as they recalled being punished ten times over for all their unjust acts toward others; those from above exulted in the good things they had enjoyed and the indescribable beauty they had observed, as "just and holy" people (δίκαιοι καὶ ὅσιοι; 614e–15c). The only group not included among the mixed crowd were the truly wicked—most of them tyrants—who were not allowed to leave the place of torment but had been seized, after their millennium of pain, by "wild men, fiery in appearance" (ἄνδρες . . . ἄγριοι διάπυροι ἰδεῖν) who carried them away for merciless torture before casting them into Tartarus (615d–16a).

After the week of storytelling, the souls embarked on another journey. In four days they came to a place where they could see the light that passes through earth and heaven and observe the inner workings of the cosmos. They realized the world is complexly but completely orderly, arranged, and driven not by capricious chance but by Necessity (Ἀνάγκη) (616c). For the reader that means, among other things, that postmortem rewards and punishments are not arbitrary but conform to how the world works.

A key feature of Er's vision is his realization that souls' destinies are not eternal, except for the truly wicked, who are sent to Tartarus. The discharged souls next journeyed to the place where they were to choose how once more to live (617d). They were to be reincarnated and so they stood at the "beginning of another mortal period, an age of life that will bring death" (ἀρχὴ ἄλλης περιόδου θνητοῦ γένους θανατηφόρου). They themselves would determine what their next life would be—no one else, not even a divine being would do so.

Even so, they did not have complete freedom of choice. Lots were cast to determine the order in which souls chose from among the large varieties of life on offer. They could opt to become wealthy tyrants or obscure nobodies or nearly anything in between: the whole panoply was available, more possibilities than souls, and including not just human lives but also animal lives for those who preferred them. The account emphasizes that even though some of the more tempting options might be scarfed up before the selection process was finished, no one would be forced into a bad choice leading to a horrible life.

Whatever kind of life a soul chose would determine its incarnate character. For Plato the mythmaker, that is the point. One needs to choose a life that is just, whatever else is involved. The narrator Socrates informs his interlocutor that most important is to "distinguish the good life from the wicked, and always, absolutely to choose the best one possible" (βίον καὶ χρηστὸν καὶ πονηρὸν διαγιγνώσκοντα, τὸν βελτίω ἐκ τῶν δυνατῶν ἀεὶ πανταχοῦ αἱρεῖσθαι; 618c). In every case, the worse life is one that will make the soul more unjust (εἰς τὸ ἀδικωτέραν γίγνεσθαι); the better, more just (δικαιοτέρον). And so, it is not extreme wealth, power, and physical pleasure that make a life good and happy; it is "righteousness." Those who have learned from life and practiced philosophy are the ones who will make the right choice.

Amazingly enough, some souls chose very badly indeed. The very first soul, one who had come from the glories of heaven, snatched up the life of a tyrant without due reflection. This soul may have just spent a thousand years in ecstasy and heard tales of alternative misery for seven days, but it was a very slow learner. Yes, it would be fabulously wealthy and powerful for its mortal existence, but it would also be corrupt and wicked and would have a millennium of hell to pay for it.

Many others made less insanely bad choices, but their mistake became clear—at least to the reader—even before they left the afterlife. A final journey was made, to the Plain of Oblivion, through a dreadful heat. The souls eventually arrived at the River of Forgetfulness (τὸν Ἀμέλητα ποταμόν), where they were required to drink in order to forget all that had already happened before being born again into the world above. Understandably, given the hot conditions, some souls drank long and deeply, enjoying their refreshment. Others took only what was required. Without saying so Plato is making a subtle point. Throughout various dialogues

Socrates insists that knowledge involves "remembering" (e.g., Meno). And so in Er's tale the souls that were headed for the unphilosophical life, who were to spend their lives satisfying their desires, quaffed an excessive amount of the water of forgetfulness. They would be severely handicapped above, not likely to "recollect" much truth, let alone engage in life-enriching philosophy. Only the philosophically inclined who took just the small amount of the water of oblivion required would have a chance to remember the lessons of the past.[59] Er himself was not allowed to drink the water at all because his mission was to tell what he had seen. He awakened on his pyre and told his tale.

Once Socrates has recounted the myth, he urges his hearers to take heed. A person can experience any extreme of good and evil in life; but the ultimate goal is to advance along the "upper path" and "to pursue righteousness with wisdom, in every way, so that we may be beloved both to ourselves and to the gods" (621c).

Plato has obviously not given us a literal description of the afterlife. This is mythos (μῦθος), a story with a point. It matters how we live. Most people do not live well. They follow their passions, seeking wealth, power, fame, influence, social standing, and bodily pleasure. In doing so they are killing their souls. They need to change, radically. In the myth, souls are said to have another chance in the life to come, after paying a thousand-year price for their poor choices. But in truth, for Plato, people have their chance now. They can change how they live and begin life anew, radically altering the direction and focus of their lives in the pursuit of righteousness, virtue, goodness, and truth. In short, they need to convert.[60]

This then is philosophical conversion. Nothing like it was on offer in "religion"—no effort to bring about a complete reorientation of a person's understanding, practice, and life—and so there was no emphasis on proselytizing.[61]

Conversion in the Christian Tradition

The matter was completely different in the early Christian tradition. Not long after Jesus's death his immediate followers insisted on an exclusivist commitment to him that involved acceptance of the crucified Messiah. The roots of their view lay in a Judaism that insisted one God was to be worshiped, and in highly prescribed ways. This God was the creator of all and the one who had called Israel to be his special people. In the apocalyptic tradition out of which Christianity emerged, a Day of Judgment was soon to take place. Those (few) who lived in obedience to God would be saved when it happened; all others would be destroyed. Jesus himself was an evangelist for the kingdom, urging people to transform their lives in light of the eschatological realities soon to come. After his death his followers continued the message, with the revolutionary twist that a right standing with the God of Israel and judge of all required a commitment to the Messiah he had sent, Jesus, who had been crucified for the sins of others and raised from the dead. Whoever rejected this salvific gift would face God's wrath when Jesus returned.

It was not many years before the newly converted Paul honed the evangelistic impulse of the earliest Jesus movement to a fine pitch and significantly broadened it to embrace the gentiles who comprised the vast majority of the world's population. More than anyone else on record, Paul promoted two aspects of this new messianic movement that set it apart from the other religious traditions of the Roman world and led, eventually, to its long-term success: exclusivism and evangelism. Paul insisted there was no way of salvation apart from Christ—certainly not pagan cultic practices but also not traditional Jewish law observance. Those who believed in Christ's death and resurrection, and acted accordingly, would be saved; all others would be condemned by the wrath of God. There was one God, one Messiah, one way of salvation. This remarkable exclusivism drove the evangelistic efforts of Paul and others like him. Like pagans, traditional Jews had virtually no reason to convert anyone to their particular cultic preferences.[62] But among followers of Jesus there was a very good reason indeed. Those who did not follow the Christ of God would be condemned forever.

We have reasonably solid information about what Paul preached to his potential converts, based on his own recollections in such passages as 1 Thessalonians 1:9–10 and 1 Corinthians 15:3–5: Christ died for the sins of others; he was raised from the dead; he is returning in judgment; people need to turn from their former cultic practices and pagan views, worship only the God of Israel, believe in his Son, and follow his dictates. If that was Paul's message, what made it convincing? Modern scholars, with good post-Enlightenment zeal and sensibilities, have long been reluctant to accept Paul's own claims about the matter, even though, as it turns out, these coincide with virtually every other early Christian source that discusses it. In his letters Paul speaks of his compelling "signs, wonders, and miracles" (2 Cor 12:12; so too Rom 15:18–19, 1 Cor 2:4). Acts of divine power provided the necessary proofs for the claims of faith.[63]

Even those committed to modern principles of reason and science can accept this explanation. We do not need to believe that Paul literally performed actions that defied natural law. Some of the people Paul addressed became convinced he was telling the truth that Jesus had been raised from the dead; that it was not a mere near death experience; that Jesus soon afterward appeared to his followers, then to Paul later; and that he is now resident with God up in heaven. They believed Paul himself was empowered by the Spirit of God to perform deeds that most mere mortals—that is, those without the Spirit of God—could never do. Wondrous deeds. Miracles. These acts confirmed for them the truth claims of Paul's message. In response, they converted.

Paul certainly did not convince most people he met, and probably few of those he encountered believed he could do the miraculous deeds he was alleged to have done. Almost certainly most of his potential converts thought the bodily resurrection of a dead man and the supposed miracles of his followers were all nonsense. Even so, Paul did not need to convince large numbers of those he encountered, day in and day out, year after year. He had to convince a few. These in turn would convince a few others—say a spouse, their children, and slaves. Maybe they would convince a single neighbor, who, some months later, convinced a cousin, who eventually convinced a single friend, who then. . . . And then the process continued year after year, in geometric growth, with more converts making more converts. The resulting exponential curve eventually became significant, not in Paul's lifetime but over the course of decades and then centuries. What made Christianity successful in the end was not merely this conversionist emphasis, but its concomitant exclusivism. Everyone (in theory) who converted to worship only the one God of Jesus was both won over to Christianity and lost to paganism; year after year, decade after decade, as Christianity grew, pagan cults shrank; since Christianity was the only religious movement doing this, by its very nature it grew by destroying the other religions in its wake.[64]

Lots of "reasons for conversion" have been adduced over the years—almost none of them convincing or, more important, with any solid ancient testimony or evidence.[65] The surviving accounts consistently follow Paul in referring to "miracles" as the key—whether in the book of Acts (e.g., chs. 2, 4, 9, 19); the apocryphal *Acts* (whether Peter, John, or the others); allegedly historical accounts (Gregory of Nyssa's *Life of Gregory Thaumaturgus*; Sulpicious Severus's account of Martin of Tours); treatises that reflect on the matter (Cyprian, *Letter to Demetrianus*) or, yet more striking, that come from the pens of enemies (Celsus, as we will see). As late as the early fifth century, Augustine is perfectly straightforward and clear: Christianity spread throughout the empire because its claims were confirmed by powerful miracles; indeed, the miracles described in the biblical texts "were published that they might produce faith, and the faith which they produced brought them into greater prominence" (*City of God* 22.7). But it is not simply old miracles that convert, according to Augustine: "Even now miracles are wrought in the name of Christ," and these lead to conversions (22.8). Augustine goes on to describe the mighty and compelling miraculous acts of God he himself has seen: healings of blindness, gout, paralysis, cancer, hernia, and, remarkably, rectal fibula.

The role of miracles in the Christian mission helps make sense of one aspect of the Christian katabatic tradition, which emphasizes the miraculous power of God and its effect on humans, not just in this life but in the life to come.

The Role of the Afterlife in Christian Conversion

It is striking that Augustine goes into this long disquisition on the miraculous acts of God precisely where he does, at the very end of the *City of God* and its lengthy account of the afterlife—both the reality of conscious eternal torment for sinners (Book 21) and the glorious eternal life of the resurrected saints (Book 22). As for many others in the Christian tradition, for Augustine the power of God transcends this world of mere mortals. It will assert itself throughout the ages, and, combined with his justice, it will affect human destiny for all time. Heaven and hell are embodiments of divine might. Anyone who does not believe in God's power while living—as seen in miracles—will experience it with exquisite clarity when dead.

This was the message of the Christians from very early times: God's overwhelming and all-encompassing might will especially be manifest in acts of judgment. Some such message came already in the apocalyptic preaching of John the Baptist: "Already the axe is laid at the root of the trees: every tree that does not give good fruit will be cut down and cast into the fire" (Matt 1:10). Jesus himself spoke of those who would be tossed into Gehenna (Matt 5:22); of the ultimate destruction of the "many" who chose the wrong path (Matt 7:13–14); of the ones cast out of the kingdom into the outer darkness where there would be weeping and gnashing of teeth (Matt 8:1–12); and of the "eternal fire prepared for the devil and his angels" where many would find "eternal punishment"

(Matt 25:41, 46). So too our first Christian author, Paul, speaks of the conversion of pagans from dead idols to the true God, to await "his son from heaven, who delivers us from the wrath that is coming" at the time of "sudden destruction" (1 Thess 1:9, 5:3).

These earliest preachers in the tradition were speaking not of eternal torment in hell but of the annihilation awaiting those who would not enter the coming kingdom.[66] But eventually within this tradition the kingdom of God on earth came to be transformed into the life of heaven above. Even after this transition the incentives remained very much the same: repent or experience the eschatological wrath of God. At the same time, with the shift away from an earthly kingdom to a heavenly eternity, Christian preaching ratcheted up the threats a significant notch. Now the wicked unbelievers would not be mercilessly slaughtered out of existence; they would be consciously tormented forever, with no possibility of escape through death.

Driving these notions was a Christian theodicy that explained how those suffering for God now would be rewarded later, whereas their persecutors would be mercilessly punished in the end—an end that would never end. And so it is interesting that some of the earliest threats of eternal torment come precisely in Christian martyr accounts. One of our earliest, the *Martyrdom of Polycarp*, recounts a telling scene.[67] When the bishop of Smyrna is brought for trial and execution in the local "stadium," the proconsul, in a terrific bit of irony, urges him to repent. Polycarp, of course, refuses, even when the proconsul threatens to burn him alive. But the saint's decision for painful death over apostasy has a compelling eschatological logic: "You threaten with a fire that burns for an hour and after a short while is extinguished; for you do not know about the fire of the coming judgment and eternal torment, reserved for the ungodly" (*Mart. Pol.* 11). To paraphrase: Yes, you can torch me to death; and in return God will torch you for all eternity. In contrast to me, you will never be able to escape, even by expiring. So which of us needs to repent?

Thus also in the *Martyrdom of Perpetua*: the day before the Christians were to be thrown to the wild beasts, they spoke with the mob that had gathered, and after they threatened them with the "judgment of God," "many" are said to come to belief (*ex quibus multi crediderunt;* 17.3). The next day, during the martyrdom scene itself, three of the Christians, Revocatus, Saturninus, and Saturus, about to be torn apart by the animals, turn to threaten the crowd in remarkably effective terse terms, "You us, but God you" (*Tu nos, inquiunt, te autem Deus;* 19.8). This notion of reversed torment can also be found in martyr accounts in which Christians regularly refuse to recant so as to save themselves from torture and death because they "fear God" (*Scillitan Martyrs* 15; *Martyrdom of Pionius*). There are things far worse than ephemeral fire and wild beasts.[68]

Christian texts threaten nonbelievers with eternal torments in all shapes and sizes. Thus we have a letter of Cyprian to the pagan Roman proconsul of Asia, Demetrianus, who had been blaming the Christians for the upheavals widely experienced during the "Crisis of the Third Century." This was a truly horrible time in the life of the Roman Empire: barbarian invasion, civil war, breakaway states, imperial political turmoil, earthquakes, drought, and epidemic. Demetrianus claimed the gods were angry at the presence of so many "atheists," that is, Christians, refusing to offer them the cultic worship they deserved. And so they should be forced to do so. As a result, Christians were subjected to persecution, and pagans were having trouble understanding why they did not simply cave in and do what the gods required, especially in such tumultuous times.

Cyprian had the opposite view: the crisis did not come from the pagan gods in retribution for the Christians; it came from the Christian God to punish the pagans who refused to recognize him. Moreover, the tortures applied to the Christians were nothing in comparison with what unbelievers would face in the life to come: "Our certainty of a vengeance to follow makes us patient. . . . The harmless acquiesce in punishments and tortures, sure and confident that whatsoever we suffer will not remain unavenged, and that in proportion to the greatness of the injustice of our persecution so will be the justice and the severity of the vengeance exacted for those persecutions" (*Letter to Demetrianus* 17).[69] The suffering in this world during the crisis marked only the beginning for those outside the church: "And since [these plagues] are of no avail in this matter, and do not convert individuals to God by such terror of destructions, there remains after all the eternal dungeon, and the continual fire, and the everlasting punishment, nor shall the groaning of the suppliants be heard there" (*Letter to Demetrianus* 9). But there was still the chance to repent, and anyone who failed to do so would pay a terrible price, forever:

> When the day of judgment shall come, what joy of believers, what sorrow of unbelievers; that they should have been unwilling to believe here and now that they should be unable to return that they might believe! An ever-burning Gehenna will burn up the condemned, and a punishment devouring with living flames; nor

will there be any source whence at any time they may have either respite or end to their torments. Souls with their bodies will be reserved in infinite tortures for suffering. (*Letter to Demetrianus* 24)

The rhetorically trained Cyprian concludes with a flourish: "Too late they will believe in eternal punishment who would not believe in eternal life."

Even pagan polemical sources maintain that Christians used their descriptions of heaven and hell both as an encouragement for insiders and as a strict warning for outsiders, with a goal of conversion. These are particularly remarkable testimonies, given how infrequently Christians appear in the writings of outsiders at all before the mid-third century. But when they are mentioned, incentives provided by the afterlife regularly come into the picture. Already Lucian, in one of his rare references to Christians, maligns those "miserable souls (κακοδαίμονες) who have convinced themselves that they will never die but will live for all time; that is why most of them despise death and willingly give themselves over to it" (*Peregrinus* 13). These words immediately call to mind the later *Meditations* of Marcus Aurelius, in his one and only reference to Christians, in which he marvels at their pure obstinacy in going to death (*Meditations* 11.3).

So too the much better informed Celsus, who mocks Christians for the "miscellaneous ideas they use to persuade potential converts," especially the "terrors they invent" (Origen, *Contra Celsum* 3.19; see also 3.80). Celsus claims Christians are "led away with vain hopes," and he "attacks the doctrine of the blessed life and of fellowship with God." In his most famous statement, the pagan antagonist pulls out the rhetorical stops:

It is foolish of them also to suppose that, when God applies the fire (like a cook!), all the rest of mankind will be thoroughly roasted and that they alone will survive, not merely those who are alive at the time but those also long dead who will rise up from the earth possessing the same bodies as before. This is simply the hope of worms. For what sort of human soul would have any further desire for a body that has rotted? The fact that this doctrine is not shared by some of [the Jews] and by some Christians shows its utter repulsiveness, and that it is both revolting and impossible. For what sort of body, after being entirely corrupted, could return to its original nature and that same condition which it had before it was dissolved? As they have nothing to say in reply, they escape to a most outrageous refuge by saying that "anything is possible to God." (*Contra Celsum* 5.14)

Finally we might note the pagan Caecilius, probably invented by Minucius Felix for the purpose of his apologetic dialogue *Octavius*, mouthing familiar pagan objections to Christian preaching: "What amazing stupidity and incredible audacity! They despise present torments while fearing the uncertainties of what is to come; and while they are afraid of dying after death, in the mean time they do not fear dying. And so a deceptive hope of comforts to come later charms away their fear" (*Octavius* 8.5). How would pagans know so well the Christians' unusual teachings of the world to come? It must have been one of the Christians' most common messages, delivered either to explain themselves in the face of opposition or to win converts or both.

Given the emphasis on the glories of heaven and the torments of hell, it is no surprise that some Christian authors produced narratives that portrayed graphic descriptions of both. Clearly these were meant in part to urge Christians within their communities to stay true to their convictions, even in the face of persecution. But they also functioned as evangelistic warnings to pagans, whether they were meant to be read by them or not.[70]

Fire and Brimstone in the Acts of Thomas

We have already seen one aspect of the evangelistic function of Christian katabasis in the second Act of Thomas: when Gundaphorus and Gad realize the fantastic afterlife benefits that will accrue, they convert to the God proclaimed by Thomas.[71] The other katabasis in the *Acts of Thomas* (Act 6, chs. 51–61) shows the flip side—the persuasive power of threats of eternal torture. In this case, the narrative does not involve a named and extremely wealthy king but an anonymous lower-class woman. Also different are the incentives for conversion. Rather than committing to give to the poor to obtain treasure in heaven, the woman converts from a life of sin to avoid the horrible torments of hell. The *Acts of Thomas* woos the wealthy but terrifies the transgressor. Both katabatic visions, as one would expect, are successful, leading to on-the-spot conversions. But the latter leads to conversion of many more people. For one thing, there are more poor transgressors than wealthy monarchs. For another, as we have seen, fire and brimstone have long been one of Christianity's most effective missionary tools.

Act 6 is possibly the strangest narrative in this book of strange narratives. It begins with a young man in Thomas's community trying to take the Eucharist, only to have his hands wither when bringing the element to his mouth. Those standing by tell Thomas what has happened, and he confronts the young man to find the reason. The young man confesses to a foul deed and reveals the backstory. His lover had been a woman "living outside the city in an inn" (ἐν πανδοχείῳ). This is usually taken to mean she was a prostitute.[72] The young man had listened to Thomas's ascetic proclamation, that "whoever has sexual intercourse in a vile union, especially in adultery, will not have life from the God I preach" (*Acts of Thomas*, ch. 51), and had converted. But when he tried to persuade his lover to follow suit by living with him "in chastity and a pure way of life," she had no interest in the idea. Rather than watch her commit adultery with someone else, he murdered her. This had just happened before he came to take communion—her corpse was still at the inn.

The apostle responds to the tale by railing against "insane sexual intercourse" and "unbridled desire" but not, oddly enough, against the man who has just committed cold-blooded murder. The apostle calls for water, instructs the man to wash his hands, and they are restored. When the man confesses that he believes, he somewhat discomfortingly pins the blame for his crime on the woman who had refused to choose chastity (ch. 52).

As readers of apocryphal *Acts* surely expect, this will all lead to a miracle. John accompanies the young man to the scene of the crime, has the woman's corpse brought outside, and prays for Jesus to manifest his power (δύναμις) by raising her from the dead, both for Jesus's own glory and for "the faith of those standing by," that is, the onlookers who have gathered around (ch. 53). A show of power produces faith.

Thomas instructs the man to take his erstwhile lover by the hand and raise her from the dead. After some hesitation he does so. Seeing the apostle she falls at his feet, grasps his clothing, and asks where "the other one" is who had been with him—the one who did not "abandon her to that fearful and awful place" (ch. 54). When Thomas instructs her to reveal what had just happened, she launches into her tale. She had been in the place of torment and indicates Thomas had been there with her.

Her tale begins at the point where she passes from life to death. A hostile man in filthy clothes appears and takes her to a place filled with pits and reeking with a ghastly stench. When she looks into the first pit, she sees people attached to wheels of fire ramming into one another. Her attendant tells her these sinners are of "her own stock" (ὁμόφυλοι); he then explains that these are "the ones who exchanged the intercourse of man and woman" (or "husband and wife"; αἱ μεταλλάξασαι ἀνδρὸς καὶ γυναικὸς τὴν συνουσίαν). That may sound like a reference to the same-sex relations condemned in Paul's letter to the Romans (1:16–17), and it is often taken that way,[73] but the immediate context suggests otherwise: the woman next sees a pile of infants who are the (ill-begotten) offspring of the men and women on the fiery wheels. Those being tormented, then, appear to have been involved with illicit *procreative* sex (exchanging sex partners?). That would also be why they are of the "same stock" as the touring sinner. It is hard to say whether they were also involved in prostitution.

The next pit is exuding worms, and in it the woman sees souls rolling about and moaning. These are women who have left their husbands in order to commit adultery. Their partners are nowhere to be seen. Possibly as men, they get off scot-free. Another pit contains various souls who are being hanged: slanderers by their tongues; immodest women by their braided hair; thieves who refused to give alms to the poor or help the oppressed by their hands; and those who merrily ran down evil paths, not caring for the sick or mourning, by their feet (not a euphemism for genitals in this case; ch. 56).

The woman's horrible attendant then takes her to a dark cave emitting a foul smell. Here she sees a number of souls trying to escape their confinement for a breath of air, but their guards do not allow it. These are souls who had already been tormented in other pits, who now will be either consumed out of existence or taken off for more torture (ch. 57). The guards ask the woman's guide to hand her over so they can confine her in the pit, but he refuses because of orders he has received. He takes her to another place, and then the Thomas look-alike ("the one who was like you"; ὁ δέ σοι ὅμοιος)—obviously Jesus—takes her, hands her over to Thomas himself in the underworld (he is evidently in two places at once), and tells him to take her because she was one who had gone astray (as if all the others had not). The next thing she knew, she had come back to life, and she begs Thomas not to send her back "to those places of torment I saw."

This is clearly an apostolic teaching moment. Thomas turns to the gathered crowd and assures them that what the woman had seen "are not the only punishments"; on the contrary "others are worse than these" (ch. 58). It is hard to imagine what could be worse, but possibly the point is precisely to make the reader imagine. The apostle then makes his pitch. If those listening to him do not turn to "this God I preach" and refrain from their ill-guided behavior, which they pursue "out of ignorance" (χωρὶς γνώσεως), they will indeed undergo such torments. There is only one solution: "Believe in our Lord Jesus Christ and he will forgive you of the sins you committed before now, and he will cleanse you from all bodily desires that remain on earth" (ch. 58). Thomas indicates the offer is good for sinners of all kinds: robbers, adulterers (a sin that is "altogether wicked before God, an evil above the other evils"), the greedy, liars, drunkards, slanderers, or simply those who pay back evil for evil. They should instead live in faith, gentleness, chastity, and hope, so they might become like God and "accept from him the gifts which only a few receive" (ch. 58).

Thus the main incentive for conversion is a dire threat, but on top of it comes a lovely promise. Within the narrative world of the *Acts*, the expected occurs: "Then the entire crowd believed." This was a true faith from Thomas's perspective: everyone begins to glory in good works, in particular giving money to help widows in need (ch. 59). Thomas goes off to preach his Gospel, healing the sick, casting out demons, and converting the masses.

The lesson of the story is none too subtle. Those who do not follow Christ and who, as a result, live in sin will pay a gruesome price for all eternity. Those who convert, come to believe, and completely change their ways, will receive multiple gifts from God reserved for only the few.

Katabasis and Incentives for Evangelism

Christian katabaseis, like all others, worked on many levels. In part they provided believers with firm ideas about the world to come, in both its horrifying and its glorious aspects. Even if authors did not really think they knew the actual details, they almost certainly believed that life after death would be either excessively awful or unimaginably magnificent. But the descriptions were never meant principally as lessons in postmortem geography, climate, or experience. They were largely parenetic, urging readers to certain courses of action before the life to come had come. At times the parenesis was negative and specific: do not sin, especially in this way or that. At other times it was positive and more broad-ranging: be unusually generous by giving your money to the poor. And sometimes it was all-encompassing: turn your life around and experience a radical transformation that only Christ can provide.[74]

Given the evangelistic emphases of some of these texts, we might return to the questions of their audience and real-life function. It seems unlikely that Christian writers or their readers could imagine pagan or Jewish outsiders having any interest in perusing at leisure the *Acts of Thomas* or the apocalypses of Peter or Paul. These surely were not meant as missionary tractates. Then what? More plausibly, katabaseis functioned like the Christian "apologies" produced during the same era, ostensibly directed to outsiders of the faith but really being in-house literature. Why would an apology "defend the faith" for readers who already accept it? Possibly to assure its readers of the truth of their faith. But also, almost certainly, because the Christian audience wanted and needed to communicate with antagonistic or at least ignorant outsiders, and these works provided them with ammunition to help them make their pitch. The apologies supplied Christians with the rhetorical weapons they needed to *defend* themselves when assaulted for their faith. Katabaseis provided tools for *conversion*, supplying "information" about life, death, and the afterlife not merely for their readers' education and edification but also for their missionary efforts. In the early Christian church such efforts almost never involved long-term evangelistic campaigns taken to unknown lands, funded by the home community. That kind of missionary work very rarely happened in our period, so far as we know.[75] The mission field was not abroad but at home, undertaken daily, even if not by all Christians, at least certainly by some. It was carried out through individual social networks. Everyone had families, neighbors, friends, co-workers, and other acquaintances. In the cities people lived and worked in close quarters, virtually piled on top of one another. They had no forms of media entertainment or money to travel. They worked and came home or they worked at home. Their entertainment was social engagement. They spent significant amounts of time with others. They talked about all sorts of things, including religion. And the meaning of life. And the realities of death.

Early Christians talking about religion had a different agenda from others in their world. Most Christians, we might suppose, or at least a good many of them, believed that everyone would be judged at the end of their lives. Loved ones and other acquaintances not in the Christian community would be condemned for failing to believe in Christ and to model their lives on the commandments of God. Katabaseis helped educate these Christians. Reading—or more often hearing—these texts brought home in unusually graphic terms the afterlife realities everyone they knew would be facing. Those not yet in the believing community had a simple choice: convert to follow Christ and enjoy utopian consequences forever or refuse and experience the eternally painful consequences. Naturally there was an urgency about the message. And so, Christians not only reported the amazing power of God that was being manifest in their midst but also described how that power would make itself felt in the life to come. Those on the side of God would experience blessings beyond imagination, forevermore. Those who rejected God would be eternally tormented. Those were the two options, and the katabaseis provided the details.

CHAPTER FOUR

The Afterlife of Afterlives

Editorial Interventions and Christology

C HRISTIAN KATABASEIS CAN sometimes do unexpected theological work. In this chapter I explore a single instance and take a circuitous route in doing so by examining the editorial alterations of the text of the *Apocalypse of Peter* as found in the Akhmim fragment (Akhmim 2). This is a major reworking of the text, done in conjunction with an editorial revamping of the *Gospel of Peter* (Akhmim 1). The editor of the two texts rewrote the *Apocalypse* to insert it as an episode into an old, no longer surviving, version of the *Gospel*. Others have made this argument for more than a century; I pursue the investigation, however, by exploring not only what the editorial work entailed but also what it was meant to achieve. My thesis is that an editor redacted the texts not because there was a problem with the *Apocalypse of Peter* but because there was a problem with the *Gospel*, whose reputation had been sullied because of its allegedly docetic Christology, purportedly maintaining that Christ only "seemed" to be a flesh-and-blood human. The editor's redactions were meant to help ameliorate the problem.

It is a vexed issue. The place to begin is by considering the evidence that has long persuaded scholars that Akhmim 2 represents a version of the *Apocalypse* that, in this secondary, edited form, was actually a part of the *Gospel* narrative.[1]

The *Apocalypse* and *Gospel of Peter* in Early Scholarship

In 1892, when Urbain Bouriant published the *editio princeps* of the Codex Panopolitanus, discovered near Akhmim, Egypt, six years earlier, he identified its second text, bound into the manuscript upside down, as a fragment of the long-lost *Apocalypse of Peter*.[2] The book had previously been known only from early church canon lists, starting with the Muratorian Fragment, and patristic references beginning with Clement of Alexandria and going up to Sozomen.[3] Since the other two major writings in the codex, *1 Enoch* and the *Gospel of Peter*, were clearly fragmentary, and since the apocalypse itself contained none of the explicit patristic quotations,[4] the text was almost immediately thought to comprise only a portion of the account otherwise known in Christian antiquity.

In the first full analysis, appearing, remarkably, the next year, Albrecht Dieterich argued that the *Apocalypse of Peter* must have undergone numerous changes, expansions, and even serious transformations over the years and so had appeared in a variety of recensions. In his judgment, the Akhmim version was actually not "the" *Apocalypse of Peter* but a portion of the *Gospel of Peter*, the preceding text in the manuscript: "We do not have an independent Gospel before us—not the *Apocalypse of Peter*—but a fragment from a Gospel . . . even the same Gospel" (i.e., the *Gospel of Peter*).[5] In other words, the scribe who produced the Akhmim manuscript was copying *two* sections from the *Gospel of Peter*—one a fragment covering Jesus's trial, death, and resurrection, and the other providing an apocalyptic discourse.

In Dieterich's view, what later came to be known in church circles as the *Apocalypse of Peter* developed out of this portion of the original *Gospel of Peter*. That is to say, a later editor extracted this portion of the *Gospel*, edited it, and published it as a stand-alone piece that became known as Peter's apocalypse. Since Dieterich and other scholars believed the *Gospel of Peter* must date to the early part of the second century, the freestanding apocalypse could only have been put in circulation somewhat later, but at least before the writing of Clement of Alexandria at the end of the century.

Some years later Theodore Zahn set out an alternative hypothesis. He agreed that eventually a *Gospel of Peter* and an *Apocalypse of Peter* circulated as independent texts. But the *Apocalypse* was not an edited version of an account originally found in the *Gospel*. It had been composed at an earlier stage and had been used by the *Gospel* writer as one of his sources, edited in order to make it fit into its new literary context. The second Akhmim text represented this edited version. It was clearly part of the Akhmim

Gospel because of their linguistic similarities, but it had been created by the editor who had altered the original, independently circulating form of the text.[6]

Thus Dieterich and Zahn agreed that the two Akhmim texts were taken from the same book, the *Gospel of Peter*. As a result, for them both, technically speaking, Akhmim 2 is not the *Apocalypse of Peter* referred to by patristic sources. It is a *Gospel* fragment.

Textual Evidence of an Older Form of the Text

Scholarship on the Akhmim text changed suddenly and serendipitously in 1910 with the publication of an Ethiopic version of the *Apocalypse* by a scholar who did not realize he was publishing it. It appeared in the second installment of Sylvain Grébaut's edition of a previously unknown Pseudo-Clementine writing discovered in an Ethiopic manuscript.[7] The publication would have passed into scholarly obscurity had M. R. James not immediately realized that the text contained a full version of the *Apocalypse of Peter*, significantly different from that already known from the Codex Panopolitanus. He began writing his article on the new discovery two days later.[8]

At the outset James saw the obvious, that the Ethiopic *Apocalypse* is significantly longer than Akhmim 2. He also recognized that in some ways it represents a better, older form of the text. Among other things, it preserves passages quoted by Clement of Alexandria and Methodius that are lacking in the Greek. James's immediate judgment was that the Akhmim version "must be regarded as something like an abridgement, or a series of excerpts from the Apocalypse";[9] that is, it had been seriously revised from the original.

The differences between the accounts will be evident to any casual reader, especially when they are laid side by side in modern editions such as those provided by W. Schneemelcher or J. K. Elliott.[10] Most obviously, unlike the longer Ethiopic version, which I summarized in Chapter 2, the Akhmim account:

- Does not begin with a lengthy description of the coming Day of Judgment.
- Correspondingly does not describe what will happen to souls after the coming apocalypse, but concerns the present state of souls after death.

- Describes the heavenly rewards for the faithful before detailing the hellish torments of the damned.
- Gives a significantly lengthier description of these rewards.
- Lists fewer sinners and the torments they endure (fourteen sets of sins and punishment instead of twenty-one).
- Removes the account of Jesus's ascension at the end, making the account a version of the Synoptic transfiguration narrative; as a result, the descriptions of the afterlife come during Jesus's ministry rather than as a postresurrection dialogue after his death.

James's article was also significant because, somewhat buried in Part II, he provides the *editio princeps* of another textual witness to the *Apocalypse of Peter.* This is a tiny and highly lacunose two-sided Greek fragment that had been uncovered in the Bodleian Library, containing just "eight to ten letters apiece on each side."[11] James dated the manuscript to the fifth century (a dating that still holds), thus a century earlier than Codex Panopolitanus. Its size belies its importance: its few lines are much closer to the Ethiopic form of the text than to Akhmim 2, thus providing support for James's claims of the relative antiquity of the former.

Further corroboration appeared in 1924 with the publication by C. Wessely of a second small Greek fragment found in the Rainer collection in Vienna, P.Vindob.G 39756. Wessely wrongly thought the piece came from an otherwise unknown portion of the *Acts of Peter.* The text was correctly identified five years later by K. Prümm and was then subjected to a relatively full analysis, again, by M. R. James.[12] It was only after James had completed his article, but before sending it off, that he came to a significant realization: the Rainer fragment (R) must have come from the same manuscript as the Bodleian fragment (B) he had published fourteen years earlier. He added a last-minute addendum to his article, pointing out that both fragments come from a manuscript with the same dimensions, the same number of lines to the page (thirteen), and the same number of letters to the line (eight to ten).[13]

The Rainer fragment is both longer and more textually significant than the Bodleian, and it confirmed the superiority of the Ethiopic edition to Akhmim 2.[14] In James's words: "We have two widely divergent texts of the *Apocalypse of Peter.* . . . Clearly the weight of external evidence warrants us in regarding this latter (represented by the Ethiopic version and B/R [= Bodleian and Rainer fragments]) as original, and the other as an edition. And internal evidence points the same way."[15] When using the term "original" James is speaking loosely: he repeatedly acknowledges that the Ethiopic text is seriously corrupt in places and hard to translate, let alone retrovert into Greek. And as we will see, it is a mistake to consider the Ethiopic standing in complete solidarity with B/R, as a single form of the text. Their differences are not merely due to difficulties of translation and simple scribal mistakes, but to editorial activity.

Reopening the Question of the Relationship of Akhmim 1 and 2

When the older form of the *Apocalypse of Peter* had appeared in Ethiopic and B, James immediately realized that the relationship of Akhmim 1 (= *Gospel of Peter*) and Akhmim 2 (= *Apocalypse of Peter*), which had been resolved in different ways by Dieterich and Zahn, needed to be reevaluated. Did the scribe who produced these texts for the Codex Panopolitanus find them in two distinct works, both of which happened to be connected with Peter, and decide to place them sequentially in the codex? In the abstract that might seem plausible—the other major text, of *1 Enoch* (produced by a second scribe), obviously came from a different work. But there are compelling reasons—already seen by Dieterich and Zahn—for thinking that Akhmim 1 and 2 came from the *same* literary work. In particular, they share numerous similarities that are otherwise difficult to explain. Of James's various pieces of evidence, the most compelling have proved to be the linguistic parallels, in particular the fact, noticed by others, that neither text uses the name Jesus (Ἰησοῦς) but prefers the title Lord (Κύριος). Even more striking is the highly unusual and distinctive phrase "we the twelve disciples" (ἡμεῖς οἱ δώδεκα μάθηται), found in both. James, as was his wont, made a full list of the similarities, which continue to be persuasive. Later, Léon Vaganay, in his celebrated commentary on the *Gospel of Peter*, argued that such linguistic parallels were insignificant and easily explained. James issued a devastating and nearly unanswerable response.[16]

Since in the Ethiopic and B we have a version of the *Apocalypse of Peter* that is earlier than that found in the Codex Panopolitanus, and since the latter account has noticeable and unusual linguistic similarities to the *Gospel of Peter* in the same manuscript, copied by the same scribe, the conclusion lies near to hand that the views of Dieterich and Zahn, set forth before the discovery of the new textual witnesses, were correct: the scribe of Akhmim's *Apocalypse of Peter* copied his account from the *Gospel of Peter*.[17]

But which of the scholars was right? Did the Akhmim *Apocalypse* begin life as a portion of the *Gospel*—say, a distinctive form of Jesus's Olivet discourse—later extracted from the *Gospel*, expanded, otherwise edited significantly, and then put into circulation as "the" *Apocalypse of Peter* that became known to later church writers (thus Dieterich)? Or was there an earlier *Apocalypse of Peter* that the author of the *Gospel of Peter* acquired, utilized, shortened, and otherwise edited in the process of producing his Gospel account (thus Zahn)?

James preferred the latter view. Some of his arguments are not altogether cogent,[18] but later scholars have tended to support his view. A good argument was put forth later by C. Maurer, who did not, however, explicate it fully.[19] The linguistic parallels to the *Gospel of Peter* occur only in the Akhmim version of the *Apocalypse of Peter*, not in the Ethiopic (B/R are lacunose at the relevant places).[20] The most plausible explanation is that the version represented by the earlier form of the text, attested in the Ethiopic, had been edited into conformity with the *Gospel of Peter* to make it fit into its broader literary context. James concluded that the author of the *Gospel of Peter* used the earlier *Apocalypse of Peter* as one of his sources for his *Gospel* narrative.

Once it is recognized that what appear as two texts in the Codex Panopolitanus came to its scribe as separate portions of the same text, the question remains why they are presented separately in the manuscript. James claimed it is unlikely that the two accounts were contiguous in the *Gospel* manuscript the scribe had copied, one account following immediately after the other. In his view, not just Akhmim 1 but also Akhmim 2 is fragmentary, beginning and ending abruptly.[21] Moreover, one needs to consider Codex Panopolitanus itself: the first quire, containing the *Gospel*, ends with two fully blank pages; the next quire, containing the *Apocalypse*, sewn in upside down, also begins with a blank page. This almost certainly means the scribe was copying a manuscript that was lacunose and so left blank pages for the gap, either hoping to fill the rest in later when he found more of the text or simply indicating a break.[22]

Either way, the implication could be significant: if the scribe was using a manuscript that was literally in tatters—that is, with disconnected pages—then there is no assurance that the sequence in which the texts were bound together later in the Panopolitanus codex is correct. That is, the passage recounted in the *Apocalypse* may well have occurred, in the original nonfragmentary manuscript that the scribe inherited in pieces, before the events narrated in what is now called the *Gospel*. That in fact seems likely, since the katabatic vision has been reconfigured as occurring in the context of Jesus's transfiguration, not as a postresurrection dialogue before the ascension. The *Gospel of Peter*, of course, narrates the end of the Jesus story, of his trial, death, and resurrection; but the vision found in the *Apocalypse* occurred before his arrest.

In a later publication James reiterated his view, summarizing it at one point as follows: "I have followed Zahn's lead and maintained that [Akhmim 2] is a portion of the Apoc.Petri embodied with changes in the Gospel by the author of the latter."[23] But it is here that James made an unnecessary and rather dubious assumption, earlier made as well by Zahn, that it was precisely the *author* of the *Gospel of Peter* who adapted the *Apocalypse of Peter* to insert it into the *Gospel* narrative. A better option was suggested years later, again by Maurer: the *Apocalypse* may have been inserted into the *Gospel* at a later stage by an editor or interventionist scribe revising both texts. As he says in his Introduction to the text in Hennecke-Schneemelcher: "The old witnesses, however, always speak of the Gospel and the Apocalypse as two separate writings. Consequently, we must assume, not that the author of the Gospel assimilated the Apocalypse (Zahn, James) but that it was a later finder of the two Greek fragments who first adapted the Apocalypse to the Gospel."[24] Maurer concludes by suggesting that the "later finder" may in fact have been the scribe who produced Codex Panopolitanus.

That an editor of the *Gospel of Peter*, not its author, inserted a redacted form of the *Apocalypse* into the longer narrative of the *Gospel* makes a good deal of sense of what else we (think we) know: we have a version of the *Apocalypse* older than Akhmim 2; Akhmim 2 has significant parallels to the form of the *Gospel of Peter* found in Akhmim 1 but not found in the older version of the *Apocalypse*; therefore, Akhmim 2 was probably edited into some level of conformity with the *Gospel of Peter* only after the *Gospel* was first composed. It seems implausible, however, that the scribe of Codex Panopolitanus himself performed the editorial work, as Tobias Nicklas points out in an important article.[25] The codex probably dates from the late sixth century. During that period, neither the *Gospel* nor the *Apocalypse* was in wide circulation, if any circulation at all. Presumably an editor who combined the two texts did so in order to improve one or both of them. But why go to the effort of improving writings no one was reading? It would make far better sense to think the editorial work was undertaken centuries earlier, when both books were known and one of them, at least, had widespread appeal and was sometimes considered to be part of Scripture. We consider the canonical status and fate of the *Apocalypse of Peter* in the following chapter. For now, it is enough to know that the scribe of Codex Panopolitanus appears to have inherited its text in a form that had been created before his day. But when was it created and, more exactly, why?

These are questions that Nicklas ponders.[26] Why would editing the *Apocalypse of Peter* in the direction of the *Gospel of Peter* make it more acceptable? There seems little in the *Apocalypse* that would be objectionable to orthodox sensitivities in the first place. There was indeed a problem in its text—as we explore more fully later—but it easily could have been resolved with a simple editorial adjustment of one passage, as in fact was done by other scribes in various ways. But why go to the radical lengths of combining the *Apocalypse* with the *Gospel?* Nicklas does not express a strong opinion on the matter but suggests that the editor wanted to bring the two Petrine texts together because of their interesting points of agreement. His editorial activities were meant simply to make them yet more closely related.

Another option, however, should be considered. Here I restate my thesis: an editor of the second or third century did revise earlier circulating versions of both the *Gospel of Peter* and the *Apocalypse of Peter,* making the latter a single episode in Jesus's ministry in the *Gospel* narrative. In doing so he was not, however, trying to solve a problem with the *Apocalypse.* The problem was the *Gospel.*

The Rewriting of Akhmim 2

It is important to stress that the textual changes in the Akhmim version of the *Apocalypse of Peter* are not merely "textual variants," that is, accidental or intentional alterations of the text. They are wholesale rewritings, the work of an editor or a reviser. The differences between Akhmim 2 and the other witnesses to the *Apocalypse* are not on the level of, say, Codex Bezae in relationship to Codex Vaticanus in the Gospels. They are on the level of the relationship of the Gospel of Matthew to the Gospel of Mark. I do not mean this as a precise analogy,[27] but in some ways the situation is similar. Even though most of Mark's account reappears in Matthew, anyone who reads Matthew is reading Matthew, not Mark. So too, anyone reading Akhmim 2 is not reading the *Apocalypse of Peter* but the *Gospel of Peter.*

Most of the major differences between the text of Akhmim 2 and the Ethiopic version make sense if the former was rewritten to fit into the

Gospel. The account is shortened, for example, by including only two-thirds of the punishments, possibly in order to keep this new section of the *Gospel* from overwhelming the rest of the narrative; the punishments are described as occurring immediately after death rather than after the future Day of Judgment, possibly because so much time has passed since the original composition of the account that Christians (or at least this editor) are generally concerned with fate postmortem rather than the constantly receding end of time; the account is placed in the context of Jesus's ministry instead of after his resurrection, possibly to keep the postresurrection appearances as the appropriate climax to Jesus's story, or possibly because a different ascension story was already found in the *Gospel of Peter,* or possibly because the editor was suspicious of postresurrection dialogues as too closely associated with Gnostic traditions, as discussed more fully below. Still, even though such alterations make sense if an editor chose to merge the accounts, they do not explain why he wanted to do so in the first place.

One oddity of scholarship is that the matter has almost never been addressed by those who have devoted considerable effort in interpreting the *Gospel of Peter,* which is by far the most studied of the two texts. But if, as is widely understood, Akhmim 2 is a form of the *Apocalypse* that was produced in order to be inserted into the *Gospel,* that necessarily means Akhmim 1 represented an edited version of the *Gospel.* Not only is the Akhmim *Apocalypse* not an "original" form, but the Akhmim *Gospel* is not either (or, if one prefers to avoid all talk of "originals," then at least it is not the *Gospel*'s earliest circulating form but has been radically altered). And yet, analyses of "the" *Gospel of Peter* (Akhmim 1) resolutely overlook the fact they implicitly acknowledge, treating the text as if it had come straight from the hand of the author. That will scarcely work. Akhmim 1 is a rewritten *Gospel.*

Why was it rewritten, and how thoroughly? We cannot, of course, determine the full extent or character of the editorial work unless an older version comes to light. But we can consider a reason the editor may have wanted to make the one change he certainly appears to have made—inserting a version of the *Apocalypse.* A place to start is by pondering the basic question: Why does any author or editor add preexisting material to an already circulating text? The obvious answer is also the most plausible: in order to "improve" it. Sometimes that improvement involves intentional alterations of the text's message, but sometimes it (probably) involves amplifying a text without realizing the broad-ranging hermeneutical significance of having done so. Yet most substantive textual changes do alter a text's meaning in one way or another. This can be seen on a number of levels. Suppose the Gospel of Luke originally lacked the textual variant found in 22:43–44, the account of Jesus's so-called bloody sweat. Without these two verses, Luke's narrative precisely lacks what is so pronounced in his source Mark, that is, numerous references to Jesus's agony in the moments before his arrest—all of them otherwise removed in the Lukan redaction. Add the verses, and now there is agony: Jesus is not above suffering but is in fact deeply in the throes of it. It is probably no accident that the verses are first mentioned in the Christian tradition by church fathers who cite them to stress that contrary to heretical teachings, Jesus really was a flesh-and-blood human who could suffer.[28]

On a much higher level: What happens when an author/editor takes the Gospel of Mark and expands it by adding a collection of sayings such as are found in the hypothetical Q source? One could probably come up with lots of answers, but here is an intriguing one. Doesn't Q shatter Mark's portrayal of the messianic secret? It certainly confuses it. Thus in Matthew 11 we have a substantial amount of material from Q (and thus *added* to Mark): the Baptist's disciples come to ask Jesus whether he is the one to come, and he reminds them that he is the one who performs the eschatological miracles predicted in Scripture (Matt 11:2–6); he proceeds by identifying John as Elijah, the one who was to come (i.e., before the messiah) (11:7–15); he then preaches woe against Chorazin and Bethsaida because they have not repented in face of the miracles he has publicly done and so will be condemned (11:20–24); and then comes the climactic "Johannine Thunderbolt," where he openly proclaims himself the Son of the "Father, the Lord of heaven and earth," to whom all things have been handed over by the Father, who alone knows the Father, and who can ease the burden of everyone's soul (11:25–30). There is no messianic secrecy here. Matthew's expanded version of Mark's narrative is no longer Mark, simply by virtue of additions from another source (even overlooking Matthew's other additions and alterations).[29] With respect to Akhmim 1: Is the *Gospel of Peter* still the *Gospel of Peter?*

We obviously cannot know how many other alterations were made when its editor combined the account with the *Apocalypse.* But how would this *one* change have affected the meaning of the text? Since we no longer have a pre-redacted version of the *Gospel,* virtually our only evidence for knowing its older character comes in discussions of the book by early authors who knew about it. That is, we need to explore the ancient history of its reception. In doing so, we are not asking whether these ancient descriptions were accurate. Our interest is in how the book was perceived—a crucial difference, not always appreciated.

The Reception of the *Gospel of Peter*

Some Christians in the town of Rhossus, Syria, considered the *Gospel of Peter* an authoritative account of the (life and) death and resurrection of Jesus, as indicated by a letter from the bishop of Antioch, Serapion, following a brief visit to the community (Eusebius, *Hist. eccl.* 6.12). The proto-orthodox Serapion himself initially approved the use of the book by the church, until he learned from others that it had been used (or composed?) by a group of ΔΟΚΕΤΑΙ (*Doketai*) and embodied suspicious teachings. Serapion then read the book. In his letter he indicates that most of the account was completely orthodox (τὰ γὰρ πλείονα τοῦ ὀρθοῦ λόγου τοῦ σωτήρος), but some parts were "added" to it (a highly unusual word: ([τινὰ δὲ] προσδιεσταλμένα). Serapion does not explicitly say, but apparently he means these "additions" were the parts that could cause offense.

In his letter Serapion went on to list the problematic, or possibly problematic, passages. To our eternal regret, Eusebius does not quote that part of the letter. Moreover, in the part that *is* quoted, Serapion does not say specifically what he found offensive about the "additions"—or even whether they were actually "heretical" or simply capable of heretical misconstrual. Strikingly, he does not indicate that they embodied a docetic Christology, only that the book was *used* by people called ΔΟΚΕΤΑΙ. They appear to have been called this by proto-orthodox Christians aligned with Serapion, not necessarily by themselves (οὓς Δοκητὰς καλοῦμεν). We obviously do not know what these people actually said, but given their name, it appears they maintained—or were thought to maintain—that Christ "seemed" to be human but was not, either at all or fully. It is worth noting that Serapion also does not say the book was written by someone who was a δοκητῆς. He does suggest that a heretical teacher named Markianos (Μαρκιανός), or Marcion, was behind the book, or at least promoted it. How we might wish that this was the famous Marcion: that would indeed solve part of the mystery. It is also not clear what Markianos's connection is to the ΔΟΚΕΤΑΙ. It is their successors (διάδοχοι) who have helped Serapion interpret the book. But the whole passage is a muddle: Why would Serapion's heretical enemies help him decipher a book he would want to condemn? Is it because they thought they could persuade him of their theological views, embodied in an authoritative account of Jesus's life and death by his closest disciple, Peter? Or does Serapion mean that he has learned how heretics interpret the book and that has made him realize why it is problematic? In any event, it certainly appears that Serapion came to see that the book was capable of a docetic construal, whether or not it actually set forth a docetic view.

The other early Christian references to the book give us no hint of its theological character or reputation: a probable reference by Justin, despite widespread scholarly refusal to admit it (*Dial.* 106.3);[30] a clear mention by Origen (*Comm. Matt.* 10.17); an additional reference by Eusebius (*Hist. eccl.* 3.1–2); a passing comment by Didymus the Blind (*Comm. Eccl.* 1.1–8); a reference in Jerome (*Vir. ill.* 1.3–5); and the Gelasian Decree. There is also, of course, the sixth-century Akhmim manuscript itself, and the fact it was buried with someone who was identified, on tenuous grounds, as a monk from the eighth century.[31] Several other fragments that have been suggested as belonging to the *Gospel of Peter* by one scholar or another include a probable case with P.Oxy 2949; a possible case, somewhat undervalued by scholars, of P.Oxy 4009; and the much less likely case of P.Vindob G 2325 (the Fayûm Fragment).[32]

Thus the book was known in proto-orthodox and then orthodox circles. But after the evaluation of Serapion, the book was not accepted as a text of Scripture, almost certainly because it was judged pseudonymous, a judgment rendered—so far as we can tell—on the basis of alleged docetic Christology argued by Serapion and somewhat emphatically implied by Eusebius. That is to say, in proto-orthodox opinion, if the book did not toe the orthodox line, then clearly it could not have come from the pen of an apostle of Jesus; even if it contained passages that could simply be *read* heretically, that was enough.

The view that the *Gospel of Peter* was docetic, even if not explicitly stated by either Serapion or Eusebius, certainly guided readers of the text in modern times. Nearly as soon as the Akhmim fragment was published in 1892 it was identified not only as the long-lost *Gospel of Peter* but also as patently docetic. H. D. Swete made the point in a study published just months later, devoting seventeen pages to the question. Here he cites the now familiar passages to show the aberrant Christology: on the cross the Lord is "silent as if he felt no pain" (v. 10); at death he declares, "My power, O power, you have left me" (v. 19); the narrator then describes his death as an ἀνάληψις (being "taken up," v. 19); Jesus later emerges from his tomb supernaturally tall (v. 40), accompanied by a personified cross (v. 39).[33]

The docetic construal of the text was standard fare among scholars until the Emory dissertation of Jerry McCant, summarized in a much-cited article of 1984, "The *Gospel of Peter:* Docetism Reconsidered," in which he argued that scholars were reading docetic views into the text rather than out of it,[34] a view that has widely caught on as the new consensus.[35] Even if the matter is not as cut and dried as most interpreters today seem to think,[36] it does not affect my argument here. In this context I am not interested in exegesis so much as reception, and it needs to be stressed: Serapion does not actually claim the text was docetic; his letter suggests it was open to a docetic construal.

Akhmim 1 as a Later Edition of the *Gospel of Peter*

A good deal of modern scholarship on the *Gospel of Peter* can be "prescribed" (in Tertullian's sense, that is, ruled out of court) because it is based on the problematic assumption that the Akhmim version of the text is the one known to Serapion and, if he had ever seen the text, Eusebius. But it almost certainly was *not* the same text; at the very least it has been expanded significantly through the interpolation of a version of the *Apocalypse of Peter.* If the editor of the text was willing to make that kind of major alteration, are there grounds for thinking he did not make other changes—possibly major changes? Scholars who know that Akhmim 1 does not preserve the text as read by Serapion simply overlook that little circumstance when arguing about whether the *Gospel of Peter* was docetic. Turning a blind eye may make sense in this circumstance, since otherwise—without having the older form of the text—there would be almost no way to evaluate Serapion's claims. But in fact there *is* no way, apart from looking for hints in the later form of the text available to us but not to him.[37]

The problem is exacerbated by another consideration that is also almost never addressed. Serapion gives no indication that the problematic "additions" to the *Gospel of Peter* occurred in the accounts of Jesus's trial, death, and resurrection—the only parts preserved in Codex Panopolitanus. Who knows what came before—or for that matter, after—the fragment? Arguing that this particular section of the *Gospel* is not docetic has no bearing on the question of whether other parts were. In that connection it should be pointed out that if other passages clearly were docetic, then certainly the passion narrative would have been read (or at least written) in light of these "reading instructions" found elsewhere.[38] They are certainly *susceptible* to that kind of construal, as is clear from the history of scholarship in the twentieth century.

Yet another point is rarely given its due by scholars attending to these matters. There is very good evidence that the text of the *Gospel of Peter* was remarkably unstable otherwise, that is, that significant editorial interventions were made with some regularity. With good reason, P.Oxy 2949 is often considered an alternative form of the *Gospel*, even though the matter continues to be debated.[39] But the highly peculiar description of a "friend of Pilate" asking for Jesus's body in both texts makes the identification unusually attractive.[40] Scholars reluctant to concede the point typically stress the textual differences otherwise between the two fragments. There are indeed a large number. In an important and detailed analysis, Jay Treat has noted: "Of the twenty-two words identifiable in Fragment 1 of POxy 2949, at least eight are different from the corresponding words in the Akhmim excerpt, and three of those changes appear to be substantial variations involving more than one word. . . . Three words . . . found in the Akhmim excerpt are definitely missing in the corresponding locations in POxy 2949. And the evidence suggests that the last four lines are materially different."[41] He goes on to ask, "At what point do we stop speaking of textual variations and begin to speak of a different version of the text?"[42] Without fully conceding that P.Oxy 2949 is part of the *Gospel of Peter*, Tobias Nicklas comes to a similar conclusion about the Akhmim fragment: it is a later form of the *Gospel*, certainly not the Urtext.[43] He goes on to suggest that the *Gospel of Peter*, as a noncanonical text, was subject to wider vagaries of textual transmission than those that made it into Scripture, even if it was altered in ways we cannot detect.

To a great extent, that is right, of course. Even with Akhmim 1, we have only a portion of the *Gospel*, and in this portion there is no way of knowing everything that has been changed. But we do know of one major alteration in the *Gospel*—the insertion of the *Apocalypse*. What is more, we have some sense of how this (apparently) same editor altered the other text that we have from his hand: we can simply compare his edition of the *Apocalypse of Peter* with the form of the text found in our better witnesses, Ethiopic and B/R. That may provide us with some plausible inferences of his general editorial proclivities, at least when it comes to this one editorial project.

The reality is that he did not simply insert a relatively unaltered form of the *Apocalypse of Peter* into an earlier circulating form of the *Gospel of Peter*. He completely rewrote the text in ways not always fully appreciated. If he did it with the *Apocalypse*, why should we think he did not do it with the *Gospel*? And if he did it with the *Gospel*, why should we think that when we are examining Akhmim 1, we are reading the *Gospel of Peter* known to early church writers?

The Edited Versions of the *Apocalypse of Peter*

The major differences between the Ethiopic and Akhmim versions of the *Apocalypse*, described earlier, have long been widely known, but these are not the only data points of interest and importance. Even though the Ethiopic version stands in the same textual tradition as the Bodleian and Rainer fragments, rarely has anyone examined these witnesses all in relation to one another in detail—not just the Ethiopic in relation to Akhmim, but also the Ethiopic in relation to B/R, B/R in relation to Akhmim, and finally all three witnesses in relation to one another at the one point of their mutual overlap.

Of the major differences between the Ethiopic and Akhmim versions, not much more needs to be said: the Akhmim gives only fourteen of the twenty-one punishments of the Ethiopic, locates them in the present, gives a much more extended discussion of heaven, and begins with heaven instead of hell. But I do need to stress an obvious and widely unacknowledged point: even when these texts have the same basic material, the Akhmim does not merely contain a few textual variants here and there; it is a wholesale rewriting of the text. Of particular significance, the editor rewrote passages even when his changes did not affect the meaning or achieve any other noticeable purpose. He has produced an entirely new version.

No detailed analysis is necessary: simply look at the three passages in Table 1, which are typical rather than extraordinary; in particular, pay attention to the words themselves. (I give the Ethiopic version in the literal translation of Buchholz and the Greek in my own literal translation.)

As might be expected, a similar result obtains from a comparison of the Akhmim and B/R, or more precisely, with B, since the only passage preserved in R was deleted in toto by the editor of the Akhmim version (Table 2). Here, if anything, the differences are even more pronounced than those between Akhmim and the Ethiopic. I give the accounts in both English and Greek, but my assessment is based on the latter. The Bodleian fragment is as restored in the edition of Kraus-Nicklas; translations are my own. Words that are significantly different in the two accounts are in **bold;** those that are the same or essentially the same (i.e., without changing the meaning) are underlined. (A more thorough analysis, of course, would need to explore why the truly insignificant rewrites occurred as well—these are clear in the Greek even if not in the English. That is, why did the editor bother to make apparently meaningless changes, if not simply because he chose to rewrite the account?)

Table 1. Comparison of the Ethiopic and Akhmim
versions of the *Apocalypse of Peter*

Ethiopic Version	Akhmim Version
9.1–2 The angel of his wrath, Ezrael, brings men and women who are half on fire. And they are put in a place of darkness which is the Gehenna of men. And a spirit of wrath whips them with every whipping and a worm which never sleeps eats their bowels. They (are) the persecutors and betrayers of my righteous ones.	27 And other men and women were burning up to their midst, having been cast into a dark place, being flogged by evil spirits and their intestines were being eaten by sleepless worms that do not sleep. These were those who persecuted the righteous ones and handed them over.
10.5–6 And near them to these . . . (one unknown word) and beneath them the angel Ezrael makes a place of fire frequently [and] (with) every idol of gold and silver, every idol the work of human hands and which resembles the image of a cat and lion, the form of reptiles, and the form of animals. But those men and women who made their images (are) in chains of fire (with) which they beat themselves in their error before them. And thus (is) his punishment forever.	33 And beside that cliff was a place filled with a very large fire. And there stood men who made for themselves with their own hands, images in the place of God. And beside these were other men and women holding rods of fire and beating one another and never ceasing from such torment.
10.8 And near to this flame (is) a pit, large and very deep. Into it [and] there flows all which is from everywhere, judgment and abomination, discharge. And their women (are) swallowed up to their necks and are being punished with great pain. Therefore these are they who abort their children and wipe out the work of God which he had formed. And opposite them is another place where sit the children whom they kept from living. And they call out to God and lightning comes [and] from among the infants (being) a drill in the eye of those who by this adultery have brought about their destruction.	26 And near that place I saw another narrow place in which the serum (or blood? ἰχώρ) and stench of those being punished flowed down and became like a river there. And women sat there with the serum up to their necks and across from them many children . . . untimely born sat weeping. And there went out from th[em. . . .] of fire and struck the women in their eyes. These were women who [. . .] and who had [or caused?] abortions.

Table 2. Comparison of the Bodleian and Akhmim
versions of the *Apocalypse of Peter*

Bodleian (B) Version	*Akhmim Version*
. . . <u>women</u> **grasping chains** <u>and</u> **whipping themselves before the deceiving idols** <u>and</u> **they will have** <u>torment</u> **ceaselessly.**	33 . . . <u>women</u> **holding rods of fire** <u>and</u> **who were beating one another** <u>and</u> **never ceasing from such** <u>torment</u>.
<u>And near</u> **them** <u>other men and women</u> **will be burning in the burning of those who are idol-crazed.** <u>These are those who</u> **aban-doned** <u>the path of God and</u> . . .	34 <u>And</u> **again** <u>other women and men near</u> **those (were) flaming and twisting and being fried.** <u>These were those who</u> **left** <u>the path of God.</u>
. . . <u>γυναῖκες</u> **κρατοῦντες ἁλύσεις** <u>καὶ</u> **μαστιγοῦντες ἑαυτοὺς ἔμπροσθεν τούτων εἰδώλων πλανῶν** <u>καὶ</u> **ἀναναπαύστως ἕξουσιν** <u>τὴν κόλασιν</u>	33 <u>γυναῖκες</u> **ῥάβδους πυρὸς ἔχοντες** <u>καὶ</u> **ἀλλήλους τύπτοντες** <u>καὶ</u> **μηδέποτε παυόμενοι** <u>τῆς τοιαύτης</u> <u>κολάσεως</u>.
<u>Καὶ ἐγγὺς αὐτῶν</u> <u>ἕτεροι</u> **ἔσονται** <u>ἄνδρες καὶ</u> <u>γυναῖκες</u> **καιόμενοι τῇ καύσει τῶν εἰδολομανῶν.** <u>Οὗτοι δὲ εἰσιν</u> **οἵτινες κατέλιπον** <u>τὴν τοῦ θεοῦ ὁδὸν</u> **καὶ προε**	34 <u>καὶ</u> <u>ἕτεροι</u> **πάλιν** <u>ἐγγὺς ἐκείνων</u> <u>γυναῖκες καὶ ἄνδρες</u> **φλεγόμενοι καὶ στρεφόμενοι καὶ τηγανιζόμενοι.** <u>Οὗτοι δὲ ἦσαν</u> **οἱ ἀφέντες** <u>τὴν</u> **ὁδὸν τοῦ θεοῦ.**

The Bodleian version contains thirty-nine words; the Akhmim, thirty-five. Approximately half the words in the Akhmim are the same as in B (<u>underlined</u>: eighteen of thirty-five of Akhmim; eighteen of thirty-nine of B), but eight of those eighteen are καί (and) δέ (and), or the article (the)—scarcely significant overlaps. Of the twenty-six *substantive* words Akhmim has in the passage altogether (words other than καί, δέ, or the article) and twenty-four substantive words of B, they share only ten—that is, well less than half. In some ways the most interesting differences involve the use of synonyms, semi-synonyms, or substitutions. Some of these actually change the meaning, but equally significant are the ones that make little or no difference, for example:

1. <u>τὴν κόλασιν</u> // <u>τῆς</u> **τοιαύτης** <u>κολάσεως</u>
2. <u>ἐγγὺς αὐτῶν</u> <u>ἕτεροι</u> **ἔσονται** <u>ἄνδρες καὶ γυναῖκες</u> // <u>ἕτεροι</u> **πάλιν** <u>ἐγγὺς ἐκείνων</u> <u>γυναῖκες καὶ ἄνδρες</u>

This again shows that the Akhmim version does not contain merely interesting textual variants.

Among the significant (or somewhat significant) differences between the two versions are the following *substitutions* (the Bodleian reading coming first):

1. grasping chains / holding rods of fire
2. whipping themselves / beating one another
3. ceaselessly / never ceasing
4. burning / flaming and twisting and being fried
5. who have abandoned / who left

There are also three significant *omissions* of text in the Akhmim in comparison with B:

1. before the deceiving idols
2. in the burning of those who are idol-crazed
3. and . . . (final line is not a complete sentence in B, but it is in Akhmim)

One could mention as well the fact that the Bodleian fragment clearly depicts punishments yet to come (future tenses of ἕξουσιν and ἔσονται) whereas the Akhmim describes the punishments occurring now (in the point of overlap the Akhmim does not contain finite verbs in parallel to those of B—although the rest of the account makes the contrast clear).

In sum, over the course of a mere thirty-nine words in B (or thirty-five in Akhmim), there are nine substantive differences, not to mention minor changes that have no significant bearing on the meaning. Clearly, this is the same account. But in what sense is it the same text?

Even less frequently assessed has been the relationship of the Ethiopic with B/R, apart from the observation made since James that they are closer to each other than either is to Akhmim. That much is clear. But how close are they? Luckily for us, the Ethiopic overlaps with both B and R, and it can be seen that alterations similar to those between B and Akhmim are evident, and some are highly significant (Table 3). It is a wonder that analyses have passed them over. Even though the basic substance of the accounts is closely parallel, just in the brief amount of textual overlap we have there have been serious and extensive textual interventions—by either the scribe(s) responsible for the Greek edition

Table 3. Comparison of the Bodleian and Ethiopic
versions of the *Apocalypse of Peter*

Bodleian (B) Version	*Ethiopic Version*
women **grasping** <u>chains</u> and whipping <u>themselves</u> <u>before</u> **the deceiving idols** <u>and</u> **they will have torment ceaselessly.**	10.6 . . . <u>women</u> **who made their images (are) in** <u>chains</u> **of fire (with)** which they beat <u>themselves</u> **in their error** <u>before</u> **them.** <u>And</u> **thus (is) his punishment forever.**
<u>And near them other men and women</u> **will be** <u>burning in the</u> **burning of those who are idol-crazed.** <u>These are those who abandoned</u> <u>the</u> **path** <u>of God</u> <u>and</u> . . .	10.7 <u>And near them (are) other men and women</u> and they <u>burn up in the</u> **heat of judgment. Their punishment is forever.** <u>These are they who abandon the</u> **commandment** <u>of God</u> <u>and</u> followed harsh (?) demons.

used by the Ethiopic translator, the translator himself, or the scribe(s) who copied the translation.

As would be expected, the Ethiopic overlaps with the Bodleian in the same place as the Akhmim, though here the variations are different. Again, I rely on Buchholz's literal translation of the Ethiopic and my own of B. In this case I have <u>underlined</u> only words that are (or at least appear to be) *exactly* the same; key differences are in **bold**.

In one place (possibly more) the English translations may differ simply because Buchholz rendered the Ethiopic words differently from how I rendered the closely equivalent Greek (does Buchholz's "beat themselves" represent a literal Ethiopic translation of the Greek "whip themselves"?). Even apart from that, any word counts obviously cannot be precise, since we are comparing an English translation from one language to an English translation from another. Even so, the overall comparison can be revealing. In these translations, the B contains forty-four words to the Ethiopic's sixty—a matter of little significance in itself. But what does matter is that only twenty-six of these words are the same (of which six are "and" or "the"). And again, a number of the differences are substantive. Here are the most obvious, with the Bodleian version given first:

1. [punishment described as future / described as present]
2. women / women who made their images
3. grasping chains / (are) in chains
4. chains / chains of fire

5. themselves / themselves in their error
6. before the deceiving idols / before them
7. in the burning / in the heat of judgment
8. burning of those who are idol-crazed / of judgment
9. (missing) / Their punishment is forever
10. path / commandment

All this in the course of fewer than two verses.

A comparison of the Ethiopic to R yields comparable results, with one major exception—the complete rewriting of the first paragraph not just to alter its meaning but in fact to circumvent its claim and reverse its meaning (Table 4). There is no point in this case to provide words in boldface or underlined.

Table 4. Comparison of the Rainer and Ethiopic versions of the *Apocalypse of Peter*

Rainer (R) Version	Ethiopic Version
I will [pro]vide my chosen and elect with whomever they ask of me from the punishment, and I will give them a beautiful baptism in the salvation of the Acherusian lake, which they call the Elysian Field, a portion of righteousness with my holy ones. And I will come forth, I and my elect, rejoicing with the Patriarchs into my eternal kingdom.	14.1–4 And then I will give my elect and my righteous ones the baptism and the salvation which they ask of me in the field of Akeroseya which is called Aneslasaleya. And I will give the portion of the righteous ones and I will go now rejoicing with the patriarchs into my eternal kingdom.
And I will fulfill with them my promises that I promised them, I and my father in heaven. Behold, I have shown you Peter and I have set forth everything.	And I will do for them what I have promised them, I and my heavenly father. I have told you Peter, and I have informed you.
And go to the city ruling over the West, and drink the cup, which I promised you, by the hand of the son who is in Hades, so that his destruction may receive a beginning. And you, acceptable of the promise . . .	Go out, therefore, and go to the city which is (in) the west and drink the wine about which I have told you, from the hand of my son who is without sin, that his work of destruction might begin. But you (are) chosen by the promise which I have promised you.

The rewriting of 14.1–2 is not a slight editorial change. It is a radical alteration, a negation of the older form of the text. In the previous chapter of the *Apocalypse*, the "elect" and "righteous" ones look down on those who are in torment and pleading for mercy; in chapter 14 of the R text, these chosen ones join in the pleas of the sinners, and God provides deliverance to *everyone* the saints request. As I argue in the next chapter, this almost certainly refers to a universal salvation and is what led to the radical rewriting of the Ethiopic version ad loc. In the edited version God does not provide heavenly admission to tormented sinners but to the saints who were bound for heaven in the first place. Sinners remain in hell forever.

There is no need for me to do a detailed comparison of R and the Ethiopic for the other two paragraphs: readers can readily do that for themselves and will see that the substance again is often the same, but sometimes with rather startling differences (who gives the cup of death to Peter: Christ or Satan?), and with wide differences of wording that simply bear out what we have already seen.

A detailed synoptic comparison of all three versions at the one and only place of overlap would be redundant. Instead, in Table 5 I simply underline the words held in common among all three texts, itself a striking graphic.

At the place of overlap, the Ethiopic is the longest of the three versions, with sixty words (in the English translation). Only sixteen of these are the same as in the Akhmim and Bodleian fragments: the words "women," "and," and "punishment" (assuming the Ethiopic translator was rendering the Greek word for torment, an admittedly tenuous assumption) and the phrases "And near them (are) other men and women," "these are they who," and "of God." If we wanted to reconstruct the text based only on the words shared among the three witnesses, what would we have?

The witnesses are clearly giving the same account. But on the linguistic level they have far more differences than similarities. We are not dealing here with a standard kind of textual tradition with three witnesses containing occasional variants. In this case the variants often involve synonyms. If these are really synonyms, meaning virtually the same thing, why would a scribe make the change? Why not simply copy the inherited text? And why make simple grammatical changes that really do mean exactly the same thing ("the path of God" as τὴν ὁδὸν τοῦ θεοῦ instead of τὴν τοῦ θεοῦ ὁδόν)? That is, why would a scribe bother, if he were in fact simply copying a text that had been acquired? On top of that, of course,

Table 5. Comparison of the Bodleian, Ethiopic, and
Akhmim versions of the *Apocalypse of Peter*

Bodleian (B) Version	Ethiopic Version	Akhmim Version
. . . <u>women</u> grasping chains and whipping themselves before the deceiving idols <u>and</u> they will have <u>torment</u> ceaselessly.	10.6 . . . <u>women</u> who made their images (are) in chains of fire (with) which they beat themselves in their error before them. <u>And</u> thus (is) his <u>punishment</u> forever.	33 . . . <u>women</u> holding rods of fire and who were beating each other <u>and</u> never ceasing from such <u>torment</u>.
<u>And near them other men and women</u> will be burning in the burning of those who are idol-crazed. <u>These are those who</u> abandoned the path <u>of God</u> and . . .	10.7 <u>And near them (are) other men and women</u> and they burn up in the heat of judgment. Their punishment is forever. <u>These are they who</u> abandon the commandment <u>of God</u> and followed harsh (?) demons.	34 <u>And other women and men again near</u> (are) flaming and twisting and being fried. <u>These are those who</u> left the path <u>of God</u>.

often the meaning is changed, and sometimes quite significantly, all in the course of just several dozen words.

It is significant that we do not appear to be dealing with a linear development of the tradition. That is to say, one cannot draw a simple stemma of transmission here, of B (the oldest form of the text) to Ethiopic (the fullest representative of that form of the text) to Akhmim (a later revision). The Ethiopic is a significant revision as well. With Akhmim we have at least some grounds for knowing just how significant the fuller revision was: it appears to be a completely new edition of the *Apocalypse*, created for the purpose of making the *Apocalypse* a part of the *Gospel of Peter*: hence the considerable alteration from the basic textual form found in the Ethiopic. But we have no way of knowing how different either of these two versions was in relation to B/R for the full extent of their texts since these are only two small fragments. What is more, there is no way to determine whether the fifth-century copy surviving in B/R faithfully represents the form of the text placed in circulation roughly three centuries earlier.

A Possible Motivation Behind the Akhmim *Apocalypse*

This highly unstable textual tradition is most clearly reflected in the re-worked edition of the *Apocalypse* found in our first-discovered witness, the Panopolitanus codex. Recognizing that it represents a wholesale rewriting of the narrative leads us back to our original question: Why did an editor do this? It was clearly not simply to condense the text or alter a few words to make them more theologically acceptable.

It scarcely need be said that we have no access to the identity of the editor, let alone to any of his internal psychological processes that could enlighten "personal motives." The same is true, of course, for a great many historical tasks in the field of early Christian studies. But that does not mean one cannot make a case. In the present instance I advance my thesis, rooted now in what appears to be a solid conclusion: the editor who produced the texts found in Akhmim 1 and 2 repurposed the *Apocalypse of Peter* to make it fit into the *Gospel of Peter.* The thesis, as already indicated, is that he did so not to improve the *Apocalypse* but to improve the *Gospel.* The editor inserted the revelation of Peter as a discourse from Jesus's ministry in order to help salvage the sullied reputation of the *Gospel.* This was presumably to make it more amenable to broader distribution and influence—that is, so it would be more widely accepted by the proto-orthodox Christian communities. To this extent I agree with the view set forth by Tobias Nicklas mentioned earlier. But I have a specific proposal to make about the matter. By expanding the narrative to include the visions of the very tactile rewards for saints in heaven and yet more graphically tactile punishments for sinners in hell, the editor worked to counteract the allegedly docetic character of the *Gospel of Peter.*

We have seen that the *Gospel* was used in proto-orthodox communities: apparently known to Justin,[44] the church in Rhossus, Serapion, and Origen. But the only surviving evaluations of the book are negative: the informers of Serapion, Serapion himself, and Eusebius. The problem was either a genuinely docetic bent or wording that could at least be read docetically. The insertion was meant to resolve the issue.

Docetism in the Early Church

Scholars often fail to appreciate the range of "docetic" options in early Christianity, at least as perceived by the proto-orthodox heresiologists. There have been needless wranglings about what Docetism "really" means and about whether both ancient heresiologists and modern historians of doctrine have done justice to the actual positions on offer.[45] For my purposes here I have no interest in jumping into those particular quagmires. For methodological reasons, my interest is not with which Christological positions were endorsed by one group or another, but rather with how heterodox views were perceived. The editor responsible for the Akhmim version of the *Gospel of Peter* was influenced by his perception of the problem, whether or not his perception was on target.

In the broadest terms, views commonly labeled "docetic" in the second and third Christian centuries came in two varieties.[46] Best known but least attested is a "phantasmal" Christology: Christ did not have a real human body like other human bodies but was, in some sense or another, only an appearance. Even if the view had earlier roots, it is clearly attested in the well-known polemic of Ignatius, especially in his letters to the Trallians and Smyrneans.[47] Ignatius stresses that Christ "really suffered" (ἀληθῶς ἔπαθεν) to bring about salvation, decidedly not, as some "unbelievers say, that he [only] appeared to suffer" (οὐχ ὥσπερ ἀπιστοί τινες λέγουσιν, τὸ δοκεῖν αὐτὸν πεπονθέναι). No, on the contrary it is these unfaithful ones who are "the appearance" (αὐτοὶ τὸ δοκεῖν ὄντες; Ign. *Smyrn.* 2). Hence the term "docetists." For Ignatius, Christ did not come in appearance but "really" or "truly": he really was born, he really ate and drank, he really suffered, he really was crucified and died, and then he really was raised (Ign. *Trall.* 9.1–2). It was not an appearance.

Later, Irenaeus attributes a phantasmal Christology to both Simon Magus ("he appeared in turn as a man, though he was not a man. He appeared to suffer in Judea, though he really did not suffer") and Saturninus ("he was believed to have appeared as a man"; *Haer.* 1.23.3, 1.24.2).[48] The view is most commonly associated with Marcion (thus Tertullian, *Contra Marcionem*, e.g., 3.8, and *De carne Christi* 1–2). Tertullian provides a sustained attack on it in *De carne Christi* (passim).

The more commonly attested view that scholars often label "docetic" is quite different and can be more appropriately labeled "separationist." Here Christ is not seen as a unitary, phantasmal being lacking body or flesh but as two entities temporarily united: the fully human (and therefore nonphantasmal) Jesus and a divine entity that came down from above to empower him for his ministry, at, say, his baptism, and then later left him to his fate at the crucifixion. This is the view Irenaeus most commonly ascribes to various "Gnostics," most famously Cerinthus (*Haer.* 1.26.1) but also the Marcosians (1.21.2), Carpocrates (1.25.2), and, oddly, even the

Ebionites (1.26.2). In this perspective, at least as portrayed by our heresiologists, Jesus was born, could suffer, and died; but that was not true of
the "Christ" (or whatever term is used to describe the divine element that
entered into Jesus): as a divine being it could not be born, could not suffer,
and could not die.

Even though the views differ, they are often lumped together as
"docetic" since both assert that the divine Christ was not actually a human
being and could not and did not suffer. This basic idea posed serious problems for proto-orthodox thinkers on numerous levels, since it involved
so many of their fundamental views, not just about the nature of Christ
but also about God as creator, the way of salvation, the future resurrection, and the path of discipleship. All these issues were intimately related
to one another: an actual, fleshly, material Christ reveals God's ultimate
concern for the material world, which helps affirm that he created it, that
it was originally good, and that it had to be redeemed through the material
means of Christ's real suffering and bodily resurrection. Moreover, since
Christ "suffered in the flesh," so too must his followers.

This issue of suffering drives a good deal of our early polemic against
both phantasmal and separationist Christologies.[49] The importance of suffering as a true follower of Christ, of course, goes all the way back to our
earliest Christian author, Paul (e.g., 2 Cor 1:5, 4:9–11, and esp. 11:23–29).
An explicit appeal to Christian physical suffering as "evidence" for Christ's
actual (not apparent) suffering comes, again, already in Ignatius:

> For if these things were accomplished by our Lord only in appear-
> ance, then I also am in chains only in appearance (εἰ γὰρ τὸ δοκεῖν
> ταῦτα ἐπράχθη ὑπὸ τοῦ κυρίου ἡμῶν, κἀγὼ τὸ δοκεῖν δέδεμαι). But
> why then have I handed myself over to death, to fire, to the sword,
> to wild beasts? . . . I am enduring all things in order to suffer along
> with him, while he, the one who became the perfect human (τοῦ
> τελείου ἀνθρώπου γενομένου) empowers me. (Ign. *Trall.* 9.2)

The connection between the suffering of Christ and of Christians becomes a staple in proto-orthodox heresiology.[50]

The importance of Christ's real flesh also takes on serious eschatological significance in the early debates about the resurrection of the body,
on all sides—from the Valentinian "Treatise on the Resurrection" (= Letter to Rheginus) to the nearly contemporary but totally contrary proto-
orthodox *De resurrectione* by Athenagoras, on through the emphatic dis-

cussions of Tertullian in *De carne Christi* and up to Augustine's *De civitate dei*.[51] From the proto-orthodox position, the three matters then tie closely together: Christology, martyrdom, and eschatology. The reality of human suffering demonstrates the true bodily suffering of Christ, and the bodily resurrection of Christ revealed the physical nature of life eternal. These three are not simply argued sequentially in a linear fashion; they connect and support each other, each serving as a demonstration of the other. It is no accident that Tertullian wrote treatises arguing that Christ had real flesh that really suffered and was raised (*De carne Christi*), urging Christian martyrs to experience torture leading to death (*Ad martyras*), and insisting that the afterlife will involve real pleasure for saints and real torment for sinners (*Spect.* 30). But one could run the equation in any direction. The fact that humans will experience exquisitely tactile afterlives can show not only why they should be willing to suffer physically now for the sake of physical rewards later and/or to avoid eternal physical agony, but also why they need to realize—as essential for their salvation—that the tangible ecstasies of heaven and exquisite torments of hell demonstrate that Christ really did come in the flesh.

Peter and Docetism

It has also never been fully appreciated how, long after his death, the apostle Peter in particular was pulled into the debates about the flesh of Christ—strikingly, both by those who attested allegedly "docetic" views and by the proto-orthodox authors who opposed them. The *Gospel of Peter* itself is an obvious case in point—initially accepted for use in the church of Rhossus, and therefore considered "orthodox" by Serapion (without his having read it), before he was alerted to its suspicious character as amenable to the views of the *Doketai*. His letter proscribing its use may well have sealed its fate. It certainly did for Eusebius. Peter, of all people, would not accept let alone author a work that denied the reality of Christ's suffering. It had long been "known" in the orthodox tradition that Peter affirmed Christ's actual suffering. Even though the New Testament Gospels declare that Peter fled the scene of Jesus's death, the pseudepigraphic 1 Peter stresses that the author "Peter" himself was "a witness of Christ's sufferings" (1 Pet 5:1). What is more, the main theme of this short letter is the suffering of Jesus's followers. The term "suffer" (πάσχω) occurs more in these five chapters than in all forty-nine chapters of Luke-Acts, despite the latter's emphasis on the suffering, persecution, and martyrdom of both

Jesus and his followers.[52] As in Acts, the stress in 1 Peter is on the actual, physical suffering of Jesus's followers, who are to suffer as Christ suffered. He "suffered in the flesh" (1 Pet 4:2) and "died in the flesh" (3:18), and his followers can expect to do the same (4:1) and in fact to "share in the sufferings of Christ" (4:13). This is real, physical suffering. Christ's bodily death brought salvation, and so his followers are to suffer as well. Here we have the roots of the later proto-orthodox connection between (1) the pain, suffering, and death of Christ; (2) Christ's fleshly/bodily nature; and (3) the physical pain experienced by his followers—all rooted in the witness of Peter.

This New Testament testimony had no effect on numerous Gnostic teachers who appealed to Peter in support of their docetic views of Christ and his suffering. One possible but faint connection may be found in Basilides, maligned by Irenaeus for proffering a phantasmal Christology (*Haer.* 1.24.3) and for promoting an unusual account of the crucifixion, in which Jesus pulled an identity switch with Simon of Cyrene on the way to execution, taking on the form and features of the innocent bearer of his cross while transforming Simon into his own double, so that the Romans crucified the wrong man. Jesus was exempt, therefore, from suffering, and, more than a little disturbingly, he stood by the cross laughing at his little trick, watching his unwilling Doppelgänger suffer a torturous death (*Haer.* 1.24.3). The potential connection to Peter is provided by Clement of Alexandria, who reports that Basilides studied under Glaukias, a disciple of Peter (*Strom.* 7.17.106).

One of the more intriguing texts from Nag Hammadi, the *Letter of Peter to Philip* (Codex VIII.2), does not provide such anecdotal explanation but nonetheless takes a strong stand in Peter's name against Jesus's full humanity and suffering.[53] Probably dating to the end of the second or the early third century, the book claims to be a letter addressed to Peter's fellow disciple and contains a Gnostic postresurrection revelation from Christ. In the account Christ affirms that he came into the world, but he puts a docetic spin on it: "I was sent down in the body (σῶμα) for the seed that had fallen away. And I came down to their mortal model (πλάσμα). But they did not recognize me, thinking I was a mortal" (*anok ourōme ef-moout*) (136.16–22). Even more telling is Peter's own account of Christ's passion in the letter. He begins by affirming a view that would in fact have been acceptable to any of the proto-orthodox of his time: "Our luminary (φωστήρ), Jesus [came] down and was crucified. He wore a crown of thorns, put on a purple robe, was hanged on wood, was buried in a tomb, and he rose from the dead." But then he insists on a docetic construal of this creedal claim: "My brothers, Jesus is a stranger to this suffering (*ouš^emmo ^empeiči ^emkah*). But we are the ones who have suffered through the Mother's transgression. For this reason he did everything symbolically among us" (literally, "in a likeness among us," *kata oueine hrai ^enhēt^en*; 139.15–25).

The most striking Gnostic narrative description of Christ's "passionless passion" comes to us in Codex VII of the Nag Hammadi library, in a writing that, perhaps not coincidentally, is also called the *Apocalypse of Peter*. Here the polemic against proto-orthodox views is unusually direct and vivid, as recognized and discussed more than forty years ago by Klaus Koschorke in his groundbreaking work *Die Polemik der Gnostiker gegen das kirchliche Christentum*. There have been long and protracted debates concerning the various Christian groups opposed in the short text, but however one comes down on the final count, it is clear that the author embraces a separationist Christology, is incensed that his proto-orthodox opponents have co-opted the apostle Peter in support of their views, and fights fire with fire by claiming Peter as one of his own.[54] In this *Apocalypse*, Christ himself states that the (proto-orthodox) opponents are "blind and have no leader" (72.12–14); they are "people of error" who are "without perception" (74.1–3) and "who do business in my word" (77.2–78.1). Tellingly, these are people "who call themselves bishops and deacons"—that is, they are the leaders of the churches. But they are not fountains of truth; they are "dry canals" (79.30–31). As an intriguing part of the polemic, Christ indicates these opponents will "denounce" him because they will be "ignorant" of him—that is, they will not understand him and will "praise" Peter "when there is no knowledge." They will at first accept the words Peter proclaims but then "turn away" to follow "the father of their error" (72.19–27). What is it that these proto-orthodox leaders of the churches claim Peter says? Apparently that Christ really suffered. "They hold on to the name of a dead man" (74.13–14).

This opposition to Christ's bodily nature is central to the polemic of the Coptic *Apocalypse of Peter*. The account continues with an unforgettable passion scene. Peter is speaking with Jesus while he also watches him (another him) hanging on the cross. As perplexing as that is, matters become far more confusing when Peter sees, at the same time, yet another Jesus above the cross laughing at the entire proceeding. The Savior standing next to Peter tries to explain what he is seeing: "He whom you saw [above] the tree, glad and laughing. This is the living Jesus. But this one into whose hands and feet they drive the nails is his fleshly part, which is the substitute, being put to shame, the one who came into being in his likeness" (81.3–23).

To complicate matters further, Peter then sees someone else approach, one who looks just like the figure laughing above the cross; this one is also called the Savior and is apparently yet another Christ, who describes the "real" situation and explains the meaning of the laughter:

> He said to me, "Be strong, for these mysteries have been given to you so that you might know clearly that the one they crucified is the firstborn, the abode of demons, the stone vessel in which they live, the man of Elohim, the man of the cross, who is under the law. But the one who is standing near him is the living Savior, who was in him at first and was arrested but was set free. He is stand-ing and observing with pleasure that those who did evil to him are divided among themselves. And he is laughing at their lack of per-ception, knowing that they were born blind. The one capable of suffering must remain, since the body is the substitute, but what was set free was my bodiless body." (82.4–83.13)

This is an unusually full exposition of a separatist Christology. It is only the shell of Christ, the kind of "stone vessel" in which people also live, the "abode of demons," that is crucified. The real Christ, the "living Savior," is set free and is (literally) above it all. The *body* can suffer, but the pain does not touch the real person of Christ; the physical being is simply a visible substitute for his true nature, his bodiless body. Peter is the one who sees and affirms this view. Others, who are only allegedly followers of Jesus, stress the real suffering of Christ and the concomitant teaching that bodies matter and are of the essence of existence. These may try to usurp Peter for their teaching. But they do not convey the water of life; they are dry canals who are ignorant, about Christ and Peter, and about reality. Ultimate reality is not connected with the body. The body must be and will be transcended by those who come to know the truth. The impli-cations for humans are clear: they too must then transcend the body. The body will be dispensed with. Eternal life will not entail a crass material existence in the stone vessels used by demons; it will be of the pure spirit that ascends from the realm of matter.

The proto-orthodox *Apocalypse of Peter* clearly has a different view. Life beyond the grave is completely tactile, involving horrific physical torment or real material pleasure. Of the two, the pain is by far the more emphasized. Because the wicked refused to accept the terrible suffering Christ endured for them, they must themselves experience torment. They have bodies, and bodies suffer.

The Two Apocalypses of Peter

Rarely are the two apocalypses of Peter examined in tandem, and for obvious reasons: one is a Gnostic account of the crucifixion, and the other is a proto-orthodox tour of the realms of the dead.[55] Even so, they share a striking number of features. Both are revelations of Christ directly to Peter, near or at the end of Jesus's life; the revelations unveil what cannot be perceived by mere human observation. Both focus directly on questions of death and life, suffering and the escape from suffering, and the innate or accidental nature of bodily existence. One is directly about the bodily nature of Christ with implications for the bodily nature of humans; the other is about the eternal bodily nature of humans with possible implications for the body of Christ. An important question for both texts is whether the material body is an essential component of God's creation. One account explores the matter through Christology, the other through eschatology. It would probably be going too far to say that one of them was written in direct response to the other; but it is striking that both are graphic and emphatic in their views of the body, even though those views are polar opposites. Does salvation come *from* the body, as in the Gnostic *Apocalypse*, or *in* the body, with the corollary that damnation itself is entirely bodily, as in the proto-orthodox *Apocalypse?*

That the proto-orthodox *Apocalypse of Peter* stresses that salvation comes precisely in the body is evident in both the grotesquely physical punishments endured by the damned and the tactile heavenly pleasures of the saved—pleasures, it might be reemphasized, that are described at much greater length in the edited version of Codex Panopolitanus.

The editor of this version, paradoxically at first glance, eliminated one of the episodes that stresses the bodily nature of the afterlife found in the earlier Ethiopic version. But he appears to have done so for a good reason. In the older account, after Peter and the other disciples observe the tangible glories of heaven—the glorious bodies, the bright light, the flowering trees, the wonderful smells—the narrative ends with Jesus's ascension, modeled on the transfiguration account of the Synoptics. As the disciples watch Jesus ascend, they see heavenly beings come to welcome the three glorious figures into the realms above. The striking feature of the narrative for our purposes here is the nature of the welcoming committee. These heavenly beings are specifically called "men *in the flesh.*" Yes, for this text that is what the afterlife entails.

Even so, the editor of the Akhmim version could not very well keep this key detail, simply because he chose not to keep the entire episode. In his version, the account occurs during Jesus's ministry in his discourse with the disciples on the Mount of Olives (v. 2), paralleling the Synoptic apocalyptic discourse before Jesus's passion. Since Jesus does not ascend in this edited version, he cannot very well meet up with the fleshly humans sent to usher him home. This very editorial decision raises an interesting question. Why did the editor of the Akhmim version decide to eliminate the ascension narrative and move the account to Jesus's public ministry? Various options may be imagined, but one possibility certainly presents itself. A well-known venue for Gnostic revelation discourses was the postresurrection appearance of Jesus, when he revealed the truth not unveiled during his public preaching.[56] As a genre, the postresurrection dialogue proved particularly conducive for Gnostic revelations: it set the context for Jesus to reveal the heavenly secrets he did not disclose during his earthly ministry—theogonic and creation myths whose emphases run precisely counter to the proto-orthodox insistence on the one true God over all, the creator, his good creation, and the essential materiality of humans in both this life and the life to come. Proto-orthodox authors resisted these postresurrection dialogues. In one instance the opposition involved a counternarrative: the pseudonymous author of the *Epistula Apostolorum* took over the Gnostic genre in order to proclaim a decidedly non-Gnostic message of the absolute importance of "the flesh," both of Christ in his incarnation and of his followers at the resurrection. Possibly the editor of the Akhmim version of the *Apocalypse of Peter* decided to take a different route by avoiding the tainted Gnostic associations altogether. That was easily done. He simply eliminated the ascension scene, which was not central to his purposes, and relocated the narrative to within Jesus's public ministry.

The *Apocalypse of Peter* as Embedded in the *Gospel of Peter*

I can now tie these various strands of my argument together to explain my proposal. The proto-orthodox *Apocalypse of Peter* was already a highly malleable text, in general. The editor who produced the form of the text specifically found in Akhmim 2 was not interested in simply producing a shorter, highly redacted version. He edited the text to insert it into the *Gospel of Peter*, a book that was recognized as basically orthodox but with docetic or possibly docetic elements—that is, it allegedly contained passages that denigrated the flesh, whether that was its author's intention or not. The *Apocalypse of Peter*, on the other hand, affirmed the opposite perspective. Here the real flesh is everything. If salvation and damnation have no tactile reality, there could be no bodies forced to stand in rivers of fire, eyes to be stabbed with fiery pokers, intestines to be infested with worms, necks to be encompassed by dragons, or genitals by which to be hung over eternal flames. Without real, physical sensations there could be no beautiful, transformed bodies, shining like the sun in the world above; no eyes to observe the lush vegetation; no noses to revel in the sweet, eternal odors.

Both the *Gospel* and the *Apocalypse* texts claimed to be written by Peter, the witness to Christ's sufferings according to earlier traditions, wrongly championed by heretics as a proponent of docetic Christologies. Some of these heretics used the *Gospel of Peter* to that end, or at least were reputed to do so. Whether the text really was docetic or not, this unknown editor decided to redeem it. We can see only one of the ways he did so, by inserting into it a radically rewritten version of an *Apocalypse of Peter*. Now the *Gospel* clearly endorses the importance of the body, a body that can feel pleasure, but also, emphasized even more, pain. The body really does matter in the divine economy, and suffering is real.

Throughout proto-orthodox thinking, human suffering in God's scheme of creation attests to the nature of Christ, who also, of necessity, had a real and suffering body. In the new, expanded version of the *Gospel of Peter*, Christ himself, through his right-hand apostle, Peter, explicitly and emphatically emphasizes the importance of material existence. And that applies not just to humans but to the Savior himself, the one who became human. The text has been transfigured to reveal a salvation that is exquisitely tactile and, as a consequence, a Savior who is as well.

It is impossible to know what else this editor did to improve his presumably beloved *Gospel* that had fallen into disrepute. Given the enormous effort involved just in creating his new amalgamated version, it would be hard to believe that he left the rest of the text untouched—especially parts that could easily be recognized as open to docetic misconstrual. If the editor did indeed attempt an extensive rewriting of parts of the rest, we obviously do not know what Serapion had read. Nor do we know whether the passages in Akhmim 1 that appear docetic to some modern interpreters but not to others represent redacted versions that retain only traces of their original form. To pick an obvious example, it would be quite easy to edit an earlier statement that Christ on the cross "was silent because he had no pain" to read that he "was silent as (if) he had no pain" (*Gos. Pet.* 10). It involves a single word. It cannot be objected that an anti-docetic editor would have been more rigorous, thoroughgoing, and consistent than to leave traces of the objectionable theological view. At least not by anyone who has spent years studying the redactional and/or scribal tendencies of early Christian writers generally.

However one evaluates the merits of this thesis, it is important to stress that the editor/scribe of the Akhmim *Apocalypse of Peter* almost certainly undertook his revision in order to facilitate its insertion in a preexisting *Gospel of Peter*, and that he must have had a reason for doing so. Presumably he wanted it to be more widely read and accepted. Why would he be particularly fond of this *Gospel?* Since all we have is a fragment (or two or three) of its text, we simply cannot say. It is at least possible that he believed it deserved a place in canonical Scripture.

CHAPTER FIVE

The Justice and Mercy of God
in Textual Conflict

T HE THEOLOGICAL INVESTMENTS of Christian katabaseis are not merely eschatological or, as we saw in the previous chapter, Christological. At the most fundamental level they concern the character of God and, in particular, two unusually important divine qualities: justice and mercy.[1] Christian history has been replete with attempts to balance the two. God is both severe and gracious; he strictly judges and he mercifully forgives. But which attribute is dominant? Theologians may argue: neither. God is both infinitely just and infinitely merciful. But when it comes to the individual—say, to the individual sinner— does mercy triumph over judgment or judgment over mercy? This has never been a purely disinterested inquiry.

For most Christian history, a large majority of Jesus's followers has affirmed, sometimes with startling alacrity, the ultimate and eternal damnation of anyone outside the faith and, indeed, even of many within it. But minority voices have always appealed to the witness of the New Testament itself to argue that in the end, all will be saved. In this view God is indeed a judge to be respected and feared. He does have laws, commandments, requirements, and demands, and violating them brings punishment. But he is also, even more fundamentally, a loving being who cares for those he created and understands them completely, not just superficially, and is intent on bringing them back to the ways of righteousness. Since he is the

Almighty Sovereign, and since this is what he desires, it is what he will do. Even though judgment awaits sinners, in the end love will triumph over all: in one way or another, God will restore everyone and be reconciled with all. Even sinners will be saved.

It is no surprise that the ancient debate over universal salvation played itself out in various Christian tours of the afterlife, and sometimes within the manuscript tradition of a single text. In this chapter I return to the oldest-known form of the *Apocalypse of Peter* and argue that it endorsed a universalistic view but that the passage in question suffered a scribal intervention. The alteration was much smaller than the complete rewriting attested in the Akhmim edition discussed in Chapter 4, but the theological effect of the change was even more significant. By changing just a few short lines, later scribes managed to alter the perspective of the account as a whole—to reverse it, in fact.

This part of my argument is not new, although I provide it with significant additional support.[2] More important, I mount an argument for why the change was made, broadly similar to what we saw in the previous chapter, to make a Petrine pseudepigraphon more suitable for Christian reading. But in this case I make a stronger claim that a scribe changed the text of the *Apocalypse of Peter* specifically to facilitate its acceptance as part of the Christian canon of Scripture.

The *Apocalypse of Peter* and the Question of Canon

Once again I approach the question from a possibly unexpected perspective, by framing the discussion of the *Apocalypse of Peter* in relation to its canonical history and by doing so in relation to another Petrine pseudepigraphon with strikingly similar theological and parenetic concerns even if, at first glance, the similarities are not obvious. The book of 2 Peter does not present a katabasis, but like the *Apocalypse* it does focus on an eschatological question—the ultimate divine judgment of sinners. It is striking that even though 2 Peter was scarcely known, let alone revered, during the first three Christian centuries, it became part of Scripture, whereas the *Apocalypse of Peter,* which was both better known and revered, disappeared into oblivion. Understanding this reversal of fortunes sheds some light on the textual problem of *Apocalypse of Peter* 14, which, in its oldest form, indicated that at the end Christ will deliver all sinners from their torments in hell.

Petrine Pseudepigrapha in the Early Church

A rather remarkable number of Petrine pseudepigrapha have come down to us from Christian antiquity. Two, 1 and 2 Peter, are obviously in the canon.[3] But why these two? Why not also the *Apocalypse of Peter*? Or the *Gospel of Peter*? And what about the Coptic *Apocalypse of Peter*, the Nag Hammadi *Letter of Peter to Philip*, the pseudo-Clementine *Letter of Peter to James*, and the *Preaching of Peter* (known today only from quotations)? Scholars have long agreed that these noncanonical works are forged. But one can argue, and many have, that so too are all our surviving Petrine texts. Few scholars, in any event, want to hold out for the authenticity of 2 Peter.[4] But it is an intriguing question, surprisingly little asked: Why is it that 2 Peter made it into the canon but the *Apocalypse of Peter* did not?

First Peter, one could argue, was more or less a foregone conclusion. Its claim to be written by an apostle was nearly everywhere accepted from the outset, and for early Christians this made it both ancient and apostolic—an absolute sine qua non for canonical Scriptures. The book also proved useful for proto-orthodox purposes because, among other things, it endorses a number of theological perspectives familiar from Paul but on the pen of Peter, thus providing precisely the kind of bridge between the two apostles deemed important, given the alternative claims of sundry heterodox groups, from Marcionites at one extreme to the "Jewish-Christians" represented in the Pseudo-Clementines on the other.[5] The other views the book endorses were seen as either relatively innocent or theologically acceptable. And so it passed the "standard criteria" for canonicity with flying colors.

Not so 2 Peter, barely known at all in the second and third centuries and well into the fourth, and widely considered pseudepigraphic by those who did know it. Yet it too made it into the canon. The *Apocalypse of Peter*, however, did not, even though it was much more widely known, used, and accepted during the period than the letter. By the mid-fourth century the preferences were reversed in favor of the epistle over the apocalypse. By the end of the century the matter was scarcely even debated. Why the turnaround? My argument is that the *Apocalypse of Peter* fell out of favor because it advocated not just the judgment of God but also God's even greater mercy, endorsing universal salvation, a view decidedly not embraced by 2 Peter. Of particular interest, when the *Apocalypse* was recognized as problematic on these theological grounds, scribes and/or editors altered the suspect passage to resolve the issue.[6] By then it was too late.

In making this argument I do not assume that the formation of the New Testament canon was a zero-sum game. There were not exactly twenty-seven slots available for Christian leaders to choose from, or a limited number of openings for Petrine options.[7] They could have had both the second letter and the apocalypse, just as they ended up with five books assigned to John and thirteen to Paul. Nor would there be a problem having two apocalypses in the collection, John's and Peter's, any more than there was a problem with having four Gospels or twenty-one letters.[8] It was not limited space but controversial views that created difficulties for the apocalypse but not for the epistle.

Part of what makes the matter interesting is that despite rather obvious large differences between 2 Peter and the *Apocalypse*—all the way from genre to thematic emphases, presupposed occasion, even on to the fine level of style—there are intriguing similarities as well. As examples: Both writings appeal to Peter's personal connections to Jesus, and specifically to traditions connected with the transfiguration, in order to establish his authority for knowing about the coming apocalypse. In both accounts Peter hears the voice from heaven, "This is my beloved Son in whom I am well pleased" (*Apoc. Pet.* 15–17; 2 Pet 1:16–19). Both stress God's future act of judgment at the end of time in retribution for moral turpitude (*Apoc. Pet.* 4–6; 2 Pet 3:5–7, 10), especially against those who have corrupted the flesh and committed slander against God (*Apoc. Pet.* 7–10; 2 Pet 2, passim, esp. vv. 12–14). These sinners will be severely punished. Both texts focus far more on punishment for sin than on reward for righteousness; the latter is mentioned but is not central (*Apoc. Pet.* 16; 2 Pet 1:10–11, 3:13). Strikingly, for both texts the coming judgment appears to involve insiders, or at least one-time insiders, of the Christian community, not just non-Christian Jews and pagans. Second Peter attacks those who have left "pollutions" of the world "through the knowledge of our Lord and Savior Jesus Christ" but then have again become "entangled" and "seized" by them and claims it would have been better for them not to have become (temporarily) upright in the first place. These continue to appeal to the authority of Paul, even though they "twist" his words (2 Pet 3:16). In the *Apocalypse*, one group of sinners are apostates; moreover, the slanderers, adulterers, infanticides, usurers, and such are not said to comprise only rank pagans but could include anyone involved in such activities (*Apoc. Pet.* 7–10). Both texts urge their readers, implicitly or directly, to reshape their behavior in light of the ultimate eschatological realities certain to come. In neither case does this entail a condemnation of souls immediately after death; it comes in a future act of God against the earth and those on it who do not follow his ways.

These similarities and others have led many scholars to question the relationship between the two books.[9] Was one used as a source for the other? The long standard view is what one would probably expect: the author of the *Apocalypse* used 2 Peter. There have always been dissenting voices of course, and the opposite view has recently come to the fore. On the margin, some have thought the books were possibly written by the same author.[10] These, however, are not the questions I address here. I am instead interested in the subsequent fates of the two texts: Despite their broad similarities, why did 2 Peter make it into the canon of Scripture but the *Apocalypse of Peter* did not, and how did debates over canonicity affect the textual tradition of the latter?

The Canonical History of 2 Peter

I do not provide an exhaustive account of the canonical history of 2 Peter here but just a brief foray sufficient to make my point: in comparison with the *Apocalypse of Peter*, it is surprising the book became Scripture, given especially its sparse support in the early centuries. I need to stress that I am not asking who was using the book then, or even who seemed to have found it useful. Second- to fourth-century Christians used numerous Christian books for various reasons without considering them Scripture. My questions instead are about when 2 Peter came to be accepted as a canonical authority and by whom.[11] The short reply is that from the time the book was placed in circulation in the early second century up until the middle of the fourth century, no surviving Christian writing explicitly describes it as canonical: texts either do not mention it (including a key canon list), reject it, or indicate it is disputed. The latter would suggest, of course, that *someone*, at least, was giving it a scriptural status; but none of our authors takes that stand. As we will see, some of the discussions of the status of the book—even those often cited unproblematically in the scholarship—are hopelessly vague and nearly impossible to evaluate.

Among Christian authorities that notably do not include it in Scripture are, early in our period, the anonymous Muratorian Fragment (late second century)[12] and, at the end, Didymus the Blind (late fourth century), who explicitly labels it a "forgery" (*esse falsam*).[13] In terms of our pre-mid-fourth-century manuscript evidence, the first attestation of the book occurs in Papyrus 72 of the third or early fourth century, but contrary to what one might think, there is nothing to suggest that the scribe considered the book part of the canon. The manuscript does contain several canonical texts—Psalms 33 and 34 and 1 Peter—but otherwise it is a rather strange collection of either "disputed" or "noncanonical" writings: the *Nativity of Mary*, *3 Corinthians*, the *11th Ode of Solomon*, Melito's *Passover Homily*, an anonymous hymn fragment, the *Apology* of Phileas, and Jude. It is impossible to know whether the scribe had a category of canon at all, or if he did, where he would have placed any of the books he transcribed.

Possibly the most intriguing manuscript evidence comes from the mid-fourth-century Codex Vaticanus, whose scribe clearly considered the book canonical. But there are good reasons for thinking it was not included in the text of his exemplar. As is true for almost all the rest of his New Testament, in the Catholic epistles the manuscript normally indicates text divisions with both an older numbering, almost certainly taken from the scribe's exemplar, and a newer one meant, probably, to bring the system up to date. But the text of 2 Peter does not include the older numbers. Apparently, these were not found in the manuscript the scribe copied, which suggests that the letter was taken from some other manuscript, not from the exemplar for the other epistles.[14] It is also worth noting that the oldest Syriac versions did not include the "shorter" Catholic epistles as Scripture, including 2 Peter. Nor is it found later in the fifth-century Peshitta.[15]

In terms of patristic evidence, several authors starting with Origen mention 2 Peter but indicate it is "disputed" (Origen, *Expositions on the Gospels According to John* 5, quoted in Eusebius, *Hist. eccl.* 6.25.6). Eusebius includes the book in the first of his two groups of Antilegomena, along with James, Jude, and 2 and 3 John; he differentiates these from other proto-orthodox works also called "disputed" but labeled, by Eusebius himself, as νόθα (that is, "illegitimate," the standard term for "forged"): *Acts of Paul*, *Shepherd of Hermas*, *Apocalypse of Peter*, *Barnabas*, *Didache*, and possibly, Eusebius suggests, the Revelation of John and the *Gospel of the Hebrews*. All these works are clearly differentiated from the writings of "heretics" (*Hist. eccl.* 2.25). Somewhat later Amphilocus reports that some receive 2 Peter in the canon, along with 2 and 3 John and Jude, but others not. He does not indicate his own view.[16]

Other relevant witnesses are difficult if not impossible to assess. Eusebius claims that Clement of Alexandria, in his now-lost work *Hypostases*, had commented on "all of the canonical Scriptures" (πάσης τῆς ἐνδιαθήκου γραφῆς) and indicates that this included the "Antilegomena" (*Hist. eccl.*

6.14.1). But that term is Eusebius's, not Clement's, and Eusebius never indicates whether the books he considered disputed were seen that way by Clement. He does say that Clement's Antilegomena comprised *Barnabas*, the *Apocalypse of Peter*, Jude, and "the remaining Catholic epistles," but he does not indicate which books Clement included among these "remaining" ones. A relatively good piece of evidence that 2 Peter was not among them comes from Cassiodorus (died 570 CE). After similarly noting that Clement commented on the entire Scripture, Cassiodorus indicates that his Catholic epistles were 1 Peter, 1 and 2 John, and James.[17]

Also difficult to construe, in general, is the canon list of Codex Claramontanus, which does include 2 Peter among the canonical books, along with *Barnabas*, the *Shepherd*, the *Acts of Paul*, and the *Apocalypse of Peter*. The list almost certainly came to the sixth-century scribe from an earlier source, normally dated to the end of the third or beginning of the fourth century, but the date—as Adolf von Harnack explicitly states—is based on the nature of the list itself. That is to say, the books included suggest the date. But since we are principally interested in the date at which a certain book was included, we can scarcely depend on a conclusion that we presuppose. Even so, a third- or fourth-century date for the source seems completely plausible; if it is right, this would be the earliest affirmation of the canonical standing of the book.[18]

Even more problematic is the "Cheltenham Canon" dated usually to around 360 CE and so named because it was uncovered in a Latin manuscript in the private library of Thomas Phillips of Cheltenham.[19] The canonical list is stichometric and involves a rather odd feature in two places. Immediately beneath its indication that the three epistles of John comprise 350 lines, the scribe wrote "only one." So too with the "two epistles of Peter," at 300 lines, beneath which is written "only one." Metzger sensibly suggests that the exemplar included all five of these Catholic letters, but the scribe copying it accepted only two of them (1 John and 1 Peter). He could not very easily change the text of the copy he was reproducing, since then the stichometry would obviously be skewed, lacking the 650 lines these letters contain. So he kept the original list but indicated that in fact only one Johannine and one Petrine letter was canonical.[20] It is hard to think of a better solution, but it does mean that the three Catholic epistles in question, 2 and 3 John and 2 Peter, were accepted early (in the fourth-century scribe's exemplar) and rejected late. Naturally one would have expected it to have been the reverse. And when would that earlier list have been produced?[21]

The canonical fate of 2 Peter seems to turn almost on a dime in the middle of the fourth century, away from being rejected, doubtful, and/or debated to being widely accepted (with a few exceptions, such as Didymus, mentioned above). The first explicit affirmation of its canonical status appears around 350 CE in the *Catechetical Lectures* of Cyril of Jerusalem, who includes it as one of the seven Catholic epistles (*Cat.* 4.36). Not long after is Athanasius's thirty-ninth Festal Letter, our first list of all the twenty-seven books that became the traditional New Testament canon. Here, 2 Peter is questioned no more than any of the others. Gregory of Nazianzus followed suit in the 380s (though he rejected the book of Revelation).[22] The third council of Carthage in 396 CE ratified Athanasius's list, and after that there was not a great deal of debate, even though Jerome expressed some doubts about 2 Peter (*Vir. ill.* 3.1).

The patristic evidence is supported by the manuscript tradition. The letter, of course, is found in all the pandects, starting with Sinaiticus and Vaticanus (though, as mentioned, it was apparently not included in Vaticanus's exemplar). Moreover, it is found in both the Bohairic and Sahidic versions—suggesting, probably, that it was already considered part of the canon in parts of Egypt at the beginning of the fourth century, possibly earlier.

It is difficult to say for certain why a book either unknown in the second century to the middle of the fourth or generally disputed when it was known should suddenly become an accepted part of the canon. It is possible, of course, that since the book had long been in circulation, even if not widely, it more or less slipped in as an innocuous compendium to 1 Peter. It too claimed to be written by Jesus's closest disciple (1:1), it embraced the first letter (3:1), and it showed clear connections with the views of Paul (not just 3:16).[23]

But in considering its later appeal one should also not overlook the fact that the book provided an apostolically sanctioned and decisive set of reflections on why the judgment of God was still certain to come. This was a particularly utilitarian message for Christian leaders dealing with the throngs of converts coming into their churches in mind-boggling numbers during the mid-fourth century. These pagan converts were, in part, enticed by the assurances of salvation the Gospel message provided, and we have records aplenty that not all converts were sufficiently invested in the demands of the new faith.[24] One cannot help noticing that this was all happening just when traditions such as those embodied in works such as the *Apocalypse of Paul* were becoming popular, traditions that warned of the eternal judgment of precisely Christian sinners. Second Peter in its own way provided similar fodder for the proponents of strict ethical behavior within Christian communities. God's judgment had been delayed by divine fiat for a time—it did not come "soon" after the days of Jesus—but it was nonetheless certain to come, and those who had not truly repented were sure to be on the chopping block, including those who were within the community but did not live up to the author's standards of belief and sanctity (3:3–13).

The Canonical History of the Apocalypse of Peter

The canonical history of the *Apocalypse of Peter* provides practically a mirror image of that of 2 Peter. It too is not widely discussed in our surviving sources of the second and third centuries, but those that do mention it typically consider it part of the canon. Then starting in the fourth century it comes to be frequently rejected, and soon after that it drops not only out of contention but also out of sight.

The late-second-century author of the Muratorian canon accepts the *Apocalypse of Peter* as canonical Scripture, along with the Apocalypse of John, but with the caveat, only for Peter, that "some among us do not want it to be read in church." It is important to note the author's language here: he explicitly states that "we" receive the book, but that "some" do not want it used as a liturgical text. That is, it was generally accepted, at least by the author and his community. This is different from saying that the matter is "disputed" (as, for example, Origen and Eusebius state about 2 Peter), a statement that probably indicates some level of indecision on the part of the author himself.

Clement of Alexandria also accepted the *Apocalypse of Peter* as canonical Scripture. As we have seen, Eusebius indicates that Clement commented on all the books of the Bible and explicitly includes the *Apocalypse* among them (unlike 2 Peter; *Hist. eccl.* 6.14.1). It is true that Eusebius classifies the book as an antilegomenon, but that is his category, not Clement's.[25] Clement's acceptance of the book is confirmed in two of his quotations, one that summarizes, quotes, and discusses *Apocalypse of Peter* 8.4 and 10, naming Peter as the actual author and calling the book "Scripture" (ἡ γραφή φησι; *Ecl.* 41.1–3) and the other that also deals with 8.4 but attributes the words both to "Peter" and to "the Divine Providence" (a term elsewhere synonymous with "God" for Clement; e.g., *Strom.* 4.12, *Ecl.* 48.1–49.2).[26]

A particularly strong and almost completely unexpected late-second-century witness to the canonical standing of the *Apocalypse of Peter* comes from a fierce opponent of the early Christian movement, the anonymous "Hellene" cited in the *Apocriticus*, the fourth-century apology of Macarius Magnes. In good apologetic fashion Macarius quotes his pagan opponent before expounding (at some tedious length) the nature of his errors. One long-standing debate among readers of the work involves the identity of the Greek opponent. Most commonly, and for very good reason, he is identified as Porphyry (232/233–305 CE), the brilliant and feared nemesis of the growing faith.[27]

Books 1 and 5 and the first part of Book 2 of the *Apocriticus* are lost, but that has little bearing on the issue we are addressing here. Most of the end of Book 2 through Book 4 provide refutations of the Hellene's polemical use of the Christian Scripture. The exposition moves through the Christian canon sequentially, as does Macarius's response. Book 2 focuses on the Hellene's discussion of the Gospels; Book 3, on his comments on the ending of the Gospel narratives, the book of Acts, and Paul. Book 4 continues with the Hellene's attack on Paul and then, at last, his denigration of the *Apocalypse of Peter*, introduced specifically by name ("For the sake of completeness, let us also consider what is said in the *Apocalypse of Peter*"; 4.6.1).

Once the Hellene completes his mockery of the book's eschatological expectations, he moves away from a refutation of Christian Scriptures to discuss specific ideas about theology, angelology, demonology, and so on. He says nothing about the Catholic epistles or the Revelation of John. It is, of course, possible that he discussed these other texts in sections of his work that no longer survive; but given the seriatim discussion of what we do have, it seems unlikely. What we know is what he considered the Christian canon of Scripture: the four Gospels, Acts, the letters of Paul, and the *Apocalypse of Peter*.

Possibly the Hellene chose to attack the Christian faith by focusing on Jesus, Paul, and Peter as its three best-known characters and so chose books specifically connected with them. On the other hand, it is hard to see how he could have imagined his refutation would be effective if he spent a portion of it attacking a book of Scripture that was not actually recognized as such by the Christian communities with which he was familiar. Almost certainly the best explanation is that the Hellene knew, or thought he knew, which Scriptures were cited generally by Christians in support of their views. Among them was not the Apocalypse of John or, as far as we can tell, 2 Peter, but the *Apocalypse of Peter*.[28]

Further confirmation of the book's occasional canonical status comes near the end of the third century or beginning of the fourth in the writings of Methodius, who refers explicitly to *Apocalypse of Peter* 8.4 (the same passage Clement used). As it happens, in this case the book is not called by name, but there is little doubt about the reference or its canonical standing: Methodius says the quotation comes from "the divinely inspired Scriptures" (ἐν θεοπνεύστοις γράμμασιν).[29]

The *Apocalypse* continues to find acceptance into the fourth and fifth centuries, though not widely. An anonymous Latin homily from fourth-century North Africa uses the book by name as an authoritative intertext to interpret a detail in the parable of the ten maidens (Matt 25:1–13), attributing it to Peter and ascribing to it the same authority as the book of Daniel. Near the mid-fifth century we have the indirect but tantalizing comment of Sozomen, who introduces the book by name but judges it inauthentic, since it has been "shown to be completely spurious by the ancients." Even so, he reports that it is still being read in "some churches of Palestine" on Good Friday, presumably, then, as a scriptural authority (*Hist. eccl.* 7.19.9). Since Sozomen came from Bethelia of Gaza, he was, of course, well-positioned to know about these churches.

Well before Sozomen's day, the book had begun to fall into disfavor. The group of "some" Christians who did not want it read in church, mentioned in the Muratorian Fragment, had obviously grown within the circles known to Eusebius. In his canon list he assigns it to the Antilegomena; but as we have seen, unlike 2 Peter, which was also a member of the group, he places it among the νόθα, that is, the "forgeries." Eusebius did not reject the *Apocalypse* as a heretical book but still sees it as orthodox, locating it in the same group as the *Acts of Paul*, the *Shepherd*, *Barnabas*, and the *Didache*.[30] Around the time of Eusebius, or possibly a bit earlier, the list of Codex Claramontanus rejects the *Apocalypse of Peter*, while accepting 2 Peter. The same is true of Macarius (his Hellene opponent notwithstanding), Jerome, and then virtually everyone else on record.

In sum, the *Apocalypse of Peter* was broadly accepted as canonical in the second and third centuries nearly as often as it was mentioned or quoted, but the support rapidly began to evaporate in the early fourth century and was nowhere to be found except in churches of Palestine in the fifth. This is the obverse reception history of 2 Peter. How do we explain the *Apocalypse*'s demise?

Several explanations have either been put forth or can easily be imagined that should be ruled out of court. It will not work to say that the book was rejected simply because church leaders realized it had not been written by Peter. In the early fourth century there were no solid grounds for making such judgments. On the contrary, questions of apostolic authorship were typically decided on the basis of orthodoxy and widespread use. Just with the two Petrine books we have already considered, Serapion rejected the *Gospel of Peter* as spurious not because he had done a detailed study of its vocabulary, style, and presupposed historical situation but because he came to think it might promote a docetic Christology. This is an authorial claim based not on linguistic assessment but on an assumption: if an apostle wrote a book, it would toe the appropriate theological line. The reverse is true of 2 Peter. Even a cursory examination of style in relation to 1 Peter and a basic knowledge of the ploys of forgers could have uncovered its pseudonymous character, but most church leaders were neither equipped to pursue that kind of analysis nor interested in doing so. The book claimed to be written by Peter, it was perfectly acceptable theologically, and it could be used to a helpful end. Therefore it was written by Peter.

The Problem with the Apocalypse

What then offended the proto-orthodox leaders who, in the end, decided the *Apocalypse of Peter* was not suitable for Christian Scripture? Most early-twentieth-century scholars agreed there was little point in even asking the question. Of course such a crass and vulgar book had no chance of becoming part of the canon, even if in the earliest centuries of the church lower-class, uneducated Christians—the majority at the time—did not have the intellectual means or good sense to recognize it. As E. W. Winstanley put it: "It fell into disrepute because it offended the finer moral sensitiveness of cultured Christians and failed to withstand the increasing perception of the dignity and reserve of the canonical writings." Indeed, "Much of what still remains extant [of the book] . . . is puerile, and frequently savage and horrible, while affording scope for fertile imagination and individual inventiveness."[31]

Even the great M. R. James could fall into this trap of canonical exceptionalism, pronouncing on literary merits with the moral superiority of an elite scholar of modernity. James assures his receptive readers that the *Apocalypse* is "not a great book" and that in the ancient world it "influenced popular imagination to a degree which . . . was wholly disproportioned to its merits." Indeed, "My impression is that the educated element realized very soon that it was a gross and vulgar book." And then comes the rhapsodic canonical contrast:

> Who that has listened . . . to the lessons in Advent or at Septuagesima must not wonder that even for a moment the Revelation of Saint John the Divine could be equated with the Revelation of Peter? Who is not shocked at the low level of perception which failed to see that the Johannine Book stands entirely alone—that, in spite of the fact that it is a mosaic of quotations, it is unsurpassed in originality, as it is in sublimity. . . . The wonder remains that *Peter* and *John* could have been classed together.[32]

This is theology, not history. But, to be fair, James directed this particular article not to fellow scholars but to a wider readership. To his own peers in the field, he had a different suggestion, one that I want to expand, elaborate, and more securely situate in the history of early Christian controversy. It involves the passage that describes the ultimate fate of sinners in hell.

The passage is missing altogether in the Akhmim fragment (see Chapter 4), possibly simply the victim of the editor's scalpel in his condensation of the text, but possibly for other reasons, as we will see. But there is a relatively unproblematic version of it in the Ethiopic version, given here again in the literal translation of Buchholz: "And then I will give my elect and my righteous ones the baptism and the salvation which they ask of me in the field of Akeroseya (Acheron) which is called Aneslasaleya (Elysium). And I will give the portion of the righteous ones and I will go now rejoicing with the patriarchs into my eternal kingdom. And I will do for them what I have promised them, I and my heavenly father" (14.1–3). There is nothing offensive to orthodox thinking here, even if the passage would have struck James's cultured elite for its deficient understanding of underworld geography (with the Acheron Lake called a "field" and identified with "Elysium"). Apart from that oddity, the passage makes good and relatively trouble-free sense in its context. After describing the horrible tortures of the wicked, which are called "eternal" and never-ending in a rather emphatic fourteen instances, the text moves on to contrast the fate of the righteous who will receive the baptism offered by Christ in the heavenly realm. These will enter their heavenly reward, along with the holy patriarchs, in fulfillment of the promises made by Christ and his Father. No real problems there.

Still, this was almost certainly not how the passage was originally written. Already in 1911, before having any manuscript evidence to prove it, James suspected that the Ethiopic text had been doctored and that originally the passage had acclaimed salvation for all sinners.[33] Some years later the Rainer fragment confirmed his suspicion. In this fifth-century witness, announced by James himself in 1931, we find the text worded as he suspected:

[παρ]έξομαι τοῖς κλητοῖς μου καὶ ἐκλεκτοῖς μου, ὃν ἐὰν αἰτήσωνταί με ἐκ τῆς κολάσεως, καὶ δώσω αὐτοῖς καλὸν βάπτισμα ἐν σωτηρίᾳ Ἀχερουσίας λίμνης ἣν καλοῦσιν ἐν τῷ Ἠλυσίῳ πεδίῳ, μέρος δικαιοσύνης μετὰ τῶν ἁγίων μου. Καὶ ἀπελεύσομαι ἐγὼ καὶ οἱ ἐκλεκτοί μου ἀγαλλιῶντες μετὰ τῶν πατριαρχῶν εἰς τὴν αἰωνίαν μου βασιλείαν. Καὶ ποιήσω μετ' αὐτῶν τὰς ἐπαγγελίας μου, ἃς ἐπηγγειλάμην αὐτοῖς, ἐγὼ καὶ ὁ πατήρ μου ὁ ἐν τοῖς οὐρανοῖς.[34]

I will grant to my called and my elect whomever they ask of me from punishment, and I will give them a good baptism in (or for) salvation in the Acherusian Lake, which they call the Elysian Field, a share of righteousness with my saints. And I and my elect will go rejoicing with the patriarchs into my eternal kingdom. And I will fulfill my promises that I promised them, I and my Father in heaven.

Needless to say, this is a radically different message. Not only do the saints pray for the wicked who are being tormented, but their prayers are entirely effectual. Everyone they ask for is removed from punishment and transferred to the heavenly realm for eternal blessings.[35] For reasons I will show, this wording is almost certainly original—or at least a close approximation of the original—and almost certainly indicates (and was taken to indicate) that all people, even the worst of sinners, would be delivered from their torment and given salvation. My thesis is that it was edited out of existence only after the damage had been done: the passage sullied the reputation of the book, leading to its almost complete demise. It fell out of favor especially when suspicions of universal salvation among numerous proto-orthodox theologians of the third century came to be exacerbated by the controversial eschatology of Origen, and even more by the later Origenist controversy. To be sure, the passage does not promote an Origenist understanding of how or why all will be saved; but universalism more or less disappeared as a viable option at the end of the fourth century and beginning of the fifth with the sustained attacks on Origen's doctrine of *apokatastasis*—the restoration of all rational creatures to a blessed unity with God.

Before exploring the relevance of the passage for the canonical history of the *Apocalypse of Peter* I need to provide a brief exegesis, not going into all the details but considering only points of particular importance to my argument. Christ is speaking here to Peter about prayers the saints have made to him and indicating how he will respond. Thus, technically, it will be he, not his Father, who grants mercy for those suffering torture in the lower realms. He does so based on the promises that both he and the Father have made. We are not told what those promises were, but they almost certainly would have been connected with the actions he performs and so involved the promises of eternal life, possibly even that everyone would eventually receive it. If so, the author may have been drawing on sayings of Jesus found in such scriptural passages as John 12:32: "And when I am lifted up, I will draw all people to myself" (cf. Rom 11:2, Phil 2:8–11, 1 Cor 15:22–28).

Those who make the requests of Jesus are his "called and elect," a group distinct from the "patriarchs" mentioned in the next sentence; the latter are almost certainly Old Testament saints, commonly referenced in the early Harrowing of Hell traditions (see Chapter 6). Bauckham has proposed that the "called and elect" are Christian martyrs, but they are not identified in that way. Possibly he has been influenced by other texts.[36] The term "elect" without further qualification would suggest the group comprises all those who have been chosen for eternal blessing.[37]

Christ indicates that he will provide salvation for *everyone* the saints request. Some interpreters have difficulty believing that this could mean absolutely everyone suffering torment and so have proposed that the saints plead only for those who had injured or killed them.[38] That, however, involves reading an idea into the text that would have been easily stated had the author had it in mind. Others have suggested that the saints are asking only for their family members and friends, an arbitrary kind of mercy that obviously creates just as many problems of justice as it solves (lucky you to have a Christian cousin!).

On the contrary, the text itself provides a clear indication of the objects of the saints' anguished concern. Recall: At the outset of the descriptions of hell, already in chapter 3, Peter and the other apostles peer into Jesus's right hand and see the "sinners" and "evildoers" separated from the saints. Those being punished are said to be in "great affliction and sorrow," weeping over their fate. The apostles respond in kind: they too weep. In fact, *everyone* who sees the sufferings of the evildoers weeps: the righteous, the angels, and even Christ (*Apoc. Pet.* 3.3). This weeping is not for a few known individuals; it is for the entire group—the masses of "evildoers" experiencing anguish in the depths of hell. More than just weep, Peter indicates he wished it were otherwise; would it not have been better if these sinners had never been born?

This reaction to tormented souls in chapter 3 is key for understanding the recurrence of the theme in chapter 14. In the later context, for whom would the saints ("all the righteous") be concerned? Surely the vast multitude of evildoers being tormented, as in the earlier chapter. These, then, would be those whom they ask to be delivered, not just family members, friends, and personal persecutors. As we will see, the text was certainly read this way. But if all of the sinners are in fact delivered, why does the *Apocalypse* indicate their punishment is "eternal"? As we will also see, it doesn't. That is an emphasis found only in the Ethiopic redaction, a redaction made in part to rid the text of its universalistic teaching.

Christ then saves them all by providing the sinners a "good baptism" before taking them to a heavenly eternity.[39] The baptism occurs in the Acherusian Lake, oddly equated with the Elysian Field (singular). This is the first reference to these Greek notions in early Christian literature, a matter that has attracted some scholarly attention.[40] Most important, they point us to the crucial intertext for the passage—the eschatological myth in Plato's *Phaedo*.[41]

The *Phaedo* myth, in some form or other, was almost certainly known to the author of the *Apocalypse of Peter*. But in many ways the striking similarities of the accounts serve to highlight their most stark difference, rooted in their varying conceptions of divine power and sovereignty: Is a person's destiny determined more or less by the nature of things, the way the world "works" (whether providentially designed that way or not), or by the sovereign will of the Judge of all, who can both dole out punishment and extend mercy, as he chooses? Within the Platonic system, at least as sketched in the *Phaedo*, the immortality of the soul and the ultimate reality of justice require rewards and punishments after death, based entirely on how one has lived one's life. It is not the decision of a divine sovereign.

The dialogue as a whole, of course, is about the immortality of the soul, which is discussed, demonstrated, questioned, and then established over a day-long conversation of Socrates and his companions before his state-appointed suicide. Once the matter of immortality has been decided to the satisfaction of all those present, Socrates draws the conclusion toward which the argument had been heading: "If indeed the soul is immortal, we need to take care of it not for this time only, which we call 'life,' but for all time. If anyone should neglect it, the danger now would appear fearful" (*Phaedo*, 107c). So far, of course, the *Apocalypse of Peter* heartily agrees: bad behavior now leads to horrible suffering later.

Much as happens at the end of the *Republic* with the Myth of Er, Socrates brings the discussion to a climax by shifting from dialectical reasoning to "mythos" (110b), introduced in his typically noncommittal way: λέγεται δὲ οὕτως ("it is sometimes said . . ."; 107d). The "tale" involves the realities of the afterlife, which are rooted in the nature of the cosmos. At some length Socrates imaginatively describes the geography of the earth and its "many and amazing places" (πολλοὶ καὶ θαυμαστοὶ τῆς γῆς), including where souls go when they die. There is a great chasm that pierces through the entire earth, called Tartarus by Homer and others (111e–12a). Into this chasm run all the rivers. One of these is the Acheron, which flows underground until it arrives at the Acherusian Lake (τὴν λίμνην . . . τὴν Ἀχερουσιάδα, 113a; cf. *Apoc. Pet.* 14). This is where "most of the souls of the dead" go. Indeed, "such is the nature of things" (τούτων δὲ οὕτως πεφυκότων).

After arriving, all souls are subject to judgment (we are not told by what or whom), based on whether their lives have been good and holy (οἵ τε καλῶς καὶ ὁσίως βιώσαντες). There are four groups. Souls that are neither entirely pure or wicked, but have lived somewhere in the middle (μέσως βεβιωκέναι), are boarded onto ships, taken down the Acheron River, and go to the lake where they are purified, penalized for their bad deeds, and rewarded for their good. By contrast, those who are incurably wicked—"having committed many great sacrileges or unjust murders and many lawless acts"—are cast by "the appropriate Fate" into Tartarus, from which "they never come out" (113e). Yet others who have committed "great" but "curable" sins, such as doing violence to parents or committing murder out of anger, are thrown into Tartarus where they are severely punished for a year and then cast out and carried by river to the Acherusian Lake. This group is key for understanding the intertextual connection with the *Apocalypse of Peter*. While in the lake, these souls shout out to those they had murdered or mistreated (presumably those who are being rewarded), begging them to have them released from their torment and "received" (presumably into the place of the blessed). If their pleas succeed, they are removed and relieved of their sufferings (114a–b). Otherwise, they are returned to Tartarus, to be punished unceasingly until (if ever?) they manage to persuade those they had harmed to grant them mercy. The final group are the blessed, who come in two subgroups. Those who have lived "holy lives" (ὁσίως βιῶναι) are taken out of the underworld prison and go to the "pure abode," to live again on the earth. It is not clear whether this entails reincarnation—as in the Myth of Er—or a permanent dwelling for eternal bliss somewhere in the earthly realm, that is, the Elysian Fields. But it will be even better for those who have been "sufficiently purified by philosophy" (οἱ φιλοσοφίᾳ ἱκανῶς καθηράμενοι): these are released from their bodies and enter "even more beautiful abodes" (εἰς οἰκήσεις ἔτι τούτων καλλίους) for all time.

Here we have a Platonically modified sliding scale of eschatological options, from the incurably wicked to the philosophically committed. The connections with the *Apocalypse of Peter* are obvious at the point of our major interest: both texts portray a group of saints enjoying a blissful existence for all eternity and a group of wicked sinners in the Acherusian Lake who plead for mercy and are, after a time, removed from their torment and granted entrance to the heavenly realm. The differences, though, are particularly revealing. Unlike the *Apocalypse*, the *Phaedo* insists there is a group of sinners who can never be cured or granted salvation; moreover, those who can eventually attain salvation make their pleas not to the righteous as a whole but to those they had harmed;[42] and they are not delivered because of the mercy of an all-powerful divine being but because their victims grant them forgiveness.

At the same time, non-Platonic characters and themes naturally permeate the Christian *Apocalypse*, including Christ, the all-powerful judge; his "chosen ones"; his Father; his "eternal kingdom"; and "baptism" for salvation, which makes the Acherusian Lake a place of sacramental redemption, not a holding pen for hopeful souls. It is particularly important that salvation depends on a sovereign act by the God over all; it is not determined by the "nature of things," or "Fate," or the arbitrary mercy of offended victims. And most significant for our purposes here, it comes to everyone. Hell is emptied out. At least according to the Rainer fragment.

The Oldest Form of the Text

There are clear and powerful reasons for taking the fragment's text as the "original," or at least as the most ancient form of the *Apocalypse of Peter*. That it is the *lectio difficilior* in a proto-orthodox context goes without saying, although we need to reflect on the matter more fully below. To be sure, it is possible to imagine the history of the text moving *toward* a *lectio difficilis*. Idiosyncratic scribes are always the bane for arguments over superior *lectiones*. But all the other evidence points in the same direction as well, making the argument of intrinsic probability stronger by accumulation.

This other evidence is all textual. First is the simple matter of the dates of our manuscripts. Our Akhmim manuscript, which does not have the passage, probably dates from the late sixth century at the earliest.[43] The two manuscripts behind the Ethiopic version are probably from the fifteenth and nineteenth centuries,[44] though the translation itself would, of course, have been made much earlier, even if it is difficult to know when. Some leverage is provided by the estimated date of the translation of other early Christian texts into Ethiopic. The New Testament as a whole was not available in Ethiopic until probably the sixth century; the Ethiopic translation of the *Apocalypse of Peter* surely would have been made only after that.[45] The Rainer fragment is thus our earliest extant witness to the text of chapter 14.[46]

More evidence comes from an otherwise seemingly unrelated text, a passage found in the *Sibylline Oracles*. M. R. James, in yet another instance of quick insight, after "two or three days" of examining the French translation of the Ethiopic version of the *Apocalypse*, recognized how closely it parallels the account of the afterlife in *Sibylline Oracles* 2.197–338, especially 255–338, for which it was almost certainly a source.[47] Like the *Apocalypse*, the Oracle begins with a description of the destruction of the cosmos, followed by a detailed exposition of sins and fiery punishments of the wicked that follow the resurrection of the dead. A number of the itemized sins are the same as those in the *Apocalypse of Peter*, not only such obvious acts as murder, adultery, and idolatry, but also usury, disobedience to parents, performance of abortion, loss of virginity before marriage, sorcery, disobedience of slaves to masters, etc. Moreover, as in the *Apocalypse*, when the wicked plead for mercy, they are initially refused on the ground that their request has come too late.

Then, as in the *Apocalypse*, the Oracle moves to a very short description of paradise and a complete reversal of divine judgment. Again, this does not come in response to the pleas of the tormented but to the prayers of the righteous:

To these pious ones the imperishable God, the universal ruler, will also give another thing. Whenever they ask the imperishable

> God to save people from the raging fire and deathless gnashing he
> will grant it, and he will do this. For he will pick them out again
> from the undying fire and set them elsewhere and send them on
> account of his own people to another eternal life with the immor-
> tals in the Elysian plain where he has the long waves of the deep
> perennial Acherusian lake. (2.330–38)[48]

As in the *Apocalypse*, the saints receive whatever (here, whenever) they ask,
and for their sake the sinners are taken from torment to eternal life at
the place of the Acherusian Lake (λίμνης . . . Ἀχερουσιάδος; same as in
the *Apocalypse*). Given the obvious literary relation of the two texts,[49] the
Oracle provides solid evidence that its author's version of the *Apocalypse*
concluded its description of hell by describing universal salvation given
because of the intercession of the saints.

The natural question concerns the dating of the second Oracle. As
with other Sibyllines, it is widely thought to be based on a Jewish original,
modified by a Christian editor. One of the perennial scholarly obsessions
has involved the complicated business of differentiating between Jewish
Vorlage and Christian redaction. A minimalist approach would be to accept
as Christian only those sections that contain a distinctively Christian feature. Within the portion I have just described, that would entail 2.338–51,
Christ's appearance with his angels in glory to judge the world, and 2.311–
12, the intercession for sinners by the Virgin Mary. But surely in this case
a more generous redactional analysis is required: the entire portrayal of
the realms of the dead is firmly rooted in, and therefore postdates, the
Apocalypse of Peter—its structure, flow of narrative, themes, and specifics.
In any event, both Jewish substratum and Christian redaction are typically
dated before the mid-second century.[50] That puts us very close, within a
couple of decades at the outside, to the original composition of the *Apocalypse*. The form of chapter 14 attested in the Rainer fragment thus almost
certainly goes back at least that far. Whether it was the "original" reading
of the text has no bearing on my argument; what matters is that it is the
oldest form of the text known to be in circulation.

The Later Fate of the Passage

Support for this view comes through an examination of the editorial tendencies of later textual witnesses of the *Apocalypse*, the Ethiopic version and
Akhmim 2. I have already noted that the Ethiopic frequently states that

the torments in hell are "eternal." This view is completely undermined, of course, by the supreme act of mercy described in Rainer 14, which has been altered out of existence in that version. But it is also worth noting that none of the references to "eternal" punishment appear in the Akhmim fragment in their places of overlap. Earlier analysis almost invariably reasoned that the term had been edited out of the text by the Akhmim scribe or by the scribe who produced his exemplar.[51] But it appears that just the opposite happened: the Ethiopic tradition has almost certainly inserted the idea into verses that originally lacked it.

Here is the evidence. The description of punishment as eternal appears fourteen times in the Ethiopic: 3.2, 6.5, 6.6, *7.8, *7.11, *8.9, *9.5, *10.4, *10.6, *10.7, 11.2, 11.3, 11.8, and 13.3. Seven of these—the ones marked with asterisks—occur in passages that overlap with the Akhmim fragment. In each case the Akhmim lacks the term "eternal." One *might* assume that since the Akhmim represents a rather radical reworking of the text, the term had been deleted. But as we saw in Chapter 4, the fifth-century Bodleian fragment overlaps with *both* of the other witnesses in one place; for our purposes, it is a very convenient point for comparison: 10.6, 7. The textual variations in v. 7 are both obvious and striking. The passage describes those who are being punished with fire for having abandoned the ways of God. The Ethiopic version explicitly states that: "Their punishment is forever." That sentence is missing from both the Akhmim and the Bodleian accounts (see Table 5). So too in the preceding verse, where idolaters are being beaten with rods or chains of fire. According to the Ethiopic, "this (is) his punishment forever." The Akhmim and Bodleian fragments, though, both state that the punishment goes on without "ceasing" or "ceaselessly." On the surface that may appear to be the same thing, but it is not. An action that occurs for a set period can be unceasing ("that crazy dog simply will not stop barking"), but that does not mean it is eternal. Yet more important, the Ethiopic text itself differentiates between punishment that does not cease and that which is eternal—as when we are later told that slaves who disobeyed their masters are doomed to chew their own tongues "without rest" and then, in the very next sentence, are further informed that "this is their eternal punishment" (11.8–9).

Just at the point of three-way overlap of our witnesses (10.6–7), then, the Ethiopic added "eternal" to a text that apparently did not have it and changed another passage by turning an unremitting punishment into an eternal one. Moreover, given the fact that the Ethiopic account stresses the "eternality" of the punishment in twelve other instances, five of them in passages shared by another witness that both lacks the term and never uses it anywhere else, we appear to have a *Tendenz* of the Ethiopic tradition. One certainly cannot argue the reverse—that the editor behind the Akhmim fragment felt a need to eliminate the term in order to remove the inconsistency created by chapter 14, since Akhmim 2 does not have the chapter.

The Ethiopic version therefore represents a form of the text later than R and—in these particular textual variants—Akhmim 2. This will come as no surprise to anyone familiar with the version generally. Even though, on the whole, the Ethiopic form stands closer to the older form of the *Apocalypse* than the Akhmim fragment on the macro-level, its text is so hopelessly corrupt that the editors of *Patrologia Orientalis* could not bring themselves even to publish Grébault's edition.[52] Nowhere is the problem worse than in chapter 14, which Buchholz, in his full study, states is "the most corrupt portion of the Ethiopic text, at least to our knowledge."[53]

Thus, the editor of the Ethiopic reworded the text of chapter 14. The Akhmim editor dealt with it differently: he simply did not include it. Rarely has it been asked why. To be sure, the editor radically shortened and otherwise altered the text when re-creating it to be inserted into the *Gospel of Peter*; and possibly he simply did not consider the passage suitable for his purposes. On the other hand, all his other major changes make relatively good sense in light of his incorporation of the account into the wider *Gospel* narrative, as we have seen in Chapter 4. Then why not include what is now chapter 14 and its clear statement that in the end mercy will triumph over judgment, that the salvation brought by Christ will come to all? The simplest answer is that the author did not appreciate or approve of its message.

Peter, Origen, and Christian Universalism

There is an even more interesting piece of textual evidence that the Rainer form of chapter 14 would have been seen as a theological problem by later scribes. It comes to us once again in the second Sibylline Oracle, this time not in the text itself but in a marginal note added by a later scribe. As we have seen, like the *Apocalypse of Peter*, and almost certainly dependent on it, the Sibyl declares that every sinner for whom the saints plead will be released from the fires of hell: "Whenever they ask the imperishable God to save people from the raging fire and deathless gnashing, he will grant it," and they will then receive "eternal life with the immortals in the

Elysian plain" (*Sib. Or.* 2.337–38). This view did not sit well with all read-ers. The manuscripts of one important strand of the *Oracles*' tradition, Ψ, reproduce a marginal comment by a disgruntled scribe: "Plainly false. For the fire which tortures the condemned will never cease. Even I would pray that this be so, though I am marked with very great scars of faults, which have need of very great mercy. But let babbling Origen be ashamed of say-ing that there is a limit to punishment." As is true of all our manuscripts of the Sibyllines, those of family Ψ are late (fifteenth century); but they obvi-ously and necessarily go back to the same exemplar, and it is impossible to know when the note was written. Plainly its author found the notion of "temporary" hellfire not just disturbing but heretical. He was wrong to ascribe the view of the text to Origen, who decidedly did not think that everyone would be delivered from torment by a sudden, unprecedented, and unforeseen act of divine mercy, as indicated in both the Sibyllines and the *Apocalypse of Peter* (see Chapter 6). But the scribe would not be the first or the last to think "Origen" whenever he saw "universal salvation." Origen was indeed the first Christian on record to explicate the doctrine at length, and the fuller implications of his view are, in large part, what led to his condemnation.[54] But the general hope that sinners would not be subject to eternal torment clearly had early Christian antecedents, even if by and large the view was rejected by the majority of church writers.

Origen's views survive most clearly in *De principiis*, an attempt rel-atively early in his career (around 229 CE) to establish something ap-proaching a theological system fuller than otherwise available among Christian thinkers. It is by no means a *summa theologica*, but it does rep-resent a strong effort to work out the important rudiments of the proto-orthodox Christian faith, including, of course, its doctrine of salvation.[55] The work builds a rather complicated and interconnected system on the foundation of doctrinal affirmations widely accepted in what Origen sees as the broad Christian community. There is no need for us here to go into the intricacies of Origen's views of creation, the preexistence of souls, and their fall into material beings.[56] What matters most for our purposes is that Origen believed that eventually all sentient beings would be restored to their original state through compelling acts of divine persuasion. It was not a simple task and would, in fact, take ages and ages. But God is sover-eign, and he will eventually have his way. In the end there will be, neces-sarily, nothing left to oppose him: "We think indeed, that the goodness of God through Christ may recall his whole creation to one end, with even his enemies being overcome and subdued" (*Princ.* 1.6.1).[57]

As always, in one way or another, Origen based his view on a reading of Scripture: Paul really meant "all" when he said that at the end God will put "all" his enemies under Christ's feet (1 Cor 15:25) and when he declared that "all things will be made subject to him" (1 Cor 15:28). Moreover, "the word subjection . . . indicates salvation" (*Princ.* 1.6.1); that is, when Paul says "all" will be in subjection to Christ, it means all will be saved. Origen finds confirmation in Paul's famous declaration of Christ's condescension and exaltation in Philippians 2: in the end, "at the name of Jesus, every knee shall bow, in heaven and on earth, and under the earth, and every tongue confess that Jesus Christ is Lord, to the glory of God the Father" (Phil 2:10–11). In Origen's view, those at the end of time who confess Christ as Lord and thus are saved will not simply be the saints or those who have at least wanted to do their best to please God. Paul is speaking of *every* creature in the entire creation ("in heaven and on earth and under the earth"), that is, even malevolent demons—or at least so Origen has often been read (*Princ.* 1.6.3).[58]

The reformation of sinners, however, will not happen suddenly in Origen's scheme, but gradually and by degrees, over many ages and at different rates for each individual soul. The current history of the world is simply one age. But God has all the ages of eternity to accomplish his will. As souls are given chance after chance, experiencing remedial suffering to help them realize the truth, they eventually will all come to understand. When administered by the ultimate sovereign of all, punishment will inevitably have its effect. It is like horrible medicine given to a sick patient: the patient may resist but eventually will recover. Origen points out that in this life an illness sometimes requires a harsh cure, even the amputation of a limb or the application of fire: "How much more is it to be understood that God our Physician, desiring to wash away the ills of our souls, which they have contracted through a variety of sins and crimes, should employ penalties of this sort, and even apply the punishment of fire to those who have lost their soul's health" (2.10.6). Eventually, the medicine will take hold and all will return to their original state of worshiping God with all their being. God will be "all in all" when "all things" are placed under submission to Christ (1 Cor 15:28).

Throughout Christian history most exegetes have thought that Origen completely misread Paul, or at least took some of Paul's statements out of context. Others have not been so certain. There are indeed other suggestions that Paul himself believed on some level that the power of God in Christ could and would not be thwarted. When Paul says, "Just as in Adam all people died, so also in Christ all people will be made to live"

(1 Cor 15:22), he is emphasizing that Christ's act was no less powerful and universal than Adam's. If condemnation came to *all* because of Adam, then so too will salvation come to all because of Christ (Rom 5:18). And God, in the end, will "show mercy to all people," not just some (Rom 11:32). There are also hints that Paul was sometimes read as universalist by some of his earliest followers, possibly already in the New Testament period. The author of the Pastorals, for example, insisted, in Paul's name, that "God is the savior of all people." When he qualifies the statement by saying "especially of those who believe," he probably means these will be the easiest cases (1 Tim 4:10): "especially" does not mean "only."

Before Origen we do not know of anyone in the Christian tradition who developed this universalistic view to its logical limit. We do, of course, have narratives that describe postmortem salvation for some of those suffering in the world to come, through the intercessory power of saints pleading for mercy for some individuals—most notably Thecla's prayer for Falconilla and Perpetua's for her brother Dinocrates (*Acts of Thecla* 28; *Mart. Perp.* 7–8). These are rare moments and they involve only particular people, but they do show that Christians imagined that God sometimes listened to pleas for mercy from those he especially cherished.[59] In most instances, however, throughout both the Jewish and Christian traditions, such pleas are to no avail; on the contrary, they typically highlight the opposite view—that God is just and cannot or will not bestow mercy on anyone who deserves to be punished.[60]

The point occurs in a number of rather remarkable passages in a variety of texts. In the Jewish tradition we have *4 Ezra*, where Ezra laments the horrible fate awaiting the great mass of humanity and asks "whether on the day of judgment the righteous will be able to intercede for the ungodly or to entreat the Most High for them." He receives an emphatic reply from his accompanying angel: "The day of judgment is decisive and displays to all the seal of truth . . . No one shall ever pray for another on that day" (7.102–5).[61]

Even more emphatic is *2 Baruch* 85.12–13: "There will not be an opportunity to repent any more, nor a limit to the times, nor a duration of the periods, nor a change to rest, nor an opportunity to prayer . . . nor intercessions of the prophets, nor help of the righteous. There is the proclamation of judgment to corruption, regarding the way to the fire and the path that leads to the glowing coals."[62] Several Christian parallels are at best ambiguous about the efficacy of prayer for the dead. Rarely do they inspire hope. The *Epistula Apostolorum* indicates that "the righteous" are "anxious about sinners and . . . pray and implore God and ask him." The disciples ask what then happens in response, and Christ replies that he "hears" them, without indicating whether he grants the request (*Ep. Apos.* 40).[63] So too the Akhmimic *Apocalypse of Elijah* claims that erstwhile Christian persecutors suffering torment will look up to see the martyrs looking down on them from heaven and comments that then "there will be grace" (*Apoc. Elij.* 27–29). But what is the grace? There is no word of deliverance. On the contrary, as David Frankfurter contends, it appears that the saints will be gloating—a decidedly different kind of "grace" from what we find in the *Apocalypse of Peter.*[64]

Even in the *Apocalypse* we find the more typical view, at least early in the account. In chapter 3, when Peter and the other apostles first see those in torment, they weep for their fate; Peter laments and suggests it would have been better for them not to have been born. Jesus forcefully disagrees and upbraids him for resisting God: if he knew just how sinful these people had been, he would agree that horrible eternal suffering is just what they deserve. To prove the point Jesus reveals to Peter some of the gory details, in the accounts we have already examined.

Such passages are among the many that belie the exuberant claims of Ilaria Ramelli, whose erudite tome on *apokatastasis* argues that virtually every Christian author of the first nine centuries maintained that, in the end, everyone would be saved—drawing into her net even the outspoken opposition members of the Origenist controversy and beyond (including even Augustine).[65] But after Origen's day, only a handful of Christian thinkers are known to have adopted a universalistic view in whole or part, most notably Didymus the Blind (313–398 CE), Macrina the Younger (327–379 CE), her brother Gregory of Nyssa (335–395 CE), Evagrius Ponticus (345–399 CE), presumably some of their followers, and, as we will see, the anonymous author of the oldest surviving version of the *Gospel of Nicodemus.* There were certainly others whose names have not come down to us, as evidenced in the unnamed targets of Augustine's invective in *City of God* 21. Augustine discusses seven groups of Christians who deny that damnation will be eternal, at least for some people.

Augustine's discussion confirms what we find from other sources, that universalism could come in different guises and with sundry perspectives in the early Christian tradition, even if there is some overlap among them:

- The Pauline texts that embrace the incredible *scope of salvation:* the work of Christ cannot possibly be less extensive than the work of Adam and so (apparently) must be universal.[66]

- Origen's view, related to Paul's but rooted less in the scope of salvation than in the *sovereignty of God.* God is the Lord God Almighty who cannot be resisted by those he created, who, to a person, will return to him as he wills.
- The Harrowing of Hell tradition as embodied in the *Gospel of Nicodemus* (as we will see in Chapter 6), which focuses on the *power manifest in the Christ event* itself. The crucified Christ is far more powerful than the devil and Hades and death, and his atoning work leads to the salvation of all immediately after his crucifixion.
- A view that focuses not on mercy but on *judicial equity:* sinners deserve to be punished for their sins, but surely God will not punish sinners forever. An eternity of torment is simply incommensurate with a short life of sin—a view that Augustine mentions only to ridicule (*City of God* 21.11).
- And *Apocalypse of Peter* 14, where ultimate salvation is not a display of sovereignty or power per se but a show of *supreme divine mercy*, which triumphs over justice when God grants the prayers of his saints and releases all sinners, another view that Augustine maligns in his discussion (*City of God* 21.18).

The History of Eternal Torment and Annihilation

In such debates Augustine was decidedly in the majority. Christian opinion from the beginning typically maintained that punishment against sinners would be "eternal." Unlike Augustine, however, in the earliest Christian tradition postmortem punishment for sinners is not conscious torment but annihilation. Jesus himself regularly speaks of the "destruction" of sinners, not their torment (e.g., Matt 7:13–14), and often, like his predecessor the Baptist, in terms of sinners being judged by "fire" (Matt 3:10, 25:41). He sometimes states that the fire is eternal, but he never indicates that the people cast into it eternally suffer. Instead, they appear to be destroyed in the apocalyptic furnace, just as "weeds" that are cast into a fire (Matt 13:36–43) or "fish" (Matt 13:47–50): once weeds and fish are burned, they cease to exist; they don't burn forever. Even in the parable of the sheep and the goats (Matt 25:31–46), those who enter into eternal fires made for the devil and his angels are not said to suffer torment there forever; on the contrary, when Jesus summarizes their respective eternal fates, one group is given eternal "life" and the other eternal "punishment" (Matt 25:46).

This is an antithesis. The opposite of "life" is not "torture," but "death." The goats, then, are *destroyed* in fire. Why is it called an "eternal" punishment? Because it will never be reversed.[67]

Paul attests the same view (1 Thess 4:3), as do his followers (2 Thess 1:9: "eternal destruction"). Remarkably to some readers, so too does the book of Revelation, which does have the wicked thrown bodily into the lake of fire (20:11–15), but that is their mode of execution, not eternal torment. Only the Beast (Rome!), his prophet, and the devil are said to be tortured in the lake forever (20:10).[68] That is precisely not said of the humans (= mortals) who follow them there. The only exception to this annihilist view in the New Testament comes in the relatively late Gospel of Luke, in the parable of Lazarus and the rich man (16:19–31). Notably, however, the passage does not say anything about the duration of the torment, let alone that it is eternal.[69]

Probably by the second century, at least, the "eternal punishment" of annihilation found in Jesus and the New Testament authors had transmogrified into eternal torment. Thus we have an intriguing riposte recorded in the *Martyrdom of Polycarp*, the martyr's reply to the proconsular threat to execute him by fire: "You threaten with a fire that burns for an hour and after a short while is extinguished; for you do not know about the fire of the coming judgment and eternal torment, reserved for the ungodly" (11.2).[70] By the mid-third century Cyprian expressed to his pagan opponent Demitrianus the common view, but with unusual enthusiasm:

> An ever-burning Gehenna will burn up the condemned, and punishment devouring with living flames; nor will there be any source whence at any time they may have either respite or end to their torments. Souls with their bodies will be reserved in infinite tortures for suffering. . . . The pain of punishment will then be without the fruit of penitence; weeping will be useless, and prayer ineffectual. Too late they will believe in eternal punishment who should not believe in eternal life. (*Demetr.* 24)[71]

This sentiment is echoed later in Jerome's *Homily* 86 (396 CE?) on the parable of Lazarus and the rich man, the latter "held fixed in never-ending torments." There is no way out for the condemned: "Vain is your repentance in the place where there is no room for repentance."[72] This is not an occasion of anguish for the rather triumphant Jerome. The unnamed sufferer is getting what he deserves, forever roasting in fire, with an unbridgeable chasm separating him from the joys of paradise. Blessed saints and tormented sinners can observe each other, but their places are fixed. Rather than mourning those suffering in the pits of hell, Jerome and his fellow saints are overjoyed and even gleeful: "We see what we have escaped; you see what you have lost; our joy and happiness multiply your torments; your torments augment our happiness."

This kind of eschatological Schadenfreude did not originate with Jerome at the end of the fourth century; it runs throughout the centuries as a rather abrasive counternarrative to what is found in the katabasis accounts of the saints who weep and agonize over those who are so mercilessly tortured. This alternative perspective of joy at the pain of others is found already in 2 *Clement*, where the fiery torments of the wicked are a source of hope and praise for the observant faithful above:

> He calls that the day of judgment, when others see those who have acted with impiety among us and distorted the commandments of Jesus Christ. But those who are upright, who have acted well, endured torments, and hated the sweet pleasures of the soul, when they observe those who have deviated from the right path and denied Jesus through their words or deeds are punished with terrible torments in a fire that cannot be extinguished, they, the upright, will give glory to their God, saying "there will be hope for the one who has served as God's slave from his whole heart." (12.6–7)[73]

Better known and far more euphoric is Tertullian:

> What sight shall wake my wonder, what my laughter, my joy and exultation? As I see all those kings, those great kings . . . groaning in the depths of darkness! And the magistrates who persecuted the name of Jesus, liquefying in fiercer flames than they kindled in their rage against the Christians! Those sages, too, the philosophers blushing before their disciples as they blaze together, the disciples whom they taught that God was concerned with nothing, that men have no souls at all, or that what souls they have never return to their former bodies.
>
> And then there will be the tragic actors to be heard, more vocal in their tragedy; and the players to be seen lither of limb by far in the fire; and then the charioteers to watch, red all over in

the wheel of flame; and next, the athletes to be gazed upon, not in their gymnasiums but hurled in the fire. (*Spect.* 30)[74]

From about the same time comes the "gloating" spectacle described in the Coptic *Apocalypse of Elijah*, mentioned above. This is the period, of course, when the *Apocalypse of Peter* was occasionally considered Scripture by proto-orthodox Christians. But its days were numbered.

The Origenist Controversy and Its Effects

The Origenist controversy erupted at the end of the fourth century and the beginning of the fifth, at the time that the canonical fate of the *Apocalypse of Peter* was all but sealed. By this time, the notion of universalist salvation came to be almost invariably connected in the Christian imagination to Origen, and it suffered badly by the taint of the association.[75] The controversy was not focused principally on the ultimate salvation of sinners, although that was certainly part of it.[76] Far more decisive was the logical conclusion of the *apokatastasis*—the salvation of the devil and his demons.[77] Even Jerome had at one time been open to the idea, as emphasized with some vigor by Rufinus, with written proof.[78] But Jerome eventually rejected salvation for all with vehemence, principally because he came to believe there simply had to be tiers of eternal reward. Surely rigorous ascetics will have superior afterlives to the lowly saints who barely manage to squeak their way in.[79] But if so, that undercuts the entire Origenist logic, since then there could not be a final unity of all.

Once universal salvation became identified as "Origenist," even "tender-hearted Christians" (as Augustine considered them) who had completely different grounds for their views faced orthodox opposition. That would include those who explicitly exempted only superhuman forces of evil from the redemption; those who could not envision eternal torture in retribution for a brief few years of sin; those who did not see the punishment as retributive but purgative, leading to a good result; and indeed, even those who did not see ultimate universal human salvation as an inevitable conclusion of divine sovereignty but as an unprecedented act of divine mercy. Any of these could be condemned as Origenist, no matter how different they were—as seen in rather striking terms, for example, in the anonymous marginal note of the *Sibylline Oracles* (see above).

All these forms of universalism ran up against an *argumentum ad absurdum*—absurd, that is, to the majority of fourth- and fifth-century

Christians: if "all" are to be saved, that must include the devil and his demons. This is the principal argument Augustine uses against the three groups of true universalists he addresses in *City of God* 21.17–24:[80] the first group adopted Origen's doctrine of *apokatastasis;* the next maintained sinners will eventually be saved by a direct act of divine mercy initiated by God himself; and the third claimed God will in the end accede to the fervent prayers of his saints—the view attested in both the *Apocalypse of Peter* and *Sibylline Oracles* 2. Augustine's chief counterargument in each of the three cases? The *argumentum ad absurdum*. If all wicked people will be saved, then necessarily, so too all wicked powers (including the devils). Moreover, Scripture explicitly denies the idea:

> Then what a fond fancy is it to suppose that eternal punishment means long-continued punishment, while eternal life means life without end, since Christ in the very same passage spoke of both in similar terms in one and the same sentence . . . [referring to Matt 25:46]. If both destinies are "eternal," then we must either understand both as long-continued but at last terminating, or both as endless. . . . Wherefore, as the eternal life of the saints shall be endless, so too the eternal punishment of those who are doomed to it shall have no end. (*City of God*, 21.24)

In rejecting the idea that mercy will ultimately triumph over judgment, Augustine does realize there remains the problem of God's character. If every sinner faces the same punishment of eternal torment in fire, why does Scripture indicate that God will never forget to be merciful or allow his wrath to exceed his mercy (Ps 77:9)? To that Augustine has a swift reply. Even as God sends sinners to never-ending torment, he shows his mercy. He will "ensure they are not tortured as horribly as they deserve" (*faciat tanta quanta digni sunt poenarum atrocitate cruciari; City of God* 21.24). Mercy may not triumph over judgment, but it does temper it. Augustine appears to find this solution remarkably satisfying.

In the *Enchiridion*, Augustine concedes yet other possible manifestations of divine mercy in the course of eternal torment. For one thing, the living can affect the fate of the dead through "the sacrifice of the mediator . . . offered for them or alms . . . given in the Church." That is, remembering the dead in the Eucharist and through almsgiving can have a salubrious effect on their destiny.[81] But Augustine stresses that this kind of human intervention works only for the deceased who are worthy and deserve the benefit. Even so, he does toss a small bone to those who hoped there may be at least some occasional respite from torture throughout eternity: "Let them think, if they so wish, that the pains of the damned are mitigated to an extent at certain intervals of time."[82]

In this rather grudging concession Augustine may have been tipping his hat to the *Apocalypse of Paul*, which, as we earlier saw, he both knew and disliked. Unlike its Petrine predecessor, the *Apocalypse* grants tormenters and tormented one day off a week. It is striking that later versions of the work altered the Pauline text at this point, and in various directions, as noted already in the classic study of R. P. Casey.[83] The Ethiopic translation provides the respite for only one night, whereas in the Syriac version God gives no response at all to the petition. On the other hand, yet other translators proved more generous than the original. The Coptic adds the fifty days following Easter to the weekly day off. Yet more surprising, in one of the late Armenian witnesses, possibly from Cilicia in the eleventh or twelfth century, the prayers of Paul and the Virgin Mary for the damned are entirely salvific: hell is destroyed and sinners are released.

Universalism lived on, then, at the margins of the Christian tradition. But only there. The earliest emphasis on "eternal" punishment proved too powerful, and the idea of everlasting torment for the wicked simply too appealing (or useful?) to the Christian imagination. Even though Origen, the greatest theologian of the first three centuries, argued for the ultimate salvation of all, the view never caught on widely, and controversy over his writings a century and a half later sealed the deal. Augustine himself delivered the exclamation point in his influential magnum opus. Thus, So-zomen's incredulity over the use of the *Apocalypse of Peter* in fifth-century Palestine comes as no surprise. The orthodox world had moved on from the glimpse of hope that all might be saved.

The Effect of the Controversy on Scribes and Editors

As happened in other venues with other issues and other texts, this ortho-dox juggernaut affected Christian scribes and translators transmitting the early Christian writings.[84] To be sure, sometimes remnants of "Origenist" universalism were allowed to stand, even if they were openly condemned: our unknown scribe of the exemplar behind the Ψ family of manuscripts of *Sibylline Oracles* 2 could not abide the idea, but he left the text as he found it and compromised only by adding an explanatory note to condemn it for his readers. Other scribes, however, did not restrain themselves and altered the texts as they saw fit. This can be seen in the fate of Evagrius's work *Kephalaia gnostica* in the Syriac tradition. Evagrius had embraced Origen's *apokatastasis:* "all" created beings in the end would come around, worship the one true God, and enter into a blessed state. A first Syriac translation of the *Kephalaia* remained true to Evagrius's perspective. A second one, however, corrupted the text into orthodox conformity, deleting the suggestions that all would be saved, especially the "devil." It was difficult to restrain a translator or scribe on a theological mission.[85]

The *Apocalypse of Peter*, of course, has a very different view of universalist salvation from Origen's. For the orthodox theological imagination, however, it may have been even worse. Origen's God is not in the least whimsical, prone to change his mind simply because people ask him to do so, reversing his course of action and compromising his just character. He is the sovereign Lord of all with a distinct plan worked out in ages past and patiently implemented, with no possibility of change or reversal. God is not punishing people in hellfire simply because of resentment or retributive wrath or to restore his sullied dignity, like a mortal tyrant. God loves his creation and wants to restore it to its original perfect state. Torment is meant to reform character, purge sin, and urge people to return to the truth. This is a perfectly just, merciful, and unstoppable plan: eventually everyone, of their own free will, will return to God so that his sovereignty will be established forever, and he will be "all in all." The soteriological corollary is that he will shower his blessings on all sentient beings, for eternity.

The *Apocalypse of Peter*, by contrast, emphasizes God's extreme mercy— obviously a hugely appealing notion. But it has problems. A critic could object that it portrays God as a ruthless lawgiver and judge who tortures people who oppose him, not to help them see the truth but as retribution, pure and simple. In this account God originally has no intention of showing mercy to those undergoing eternal torment. On the contrary, he both wills and wants them to suffer, with no end ever in sight. He has no ear for the shrieks and pathetic pleadings of those undergoing unbearable torture. But then like a fickle but powerful leader who acts on a whim, he changes his mind, reluctantly caving in to the wishes of the saints, those who are "weak-minded," in Augustine's words, because, unlike God, they are driven more by kindness and a concern for the welfare of others than by a desire for vengeance.

Whatever one thinks of this portrayal of the Almighty, the notion that all would be saved proved too much for later readers. The editor of the

Akhmim version excised the passage, and possibly not simply out of a general desire for brevity. The Ethiopic translator (or his scribal predecessor) retained it but altered it beyond recognition, reversing its teaching. It is clear how most readers of the fourth century would have dealt with it. They would have condemned the passage as "plainly false," in the words of the scribe of *Sibylline Oracles* 2, who was incensed at the rewritten version of the passage he found in the text he was copying.

Petrine Pseudepigrapha and Canon

The universalist salvation promoted by the earliest known form of the *Apocalypse of Peter* provides the best explanation of why, in the end, it did not become a part of sacred Scripture. It did not fail to pass muster because it was scarcely known: it was both far more widely used and cited as Scripture in the early centuries than 2 Peter. Nor was it rejected because critics came to realize it had not been written by Peter. They came to this conclusion because they rejected its teaching, not the other way around. Apart from the problematic passage of chapter 14, the text posed no particular difficulties for the sensibilities of emerging orthodoxy. Early on, even that passage was not seen as especially troublesome. Other Christian writings celebrated the ultimate mercy of God and its triumph over judgment in a universal salvation of all sinners. Some such view occasionally appears, or at least seems to appear, in writings of Christianity's greatest apostle, Paul, and in its greatest pre-Nicene theologian, Origen. Moreover, the *Apocalypse* itself focuses on God's inexorable justice, enacted in unusually severe judgment upon all who disobey him. Salvation comes only after horrible torture. God is both just and merciful.

Still, the theological tide shifted decisively with the Origenist controversy, and it was not enough to acknowledge that God was just. His justice had to last forever, and sinners therefore had to face his wrath in neverending torment—a matter of delight for some of those who felt assured of eternal glory. For the burgeoning orthodox communities of the late fourth and fifth centuries, God does not revoke his judgments or change his mind—least of all because of the weak pleas of the faint of heart who would defy God's just character in order to relieve eternal pain for those who in fact deserve worse than they are getting. Anyone who might claim otherwise is frail, weak-minded, and unorthodox. The great apostle Peter was anything but unorthodox. He therefore could not have written the *Apocalypse*, and so, the salvation of all spelled its condemnation.

What about the other Petrine book with which we have contrasted the *Apocalypse?* Second Peter was far less popular in the early centuries; it was either unknown, ignored, or only weakly considered an option, scarcely a "catholic" writing. On the other hand, nothing about it offended the dictates of orthodoxy or raised any particular suspicions of authenticity. The author directly claims to have been present at Jesus's transfiguration and indicates this is the second letter sent to his reader. Everyone already knew his first letter. Moreover, he reveres the apostle Paul, showing the unity of the original apostolic band, even labeling Paul's writings as Scripture. Most important, his message coincides with apostolic norms. God is the judge who exacts his judgment on the earth. He has done it before, casting the sinful angels into the place of torment and destroying the world in the days of Noah. He will soon do it again. He has delayed his action for the time being only to allow more people an opportunity to repent. But those who remain recalcitrant need to pay heed: they will bear the full brunt of his divine judgment when Christ comes in power to destroy everything and everyone that is ungodly. Here we find no trace of universal salvation, only a final and decisive judgment that will bring destruction to the enemies of God. After that a new heaven and a new earth will appear.

In broad terms this sounds like the teaching of both Jesus and Paul. Moreover, its warnings against those who pervert the truth helped assure readers of its own orthodoxy. In the end, it was tacitly agreed that even though 2 Peter was not the most important apostolic Christian writing or even much used, it was indeed written by Peter and so deserved a place in Scripture. The letter of Peter was delivered from its fate of near oblivion, while the *Apocalypse* was cast into the outer darkness, from which it would never return.

CHAPTER SIX

The Power of Christ and the
Harrowing of Hell

E ARLY CHRISTIAN KATABASEIS are less interested in the geogra-
phies, climates, and venues of heaven and hell than in their inhabitants. Ultimately, these narratives are driven by soteriological
concerns. Who receives punishment after death? Who salvation? On what grounds? For how long? Before the "birth of purgatory,"
the final question received a resoundingly majority response: both torments and blessings are eternal.[1] The prime exceptions were universalists,
who struggled to gain traction on the margins of both learned and popular
opinion.

Intrinsic to the universalist views advanced by both the *Apocalypse of
Peter* and Origen was the idea that the postmortem salvation of sinners
required some kind of human action—either the petitionary prayers of
the saints or the eventual enlightenment of the sinners. Not so in the
Harrowing of Hell tradition, which presents a different universalist option
that, like the others, also came to be suppressed. In its most extreme form,
found in the oldest version of the descent narrative of the *Gospel of Nicodemus*, humans play no role at all in their ultimate salvation. Christ descends
to hell and with a manifestation of his irresistible might breaks its bars,
smashes its bonds, subdues its forces, and sets all people free, gloriously
triumphing over everything aligned against the divine creator and his creation. This account is about raw, divine power. Christ delivers the entire
human race, saints and sinners alike, from the forces of death, Hades, and

the devil.[2] It is an unusual kind of katabasis, but a katabasis it is. Christ journeys to the realms of the dead below and removes all its occupants to heaven above, as recorded by eyewitnesses to the event.[3]

My thesis in this chapter is that this notion of the complete Harrowing of Hell came to be modified over time in ways analogous to the universalist teaching of the *Apocalypse of Peter*. Orthodox scribes and editors simply could not abide the idea that sinners would escape punishment, especially sinners who did not repent. These later transmitters of the text continued to affirm Christ's incomparable power and his complete conquest over the infernal powers that held souls captive, but they refused to compromise the requirements of divine justice and the eternal punishment of sinners. These competing views led to confused and confusing textual productions in which Christ is affirmed as completely harrowing hell and saving all people when, in fact, many continue to be damned.

The notion of Christ's descent to hell has a long and complicated history that requires a book-length, sustained analysis. Fortunately, we already have one in an extensive study of Rémi Gounelle. Here I simply summarize the salient issues.

The History of Christ's Descent to Hell

The idea that Christ descended to hell after his death to liberate its captives almost certainly originated from deductions based on widespread beliefs and assumptions at the heart of Christian theology: Christ brought salvation to the world through his death and resurrection, and he did not simply cease to exist in the interim between these two salvific events. Since he was himself "fully human," he experienced the fate of all others by going to Hades; but while there he must have continued, in some way, the work he had done on earth above.

The earliest references to Christ's death and resurrection give no clues about what he was doing during the interim period. Both the brief creedal statement of 1 Corinthians 15:3–5 ("he died for our sins . . . and was buried; he was raised on the third day . . . and he appeared") and the full passion and resurrection narratives of the Gospels (Matt 27–28, Mark 15–16, Luke 23–24, John 18–21) are silent on the matter. The first hints of divine activity during the "missing period" do not provide much help either. Thus we have Peter's speech at Pentecost in Acts 2:23–28: "God raised him, having loosed the birth-pangs of death" (v. 24), followed by the quotation from Psalm 16, "For you did not abandon my soul to Hades, /

nor did you allow your Holy One to see corruption" (v. 27). Here Christ is understood to have been in Hades and then delivered, but there is no hint about what, if anything, he was doing there. The question raised in Ephesians 4:9 is scarcely more instructive: "What does it mean that 'he ascended' if not that he had (earlier) descended into the lowest parts of the earth?"

Of greater importance for later speculation was that most intriguing and perplexing of passages, 1 Peter 3:18–20: "For Christ died for sins once and for all . . . having been put to death in the flesh but being made alive in the spirit, in which also, having gone to the spirits who were in prison, he preached to those who were formerly disobedient, when God's patience waited during the days when Noah was preparing the ark." The passage was often read, naturally enough, with the equally enigmatic statement of the following chapter, which is nearly as difficult to translate as to interpret: "For to this end, proclamation was made to the dead, that they might be judged in the flesh like humans but live in the spirit like God" (1 Pet 4:6).[4] These texts, separately or together, have exercised interpreters for as long as there have been interpreters and have proved more fruitful for speculation than helpful for guidance, down to the present time, as both textual emendations and exegetical monographs attest.[5] In early times, a variety of views emerged to explain Christ's activities immediately after his death. These views did not develop in a linear fashion: newer views never supplanted older ones, and different views could be held by different people at the same time or even simultaneously by the same person.

An obvious conclusion drawn from the passages in 1 Peter was that Christ descended to Hades precisely to proclaim his message of salvation there as he had done in the world above.[6] At first the idea was simply expressed with no specifics about whom Christ addressed or what effect he had. In the narrative of the *Gospel of Peter* (also falsely attributed), when Christ and his cross emerge from the tomb, the voice from heaven asks, "Have you preached to those who are asleep?" and the cross replies, "Yes."[7] Strictly speaking, it is the cross that has preached to the residents of the world below, but presumably it is a metonymy.[8]

Soon, however, the tradition begins to specify an audience for Jesus's underworld proclamation. Most often it is the righteous of Israel, beginning with (or sometimes only) the patriarchs and the prophets.[9] This is the view, for example, of Justin, Irenaeus, and other second-century sources. The popularity of the view is evidenced by the fact that the second-century pagan critic Celsus mocked it, asking whether anyone could really believe that Christ tried to make converts in the world below. Origen, naturally, rebuked his opponent and argued that this is precisely what happened (Origen, *Cels.* 2.42).

An intriguing variation on the theme, attesting again to its wide acceptance, is found in Marcion, at least according to Irenaeus. Consistent with Marcion's distinctive perspective, Christ went to Hades to preach salvation not to the righteous Israelites but to Cain, the Sodomites, the Egyptians, "and all the pagans." These are the ones who were then taken to the heavenly realm. Abel, Enoch, Noah, and all the patriarchs and prophets were left behind to be punished in Hades (Irenaeus, *Haer.* 1.27.3).

Still in the second century an alternative explanation of Christ's descent arose—that he went to Hades not to preach salvation but to manifest his power. This idea may be suggested already in the *Ascension of Isaiah*, which speaks of Christ having "plundered the angel of death" (9.14).[10] A clearer reference comes nearer the end of the century in the *Paschal Homily* of Melito of Sardis, where Christ identifies himself by affirming his display of power in the world below:

> I am he who destroys death,
> and triumphs over the enemy,
> and crushes Hades
> and binds the strong man
> and bears humanity off to the heavenly heights. (102–3)[11]

A similar conceit appears in Gregory Thaumaturgus, *On All the Saints:* "Hades and the devil have been despoiled and stripped of their ancient armor, and cast out of their peculiar power. And even as Goliath has his head cut off with his own sword, so also is the devil, who has been the father of death, put to rout through death."[12] Eventually, this became a standard view, as seen much later in a comment of Ambrosiaster, for example: "After he despoiled hell by the power of the Father and arose after conquering Death, he ascended to Heaven with the souls he had snatched away. For all those who had seen the Savior in hell hoped for salvation from him and were set free, as the apostle Peter testifies" (*Epist. ad Rom.* 10; *PG* 17.143).

Closely related to and often intertwined with the question of why Christ descended—to preach or to assert his power—is the issue of the salvific effect of his descent. At an early stage, the answer appears to have seemed rather obvious: Christ went to Hades to save the patriarchs and prophets of Israel, that is, the saints who lived before Christ who could not, technically, believe in his salvific death and resurrection except pro-leptically. Once he fulfilled his earthly task, however, they were delivered from the darkness of Hades and brought to their heavenly reward (thus, e.g., Irenaeus, *Haer.* 4.27.2; *Ep. Apos.* 72; and even up to Augustine, *Sermo de symbolo* 7). Very soon—possibly immediately—other righteous Israelites (who did not happen to be named in the Old Testament) came to be in-cluded among those delivered by Christ at his descent. This, for example, is the view attacked indirectly by Marcion, who left "all the righteous" (as Irenaeus termed them) in the infernal realm. Further questions of eq-uity arose, however. If righteous Jews were saved from Hades, why not righteous gentiles? Clement of Alexandria addresses the question head-on by expanding Christ's infernal mission: he preached salvation to all the upright in the netherworld, both Jew and gentile (*Strom.* 6.6, based on a clever exegesis of Isa 42:6–7). Soon thereafter Origen appears to agree: he speaks of Christ's mission to convert the denizens of Hades but nowhere indicates Christ directed his efforts only to Jews.

Whether Christ went to save righteous Jews, or all Jews, or Jews and gentiles, there is still the question of how effective he was. If his goal was to preach his gospel of salvation, did he speak literally to everyone or just to those he knew would accept his message? Was he declaring them saved or giving them an opportunity to accept an offer of salvation? If he went to destroy the powers below, did he do it completely or only in part? If com-pletely, did he provide an alternative arrangement for justice, some other form of punishment outside of Hades? Or did he deliver every single soul from damnation? Lots of interpretive options were on offer.

Those who wanted to magnify the glorious effects of Christ's appear-ance in the world below often engaged in considerable rhetorical excess. If Christ's preaching really was irresistible, or if his power actually was unstoppable, surely all would be saved. No one could resist. Some authors do say that, but most then qualify their claims. We see qualified exuber-ance already with our first surviving Christian author, Paul, who does say that in the end all creatures everywhere will worship Christ (Phil 2:10–11) and that all who participated with Adam in sin (that is, every human be-ing ever) will also participate with Christ in salvation (Rom 5). But he still speaks of divine wrath against sinners, coming destruction, and the judg-ment seat of Christ (e.g., Rom 1:18, 2:6; 1 Thess 5:3). So in what sense will everyone be saved?

Later admirers of Paul made similar bold claims, but often it is easy to see beneath the rhetorical excess. Origen can say that at his descent Christ destroyed the kingdom of death and led away its captives, liberating those who were held there (*Comm. Rom.* 5.1.37, 5.10.12; *In Lib. Reg. Hom.* 2); but given his teaching of the *apokatastasis*, he clearly did not really mean it as a literal description of what happened.[13] So too Cyril of Alexandria, who describes the descent as having a universal effect: Christ descended "and preached to the spirits in Hades; he appeared to those confined in the house of prison, and he freed everyone from their bonds and pain" (καὶ πάντας ἀνῆκεν δεσμῶν καὶ ἀνάγκης; *Commentary on Luke* 4.18, PG 72.537). But the fact that he does not mean "everyone" becomes clear elsewhere, most notably in his *Commentary on John* 3.36 (*PG* 73.286–88), where he affirms that everyone will be raised from the dead, but not necessarily to "see life." Those who do not believe will never see life; after their resurrection they will experience punishments far harsher than death itself (*PG* 73.286–88).[14]

Many early theologians who wanted to affirm universal salvation that Christ brought at his descent but also the judicial need for eternal damnation simply claimed that Christ made salvation *available* to everyone in Hades—even the worst of sinners—but that not everyone accepted the offer. Even this idea was often challenged by orthodox thinkers; surely sinners would not be given a second chance after death. And so, we have the polemic of Filaster of Brescia: "There are some heretics who say that the Lord descended to Hades and announced to all who were there after death that if they confessed their faith there they would be saved" (*Liber de Haeresibus* 125.1).[15] It is somewhat odd that Filaster reacts to this view by insisting that sinners would indeed be condemned, a point that so far as we know his opponents never denied. But he did indeed attack a "universalizing" view (all *could* be saved) by discounting universalism (all *will* be saved). Possibly he was simply knocking down a scarecrow.[16] Gregory the Great opposes a similar view.[17] Indeed, in his full study, Gounelle maintains that a universalizing view was not just the position of a single group of "heretics" but was almost ubiquitous in parts of the West.[18]

Perfectly orthodox theologians also wrestled with the issues connected with the salvific effects of Christ's descent. The most famous instance involves an exchange of letters between Augustine and his friend and fellow bishop Evodius. Evodius had inquired about the interpretation of 1 Peter 3:18–21, Christ's descent "to preach to the spirits in prison." He maintains that the "spirits" were in hell (*in inferno*) and that "Christ descended and proclaimed his gospel to all of them" (*descendens Christus omnibus evangelizavit*). Evodius argues that Christ freed "all of them from their darkness and punishments" through his grace, so that at the time of the Lord's resurrection, "judgment could be anticipated" (= they could wait for judgment, *judicium exspectetur,* now that "the nether regions had been emptied"). Evodius ends on a humble note: "What your Holiness thinks about this matter I would like to know" (*PL* 33, 3.709). Is it right? Were all those in Hades set free?[19]

Augustine's response does not attack Evodius's proposal per se or warn him that he is on the brink of heresy. He responds gently, admitting the many problems of the passage, reflecting on possibilities, showing why some are better than others, and finally coming up with what strikes him as the most plausible solution. In the process he indicates that he can see how some readers might take the passage to mean Christ delivered all people at his descent and admits that it would indeed be an attractive option: "If we could say that altogether everyone who was found there was set free, who should not rejoice—if we could show it?" (*PL* 33.10). It is hard to know if he is ingenuous, especially in light of his following insistence that he too would prefer that sinners (or at least the pagan literati!) could "be freed from the pains of hell, were not the verdict of human feeling different from that of the justice of the Creator." For Augustine, of course, God's judgment demands retribution, and the torments will be eternal, expressed nowhere more forcefully than in *City of God* 21.

As to his solution to the conundrums posed by the passage, Augustine paints himself into a corner but then manages to get out. On one hand, Christ must have descended to hell—not some other place—because Scripture says in Psalm 16:10, "you will not leave my soul in hell," and Acts 2:24 indicates that God "loosed the birth-pangs of death." On the other hand, he did not descend to save the saints, since none of them would have been there. The parable of Lazarus and the rich man (Luke 16) shows that the righteous, even before Christ's death, were not sent down to Hades but up to Abraham's bosom. So what was Christ doing in hell? He must have been preaching his salvation to others, and surely his efforts would not have been in vain. He must have brought salvation to sinners. But he could not have planned to save simply everyone: if everyone attains salvation after death, there would be no need for the Christian mission to save people while living (Augustine's *argumentum ad absurdum*). So whom did Christ deliver? He must have saved only those few "whom he judged worthy" (Augustine, *Letter* 164.5).

Narrative Descriptions of Christ's Descent

A number of narrative descriptions of Christ's descent to hell survive, many of them connected in one way or another to the *Gospel of Nicodemus* and all of them providing answers to the key questions we have been addressing: whether Christ went to hell to preach or to manifest his power and whether he delivered only the Old Testament saints, all righteous people, all who confessed faith in him at the time, or everyone altogether.[20] Some of these traditions come to us not as freestanding narratives but in homiletic summaries. One of the most important is Pseudo-Augustine's *Sermon 160, De pascha II*, shown by Gounelle to be genealogically related to the *Gospel of Nicodemus*, not as a direct source but as a sibling to a common archetype.[21] Early in the sermon the homilist appears to embrace a universalist understanding of the descent, quoting John 12:32 to encapsulate Christ's intention for going into Hades, "that I might draw all people to myself." But immediately he clarifies what he means: by "all" he refers to all of "his elect" (*de electis suis apud inferos*). None of these will be left behind. Nonbelievers (*infideles*), however, will be eternally punished for their offenses against God (*pro suis criminibus*). "The righteous," known by their "faith and works," had been in Hades only because of "original sin" (*originali peccato*). Christ descended to take them to their heavenly reward.

Something similar may be found in Pseudo-Epiphanius's *Homilia 11*, possibly from the sixth century,[22] a highly rhetorical sermon that celebrates the descent by stressing that Christ went into Hades as "God." His mission was not to save all people but just "those who believed," that is, Adam, Eve, and "many other bodies of the saints who had been asleep for ages."[23] In this case the descent was not a matter of persuasion but of power, as rather emphatically stated in the homilist's remarkable exhortation to his audience to "go to Hades in our mind," to see how "with the *power* of his *power* he [Christ] *overpowered* the *powerful* tyrant who was *powerful* in *power*" (τὸν τῷ κράτει κραταιὸν κατὰ κράτος κρατεῖ τοῦ κράτους κρατοτύραννον).

A more ambiguous perspective comes in another closely related text, a Paschal Homily of Pseudo-Eusebius of Alexandria, *In sancta et magna parasceve, et in sanctam passionem Domini* (PG 62.721–24). Here, however, we find a summary of key events of the Gospel passion narratives, including a descent narrative. The homilist begins his account with the trial of Jesus before the Jewish council, placing a special emphasis on the robber (*lestes*) Jesus forgave on the cross in Luke 23:43; but he then devotes half his narrative to the descent, including a discussion between a personified

Hades and the devil over the disastrous and decisive defeat they are soon to experience when Christ arrives. At first glance the description seems to involve a complete Harrowing of Hell. Christ destroys the gates of hell, smashes the bars, and tramples the powers, loosing the pangs of death. He then captures the devil and robs him of all his power, binding him with unbreakable chains and spreading him out over fire with worms that never sleep. The forces of evil appear to be completely disempowered. Moreover, when the deed is done, the saints glorify Christ for his great victory, as David cites his own psalm in praise: "All nations (πάντα τὰ ἔθνη), clap your hands and shout out to God our savior"; "For the King has fought and won the victory for us" (see Ps 47:1–2).

Does "all nations" mean "all people"? The conclusion to the scene seems to suggest so: "When he rose from the dead he set the world free" (τὸν κόσμον ἐλευθερώσας) and led "all people into heaven" (πάντας εἰς οὐρανούς). On the other hand, the emphasis of the account is entirely on the salvation of the saints. When Jesus was said to arrive in Hades, the imprisoned "prophets" rejoice and come to him. At the harrowing itself, Christ takes specifically the prophets out of their confinement and tells them to go to paradise; they eagerly leap out and up. After their arrival above, only one sinner is mentioned in the heavenly realms—the recently saved robber who had repented while on earth and therefore went straight from his cross to paradise. Probably decisive to the homilist's understanding is his concluding exhortation, as he urges his hearers to sing praises to the crucified and raised Christ "so that he might take us from the darkness of our sins and make us heirs of his kingdom."[24] His hearers thus are not assured of the kingdom but may still have to pay for their sins away from the kingdom. Salvation appears to be conditional and reserved for some, not unconditional for all.

The Questions of Bartholomew

The most important predecessor of the *Gospel of Nicodemus* is the *Questions of Bartholomew*, our oldest surviving narrative of the Harrowing of Hell, with roots going back into the second century.[25] It is found in only six manuscripts, two each in Greek, Latin, and Slavonic. The relationship among them is complicated, and the variants they present create serious difficulties for interpretation. As a result, textual specialists do not agree on the oldest form of the text or the corresponding genealogical relationship of the witnesses. Jean-Daniel Kaestli expresses a strong preference for the text of Latin C (for most of the portion of the account we focus on), but more recently Christoph Markschies maintains the superiority of Greek H and proposes a stemma of the witnesses (and lost exemplars) to justify the decision. As we will see, the choice of the oldest form of the text plays a significant role for the issues we are pursuing here.[26]

The book presents questions the disciple Bartholomew raised after the resurrection, mainly with Jesus but also with his mother Mary. The first question involves Christ's descent. Bartholomew indicates that when all the other disciples had fled the scene of Jesus's crucifixion, he had stayed, keenly watching Jesus on the cross. But then Jesus disappeared, and Bartholomew heard voices below the earth and felt an earthquake. He wants to know where Jesus went.[27]

In the discussion that follows, Jesus explains that he left the cross to descend to provide salvation to those in Hades. Immediately at this point our textual witnesses begin to stand at odds. In the oldest Latin version, supported by the two Slavonic manuscripts, Jesus indicates he went below to deliver "Adam and all the patriarchs, Abraham, Isaac and Jacob" (v. 9), a view consistent with what we have seen before: salvation comes to the Old Testament saints. But the sole surviving Greek witness at this point (H) indicates he went to save Adam and "all those who were with him" (καὶ πάντας τοὺς μετ' αὐτοῦ). Presumably those "with" Adam would be all his descendants—that is, the human race. Which variant reading represents the older form of the text? Was salvation restricted to saints, or was it for all people? Whichever reading was older, one or more scribes decided to change it.

Difficulties continue with the next reference to the recipients of salvation. In Greek H, in apparent tension with its own text of v. 9, Christ indicates that he led "all the Patriarchs" out of Hades but says nothing about everyone else who was there (v. 20). Now the Latin witness C, in apparent tension with its own text of v. 9, provides a universalizing change, this time through an addition: Christ led forth all the patriarchs "and all who were detained in the same place" (et omnes qui ibidem detinebantur). The question is not simply which reading is older but why the older form of the text in each of the two witnesses appears to be at odds, not just with the other witnesses but also with itself.[28]

Matters are not helped by the following verse. In Latin C and L Bartholomew indicates that he had "again" seen Christ (later) hanging on the cross, and "all the dead (omnes mortuos) rising up and worshiping" him before "again ascending in(to) (their?) memorials" (iterum ascendentes in *memoria;* L adds *suas*). This last clause is particularly thorny. *Memoria* here surely must mean "monuments," that is, one would assume, "tombs." But why would they return to their tombs? Is the text suggesting, possibly through an allusion to Matthew 27:52–53, that the dead who came back to life at Jesus's crucifixion worshiped him and then returned to their places of entombment until the future resurrection of the dead?[29] That seems implausible in light of the earlier statement that Christ actually liberated these people from Hades (v. 9); presumably they did not then return to Hades or wherever they had been before.

If "into their tombs" does not make narrative sense, we should consider whether "*in memoria (suas)*" is a textual corruption, an addition made in an archetype of L and C. If so, the older form of the text would have ended with *ascendentes* and also lacked, then, the preceding *iterum*, simply stating that after "all" the dead had risen and worshiped Christ, they "ascended" directly into heaven. The scribe of the archetype of our two Latin witnesses would have found the statement discomforting for obvious theological reasons ("all" the dead ascended to heaven) and altered the text. But by doing so he inadvertently created the incongruous claim that the dead "ascended" (instead of "returned" or "descended") to their places of interment.

If that is indeed the transmission history of the passage, we can make better sense of a variant later attested in the Slavonic version. There, in an addition to the text of v. 21, Bartholomew reports that he had seen "the angels" standing before Christ as he was hanging on the cross, and, as in L and C, "all the dead rising up and worshiping you." But both Slavonic manuscripts omit precisely the problematic phrase, "and again ascending into their tombs." This omission is easily explained: the scribe of the Slavonic archetype also found the comment about "all . . . ascending" (to heaven) troubling but made a simple edit by eliminating it. I would suggest, then, that the archetype lying behind both the Latin and Slavonic traditions ended with *ascendentes*, denoting a universal salvation.[30] The most remarkable change of all comes in the lone Greek witness with text at this point: H omits the entire sentence. Now the narrative says absolutely nothing about "all the dead," or in fact any of the dead, rising up to worship Christ on the cross, let alone ascending to heaven. Any trace of universal resurrection and thus salvation has now been removed. That may not be consistent with the scribal inclination evidenced in v. 9 (shifting the focus to a universal salvation)—if that indeed represents an alteration of the text inherited by Greek H—but it is consistent with scribal inclination generally in the passage, of randomly removing various indications of universalism. This kind of textual inconsistency is indeed striking but not unfamiliar to anyone who has worked extensively on the theological tendencies of scribes copying early Christian texts.[31]

Still, why should we think that the tradition moved in this particular direction, away from a universalist to a restrictive understanding of the salvation brought by Christ? For a rather simple but powerful reason: restrictive salvation was by far the dominant view throughout the Christian tradition, especially in the centuries when such scribal changes of this narrative in particular would have been made. It is far more likely, therefore, that independent scribes working separately would be far more inclined to a restrictive than a universalist view.[32]

Not everyone agreed with this restrictive view. In particular, it was not shared by the author of the oldest surviving form of the descent narrative, found in the much later *Gospel of Nicodemus*. In this case we have a katabasis that recounts a complete Harrowing of Hell and salvation for all its inhabitants.

The Gospel of Nicodemus

The *Gospel of Nicodemus* was by far the best-known katabasis through the Middle Ages, even though it has attracted relatively sparse attention among modern scholars.[33] At first glance it might seem inapt to label the descent narrative in the Gospel a "katabasis." It is, after all, the divine Christ who descends to hell, he is not given a guided tour, and there is a scant description of the place. All three objections, however, are readily answered. In reverse order, even though the account is less concerned with the physical features of hell or the suffering being experienced there, it is described by two sons of Simeon who were there temporarily: it is deep below the earth and completely dark; it is inhabited by all those who have died from Adam on, who are imprisoned with unbreakable chains; it is controlled by Satan and his demons in conjunction with death and a personified Hades; it has gates of brass and bars of iron. It is true that Jesus does not (obviously) need a guided tour of the place, but tour guides are absent from other katabaseis as well, most notably Homer's *nekuia*. And finally, Christ is portrayed as a divine invader here, but he goes to Hades precisely because he is also a mortal, a human who has died; moreover, other katabatic traditions also portray a divine visitant to the underworld, most famously Dionysus in Aristophanes' *The Frogs*.

The "original" form of the account, composed in Greek, lacked the descent narrative (chs. 17–27) and was probably titled "The Acts Accomplished Under Pontius Pilate."[34] It was almost certainly in circulation at some point during the first three-quarters of the fourth century. This narrative provides a distinctive and memorable account of the trial of Jesus before Pontius Pilate (most famous for the episode of the Roman standards bowing down to worship him), his death, and events that happened in the aftermath of his resurrection. This version was soon translated, most importantly into Latin but also into Coptic, Armenian, Georgian, Syriac, and Aramaic. At some point in the sixth or seventh century an account of the descent to Hades was added to the Latin version. Rémi Gounelle and Zbigniew Izydorczyk, in particular, have compellingly argued that this descent narrative did not originate as a separate composition for independent circulation but was written precisely to fill out and complement the *Acts of Pilate*.[35] It was this expanded account that became widely disseminated throughout the centuries and retitled the *Evangelium Nicodemi* around the twelfth century. It was then translated broadly, "in nearly all the vernacular languages of the West."[36] Some 450 Latin manuscripts still survive and around 320 in some twenty European vernaculars.

As might be expected, this kind of broad interlingual circulation led to extensive textual manipulation involving revision, redaction, and alteration. The most widespread form of the descent narrative appears in what happens also to be the oldest version, Latin A, which can be quickly summarized. After Jesus's resurrection, Joseph of Arimathea informs the Jewish leaders Annas and Caiaphas that among those who had been raised from their tombs (see Matt 27:52–53) were Karinus and Leucius, two sons of the Simeon who had blessed Jesus as an infant (Luke 2:25–32). The Jewish leaders track the brothers down and ask them to tell what had happened. They independently produce the same account, word-for-word, in writing: They had been in Hades, with everyone else,[37] in the everlasting darkness, when a great light shone, and a series of prophets (Isaiah, Simeon, John the Baptist, Adam, and Seth) came forward to proclaim that it was the coming of Christ. The scene then shifts to a long dialogue between Satan, the leader of death, and a personified Hades, who complains that by stirring up the Jewish people to have Christ killed, Satan has brought their domain to an end. Hades will be emptied of every single inhabitant. While the two powers of darkness bicker, a thunderous voice sounds out an order: "Lift up your gates . . . and the King of Glory shall come in" (Ps 24:7). David and Isaiah confirm this is the coming of the one they had predicted. As Satan and Hades raise a loud protest, Christ bursts in, effort-lessly overwhelms his enemies, and releases all the imprisoned. He then dispatches Satan into Hades for eternal torment as its lone inhabitant and delivers his "saints" (now the term used for all those saved) up to the arch-angel Michael, in the heavenly realm. There they meet Enoch and Elijah, the two mortals who had been taken directly up to heaven without dying, and the robber who had been granted the kingdom by Christ on the cross (Luke 23:43). The saved all bless Almighty God for the joys of paradise, and this brings Karinus's and Leucius's accounts to an end.

As Gounelle has repeatedly stressed, this account of the descent is far less interested in describing hell than in celebrating the salvation that Christ brought there. That too is my focus. To amplify the thesis I stated at the outset: The oldest attainable form of the text narrated a complete har-rowing, in which all the dead from Adam onward, sinners and wicked, were delivered from their imprisonment and taken to the heavenly realm. As the account came to be broadly transmitted, edited, and retranslated, that em-phasis shifted. In one other major form of the tradition it was specifically and directly reversed, and in yet another it was modified out of existence. I do not consider all the variations on the theme—an impossible task at this stage of research, since the exceedingly few but hardy scholars committed to evaluating all the textual witnesses, especially Izydorczyk, have not yet been able to publish all their collations, let alone analyses of them.[38] In-stead, I look at the three most important strands of the tradition that have come down to us: the oldest form, previously mentioned, Latin A; a later revision of it known as Latin B; and the Byzantine Greek tradition, now known as Greek M, descended not from the purported original Greek ver-sion but from a back translation into Greek from something like Latin A.[39]

Latin A

The earliest Latin witness to the *Acts of Pilate*, Vindobensis 563, the "Vi-enna palimpsest," dates to the fifth or sixth century but lacks the descent narrative.[40] The account is found, however, in the other Latin forms of the text: Latin A, B, and C, the Troyes Redaction, and their various sub-groups and intermediaries.[41] As indicated, Latin A provides us with the earliest version. Regrettably, no critical edition yet exists, and so I follow standard practice by citing the text as found in one of the oldest and best witnesses, the tenth-century Codex Einsidlensis (Einsiedeln Stiftsbiblio-thek, MS 326).[42]

It has been widely recognized that this account does indeed present a complete Harrowing of Hell, achieved by the unstoppable power of Christ who robs Hades of all its human inhabitants and sends them to heaven. As Gounelle and Izydorczyk emphatically stated in their popular 1997 introduction to the text, the account narrates "the deliverance of Adam and all his children, without exception (that is, all of humanity) from the world of the dead to bring them to paradise."[43] Gounelle independently argued this case for some years but more recently has set forth the alternative view—that the harrowing brought salvation only to the saints, not to the wicked as well. His original view is more convincing.[44]

It is true that the clear emphasis in the text, as noted above, is on the "saints." They are the only humans provided with speaking parts in Hades (e.g., in chs. 18–19)—Adam, Isaiah, Simeon, John the Baptist, and Seth—and are expressly the ones repeatedly filled with joy (e.g., "Adam, the father of the entire human race, with all the patriarchs and prophets, rejoiced," 18.1; "the patriarchs and prophets rejoiced," 19.2; "all the saints rejoiced," 20.1). They are also the ones, obviously, who proclaim that what they had earlier predicted is now being fulfilled: Christ has come to bring salvation. But this proclamation of salvation extends not just to the saints but also to everyone else dwelling in the darkness, as anticipated already in an early part of the narrative, where Isaiah declares that Christ's appearance fulfills his prophecy: "O land of Zebulon and land of Nephtali across the Jordan, Galilee of the gentiles. The people who sit in darkness will see a great light, and the light will shine upon those who are in the region of the shadow of death" (quoting Isa 9:1–2). That light has now come and enlightened "we who sit in death" (*Gos. Nic.* 18.1).

That Christ's salvation extends to all becomes clear in the feverish discussions between Satan and Hades. Hades frets that "no one is able to resist [Christ's] power" (20.2), which, for him, means that if Christ arrives in Hades, "He will release all those who are shut up here in the unbelief of prison and held by the indissoluble chains of sin; and he will lead them to life by his own divinity, for eternity" (20.3). The key terms, for our purposes are "all" and "indissoluble chains of sin." None of the sinners remains bound, even though their chains are (or were thought to be) unbreakable. So too the legions of demons and death bemoan Christ's imminent appearance "to deliver *everyone* (*omnes*) from their chains," as one who would "receive the dominion of the *whole* world" (*potestam totius mundi;* 22.1).

When Christ appears, these fears are fully realized. He puts to flight "*all* the darkness of death by his own brilliance" and casts forth all the imprisoned. Hades now complains to Satan: "*Everyone* (*omnes*) who has long sighed under our torments abuses us," and in fact *no one* of the entire human race stands in any fear before them (23.1). This comprises all who have ever lived, including those who had no hope of salvation: "Those who from the beginning until now had despaired of salvation and life— now none of them (*nullus eorum . . . solito*) can be heard howling . . . nor can a trace of tears be found on any of their faces" (23.1). The text removes all doubts about whether this is a universal salvation when Hades lambastes Satan for allowing Christ to remove all the wicked (specifically the wicked) from his realm: "Why for no reason did you dare to crucify him unjustly and bring that innocent and righteous one to our region, and lose the guilty, impious, and unrighteous of the entire world" (*et totius mundi noxios, impios et iniustos perdidisti*; 23.1).

Following Hades' verbal barrage, Christ appears and delivers the entire human race—"Adam and his children"—speaking of them as "you my holy ones (*sancti mei omnes*), who have my image and likeness" (24.1). The "image and likeness," of course, refers to the creation of *humans* in Genesis 1:26, not just to saints. For this text, it is "all" the "children" of Adam (*omnibus filiis*), all who were affected by his sin. All of Adam's descendants have been "sanctified" and made "holy" by the salvific act of Christ. The "guilty, impious, and unrighteous" (*noxii, impii, et iniusti*)—all those condemned by sin—are now "my holy ones" (*sancti mei*). The tree of Christ's obedience (the cross) and the salvation it brings have conquered the tree of Adam's disobedience (the tree of the knowledge of good and evil) and the condemnation it effected—on all people. Christ proclaims: "You who had been condemned by the tree, the Devil, and Death, now see the Devil and Death condemned through the tree" (24.1). The devil is assigned to become the lone inhabitant of Hades, to be tormented forever, and death is no more. From this point in the account, the saved are "righteous"—and that is "all" the children of Adam, as Jesus himself indicates: "Peace be to all of you, my just ones" (24.1).

What is more, this universal salvation applies not only to those who had previously died and been delivered from Hades but also to those who are still alive at the time or have not yet been born. The saints whom Christ has delivered implore him: "Lord, place the sign of your victory through your cross in Hades, so that death may no longer have dominion" (24.1). The cross planted in Hades serves not merely as a reminder that Christ had once been there; it is the power that prevents anyone from entering that realm again, both an emblem of the victory and a protective shield to ensure that the conquest of hell will never be compromised. Salvation, as Izydorczyk and Gounelle stressed, is both universal and eternal.[45]

Christ ascends to heaven, taking with him the descendants of Adam, all of them now saints (*omnes sancti*; 24.2).[46] They are not saved because they became convinced by Jesus's preaching once he arrived in Hades, but because he is all-powerful and the forces opposed to God could not resist him. His power is stressed throughout the text, nowhere more emphatically than in Hades' opening words to Satan (Latin *potens* and derivatives emphasized here):

> Who is this one who is so *powerful* if he is a man fearing death? For all the *powerful* people on earth whom you have led (here) subject to your *power* are held, subjected to my *power*. If then you are *powerful*, what sort of man is that Jesus who opposes your *power* even though he is afraid of death? If he is so *powerful* in his humanity, truly I tell you that he is *all-powerful* in his divinity, and no one is able (= has the *power*) to resist his *power*. (20.2)

Christ harrows hell, in its entirety, because he has the will and sheer power to do so.

Latin B

The manuscripts of Latin B present a very different form of the text, not just in numerous differences of wording in shared passages but also in significant additions, omissions, and changes of narrative sequence.[47] Here we focus on just one kind of alteration—a radically different portrayal of the salvific effect of Christ's descent. Gounelle and Izydorczyk somewhat understate this difference by calling Latin B "more cautious" than its ancestor text. But it is not merely more cautious; it is contradictory, at least in its soteriological view. As they too acknowledge, here Christ explicitly does not harrow hell completely. Only the righteous are saved; the wicked are emphatically not.[48]

A few remnants of a (possible) universalist view do remain. When Hades speaks with Satan, in a much shorter back and forth than in Latin A, he expresses his fear that "all my prisons (*omnia vincula mea*) are about to be opened" and adjures Satan not to bring Christ into his realm, "lest when we wish to capture him, we are taken captive by him" (19.1). But we are not told what Christ would do with those emptied out of Hades once it is taken captive. So too, when Christ is later praised as "Savior of all" (25.1), it could simply mean "the Savior of all who are saved," as the text then indicates (25.2).

Reasons for doubting a universalistic message come at the very outset of the account. When the two sons of Simeon are first located—even before they begin writing their experiences—they announce that their return to life shows that the "gates of death and darkness have been destroyed" and that "the souls of the saints" (*animae sanctorum*) have been taken out and ascended with Christ to heaven (17.2). Thus, it is true that Hades was conquered, but only the saints went to a heavenly reward.

So too, in their description of the event, Seth recalls his encounter in life with the archangel Michael, when Michael assured him that it would be after the Son of God appeared in the world that his father Adam would receive the "oil of mercy," as would "all who believe in him" (*omnes credentes in eum*), and that "the kingdom of those who believe in him" would last forever (20.3). Salvation is for believers.

All residual doubt about the possibility of universal deliverance from punishment is erased in a short but conclusive addition to Latin B's description of the harrowing itself: "Then the Savior, after examining all people, lay hold of Hades, and immediately cast some into Tartarus and led some with him to the realms above" (*partem deiecit in tartarum, partem secum reduxit ad superos;* 9.2). Hades is indeed emptied out, but that is not good news for everyone. The wicked are removed, but not for salvation. They are sent off to the pits of hell for eternal torment (cf. Cyril of Alexandria, above).

Moreover, the vacancies created by this harrowing of Hades are soon to be filled. Here, as in Latin A, the saints ask that the cross of Jesus be set up as a "sign of victory" in the underworld, but it is not to assure the everlasting emptiness of the place. On the contrary, it is now there to prevent anyone from entering the infernal realm by mistake. The cross keeps the wicked servants of the place from retaining any of those the Lord had absolved of guilt (26.1). True offenders will continue to descend into its darkness.[49]

Greek M

When we come to the Greek version of the descent, we are in the fortunate situation of having a critical edition, thanks to the unflagging efforts of Rémi Gounelle.[50] Gounelle has identified three subgroups within the

Greek M (= medieval) tradition, and unlike the manuscripts of Greek A, each of them contains a version of the descent narrative—two of them (M1 and M2) very similar to one another and the latest (M3) significantly different. Among Gounelle's most important findings are that Greek M was a translation from Latin A, rather than from an earlier Greek original or Latin B.[51] Gounelle dates the Greek version to the end of the ninth or tenth century.[52]

Again there is no need here to provide a detailed analysis of all the variants. Our question is a narrow one. Did Christ harrow hell in toto or in part? Unlike Latin A and B, Greek M is notably ambiguous on the question, but in an intriguing way.[53] It appears to represent a compromise position made possible by a shift in the understanding of the purpose of Christ's descent. Here it is not to assert divine power but—as in other elements of the tradition—to engage in persuasive preaching. The big question is whether everyone is persuaded.

On one hand, as in Latin A, there seem to be clear indications of a universal salvation. We are told that all the dead are together in Hades, "everyone who had fallen asleep from the beginning" (1.2). There are not separate compartments for saints and sinners. As expected, the patriarchs and prophets receive the most attention, but in his discussion with Satan, Hades is afraid that he will lose "all (πάντες) those whom I devoured" from ages past, that Christ will come to raise everyone out of the darkness, and that "none of the dead will be left to me" (οὐδείς μοι τῶν νεκρῶν ἐναπολειφθήσεται; 20.3).

Moreover, that does appear to happen once Christ performs his task: "All the dead were freed from their bonds" (πάντες νεκροὶ ἐλύθησαν τῶν δεσμῶν) and "all the dark places of Hades were enlightened" (21.2–3). Afterward Hades complains to Satan that ultimate disaster has struck: "None of the dead is left in me (οὐδεὶς νεκρὸς ἐν ἐμοὶ κατελείφθη)" and "everything (πάντα ὅσα) you gained through the tree of knowledge you have lost—all of it (πάντα)—and all your joy has been transformed into grief" (23.1). The assessment of Hades is confirmed by the King of Glory himself. When he raises Adam, he turns to all the others and says, "Come with me, all (πάντες) you who died through the tree that this one touched; for see I am raising all (πάντας) of you through the tree of the cross" (24.1). He then "cast them all (ἀπάντας) out" of Hades (24.1).

Even though these statements seem unambiguous, an earlier passage calls the matter seriously into question. The passage is unique to this version and occurs at the very outset of the descent narrative, suggesting that it should set the interpretive frame for what follows. As soon as the great light appears in Hades to brighten the darkness in fulfillment of the prophecy of Isaiah (Isa 9:1–2), John the Baptist appears and launches into a long and unusually important speech. He begins by indicating that he had himself been the "last of the prophets" (18.3) and that he had proclaimed that Christ was the "lamb of God who takes away the sin of the world" and that he had witnessed God's confirmation of Christ's identity at his baptism. Now, once again, he is proclaiming the coming of the Son of God and, most important, declares he has come for the same reason: "So that whoever believes in him will be saved, but whoever does not believe in him will be condemned" (18.2; see John 3:18). This is the key passage for understanding the salvific effect of Christ's descent in this form of the narrative. According to the Baptist, those in Hades can be saved from punishment if and only if they repent, and this will be the last opportunity for them to do so. He goes on to say that the moment must be seized: "For this reason I say to all of you (Διὰ τοῦτο λέγω πρὸς ἅπαντας ὑμᾶς) . . . Now alone is the time for you to repent (ὅτι νῦν μόνον ἐστὶ πρὸς ὑμᾶς ὁ τῆς μετανοίας καιρός). . . . At another time this will not be possible" (ἐν ἄλλῳ δὲ καιρῷ τοῦτο γενέσθαι ἀδύνατον; 18.3). And so salvation is *available* to all, made possible only through Christ's ultimate power over the forces of Satan and Hades.[54] But—a very big but—it requires a human response. All *can* be saved, but only if they repent and believe.[55]

How then are we to reconcile these competing views within Greek M? Was everyone delivered, or only those who chose to repent? Possibly both are right: to be saved, everyone had to repent, and everyone did so. It would be easy to see why. Remaining in Hades would surely not be an attractive option. Moreover, in the narrative Christ has been revealed as the true God and shown idolaters and sinners that they had been seriously misled and mistaken. Who would choose to remain in error, darkness, and Hades forever? On the other hand, the history of Christianity is replete with perplexed believers musing over why sinners would spurn a free offer of salvation. The truth seems so obvious, error so invidious, and stubbornness so eternally inauspicious—who would possibly refuse to repent? And yet most do. Humans are difficult to explain.

True to the idea of a restrictive harrowing, the individuals who escape the confines of hell and "spring up" to heaven are identified as the saints. At the harrowing event itself, we are told that Adam, the prophets, and the saints thank Christ for it, and Christ responds by blessing Adam with the sign of the cross on his forehead and doing so also for the patriarchs.

He then takes *them* out of Hades, and these are followed by "the holy fa-thers." When they arrive in heaven, it is Adam and "all the righteous" who are greeted by Michael. Of course it may be possible that, as in Latin A, all these "saints" include sinners as well (all of them?), who were persuaded by Jesus's infernal preaching, recognized the error of their ways, repented, and so received postmortem sanctification. But if so, the text does not say. What is clear is that the unambiguous universal salvation through Christ's power endorsed by Latin A has been altered, but not to the degree of absolute denial, as in Latin B. This then is a mediating position, one that could be read in different ways. The compromise was achieved by mak-ing Christ's mission to Hades not a manifestation of raw power that can-not be resisted but a proclamation of the Gospel that provides sinners a final chance for salvation. They are not necessarily condemned forever. If they foolishly refuse to repent even in the darkness of Hades, they will be lost eternally.[56]

The Universal Harrowing of Hell

We have seen an intriguing range of early Christian texts that in one way or another make the strongest soteriological claim possible: in the end, all will be saved. Whether based on the incredible scope of Christ's salva-tion (Paul), mind-boggling divine mercy (*Apocalypse of Peter*), or irresistible divine sovereignty (Origen), all these universalist views in the end share an underlying theme: salvation ultimately derives from the unstoppable power of God. In the oldest form of the descent narrative found in the *Gospel of Nicodemus* (Latin A), this divine power becomes the single focus of attention. When Christ assaults and disables the powers aligned against God and humans, the devil, death, and Hades, they cannot lift a finger to stop him. This show of divine force does not presuppose, let alone re-quire, the prayers of the saints. It will not take ages and ages. And it does not demand human consent. This is all about God. He has a will and the full power to bring it to pass. No one can resist it, even those he chooses to save.

Later scribes and editors could not abide this message. For them, God is just and sinners must pay. And so universalism came to be written out of the text, and eternal punishment continued to thrive throughout the Christian tradition. For the majority of Christians in the world today, it remains a fearful reality. Hell has still not been emptied of its occupants.

Afterword

F EW LITERARY GENRES FACILITATE deeper reflection on the pro-
fundities of life than tours of the realms of the dead. It is no
accident that they lie at the heart of some of the great literature
of the Western tradition, literally central to both Homer's *Odyssey*
and Virgil's *Aeneid* and the entire framework of Dante's *Commedia*.

Despite their generative power, otherworldly journeys play a relatively minor role in the literature of antiquity, including the writings of
the early Christians. That certainly does not mean that followers of Jesus
did not take the afterlife seriously. On the contrary, unlike other religions
of Greek and Roman antiquity, the Christian movement placed an unusually high premium on heaven and hell, as seen in its theological debates,
polemics, evangelism, and moral instruction. No one can read the final
books of Augustine's *City of God* and fail to see how deadly seriously the
greatest theologian of Christian antiquity took afterlife realities. This level
of sincerity was not a new development: Augustine stood in a long and so-
ber line of Christian tradition that can be traced all the way back to Paul
and Jesus himself. For a broad swath of the early Christian movement, life
after death was to guide life here on earth, affecting beliefs, perspectives,
values, ethics, life choices, and daily action.

Nowhere is the reality of the afterlife and, correspondingly, the fate
of the soul expressed more emphatically and even enthusiastically than
in Christian narratives of tours to the realms of the dead. That should
at least raise the question of whether these accounts were thought of as
imaginative literature—what we today might call fiction—by either the

authors or their readers. However that matter is decided, Christian katabaseis were clearly never meant to be purely descriptive, providing factual
information for those curious about the life beyond. The narratives were
indeed instructive; but the instruction carried parenetic weight, showing
people not only what to think or "know" but also suggesting, often none
too subtly, what they should do about it. The same can be said of all the
accounts we have examined—Greek, Roman, and Jewish.

That remained the case after the early Christian centuries, and still is
so today. Obviously a rather intense interest in life after death continues
apace, all these centuries later, and discourse about the fate of the soul
continues to guide life in the body—or at least strives to. Belief in a literal
heaven and a literal hell still dominates not just the Christian tradition but
somewhat more unexpectedly the vast majority of the population of the
United States and most other countries that have adopted a traditional
form of the Christian faith.[1] These beliefs in the afterlife inspire genuine
hope and fear and, as a result, often guide action. Where I live, in the
southern United States, many, many people do not understand why one
would fight for justice and work to end poverty, racism, gender bias, xe-
nophobia, discrimination, bigotry, and intolerance of every kind if there
is not an afterlife. Many of my students tell me that personal ethics could
have no grounding apart from the hope for heaven and the fear of hell.
If there is no afterlife, why bother with morality at all? Why not simply
indulge every desire and whim and live completely oblivious to the needs
and desires of others? These students have inherited their views, of course,
from their families and environment.

Even so, this remnant of the Christian tradition is beginning to fade.
In particular, for some decades now, increasing numbers of people have
abandoned a belief in a literal hell, even within the conservative evangelical segment of our population.[2] Only to a lesser extent have they given up
on the belief in a literal heaven. Possibly, people are more inclined to jet-
tison fear than hope. In response to such shifts in religious belief we have
seen a conservative reaction, some of it driven by traditional religion but
some coming in secular forms that insist that there is life to come and we
should live in light of it. The TV series *The Good Place* was emblematic,
not avant-garde.

Over the past few decades this move to salvage the afterlife has mani-
fested in a modern form of katabasis, the literary near death experience
(using "literary" in a rather loose sense). Such experiences go way back in
the Western tradition, of course. We have seen examples in the Myth of

Er and twice in the *Acts of Thomas*. But our contemporary iterations come with a very modernist twist, packaged in post-Enlightenment wrapping, even among fundamentalists. The accounts are not meant to be read as "fiction," simply a "bunch of stories." They present themselves as "objective" descriptions of historical realities. They really happened. They can be proved. They constitute scientific evidence. They are "true" stories in the modern deracinated sense. If they didn't "really happen," they would be meaningless.[3]

It would be a mistake to read ancient otherworldly experiences this way. Of course, we have no way of knowing in some cases if they too were meant to be taken "literally." Certainly not Homer's *nekuia*, Plato's Myth of Er, and Lucian's *Downward Journey*. What about the Christian iterations? Surely the author of the *Apocalypse of Paul* did not think his narrative had really happened. (Surely?) But did he genuinely think that it closely approximated what the afterlife would entail? One might suppose so, but not only can this not be shown, it also cannot be shown to matter.

This is true of all ancient accounts of otherworldly journeys. Whatever else they are, they are literary productions, meant to entertain, provoke thought, inspire emotions, and—most important—affect the way life is lived. They are meant to inform and guide readers' views, commitments, priorities, values, beliefs, interactions, and—and everything else involved with being human. For now, we live. We may not know for certain what will come after death, but whatever we imagine it will entail should direct us along our path getting there. Ancient otherworldly journeys are meant to spur our imagination and guide the way.

Delving into the ancient Christian afterlife journeys means exploring this imagination in the minds, or at least the words, of others—other authors, editors, scribes, and even, before all that, oral storytellers. But these imaginations never come in or out of a vacuum. They come in relation to the world and lived experience. They come in relation to history and culture. They come in connection with other people, their thoughts, views, perspectives, commitments, priorities, beliefs, practices, and histories. And they come in relation to other products and productions of meaning, including the other stories we tell and hear, write and read, all of which can generate reflection and affect how we live as a result. The effect can be multiplied in proportion to the exempla. And so, the study of ancient katabasis is not simply a dry academic discipline—or at least it does not have to be. It can also be transformative. In part, that is what makes it an unusually ripe field for further harvesting, eager for more workers to pluck its fruit.

Notes

Introduction. The Well-Trodden Paths

1. With the exception of the *Apocalypse of Peter*, as we will see. But even there the scholarship is less than abundant.
2. Bouriant, "Fragments du texte grec"; for a discussion of the discovery and an analysis of the manuscript, see van Minnen, "Greek *Apocalypse*."
3. The fullest histories of early research are Bauckham, "Apocalypse of Peter: An Account," and Buchholz, *Your Eyes Will Be Opened*, pp. 82–118. See also Himmelfarb, *Tours of Hell*, pp. 41–45, and more recently Bremmer, "Apocalypse of Peter."
4. "Der· Ursprung dieser Phantasien ist nicht jüdisch, sondern griechisch-orphisch"; von Harnack, "Bruchstücker des Evangeliums," p. 954.
5. "Zur Lösung dieser Frage nach der Herkunft und den Quellen der Petrus-apokalypse"; Dieterich, *Nekyia*, p. 1.
6. Bauckham, "Apocalypse of Peter: An Account," and Buchholz, *Your Eyes Will Be Opened*. A brief resurgence of interest occurred with the publication in 1911 of a longer Ethiopic version of the *Apocalypse*, almost immediately recognized as preserving a "more original" form of the text than the Akhmim manuscript (see Chap. 4). This led to renewed questions of the editorial history of the book and in particular of the relationship between the *Apocalypse of Peter* and the *Gospel of Peter* presented in the same manuscript. If the Akhmim version was a later edition, had it been edited with an eye toward the *Gospel*? Again such matters were not much or long pursued, despite the discovery of two Greek fragments that shed light on the history of the textual tradition and introduced other interesting and important new issues.
7. Bauckham, "Apocalypse of Peter: An Account."
8. See also Bremmer, "Apocalypse of Peter."
9. See the brief remarks of Bremmer, "Apocalypse of Peter," pp. 1–6.
10. For one particularly insightful assessment of the broader intellectual history, in relation specifically to textual criticism, see Lin, *Erotic Life of Manuscripts*.

11.   I cite numerous instances throughout, but to give some sense of the approaches and ranges, consider the following: Bauckham, *Fate of the Dead*; Gounelle, "L'enfer selon l'Évangile de Nicodème"; Kraus, "Acherousia und Elysion"; Nicklas, "'Insider' und 'Outsider'"; Henning, *Educating Early Christians*; and Fiori, "Death and Judgment."

Chapter One. The Realities of Death and the Meaning of Life I: Journeys to Hades in Homer and Virgil

Translations of Greek and Latin sources are mine unless otherwise indicated.

1.   I do not delve into the various Homeric conundra here. My basic views on issues that matter to my analysis are these: I take the *Iliad* and *Odyssey* to be compositions of the eighth or seventh century BCE. I do not see them as entirely coherent either internally or in relation to one another, narratively or thematically. In particular, as I argue, a major thematic emphasis of the *Iliad* appears to be undermined by the dominant theme of the *Odyssey*. I am not invested, however, in arguing for separate authors for the two works: authors often develop their thoughts over time and write for a variety of purposes. I therefore continue to refer to a single author for both and am happy to call him Homer. I accept the view that he was dependent on a large number of otherwise unattainable oral traditions, many of which stood at odds with one another. This may have led to many of the famous inconsistencies of the two accounts. But I do not find it particularly helpful to fixate on these sources and/or their later Homeric redactions when seeking a "solution" to the problems posed by the surviving texts. At least for the purposes of my analysis I am content to deal with Book 11 as it has come down to us, as reconstructed in West, *Homerus*, which I use with only minor typographical differences. I will not be dealing with the "second *nekuia*" of Book 24.

2.   The literature on Book 11, of course, is extensive. The fullest discussion is Tsagarakis, *Studies in Odyssey 11*. Among commentaries focused on interpretation, see esp. Heubeck and Hoekstra, *Commentary on Homer's Odyssey*; Book 11 is by Heubeck. See also the older commentary of Stanford, *Homer*. For a nice overview of many of the issues and tensions in Book 11, see Sourvinou-Inwood, *"Reading" Greek Death*, ch. 2. A significant recent study that, unlike the present analysis, deals at length with questions of origins and sources and is particularly invested in reconciling all of the incoherencies of the text is Matijević, *Ursprung und Charakter*; the most important recent work is Gazis, *Homer and the Poetics of Hades*. This is a very smart account by a sensitive reader, attuned to nuance, who focuses on poetics to see how a narrative set on the other side of life, outside the realms of sight, beyond the gaze of gods and muses, allows Homer to violate rules of narrative and reverse judgments and values embraced in the world above. Much of Gazis's reading is persuasive, but in my judgment an exclusive focus on poetics can occlude the larger significance of Book 11 for the narrative as a whole. Much

of what Odysseus learns in Hades confirms, rather than reverses, the thematic emphasis of the epic. See further note 10.

3. For necromantic and katabatic traditions in tandem, see, as representative, R. Clark, *Catabasis*, pp. 54–55, 74, and, at fuller length, Tsagarakis, *Studies in Odyssey 11*, pp. 26–44. A number of earlier analytical studies proposed that on the macro level, the book combined a preexisting *nekuomantia* (as in the sacrificial rites) and a katabasis. For a brief description with important bibliography, see Heubeck and Hoekstra, *Commentary on Homer's Odyssey*, pp. 76–77, which provides the rather damning summation: "There have been many such attempts at analysis. . . . However, no sure results have emerged, nor can any be expected" (p. 77).

4. The account therefore, in the words of Johnston ("Delphi and the Dead," pp. 288–89), is "properly understood as another variation of the heroic *katabaseis* known from the stories of Heracles and of Theseus and Pirithoös." It is worth noting that Odysseus's ritual acts do not bring spirits to the upper world out of Hades: Circe herself indicates that he is to perform the sacrifice after he is already "in Hades" (εἰς Ἀίδεω; *Od.* 10.512–13). They come up from Erebus, apparently *part* of Hades (from farther below?).

5. S.v. νέκυια, Henry George Liddell, Robert Scott, and Henry Stuart Jones, *A Greek-English Lexicon*, 9th ed. with rev. supplement (Oxford: Clarendon, 1996).

6. These appear to be shades that have arrived in Hades prematurely, the "untimely dead." Death should come to those who have lived long and productive lives—literally productive, in having offspring to continue the family name and the clan. Most of these have died before their time (including the soldiers) and/or have not yet produced children, either because they were unmarried or their spouses died too soon. The only exceptions are the "long-suffering old men" (πολύτλητοί τε γέροντες; *Od.* 11.39), but no one knows who these are or why they are included with the others. It may well depend on what they had "endured" for so long. Johnston, *Restless Dead*, pp. 10–11.

7. Not least of which is that many of them also or entirely involve *anabasis* (a "going up").

8. Readers often object that Tiresias does not actually provide much helpful advice about how to return to Ithaca and point out that Circe later tells Odysseus everything he needs to know in Book 12. She could have saved him the trip. But in some respects, this is a misreading of the text. See note 20.

9. On the distinctive poetics of the book, see Gazis, *Homer and the Poetics of Hades*.

10. For a recent useful discussion of the incongruities in Homer in general, see O'Hara, *Inconsistency in Roman Epic*, pp. 8–18. For a full discussion of "sight in the dark" in Hades, see Gazis, *Homer and the Poetics of Hades*, who makes a considerable point of the complete invisibility of the realms—it is the basis of his examination of the poetics—but makes more of it than does

Homer himself, who is not at all inclined to reconcile the various physical impossibilities of his account. One of the more famous other examples of incongruity is the terror of shades in the face of both Odysseus's sword and Heracles' arrows even though the shades are immaterial and as a result cannot be physically touched (Odysseus's arms pass through thin air when he tries to hug the shadow of his mother). We will see this particular inconsistency again in *Aeneid* 6. Commentators intent on reconciling such passages have suggested creative solutions, for example, that metal (in the sword) had apotropaic powers (suggested, e.g., by Ogden, *Greek and Roman Necromancy*, p. 180). For a rather remarkable recent attempt to show that from beginning to end Homer's portrayal of the dead is fully coherent, see Matijević, *Ursprung und Charakter.* As he states in summary: "Schlussfolgerung ist, dass das vermittlete Bild von den Toten im Jenseits bei Homer durchaus einheitlich" ("The conclusion is that the portrayal of the dead in the afterlife conveyed in Homer is quite uniform," p. 154).

11. A characteristic statement of the extreme view is Heubeck and Hoekstra, *Commentary on Homer's Odyssey*, p. 76: "In fact Odysseus does not cross the threshold into Hades." A mediating view concedes that by the end of the narrative Odysseus has somehow come into Hades itself, since he observes the torment of the three famous sinners (*Od.* 11.576–600). See, e.g., Bauckham, *Fate of the Dead*, pp. 26–27. See further the following note.

12. The shades that appear in 11.36–41 do not come up from Hades but from Erebus; the text never indicates where that is, though it is obviously somewhere below Odysseus, possibly being one region within Hades (see Hesiod, *Theogony*). But Odysseus is repeatedly said to have been "in" Hades, to have gone "down to (or into) Hades," to be about to go "out of Hades," and so on (e.g., 11.22, 65, 69, 94, 164, 475–76). In addition to what we find in Book 11, it should be recalled that in preparation for his journey Circe twice instructs Odysseus go to (or into: εἰς) the house of Hades (10.491, 512). And toward the end of the epic when speaking to Penelope, he refers to his adventure as "when I went down into the house of Hades" (ὅτε δὴ κατέβην δόμον Ἀιδος εἴσω; 23.252). Possibly, readers who are inclined to think otherwise are persuaded by the fact that Hades is portrayed here as being not below the earth but at the end of it, reachable by boat. And there are, of course, incongruities—such as why he is said to go "down" into the place if there is no record of a descent and why Tiresias is said to have gone "into the house of Hades" (11.150) after he had been speaking with Odysseus precisely while he was "in Hades" (see 11.65, 69, 94, 164). See further the discussion of Matijević, *Ursprung und Charakter*, pp. 102–11.

13. It is often assumed that Elpenor is one of those who has risen from the pit. But if this is so it is not clear how he belongs among the groups, whether, for example, he is one of the "unmarried young men" or whether, instead, he represents a sixth group, the unburied. When he is called the "first" who came to Odysseus, it must mean he was the first shade (of any kind) Odys-

seus met, not the first from one of the five groups, since most of the others he encounters (e.g., the very next shade he sees, Anticleia) do not belong to the groups.

14. This stands in contrast with the second *nekuia* of Book 24, where shades do retain their memories of life.

15. Although it often is read this way. Thus, e.g., Heubeck and Hoekstra, *Commentary on Homer's Odyssey*, "Only on burial will his soul be able to enter Hades." As a rule, commentators are too quick to turn not only to the *Iliad* but also to the description of Palinurus in *Aeneid* 6 for interpretive leverage (whether explicitly cited or not).

16. Apart from eternal conscious torment, of course. On the other hand, possibly the text simply emphasizes the ubiquitous fear of death without proper burial in antiquity.

17. Thus 11.75–78; cf. 10.552–53: Elpenor was young, foolish, not brave, and a bit dim.

18. The sparsely attested ἴδεν ὀφθαλμοῖσιν is clearly the *lectio difficilior* and so preferable to the widely attested but completely unproblematic πίεν αἷμα κελαινόν (see Heubeck and Hoekstra, *Commentary on Homer's Odyssey*, pp. 100–101, and the bibliography cited there).

19. Homer himself intimates it is not Odysseus's most important or interesting encounter even by how he sets it in its narrative context: he brackets the scene with references to the appearance of Odysseus's mother, Anticleia. She arrives immediately in the wake of Elpenor but says nary a word; Odysseus feels deep compassion for her but keeps her away from the memory-inducing blood until he speaks with Tiresias. Only then does he have his pathos-filled reunion with her, a scene that, unlike the encounter with Tiresias, proves unusually significant for the thematic concerns of the book and, indeed, of the entire epic.

20. Still, it may be that interpreters who fault Tiresias for not giving more instructions are asking too much. Circe had said nothing about Tiresias providing a road map for Odysseus's return or navigation points: she simply instructed him to speak with the prophet to learn what was to happen. And Tiresias does tell him that. It is also not quite fair to claim that Circe gave him the exact same information later: in fact (why isn't this generally pointed out?), much of Tiresias's foreknowledge is about what will happen after Odysseus arrives home and slays the suitors who are devouring his earthly goods and wooing his wife. These are matters Circe never addresses. Moreover, Odysseus and the reader both are provided prophetic assurance about how it will all end well, at least for the hero. Oddly enough, much of the predicted happy ending is never narrated in the larger epic: Tiresias tells Odysseus what to do after the suitors have been disposed, and he predicts Odysseus will have a long and happy life, ending in a peaceful death. The epic, of course, finishes long before that, naturally leading the reader to speculate about why the prediction is in the text.

21. One way the narrative stresses the extraordinary character of Hades is through the repeated refrain "how did you get here?"—the first words to be spoken in most of the key encounters in the book: Odysseus asks it of Elpenor (11.57–58); Anticleia, of Odysseus (11.155–56); Odysseus, of Anticleia (11.170–73); Odysseus, of Agamemnon (11.397–98); and Achilles, of Odysseus (11.473–76). All these instances also involve grief and weeping. The dead are only to be pitied, a leitmotif of the account.

22. The option that she is simply softening the blow of reality does not comport well with the rest of the account. Among the dead, only Tiresias knows what is happening in the world above; shades in Hades have no access to news from the land of the living. Thus, for example, both Agamemnon and Achilles are eager to learn what has been happening to their sons since they died. That reality would also call into question another explanation for Anticleia's assurances to her son, that Homer is here being respectfully mindful of the timing of the katabasis: since it is narrated as a flashback, the account occurs seven years before he leaves Calypso to head home to Ithaca, and possibly Anticleia is reporting what was still the case at the moment of their encounter. If that were so, Tiresias's warnings would be predictions of what had not yet started (the wooing of Penelope, 11.115–17). But the solution does not work: three years after the Trojan War Telemachus would have been only fourteen years old; he scarcely would have been managing the estate and being wined and dined by others of his class. See Stanford, *Homer*, p. 388.

23. Thus Dova, *Greek Heroes*, p. 9: the encounter with Agamemnon "functions as a negative variation of the entire *Odyssey*, the model of a disastrous *nostos* that Odysseus, who leaves the scene with a clear benefit to his image, will manage to escape." At this stage of the narrative, of course, Odysseus does not know whether Penelope is faithful and devoted.

24. The event is not recounted by Homer, of course, but presumably it was part of the backstory. For later renditions, see Aeschylus, *Agamemnon*, and Euripides, *Iphiginia in Aulis*.

25. The one exception seems to be Achilles finding joy in the accomplishments and welfare of Neoptolemus (11.540), but it should be stressed that his reaction concerns the living, not the dead. There is nothing good down below; it is only prowess up above that matters. See below.

26. As Dova (*Greek Heroes*, p. 16) expresses it, this encounter is "the ultimate confrontation between the heroic ideals embodied by the two heroes." It is commonly argued that after death Achilles comes to embrace Odysseus's ideals of life, a view that I heartily support. Not all interpreters have seen it that way, however, most famously Schmiel, "Achilles in Hades," who argues that in Hades Achilles has not changed perspectives. I deal with his view below. See note 29.

27. The phrase ἐπάρουρος ἐὼν θητευέμεν ἄλλῳ is difficult; it may as well mean "to be working the land (above), serving another as a menial."

28. Schmiel, "Achilles in Hades."

29.   Schmiel ("Achilles in Hades") points out that the precise construction Achilles uses to describe his "preference" (βουλοίμην κ'/ἂν + infinitive + ἢ + infinitive) is used three other times in Homer (*Il.* 23.592–95; *Od.* 3.232–35, 16.106–7), and in each case it is a contrary-to-fact condition, so that Achilles' alleged reign in Hades is also "contrary-to-fact." It is an interesting argument and appears to have convinced other readers, but there is a problem with it. In each of these other passages, the speaker is setting out a hypothetical situation that might happen in the future (which does not actually happen) and indicates what the result would be if it did. It is true that both the protasis and the apodosis in these hypothetical predictions are contrary to fact. But the apodosis is necessarily so because the protasis is. In Achilles' statement, however, he is not arguing what he would prefer to happen *if* something else did. He is saying that he would prefer one potentially present state of affairs to another. And so, this time the statement is not contrary-to-fact. Achilles does not deny being the ruler of the dead or affirm it either. He simply ignores the comment.

30.   Reece, "Homer's Asphodel Meadow."

31.   For a fuller discussion, see Matijević, *Ursprung und Charakter*, pp. 137–42.

32.   So Johnston, *Restless Dead*, p. 13. She goes on to suggest they are exceptional in part because unlike the human shades, they had never died. There have long been debates about whether the passage of the three sinners, in fact all of lines 568–627, were "original" to the text. See, e.g., Stanford, *Homer*, p. 401, and Heubeck and Hoekstra, *Commentary on Homer's Odyssey*, p. 111.

33.   For example, special punishments for those who break their oaths (*Il.* 3.276–80).

34.   It's an odd exchange, but it certainly can be explained by its place in the narrative. Homer may be playing with his readers. Recall: this is the story Odysseus is telling to his Phaeacian hosts, presumably looking forward to their assistance. He concludes the episode with words by the demigod Heracles himself, who remarks on how similar the two of them are. On whether the passage is an interpolation, see Sourvinou-Inwood, *"Reading" Greek Death*, pp. 86–87.

35.   In Rohde's classic study *Psyche*, p. 4.

36.   In addition to the bibliography cited for specific points in the notes below, see esp. the fuller treatments of *Aeneid* 6 in the commentaries of Norden, *P. Vergilius Maro*, and Austin, *P. Vergili Maronis Aeneidos*, along with the recent bibliographically rich Horsfall, *Virgil*. For a broad treatment in monograph form, see R. Clark, *Catabasis*, esp. chs. 6–7. I use the text of Mynors, *P. Vergili Maronis Opera*.

37.   The normal assumption is that he composed in order to make a living and worked diligently at his craft to make an even better one, as Sarah Iles Johnston has commented to me in a private communication.

38.   Thus Horsfall, *Companion*. After a full examination of the evidence Horsfall asks whether Augustus instructed Virgil to write the account or discuss

the matter with him at all ahead of time, or whether his advisor Maecenas dropped some hints about the matter. His conclusion: "We have truly not the faintest idea" (pp. 18–19). My thanks to James O'Hara for this reference.

39. Clausen, "Interpretation of the *Aeneid*," p. 143; Parry, "Two Voices of Virgil's *Aeneid*" and note 85 below.

40. The other much noted, immediate influence is Cicero's *Somnium Scipionis*. In this case the similarities are more formal: a son meets his father in the heavenly realms and receives instruction about his role in affairs of state. Cicero uses the motif to very different ideological purposes, however, and so I do not consider the *Somnium* at length here. For discussion, see Feeney, "History and Revelation."

41. On the complicated question of why Plato would resort to myth in a work that condemns myths on the pens of poets (including Homer), see Edmonds, *Myths of the Underworld Journey*, pp. 159–220.

42. Stoic concepts are the more obvious: e.g., *spiritus intus*; *igneus vigor*; see the classic statement of Arnold, *Roman Stoicism*, p. 265. But the ironic Epicurean connections have also long been recognized; thus, Michels, "Lucretius and the Sixth Book of the *Aeneid*." Michels points out that despite the many conceptual and linguistic parallels to Lucretius, Virgil's vision of life in the world (the summum bonum) is emphatically different—the contrast between removing oneself from the world to live a life of quiet and subjugating the world through military and political involvement (see esp. *De rerum natura* 5.1129–30 and *Aen.* 6.851–53). And so: "Vergil has hoist the Epicureans with their own petard. He has used their own physics, the material and often the very words of their greatest exponent, to preach against the principle on which their secure and peaceful lives were founded, and he sends out his hero, following a dream, to labor for a future he will never see" (p. 148).

43. Thus Norden, "Vergilstudien."

44. Norwood, "Tripartite Eschatology," p. 16.

45. Originally with Cartault, *L'art de Virgile dans l'Enéide*, pp. 461, 475, 490. See also Norwood, "Tripartite Eschatology." For a particularly clear expression of this view, see Solmsen, "Greek Ideas of the Hereafter," and his later but more developed analysis, "World of the Dead."

46. O'Hara, *Inconsistency in Roman Epic*, ch. 4. O'Hara argues that a good deal of the inconsistency in the poem is deliberate: there are "clearly too many" of them "for all of them to be accidental, and they seem too thoroughly woven into the fabric of the poem" (p. 90). Moreover, many of them "help to make certain specific thematic points, and to create a more general sense of doubt or uncertainty about what is going on in the poem, and about what kind of world we are reading about" (p. 90). The uncertainty occurs on the most basic level: Will there in fact be a Roman *imperium sine fine* (1.279; p. 81)?

47. Here of course we find a major difference from Homer. Aeneas, like other mortal visitors to the underworld, is provided with a guide. Earlier, the

prophet Helenus had instructed him to visit the Sibyl once he landed on Italian shores to learn what was yet to come on his journey and to receive divine assistance for it, but he says nothing about going with the assistant into the underworld (3.441–62). Anchises' instruction provides the new element.

48. Again, cf. the sword of Odysseus and the arrows of Heracles in the *nekuia;* see above, "Final Encounters."

49. Probably the last. Among the flat-out discrepancies: Did a god cause his death as in Book 5 or not, as Palinurus explicitly states? Did it happen the day before Aeneas's descent as in Book 5, or three or four days earlier as in Palinurus's version? Was the sea calm at the time as in Book 5, or wild and stormy as Palinurus says?

50. R. Clark (*Catabasis*, p. 163, n. 43) rightly argues against Norden's view that these various kinds of untimely dead wait in limbo until the term of their full life would have ended (Norden, *P. Vergilius Maro*, pp. 11–13). Norden bases his argument in part on Lucian, *Cataplus* 5–6; Macrobius, *Somnium Scipionis* 1.13.10–11; and esp. Tertullian, *De anima* 56, but Tertullian, for example, indicates that souls are banished from the underworld during this period, whereas for Virgil they are clearly in it. Moreover, nothing in the text suggests that these souls will ever experience another fate from that which Aeneas observes.

51. Sisyphus is not named, though his punishment is mentioned in 6.16. It is widely thought that the text is corrupt at lines 601–2, with an accidental omission of an explicit reference to Tantalus.

52. This is national propaganda, of course, but it is interesting that the tradition of the "godly line" of Teucer goes far back into our sources; see the Homeric *Hymn to Aphrodite* II, 200ff., where the Trojan Race is "nearest to the gods."

53. Thus, O'Hara (*Inconsistency in Roman Epic*, p. 94) on the deliberate interweaving of inconsistent views: "[I]t is also possible, and arguably truer to the experience of reading Book 6, to see the poet as presenting a variety of incompatible beliefs, from different poetic, religious, and philosophical sources, and to admit that the views are incompatible." O'Hara, however, rejects the idea that the myth of Anchises should be seen as the ultimate point of the narrative and simply prefers to allow the inconsistencies to stand.

54. The term "innumerable" (*innumerae*) is especially significant, in light of what Anchises will say later, that only a "few" (*pauci*) are allowed to remain in Elysium without being reincarnated (6.744).

55. The descendants of Anchises are clearly only some of the multitude at the river Lethe, since it comprises "innumerable clans and people." At the same time, the Roman ancestors do number among the multitude, since Anchises has been eager to tell Aeneas about them (the multitude), but he in fact speaks only of their descendants (in the Parade of Heroes). One should not think that, according to this myth, the future greats of Rome come to life for the first time in their Roman incarnations; they have already been through the requisite purging from earlier lives.

56. For the problem of *tarda corpora* as detriments to the soul, see 6.731–32.

57. For older scholarship and expositions, see Austin, *P. Vergili Maronis Aeneidos*, pp. 220–32, and more recently Horsfall, *Virgil*, pp. 486–508. In a particularly insightful but rather overlooked contribution, R. Clark, "'Wheel' and Vergil's Eschatology," points out that R. D. Williams differs completely from Mynors on punctuation and therefore interpretation, with the remark that even though both scholars are highly eminent and influential, "The fact that their solutions of this notorious crux are so divergent as to be totally irreconcilable is therefore all the more disturbing. And the matter is crucial, for Vergil's eschatology is at stake" (p. 122). For a more succinct but characteristically insightful account, see R. Clark, *Catabasis*, pp. 177–83. Among the many other interpretations, two learned, insightful, but now-dated psychological readings provide important insights, but they differ significantly from what I advance here: Otis, "Three Problems of *Aeneid* 6," and Williams, "Sixth Book of the *Aeneid*."

58. Stoic ideas are strongly represented in lines 724–32. See note 42 above.

59. For the "wheel" as a reference to torture, see R. Clark, "'Wheel' and Vergil's Eschatology," pp. 130–31.

60. See the extended discussion of options and arguments in R. Clark, "'Wheel' and Vergil's Eschatology."

61. An exception: Heyne, *P. Virgilii Maronis Opera*, p. 958, as quoted in R. Clark, "'Wheel' and Vergil's Eschatology," p. 136, n. 9.

62. R. Clark, *Catabasis*, p. 178, n. 82, notes that the transposition appears in the *Editio Parmensis* of 1793 (correcting his earlier statement in "'Wheel' and Vergil's Eschatology" that it appeared in the *Editio Parmensis* of 1475). It also can be found in Fairclough, *Virgil* (Loeb edition revised by Goold), p. 584, based on the dubious claim that the transcriptional error arose through parablepsis occasioned by homoeoteleuton—*per amplum* 6.743/*per annos* 6.748. Surely this is a stretch. Even if the wording (lettering) were exact, the explanation would not work: for 743–44 to have been inadvertently skipped, the parablepsis would have had to be occasioned by the *igni* of 6.742. That is, if *amplum* did lead to the error, that line would have been copied in the correct place; it is the next line(s) that would have been skipped. Nor could *igni* have led to the parablepsis (because of the following *ignem*), since the copyist then would have left out five lines, not the two in question. This in turn shows why the suggested reinsertion based on *ignem* (6.742)/*igni* (6.747) also does not make any transcriptional sense.

63. The idea of "a sliding scale" of purgation goes all the way back to Servius, who, however, maintained that even the *pauci* were to be reincarnated. See the discussion of R. Clark, "'Wheel' and Vergil's Eschatology," pp. 123–24.

64. As opposed to Platonic *myth*. The model itself is not evident, however, in the Myth of Er, where a set amount of time is spent by souls either being rewarded or punished.

65. Even, to some extent, the demi-human Heracles—or at least his "image," while his true self is above with the gods (*Od.* 11.601–4).

66. Thus, among many, Zetzel, "Romane Memento," esp. p. 266.

67. Zetzel, "Romane Memento," p. 267.

68. See R. Clark, "'Wheel' and Vergil's Eschatology," and Zetzel, "Romane Memento," p. 267.

69. Feeney, "History and Revelation."

70. Feeney, "History and Revelation," pp. 2–3. In particular, Feeney's article draws a sharp contrast between Virgil's view in the *Aeneid* and Cicero's in *Somnium Scipionis*. See note 40 above.

71. Thus W. R. Johnson in a classic study, who notes that the description of Augustus in 6.791–807 is preceded by thirty-four lines and followed by thirty-eight (*Darkness Visible*, p. 108).

72. A particularly trenchant observation comes in W. R. Johnson, *Darkness Visible*. Anchises' denigration of Roman artistic abilities and nonmilitary accomplishments is a rare moment of Virgilian wit, as Virgil's entire career has been an attempt to vie with the Greeks, "an obsession throughout his career as poet" (p. 109).

73. Thus Feeney ("History and Revelation," p. 15): "Augustus' designated heir receives high praise, but waste and futility are the ruling tones."

74. See, e.g., Feeney ("History and Revelation," p. 1), who sums the matter up brilliantly in his opening statement: "Virgil's parade of heroes" is "a panegyric that becomes a threnody."

75. More subtly, as Feeney has pointed out, the towns constructed by the superb and vibrant "young men" in the early days had all lost any semblance of prestige in Virgil's own day, often in inglorious ways. Could Virgil be imagining the same could be true of Rome? Will it indeed be an *imperium sine fine* (1.279)?

76. Thus Feeney ("History and Revelation," p. 16): it is "bewildering to be promised an elaborate revelation which ultimately declares that there is in fact nothing more than the mixed uncertainties of history."

77. For an overview of suggestions up to the mid-twentieth century, along with important critique, see Otis, "Three Problems of *Aeneid* 6," pp. 173–76.

78. See the discussion in Austin, *P. Vergili Maronis Aeneidos*, pp. 275–76.

79. Norden (*P. Vergilius Maro*, p. 339): "Wenn Aeneas also durch das Tor der falschen Träume entlassen wird, so liegt darin nichts weiter als die Zeit bestimmung, 'vor Mitternacht'" ("So when Aeneas is released through the gate of false dreams, there is nothing more to it than an indication of the time: 'before midnight'"); Clausen, "Interpretation," p. 147.

80. Otis, "Three Problems of *Aeneid* 6," pp. 175–79.

81. See note 78 above.

82. R. J. Tarrant, "Aeneas and the Gates of Sleep."

83. Just as Penelope suspected that her dream was "false" in this sense: a hope that would not be realized.

84. Thus Zetzel ("Romane Memento," p. 282) takes it farther: "Virgil is neither a panegyrist nor a philosopher, he is, as Clausen saw, 'his country's truest historian'" (quoting Clausen, "An Interpretation," p. 146).

85. Recognized with particular clarity by Parry ("Two Voices of Virgil's *Aeneid*," p. 76) starting with the stark contrast between the *Aeneid* and the *Odyssey:* "Everything in the *Odyssey* prepares us for a fuller end to Odysseus' labors: we are made always to expect his reinstatement in kingship, home, honor and happiness. In the *Aeneid* every prophecy and every episode prepares us for the contrary: Aeneas' end, it is suggested, will see him as far from his fulfillment as his beginning. This other Italy will never cease receding into the distance." Thus: "The *Aeneid*, the supposed panegyric of Augustus and great propaganda-piece of the new regime, has turned into something quite different. The processes of history are presented as inevitable, as indeed, they are, but the value of what they achieve is cast into doubt." It is true: *Imperium sine fine dedi* (1.279), but Virgil "insists equally on the terrible price one must pay for this glory" (p. 78). Among others, see also Zetzel, "Romane Memento," pp. 282–84.

86. W. R. Johnson, *Darkness Visible*, p. 110.

Chapter Two. The Realities of Death and the Meaning of Life II: Jewish and Christian Journeys

1. Himmelfarb, *Tours of Hell*, p. 2 and passim.

2. The book comprises five major compositions by five different authors, later combined into the fuller ensemble we now have. For analysis of the "Book of the Watchers," see esp. the commentary of Nickelsburg, *1 Enoch 1*. The fullest analysis of the key passage comes in Wacker, *Weltordnung und Gericht*. For a brief discussion, see also Knibb and Ullendorff, *Ethiopic Book of Enoch*.

3. On the complication of whether the journeys of Enoch are katabaseis, see note 12. For the Jewish tradition of otherworldly journeys generally, see esp. the two books of Himmelfarb, *Tours of Hell* and *Ascent to Heaven*, as well as Bauckham, "Early Jewish Visions of Hell," and "Visiting the Places of the Dead in the Extra-Canonical Apocalypses," in Bauckham, *Fate of the Dead*, pp. 48–96.

4. Presumably, the compiler of the codex saw the utility of including two accounts of an underworld journey in a book (to be?) buried in a Christian tomb; the codex includes as well a fragmentary copy of the *Gospel of Peter*, not simply because it, like the *Apocalypse*, is attributed to Jesus's closest disciple, but more likely because this version of the *Apocalypse* was actually *part* of the *Gospel of Peter*, as we will see in Chap. 4.

5. For a fuller introduction, see Nickelsburg, *1 Enoch 1*, "Introduction," esp. pp. 7–20.

6. Throughout, I use the translation of Nickelsburg, also available in Nickelsburg and VanderKam, *1 Enoch*.

7. The Genesis passage is much disputed, especially with respect to whether the Nephilim are the sons of God or their offspring. See the standard commentaries. For a concise treatment, see Nickelsburg, *1 Enoch 1*, pp. 184–85.

8. The phrase "until the consummation of their generations" does not indicate a length of time for the punishment; it means that the punishment will apply until the entire generation is consumed by it.

9. Nickelsburg (*1 Enoch 1*, p. 225) expresses doubt about the interpretation that "both watchers and people will have the same place of punishment," in part because of later statements of *1 En.* 21.7–10, 27.2–3, 90.24–27, and 103.7–8. I count the final two references as of no relevance: they come from different sections of the book by different authors. The other tensions are real but not unexpected, given the inconsistent nature of afterlife traditions in general. Nickelsburg's subsidiary point that the view is found in "only such late texts as Matt 25:41 and Rev 20:10, 15" (p. 225) also seems irrelevant; in comparison with the "Book of the Watchers," all the Jewish and Christian portrayals of the place or places of punishment are "late" (two and a half centuries removed), and even so, their relative date does not have any direct bearing on whether this passage means what it says.

10. For composition theories generally, see Wacker, *Weltordnung und Gericht*; for the sequence of composition of the journeys, see below. Nickelsburg (*1 Enoch 1*, p. 290) depends on Wacker's reconstruction and provides some additional evidence.

11. This reading depends on a transposition of 19.1–2 between 18.11 and 12, urged by Dillmann, *Buch Henoch übersetzt und erkärt*, p. 118, followed by Nickelsburg, *1 Enoch 1*, p. 287, with strong arguments. The text also indicates, in a rather surprising statement, that the women the watchers seduced were turned into "sirens." See comments in Nickelsburg, *1 Enoch 1*, p. 288.

12. For an attempt to unpack this second journey, see Sock-Hesketh, "Circles and Mirrors." The account sometimes portrays the second journey as an *anabasis* (particularly appropriate for the biblical Enoch, of course), since at first he is taken into the realms above (see 14.8, 18, 20), even though the geographical descriptions within the journey suggest that, as in Homer's *nekuia*, Enoch is traversing earthly realms beyond human habitation. At one point, for example, he sees a mountain that reaches "to heaven" (17.2). But there are some confusions: while in that place he sees the treasure house of the stars and other heavenly luminaries, the river of fire that flows "down" into the sea, the pillars of heaven above the earth, and the paths of angels. Moreover, the ultimate destination of the saints is above (ch. 25). In any event, whether Enoch's journey is above, below, or in the remote reaches of the earth does not affect my analysis. See Bauckham, *Fate of the Dead*, p. 84.

13. Among the most noted perplexities: 22.1 implies one angel, but 22.3 mentions Raphael, who is identified as one of several. Seven angels are named in ch. 20, but it is not clear whether they are all with Enoch at every point; altogether, only four are mentioned by name during the tour.

14. The passage is riddled with textual problems, most famously "hollow" places. This is the reading of the Akhmim text, κοιλοί, but the Ethiopic reads "beautiful" places, obviously a translation of καλοί. Which is the corruption? E. Isaac ("1 [Ethiopic Apocalypse of] Enoch") prefers the latter; but in the context surely the former makes better sense as a place of confinement, especially since three of the four places are anything but beautiful. Thus Nickelsburg and many others.

15. There follow a rather confusing three verses, fitting uncomfortably in the narrative, about the spirit of Abel "that makes suit" against Cain "until his seed perished from the face of the earth." Apparently, the righteous pray that the sinners will be destroyed, an obvious allusion to Gen 4:10 (God speaking to Cain: "Listen; your brother's blood is crying out to me from the ground!"). The prayer will be answered in Genesis with the flood and in this narrative with the coming Day of Judgment.

16. Wacker, *Weltordnung und Gericht*, pp. 35–131, esp. 122–31, largely followed by Nickelsburg, *1 Enoch 1*.

17. For a brief but incisive explanation of the passage, see Stuckenbruck, "'Otherworld' and the *Epistle of Enoch*," pp. 82–85.

18. Or is Raphael indicating that while these souls reside in the pit "here," they are not tormented at all, apart from being in a dark and arid place and, presumably, in serious dread; instead, are they simply waiting for a future judgment, when they will be bound forever—as well as scourged and tortured? The interpretation I've given in the text seems more plausible since the contrast is between "here" (scourging and torture) and "there" (eternal binding). In any event, that is how the sentence is understood by both Wacker (*Weltordnung und Gericht*, pp. 68–69) and Nickelsburg (*1 Enoch 1*, pp. 300–307).

19. See Wacker, *Weltordnung und Gericht*, pp. 179–92.

20. Stuckenbruck, "'Otherworld' and the *Epistle of Enoch*," p. 85.

21. See Wacker, *Weltordnung und Gericht*, pp. 193–95.

22. As Tobias Nicklas has pointed out to me, the account appears to be rooted in a theology of God as creator of the world, not simply as the God of Israel or of "Jews."

23. Elsewhere the narrative claims that the righteous will live forever (27.3)— yet one more inconsistency.

24. Presumably it refers only to the souls of Pit 2 and those of Pit 3 who receive condemnation. But now the issue does involve a proper relationship to God himself, a matter not mentioned earlier.

25. All quotations of the Hebrew Bible come from the New Revised Standard Version. All translations of the New Testament and other Christian texts are mine unless otherwise indicated.

26. Thus, pithily, Nickelsburg (*1 Enoch 1*, p. 322): "The raison d'être for this section of the journey is more difficult to determine."

27. For the idea that Sheol is simply the "grave" rather than a Jewish form of Hades (i.e., a gathering place for deceased souls), see my discussion in Ehrman, *Heaven and Hell*, pp. 83–88.

28. This amalgam gives the lie to older claims that "the Jewish" view was always resurrection and "the Greek," in contrast, always immortality. See the classic statement of Cullmann, *Immortality of the Soul?* There is, of course, some truth to Cullmann's generalized dichotomy, but it cannot be pressed—as *1 En.* 22 itself so elegantly demonstrates (note the "spirits" in the pits).

29. The most important study is Diebner, *Zephanjas Apokalypsen;* see also Denis "L'Apocalypse de Sophonie"; Wintermute, "Apocalypse of Zephaniah" (with important notes); and, briefly, Witakowsky, "Apocalypse of Zephaniah." Most recently, see Sommer, "Between Jewish and Egyptian Thinking." The standard critical text remains Steindorff, *Apokalypse des Elias.* I use Wintermute's translation, but it is helpful to consult Diebner's as well.

30. Himmelfarb (*Tours of Hell*, pp. 13, 15–16) acknowledges that since the manuscripts preserving the text are Coptic, they were produced by and for Christians; she thinks, however, that the original composition was probably "a relatively early Jewish work."

31. For an account of the complicated textual problems, see Denis, "L'Apocalypse de Sophonie," pp. 796–98, and esp. Diebner, *Zephanjas Apokalypsen*, pp. 1143–51.

32. See the balanced discussion of Diebner, *Zephanjas Apokalypsen*, pp. 1171–84, and note 35.

33. Cf. the Akhmimic fragment at 4.4: avenging angels with tusks and long hair, and fiery scourges, responsible for sending sinners to eternal punishment (and see *Apoc. Paul* 11).

34. This certainly appears to be a Satan figure (from the book of Job), and Bauckham (*Fate of the Dead*, p. 91) has no qualms about naming him that. The text, however, does not do so.

35. Another early indication that the text may be Christian, or at least influenced by Christian tradition, comes at the outset of the Akhmim fragment, where the seer observes "two men walking together on one road" and "two women grinding together at a mill" and "two upon one bed" (2.2–4). The parallels with Matt 24:40–41 and Luke 17:34–35 are often noted and almost always just as often dismissed (e.g., Wintermute, "Apocalypse of Zephaniah," pp. 509–10). Most interpreters seem bound and determined to understand the text as "Jewish," with nothing "Christian" about it. See further the discussion of "catechumens" below.

36. See Wintermute, "Apocalypse of Zephaniah," p. 512, n. 5c, and Diebner, *Zephanjas Apokalypsen*, p. 1213.

37. Sins and good deeds literally weighed at death is a leitmotif of the *Testament of Abraham.* Saints becoming angels is later attested, for example, for Enoch (*2 En.* 22.1–10) and for the Christian martyrs (*Mart. Pol.* 2.3).

38. Diebner, *Zephanjas Apokalypsen*, p. 1225.

39. For "catechumens" the text uses the Greek term, κατηχόυμενος.

40. See Josephus, *Life* 6.366; Philo, *Embassy* 198 (Wintermute, "Apocalypse of Zephaniah," p. 515, n. b). Wintermute further argues that Christian texts use the verb only for proselytes, whereas this text says nothing about them being converts. I find the comment perplexing, since the text also does not say they were not converts. On the contrary, since these are people who were expected to come to perfection through instruction, it seems safest to assume they were indeed converts who had not been transformed as expected.

41. "And so we should repent from our whole heart, lest any of us perish. For since we have his commandment and drag people from idols, giving them instruction (ἀπὸ τῶν εἰδώλων ἀποσπᾶν καὶ κατηχεῖν), how much more must we keep a person from destruction when he has already come to know God" (2 *Clem.* 17.1). And so the Christian "catechesis" comes upon conversion and is expected to lead to reformed behavior.

42. But see also note 35.

43. Diebner (*Zephanjas Apokalypsen*, p. 1226) takes a good stab at the issues by trying to make sense of the "pre-Christian" views of hair in the Hebrew Bible and Second Temple texts such as 2 Maccabees, arguing that absence of hair represents holiness, as in cleansing rituals that involve shaving the head (e.g., Lev 14:8–9, Num 8:7, Deut 12:12), with the implication, then, that those suffering with all their hair in place are not in a state of holiness. It is an intriguing but not a completely convincing interpretation: nothing else about these sinners connects them with purification rituals, or lack of them, as opposed to the other groups who are involved with moral failings.

44. Neither Wintermute nor Diebner comments on it. I once gave a public talk on katabasis and mentioned a similar passage in the *Apocalypse of Peter* where "bankers" who take interest are doomed to stand forever in excrement up to their knees. A fellow on the back row commented that it sounded like a day at the office.

45. It bears repeating that nothing in these two Jewish texts suggests that members of the covenantal community have any advantage in eschatological destinations.

46. Niebuhr, *Nature and Destiny of Man*, p. 294.

47. There is, of course, a relatively large scholarship. For a full survey up to the mid-1980s, see the important contribution of Bauckham, "Apocalypse of Peter: An Account." Among the most important works are two wide-ranging collections of essays: Bauckham, *Fate of the Dead*, and Bremmer and Czachesz, *Apocalypse of Peter*. Equally significant are the introductory discussions in the following editions of the Ethiopic and Greek texts: Buchholz, *Your Eyes Will Be Opened*; Marrassini, "L'apocalisse di Pietro"; and Kraus and Nicklas, *Petrusevangelium und die Petrusapokalypse*. The most recent study is Beck, *Justice and Mercy in the Apocalypse of Peter*. I gained access to Beck's interesting study only after I had written this chapter, so I am unable to give a sustained assessment of it; but for an evaluation of the main thesis, see note 80.

48. The "Book of the Watchers" does view the future homes of the saved and the damned, which are empty of inhabitants in this interim period.

49. As Augustine complained with respect to the later author of the *Apocalypse of Paul* who broke the silence to describe at some length Paul's observations of the deceased and their rewards and punishments. See Augustine, *Tractates on the Gospel of John* 98.8 (Corpus Christianorum: Series Latina 36,581).

50. See Hauge, *Biblical Tour of Hell,* and Lehtipuu, *Afterlife Imagery.*

51. The author of Revelation does, of course, describe the heavenly Jerusalem as the future dwelling place of the saints. The place is empty, however, until after the millennium; it is not a place of current ecstatic enjoyment. So too its antithesis: the lake of fire. But is the lake of fire the eternal place of residence for sinners? That may, in fact, be a misreading. See my discussion of Rev 14:10–11, 20:11–15 in Ehrman, *Heaven and Hell,* pp. 223–28.

52. Bauckham, *Fate of the Dead,* pp. 176–94; the argument was already developed by Buchholz, *Your Eyes Will Be Opened,* pp. 408–12, and was proposed as far back as Weinel, "Offenbarung des Petrus."

53. For Bauckham the decisive passage comes in the parable of the fig tree in ch. 2 of the *Apocalypse,* where Christ predicts the appearance of a "false Christ" who is rejected by others—presumably believers in the true Christ—whom he then executes as martyrs. Bauckham ties the account to the report about Bar Kokhba in Justin, *1 Apol.* 31, and thus establishes a plausible *Sitz im Leben.* See Bauckham, "*Apocalypse of Peter:* Jewish Christian Apocalypse"; reprinted in Bauckham, *Fate of the Dead,* pp. 160–258. There are major difficulties with the view. For one thing, Justin does not indicate that Christians were martyred under Bar Kokhba, only that he tortured them; more important, he never indicates that these were Christians who refused to acknowledge he was the messiah. In fact, the Justin passage does not discuss the messianic claims of Bar Kokhba or any of his alleged miracles; it certainly says no word about anyone refusing to acknowledge his miracle-working messiahship. For detailed argumentation, see Kraus ("Griechische Petrus-Apokalypse," p. 94) who in conclusion argues: "weder dieses Gleichnis [ch. 2] noch die Vision am End [chs. 15–17] müssen exklusiv au seiner solchen jüdisch-christlichen Perspektive zu lessen sein, die genau diese Verfolgungssituation zugrunde legt. An Märtyrern und falschen Messiassen mangelte es in der damaligen Welt keinesfalls" ("Neither this parable [ch. 2] nor the vision at the end [chs. 15–17] has to be read exclusively from this Judeo-Christian perspective, based precisely on this situation of persecution. There was certainly no shortage of martyrs and false messiahs in the world at the time"). See also Tigchelaar, "Is the Liar Bar Kokhba?" More recently, see esp. the strong arguments in Nicklas, "'Insider' und 'Outsider.'"

54. For excellent surveys of the patristic evidence, see Buchholz, *Your Eyes Will Be Opened,* pp. 20–81, and esp. Kraus and Nicklas, *Petrusevangelium und die Petrusapokalypse,* pp. 87–99.

55. A superb account of the discovery and codicology is in van Minnen, "Greek *Apocalypse*." For the dating of the Akhmim manuscript, see Kraus and Nicklas, *Petrusevangelium und die Petrusapokalypse*, p. 29.

56. Grébaut, "Littérature éthiopienne"; M. R. James, "New Text."

57. See both the classic analysis of M. R. James, "Rainer Fragment," and the more recent authoritative account of Kraus, "*P.Vindob.G.*" I discuss the matter further in Chaps. 4 and 5.

58. Arguments already in M. R. James, "New Text"; see the summary of the case in Bauckham, *Fate of the Dead*, pp. 163–64. The Ethiopic version is now known in two manuscripts; see Buchholz, *Your Eyes Will Be Opened*, pp. 119–39.

59. Schneemelcher, *New Testament Apocrypha*, pp. 625–35; Elliott, *Apocryphal New Testament*, pp. 600–612.

60. For more extensive interpretation, done thematically, see Bauckham, *Fate of the Dead*, pp. 194–236.

61. For the Ethiopic version I use the literal translation of Buchholz, *Your Eyes Will Be Opened*.

62. In the readers' lifetime? See notes 52 and 53. Since the book will conclude with a rewriting of the Synoptic transfiguration scene (Mark 9:1–9), a first reading might suggest the entire narrative is thus presented as a conversation held during Jesus's ministry. But as Bauckham in particular has emphasized, the closing scene, though modeled on the transfiguration, is actually an ascension. It is better, then, to see the account as a postresurrection appearance of Jesus, instructing his disciples about the "final things" just before returning to his heavenly home (Bauckham, *Fate of the Dead*, pp. 165, 242–44). See further Chap. 4 (on the editing out of this feature in the Akhmim version).

63. See the previous note.

64. Many of the details, of course, differ in the Akhmim fragment; see Chap. 4.

65. Is denying righteousness a verbal expression of disbelief? An explicit rejection of God's demands? Of Christian claims? Is it manifest in action? An action against Christians or just a refusal to behave in a righteous manner? If the latter, why aren't all sinners in this pit?

66. The translation of the passage found in Elliott is especially confused, as Buchholz has emphatically shown (*Your Eyes Will Be Opened*, pp. 213, 328–29). Contra Elliott, these are not those who have "cut their flesh as apostles of a man"—which might make a reader think of religiously inspired castration, performed by some Christians, most famously, allegedly, Origen (reported by Eusebius but not sustained by anything Origen says in his vast corpus). This is just a mistranslation. The passage is referring to men who "make themselves women" (though Buchholz translates it as "they who cut their flesh, sodomites," p. 215). On the specific connection between idolatry and homosexual activity, see Rom 1:24–27.

67. As might be expected from such a text, the males who have sex with them are not singled out for punishment.

68. Fiensy ("Lex Talionis," p. 257) recognizes that there is not *always* a logical connection between sin and punishment, but he concludes by claiming, "Nevertheless most of the punishments do correspond logically to a particular vice." That is an overstatement. It is true that a number of them correspond, but enthusiastic interpreters have been overtaken by the obvious examples, e.g., the wretched souls hanged for eternity by their tongues, hair, or genitals. See Bauckham, *Fate of the Dead*, pp. 215–21. Among more recent studies, see Grünstäudl, "Enthüllung im Fragment," and Sommer, "Von Monstern und Männern."

69. See the previous note and Callon, "Sorcery, Wheels, and Mirror Punishment," who makes a good argument for the fiery wheels reserved for sorcerers but too readily concedes the principle of talion for every other instance.

70. The word *didymus* means twin and is also used in reference to the male "twins": the testicles. Quoted by Czachesz in his terrific little article "The Grotesque Body in the *Apocalypse of Peter*." See also Lucian, *True History* 2.26 and 2.31, and in later Jewish texts, as noted by Himmelfarb, *Tours of Hell*, pp. 85–86 (Soṭah 1.7; Sifre Numbers 18: "The limb which began the transgression, from it will begin the punishment").

71. Bauckham, *Fate of the Dead*, pp. 215–21.

72. Lieberman, "On Sins and Their Punishments," p. 48: "Some of the cruel punishments used by the Roman authorities were inserted into Gehenna from real practice, and the authors were only speaking of the ordinary custom. . . . It is only just that the wicked who dishonored heaven should not be punished less than those who dishonored a king of flesh and blood. One is, therefore, driven to conclude that our sages did not refrain from learning from the conditions below concerning what was above."

73. For a broad and detailed analysis of the phenomenon, see Kraus, "Fürbitte für die Toten."

74. In trying to explain the about face from Peter's own pleas for mercy in *Apocalypse of Peter* 3, Bauckham (*Fate of the Dead*, p. 234) maintains that God cannot answer the apostle's earlier pleas because torments in hell are inflicted for sins against other *people*, rather than against his almighty self. Therefore, it would not be up to God to forgive these sinners; mercy has to come from those who are wronged. The petitions of the saints, in ch. 14, on the other hand, are for those who are being punished for harming the followers of Christ. This interpretation is clever but not viable. Some of the sins in chs. 3–13 are indeed against God, not humans (e.g., slander of God's righteousness and idolatry). Even more important, surely Christian saints were not the only victims of the sinners' moral transgressions (e.g., adultery, usury, infanticide). So even on Bauckham's reasoning, the prayers of ch. 14 that save *everyone* should not work.

75. Even though, strikingly, for the *Apocalypse of Peter*, the final judgment of God comes to be reversed in the most extreme divine change-of-mind in cosmic history. But this is not because sinners have an opportunity to reform; it is

instead a divine response to the prayers of the saints, making sinners the beneficiaries of incredibly unmerited favor.

76. One thinks of other proto-orthodox writings of the period: the *Epistle of Barnabas* and its claim that Jews always followed a false religion and did not understand their own Scriptures; Justin's *Dialogue with Trypho*, which tries to prove it; and eventually Melito of Sardis's *Passover Homily*, which, for the first time, charges Jews with deicide.

77. Later see Origen, *De oratione* 12, and later still, Cyril of Alexandria, *Commentary on Isaiah* 29.13 (PG 70.656).

78. Are the "doubters" also members of the community who are no longer certain of their faith?

79. One might think that since he reserves some punishments for those who worship idols, the remaining categories are for other transgressions instead— which would make them Christians or Jews. On the other hand, surely most kinds of sinners engaged in more than one kind of transgression—those who refused to honor their parents, for example, presumably did other hideous things as well.

80. That the parenetic point of the text is to avoid sin does not seem obvious to Eric J. Beck, who has produced the most recent full study, *Justice and Mercy in the Apocalypse of Peter*. Beck has an interesting counterthesis—that the main purpose of the account is "to encourage the righteous to show compassion to the wicked" (p. 18). I find the view attractive, but not compelling. The overwhelming focus of the book is sin and the horrible price sinners will have to pay for it—a theme that appears page after page, chapter after chapter. The compassion of the righteous does appear, of course, and it is important—but it is scarcely emphasized, let alone central. It first appears in ch. 3, when the apostles, the angels, and even Christ weep. But for what is Christ weeping? When Peter asks whether it would have been better for sinners not to have been born than to suffer such torment, Christ reproves him for opposing the justice of God. God did show mercy on them by bringing them into the world in the first place, but they disobeyed him, and so they are getting what they deserve. Peter, Jesus states, is simply demonstrating a human weakness, being "sad" over what he is seeing. God and Christ are above that. And so, is Jesus weeping because he feels compassion for these people in such incredible pain? Or rather, is he sad because God's own creatures chose to disobey him? In either event, he thinks the punishment is fully deserved and goes on to explain why. He provides no encouragement for saints to seek mercy— just the opposite. Moreover, at the end, when he shows mercy to the sinners by removing them from their torment, there is no word of his compassion. The righteous in heaven, of course, are compassionate, just as they were earlier. But nothing indicates that Christ has suddenly become compassionate for sinners. He provides mercy because he loves the saints and decides to grant their prayer. So is the text as a whole encouraging compassion? It is possible, but if so, it is portraying it as an ungodly condition. God is a God

of justice, and he reverses his judgment only to appease others, not because it is in his nature to do so. For Christ, compassion is a human weakness, not an admirable quality. I do not want to underplay the significance of Christ's incredible show of mercy in ch. 14; I later devote a chapter to it (see Chap. 5). But I do not think it undercuts the message of the rest of the book. Sin is horrible and will be punished, even if in the end God shows mercy.

81. The first relatively full modern analysis is Casey, "Apocalypse of Paul"; the most thorough treatment is Carozzi, *Eschatologie et au-delà.* For more recent evaluations, see the collected essays in Bremmer and Czachesz, *Visio Pauli.*

82. For a discussion of the manuscript history, see Piovanelli, "Origines." Our best witness is the Long Latin text, for which, see Silverstein and Hilhorst, *Apocalypse of Paul.* I base my translations and comments on that tradition, as found in the Paris manuscript (the other "long" manuscripts lack chs. 45–51). For editions of Latin, Old Czech, and German manuscripts, see Jirouskova, *Visio Pauli.* For a work like this, it is important, for a fuller analysis, not only to establish an "original text," or at least the "oldest available form of the text," but also to see its malleability as it came to be changed according to social, historical, and religious circumstances.

83. The discovery narrative, of course, serves to explain why no one had ever seen the book or referred to it for three centuries: Paul hid it. See my discussion in Ehrman, *Forgery and Counterforgery,* pp. 123–26. For comparanda, see Piovanelli, "Miraculous Discovery."

84. Early on, Tischendorf endorsed a late-fourth-century date; the classic statement is in Casey, "Apocalypse of Paul." See the full discussion of the debate in Piovanelli, "Origines," pp. 45–59. The later dating to ca. 412 was most seriously advanced by Silverstein, "Date of the *Apocalypse of Paul,*" and briefly restated in Silverstein and Hilhorst, *Apocalypse of Paul,* p. 11, and esp. pp. 18–19, n. 3. Piovanelli provides a sustained critique ("Origines," pp. 51–53).

85. Casey, "Apocalypse of Paul." Doubts are expressed, e.g., in Piovanelli, "Origines," pp. 45–59, and Roukema, "Paul's Rapture," pp. 279–80.

86. Augustine, *Tractates on the Gospel of John* 98.8 (Corpus Christianorum: Series Latina 36,581). On the vexed question of dating the tractates, see Rettig, *Augustine,* pp. 23–31.

87. Thus Piovanelli ("Origines," p. 32), "l'une des sources, sinon la source principal," and Carozzi, *Eschatologie et au-delà,* p. 47, with detailed comparisons on pp. 107–10. For a convincing analysis, see Kraus, "Griechische Petrus-Apokalypse," who concludes, "Diese Indizien zusammengenommen mögen durchaus auf eine literarische Abhängigkeit schliessen lassen" ("Taken together, these clues may suggest a literary dependence," p. 93). The point has been disputed in some studies. Himmelfarb (*Tours of Hell*), for example, while agreeing that the author of the later apocalypse "knew the *Apocalypse of Peter* or a close relative" (p. 140) denies there is sufficient evidence of direct literary dependence (pp. 6–8, 142–44). See also the doubts of Bauckham,

"Apocalypse of Peter: An Account," p. 471, partly in dependence on Peterson, "'Taufe' im Acherusischen See," pp. 7–10, who is obviously focused on one topos in particular. Again, the issue does not affect my analysis. For interesting parallels to the *Apocalypse of Zephaniah*, see Himmelfarb, *Tours of Hell*, pp. 147–51.

88. A good deal of the problem relates to the extended descriptions of the heavenly realms, where Paul is said first to have entered the "gate of Paradise" (ch. 20); then to have gone to the Land of Promise where souls await the second coming of Christ in power (ch. 21); then to the City of Christ, where the saints will dwell for eternity, but where some proud Christian ascetics are waiting to get in (ch. 22; why are they not in the Land of Promise?); and then, after observing the torments of hell, to the original paradise of Adam and Eve, where he meets a number of Old Testament saints, including, apparently (there is a textual issue), Elijah, whom he already met in the Land of Promise (and why aren't all the saints there?). For an attempt to bring order to the specifically geographical confusions, see Rosenstiehl, "L'itineraire de Paul dans l'au-delà," who provides a complex reconstruction of the compositional history that requires significant textual displacements. For a reflection of the broader significance of the heavenly landscape in relation to the ethical concerns of the author, see Aitken, "Landscape of Promise."

89. Full analyses in relation to the "Book of the Watchers" and the *Apocalypse of Zephaniah* would be fruitful as well. See the comparative assessments of Himmelfarb, *Tours of Hell*, pp. 106–26.

90. See further note 87.

91. Thus, for example, the concluding proclamations to the souls of the saved and the damned in chs. 15, 16, and 17, whose current fates will hold "until the day of the resurrection," after which they will be made final.

92. On the significance of the fourth-century date for the de-apocalypticized eschatology, see Piovanelli, "Miraculous Discovery."

93. For a comparison of the sins and punishments between the apocalypses of Peter and Paul, see esp. Czachesz, "Torture in Hell and Reality." So too, for broader comparisons, see Bremmer, "Christian Hell."

94. For a compelling analysis of the passage to establish an enlightening fourth-century-Egyptian-monastic *Sitz im Leben*, see Fiori, "Death and Judgment."

95. As Carozzi (*Eschatologie et au-delà*, pp. 21–31) notes, the manuscripts of the Long Latin version diverge markedly in the descriptions of hell, as can be seen clearly in the parallel columns of Silverstein and Hilhorst, *Apocalypse of Paul*. I continue to use the Paris manuscript for my discussion.

96. In case the reader wonders, the angel emphasizes that his "punishment will never end." That is true of all the torments, as will become clear later.

97. See Dwyer, "Unstudied Redaction."

98. Czachesz ("Torture in Hell and Reality") argues that this account reserves the most cruel punishments for members of clergy: here, "Hell became a tool of discipline" (p. 133).

99. *Non exibendas agapes*—not, as in Elliott, *Apocryphal New Testament*, "did not maintain a single Agape" (taken from M. R. James).

100. This could be either a second-century variety or a later manifestation here likened to views of earlier arch-heretics. There are numerous parallels to the complete condemnation of those who see themselves within the Christian community who nonetheless doubt Christ's real flesh appearance and the connection of the sacraments to the "real" body and blood of Christ, starting, of course, in much earlier times. See, e.g., 1 John 4:2–3; Ign. *Trall* 9–10; 3 Cor (passim); *Epistula Apostolorum* (passim); Irenaeus, *Haer.* 5.2.2; and so on. See the discussion in Ehrman, *Orthodox Corruption*, pp. 212–306.

101. See discussion in Ehrman, *Forgery and Counterforgery*, pp. 460–80.

102. "Tout cela est parfaitement contradictoire," speaking specifically in reference to the relationship of the Land of Promise and the City of Christ: Is the first for married people and the second for virgins, as suggested in ch. 22 immediately before Paul goes on to learn about the City of Christ? Or not, as he learns once he does so? Carozzi, *Eschatologie et au-delà*, pp. 47–48; Casey, "Apocalypse of Paul," p. 20.

103. See, e.g., the sketch of Casey, "Apocalypse of Paul," pp. 20–25.

104. In an interesting article, Copeland ("'Holy Context'") maintains that this passage helps show that competition for greater heavenly rewards leads to this idea of graduated layers of heaven, leading her to conclude: "No matter how pleasant the deserved afterlife seems, the realization by the righteous but imperfect soul that eternity could have been more delightful is torture" (p. 389). It is an attractive view, but I am not sure it is supported in the text. There certainly were competitions in late ancient Christian asceticism (see the following note); but as Copeland acknowledges in a footnote, she is relying here on the Coptic version of the passage. It is difficult, however, to see the Coptic as a superior witness to an old or even widespread form of the text. On the textual tradition, see Piovanelli, "Origines." In any event, at the least Copeland shows that her view could be found in one time and place (that of the Coptic translator).

105. A common problem among fourth-century ascetics, as one might imagine, and well documented in other sources. For the theme of ascetic competition, see Wortley, "Spirit of Rivalry."

106. It would never occur to this writer that anyone being constantly disemboweled in a river of fire for all eternity suffers significantly more than someone crucified for six hours. In any event, for the idea that God would reject pleas for mercy, see, e.g., *4 Ezra* 7. For further references and analysis, see Bauckham, *Fate of the Dead*, pp. 140–41.

107. As suggested, another interpretation, sometimes assumed, is that he means every Easter, once a year instead of once a week. Other interpreters have trouble imagining that even this author could be that calloused.

108. The Coptic version extends the exemption from torment to the fifty days following Easter. If this implies that the translator (probably wrongly)

understood that the older text provided for an annual day of relief instead of weekly (see previous note), his alteration in the end provides about the same aggregate amount of respite as the more widely accepted interpretation—but to be taken as a long vacation rather than as a day of rest each week. For the manuscript variants and history of the text, see Carozzi, *Eschatologie et au-delà*, p. 32, and esp. pp. 127–29.

109. For rates of growth and estimates of numbers of converts, see the data, discussion, and final chart in the appendix of Ehrman, *Triumph of Christianity*, pp. 287–94.

110. On intolerance of and then legislation against Jews, see, e.g., the Theodosian Code (16.8, 1 and 8); more generally, see Carroll, *Constantine's Sword*.

111. Thus the words of Jesus already in our earliest Gospel, Mark: "For those who want to save their life will lose it; and all those who lose their life for my sake, and the sake of the Gospel, will save it" (8:35).

Chapter Three. Incentives from the World Beyond: Christian Ethics and Evangelism

1. In an interesting analysis, Henning (*Educating Early Christians*) stresses the "pedagogical" and "didactic" function of early Christian apocalypses, but she explicitly recognizes that more was involved than simply conveying descriptive information to interested readers. See, e.g., her helpful comments on parenesis, pp. 211–16.

2. We also find a good deal of cross-cultural overlap, of course, characteristic of multicultural ethical codes. One should not murder without just cause, for example, or steal someone else's spouse.

3. Experts have widely disparate views of the matter. Among recent studies, most helpful for my purposes is the cautious and carefully reasoned analysis of William V. Harris, *Rome's Imperial Economy*, especially ch. 11, "Poverty and Destitution in the Roman Empire," pp. 27–56. Alternative views can be found among the collection of essays in Atkins and Osborne, *Poverty in the Roman World*. My thanks to Prof. Mary Boatwright for suggesting these works. For an interesting analysis of wealth in the Roman Empire at the time of the rise of Christianity, see the demographics charted and defended by Friesen, "Poverty in Pauline Studies."

4. Thus Harris, *Rome's Imperial Economy*, "at least 80 per cent of the population," "even at the height of Roman imperial urbanization" (p. 37).

5. I am using Friesen's numbers ("Poverty in Pauline Studies") but rounding them off from their somewhat distracting precision (e.g., elites comprised "1.23% of inhabitants of the Roman empire," p. 340). Friesen does, of course, recognize that the figures principally serve to give us an idea. For my analysis the exact numbers are of little importance.

6. There is a copious literature on wealth in pagan and Christian antiquity, much of it dealing not just with economic analysis and demographics but

with ethical discourses connected with the "problem" of wealth and the concomitant issues of giving and charity. The first major study was Chastel, *Études historiques;* the classic is Bolkestein, *Wohltätigkeit und Armenpflege,* which, among many other things, contrasts pagan public benefaction with Jewish motives of virtuous generosity. A standard treatment in English, but notable for its elitist attitude, often lacking in basic sympathy for the plight of the poor, is Hands, *Charities and Social Aid.* Two unusually important and influential studies, by master scholars of late antiquity, are Veyne, *Bread and Circuses,* and Brown, *Through the Eye of a Needle.* See also Brown's *Ransom of the Soul.* Focused as well on a period later than my concern here is Finn, *Almsgiving in the Later Roman Empire.* An unusually clear, learned, and helpful overview, based in large measure on Bolkestein, is Lampe, "Social Welfare in the Greco-Roman World." Among the more helpful works concerned specifically with biblical and early Christian discourses are Countryman, *Rich Christian;* the collection of essays in Holman, *Wealth and Poverty;* Anderson, *Charity,* which focuses on Tobit and Sirach; and Downs, *Alms.* For a useful anthology of relevant early Christian texts, see Rhee, *Wealth and Poverty.*

7. For a nice succinct overview of the history of scholarship, see Jones, *Culture and Society in Lucian,* pp. 1–5.

8. Among the studies of particular relevance to our discussion here are Jones, *Culture and Society,* with biographical details in ch. 2, pp. 6–23; Branham, *Unruly Eloquence;* Nesselrath, "Lucien et le Cynisme"; Halliwell, *Greek Laughter;* Mestre, "Lucien"; Lauwers, *Philosophy, Rhetoric, and Sophistry;* Nesselrath, "Skeletons, Shades, and Feasting Heroes"; and Oikonomopoulou, "Journeying the Underworld."

9. See esp. Nesselrath, "Lucien et le Cynisme"; Mestre, "Lucien"; and Lauwers, *Philosophy, Rhetoric, and Sophistry.*

10. "Photios manifest une grande vérité sur Lucien: on ne sait jamais ou il est lui-même"; Mestre, "Lucien," p. 79.

11. "Lucian n'a pas de philosophie et voilà tout"; Reardon, *Courants littéraires grecs,* p. 39B.

12. Desmond, *Cynics,* pp. 66–67. For the purposes of my analysis I do not need to go into the complications of establishing the life of the "historical Demonax," who is known, in fact, principally from Lucian himself.

13. The classic study is Dudley, *History of Cynicism.* Among the most useful modern treatments are Branham and Goulet-Cazé, *Cynics;* Desmond, *Greek Praise of Poverty;* and Desmond, *Cynics.*

14. For example, when Stoics sympathetic to Cynic teachers or praxeis use them to establish the credentials of their own views. There are sometimes heated though probably unnecessary debates about whether the movement should be traced back to Diogenes (412 or 403–324 or 321 BCE) or his teacher Antisthenes (445–ca. 366 BCE). The early phase of the movement was principally fourth to third century BCE in Greece, with such names

(following Diogenes) as Crates, Hipparchia, Menippus, Bion, and Teles; the second was in the Roman period from the first century CE into late antiquity and was not dominated by individual philosophers so much as by praxis, though Peregrinus, Demonax, and Oenomaus of Gadara, for example, are known; we also have the Cynic epistles as sources of the period. The praxis can especially be seen in the many anecdotes preserved in the "lives," starting with Antisthenes and Diogenes, found in Diogenes Laertius, *Lives of the Philosophers.*

15. In addition to the lives found in Diogenes Laertius, nice synopses of the Cynic perspective come to us from Epictetus (*Discourses* 3.22, 4.8.30–43), who almost certainly idealizes it in order to promote his own Stoic investments; but the basic outline nonetheless appears generally valid.

16. On why a Stoic would affirm the views of a Cynic, see note 14.

17. See the discussion in Desmond, *Cynics,* p. 98.

18. Desmond, *Cynics,* p. 103.

19. Seneca does take a somewhat harder stance to money in *De tranquillitate animi* 8, where he admits that the poor are often more cheerful than the wealthy and claims that the best approach to money is to avoid poverty but to be not far removed from it. He himself, of course, made certain poverty came nowhere near him.

20. Thus, for example, Plutarch, "On Love of Wealth." Plutarch emphasizes that money cannot buy happiness: it does not free people from pain or give them more peace, serenity, or even *autarkeia* (*Love of Money* 1). But that is no reason to avoid it: "Having wealth is not the same as disdaining it and having abundance is not the same as not needing it" (ch. 11). The problem with wealth is not the money but the attitude, especially for those who are insatiable. Avarice is unlike virtually any other desire: the desire for water is satisfied by drinking, but nothing can satisfy the avaricious. They want more and more and are never sated. The worst offenders are the misers, who accumulate wealth but never spend it, having the desire but being "cheated of the pleasure" (ch. 5). They are like a bath-keeper's donkey, constantly carrying the firewood and kindling into the bathhouse, always fouled with smoke and ashes but never getting warm or clean by having a bath (ch. 5).

21. Veyne, *Bread and Circuses,* p. 5.

22. Veyne, *Bread and Circuses,* p. 5.

23. See Veyne, *Bread and Circuses,* p. 10.

24. As stressed recently by Lampe, "Social Welfare in the Greco-Roman World," p. 7, in agreement with a major point of Bolkestein (see note 6). Already in Aristotle those with means gave to help those on their own social level—for example, friends who were expected then to return payment. A truly magnanimous gesture involved giving to such people without expecting a return (*Nichomachean Ethics* 1162b and 1167b). Rarely did such giving involve providing for someone who was known to be *unable* to repay. Thus, almost none of the elites' benevolence went to citizens who were at or below subsistence level, let alone to poor noncitizens.

25. Quaintly titled "Three Bob Day" in the Loeb edition, which I use here: Nixon, *Plautus.*

26. For a somewhat more optimistic view, see the recent study of Parkin, "'You Do Him No Service.'" Parkin acknowledges that the destitute were "never *en masse* targets of aid" in the Greco-Roman world and that the large section of the poorest were rarely the beneficiaries of munificence of euergetism (p. 60). But she does try to make a case that some people did give to beggars, even though the primary sources say very little about it; in her view, these sources mask "a reality of desultory, but habitual, giving." I am inclined to accept her view of a largely hidden social reality—*sometimes* people gave to those in need—but since I am principally concerned here with discourse, it would not much affect my analysis.

27. Brown, *Eye of a Needle, pace.*

28. Thus his full name, Didymus Judas Thomas; Thomas is Aramaic for "twin," and Didymus is the Greek equivalent.

29. The literature on the *Acts of Thomas* is not as vast as one might hope. The classic study is Bornkamm, *Mythos und Legende;* the major commentary is Klijn, *Acts of Thomas* (which unfortunately is not overly helpful on many key interpretive issues). Among the more important relatively recent studies are Tissot, "Actes apocryphes"; Tissot, "L'encratisme des Actes de Thomas"; Attridge, "Original Language"; Attridge, "Intertextuality in the *Acts of Thomas*"; the brief but informed introductions in the new translation of Attridge, *Acts of Thomas,* pp. 1–15; and esp. the essays in Bremmer, *Apocryphal Acts of Thomas.* I use the text of Lipsius and Bonnet, *Acta apostolorum apocrypha.*

30. The widely accepted view since Jesus himself; see, e.g., Brown, *Through the Eye of a Needle* and *Ransom of the Soul,* passim.

31. Veyne, *Bread and Circuses,* p. 26.

32. Veyne, *Bread and Circuses,* pp. 19, 33.

33. Again I stress that some scholars, even the most prominent, who recognize the importance of the shift, do not see it is as a major sea change. See note 6. Others cannot escape the fact that the noncitizen indigent appears to have been absent from the mind, let alone the conscience, of the elite givers of pagan Rome, and that the entire motivation for giving had changed.

34. Among many others, see the works of Countryman, Holman, Anderson, Downs, and Rhee in note 6.

35. These injunctions, of course, are directed specifically to Israelites in connection with poor Israelites, but they also applied to non-Israelite resident aliens; see Lev 19:34.

36. Passages are easily multiplied; see, e.g., Sir 3:30–31, 4:1–10. For a discussion focusing on biblical views, but especially those of Tobit and Sirach, see Anderson, *Charity.*

37. See the fuller discussion of Bauckham, *Fate of the Dead,* ch. 4, "The Rich Man and Lazarus," esp. pp. 103–8.

38. Other passages can be easily cited. Among others, see the strictures of Jas 2: 1–7, 14–16.

39. Eventually, of course, almsgiving became a soteriological focus. See esp. Garrison, *Redemptive Almsgiving;* Downs, *Alms;* and, for a later period, Brown, *Ransom of the Soul.* One could argue that care for the needy was central already to Jesus's "message of salvation," as seen, for example, in the parable of the sheep and the goats (Matt 25:31–46); here it is not necessarily a matter of "wealth," of course, but simply of providing for those in need.

40. It is completely plausible to think that repeated stress on Gundaphorus's desire to be "worthy" of the mansion in the sky would suggest that he realizes there is more to it than giving away alms to the poor. On the other hand, it is striking that when the narrative explains what Gundaphorus and Gad did in order to show themselves worthy, it mentions only their financial assistance to the needy (26.1). How did they treat their slaves, lovers, enemies, and so on? The text is not concerned with the issue.

41. I will not obsess about the term; anyone who objects to it can simply substitute a different one. For full discussion, see Rambo and Farhadian, *Oxford Handbook of Religious Conversion.*

42. To forestall the obvious objections, I need to emphasize that I am not making any claims about what really happens in lived experience, such as that "conversion" requires a blinding-light experience and a total transformation of the being, in the William James–Arthur Darby Nock mode (i.e., W. James, *Varieties of Religious Experience;* Nock, *Conversion*). I am speaking of the rhetoric of the early Christian katabatic texts.

43. In this context, by "religion" I am referring to pagan worship practices but also to more than that, something like "cult, discourse, and human activities connected with the gods," that is to say, individual and communal ritual acts of sacrifice, prayer, and divination; tales, ideas, and opinions connected with divine beings; and any behaviors outside of the cult of interest to such divinities (patricide, oath-breaking, "piety"). Ancient people did not have a word for this confluence of things and normally did not see them as bound together into a single holistic entity that they imagined but could not express easily. But since my interests here are etic not emic, I am speaking simply of the various aspects of human relations to and reflections on the gods, something we today would call "religion." For religion as a modern construct, see Nongbri, *Before Religion.* A response can be seen in Whitmarsh, "Invention of Atheism." For "religion" in an ancient Roman context, see the sensible discussion of Rives, *Religion in the Roman Empire,* esp. Introduction and ch. 1; and Rives, "Religious Choice."

44. Nock, *Conversion.* One of the many problems with the book, despite its unusual erudition and insights, is its dependence on a Jamesian psychological model. See W. James, *Varieties of Religious Experience.* For more recent and compelling work on proselytizing and conversion, without the Jamesian model, see Goodman, *Mission and Conversion.*

45. For older views, see Nock, *Conversion;* more recently, Goodman, *Mission and Conversion,* and Rives, *Religion in the Roman Empire* and "Religious Choice," along with the works cited in note 47.

46. See the essays in Mitchell and van Nuffelen, *One God*.

47. Still worth reading are the now-classics of MacMullen, *Paganism in the Roman Empire*, and Fox, *Pagans and Christians*. Particularly useful is the fuller two-volume collection of sources and analysis of Beard, North, and Price, *Religions of Rome*.

48. For a brief but helpful discussion of philosophy in relation to religion, see Rives, *Religion in the Roman Empire*, pp. 37–42; for various topics and figures in Greek and Roman philosophy throughout the periods we are discussing, see Long, *Cambridge Companion to Early Greek Philosophy*; Long and Sedley, *Hellenistic Philosophers*; and Sedley, *Cambridge Companion to Greek and Roman Philosophy*.

49. Barring Skeptics, of course, who somewhat delighted in the exclusive but contradictory truth claims of others.

50. See the next note.

51. See the significant assessment of Annas, "Plato's Myths of Judgement," and esp. the cogent response in R. Johnson ("Does Plato's Myth of Er?"), who stresses the full coherence of the Myth of Er to the rest of the argument. Among other quality studies, see Edmonds, *Myths of the Underworld Journey*, esp. the Introduction, pp. 1–28, and ch. 4 ("The Upward Path of Philosophy"), pp. 159–220; the essays in Partenie, *Plato's Myths*, including, for a helpful overview, Partenie's own Introduction on pp. 1–27; Albinus, "Katabasis of Er"; Tarrant, "Myth as a Tool"; and more recently Tarrant, "Literal and Deeper Meanings."

52. In addition to the works cited in the previous note, a most helpful overview and discussion of key interpretive issues is Vorwerk, "Mythos und Kosmos." For a helpful assessment of the eschatological myths more broadly, see Inwood, "Plato's Eschatological Myths."

53. Obviously Plato's work, and the *Republic* in particular, was not directed simply to the attitudes and behaviors of the individual but toward broader social and political issues as well. But for the sake of my comparative analyses here I am focusing on the question "How then should one live?"

54. R. Johnson, "Does Plato's Myth of Er?," p. 9.

55. "Der Mythos hat nach dem Schlusswort des Sokrates (621b-8-d3) die Funktion, seine Hörer zu retten, indem er die Unsterblichkeit der Seele bekräftigt und so zu einem gerechten Leben anspornt, damit es der Seele im Jenseits gut ergeht"; Vorwerk, "Mythos und Kosmos," p. 54.

56. So, e.g., Annas, *Introduction to Plato's* Republic, pp. 349–53. Annas made an interesting effort to reevaluate her views just a year later in "Plato's Myths of Judgement." See the other works cited in note 51.

57. Most helpfully, R. Johnson, "Does Plato's Myth of Er?"

58. For fuller analysis, see the works cited in notes 51 and 52.

59. Thus R. Johnson, "Does Plato's Myth of Er?," pp. 10–11.

60. Cf. Cyniscus in Lucian's *Downward Journey*. He began life by doing evil but converted to philosophy. When his day of judgment arrived, the marks on

his soul from his previous waywardness had all faded. As a result he is sent to the Isles of the Blessed.

61. As MacMullen (*Paganism in the Roman Empire*, pp. 98–99) put it most directly: "Of any organized or conscious evangelizing in paganism there are very few signs indeed." For support, see the equally impressive study of Goodman, *Mission and Conversion:* There was virtually no parallel to the proselytizing mission of the Christian church in antiquity—not just among the traditional pagan cults but also in Judaism. Christians were practically alone in competing for converts: "Such a proselytizing mission was a shocking novelty in the ancient world"; indeed, "For most of the period before Constantine's conversion, such Christians will have been running in a race of whose existence most of the other competitors were unaware" (pp. 105, 160). To be sure, as I indicated, members of other cultic groups were generally happy to have outsiders join them, and they offered benefits for doing so—as in the Isis cult mentioned. Often these benefits did include a better afterlife—as seen already in classical times with the happy "initiates" of Aristophanes' *Frogs*, prancing and singing in happy blessedness while others are stuck in the muck. But we have no evidence of sustained missionary work undertaken by devotees of mystery cults, not even among the Mithraists, where some have suspected it. See, e.g., Beck, "On Becoming a Mithraist."

62. On the lack of a Jewish "mission," see Goodman, *Mission and Conversion.*

63. MacMullen continues to persuade in *Christianizing the Roman Empire;* I develop MacMullen's view by examining additional sources and discussing problems with alternative views in Ehrman, *Triumph of Christianity*, pp. 131–59.

64. This is another key point of MacMullen, *Christianizing the Roman Empire*, which I lay out for a broader audience in *Triumph of Christianity*, ch. 4, "Reasons for the Christian Success," pp. 104–30. In particular I crunch the numbers, modifying the model first set out by Stark in *Rise of Christianity*. Stark's book is problematic in many ways, in particular because of its treatment of ancient sources. But no one can crunch numbers better than a sociologist, and in my discussion, I show why, with significant caveats, I think the basic concept is correct.

65. See note 63.

66. That Jesus was not speaking of eternal torment is clear from his many references to "destruction." The "eternal punishment" in Matt 25:46 is not everlasting "torment." It is placed in antithetical parallelism with "eternal life." The opposite of life is not torture but death. This punishment is "eternal" not because it is consciously experienced but because it will never end. So too all the Gospel references to being burned with fire: when, in the parable, "weeds" are tossed into the furnace (Matt 13:36–41), they don't live in the fire forever burning; they are destroyed. So too the sinners gathered up by the angels of the Son of Man; they weep and gnash their teeth, but like everyone burned at the stake, that lasts only until they expire.

67. Older questions about the authorship and dating of the *Martyrdom of Poly-carp* have revived with vigor. Traditionally placed on the pen of an eyewit-ness in the second half of the second century (156 CE? 177 CE?), the text has recently been considered a forgery from the early third century; see Moss, "On the Dating of Polycarp"; and Ehrman, *Forgery and Counterforgery*, 493–508. I use my translation in Ehrman, *Apostolic Fathers*.

68. There were, of course, Jewish antecedents for this approach to martyrdom; see most famously 2 Macc 7.

69. Trans. Ernest Wallis in Roberts and Donaldson, eds., *Ante-Nicene Fathers* 5.

70. The evangelistic point of a katabasis is sometimes made explicit in its fram-ing narrative. Thus the longer ending of the *Apocalypse of Paul* (15.12–13): "Send and reveal it for its sake so that people may read it and turn to the way of truth that they may not come into these bitter torments"; and the afterlife warnings of the (Christian) Greek *Apocalypse of Ezra* 7.9–12: "As many as have not believed in this book shall be burnt up like Sodom and Gomor-rah" (translations in Henning, *Educating Early Christians*, pp. 211 and 212, n. 130).

71. For the *Acts of Thomas* generally, see the works cited in note 29; for this epi-sode, see Klijn, *Acts of Thomas*, pp. 127–41.

72. Attridge, *Acts of Thomas*, p. 54.

73. Attridge, *Acts of Thomas*, p. 56.

74. I am not discussing here the ultimate motivations for such paraneses, but it would be difficult to imagine it was purely an altruistic concern for the welfare of individuals, even if that was (often? usually?) part of it. There were also, of course, such matters as social, ecclesiastical, and political con-trol. Still, whatever the motivation or set of motivations, the injunction itself involved a radical transformation of the self.

75. Thus MacMullen, *Christianizing the Roman Empire*.

Chapter Four. The Afterlife of Afterlives: Editorial Interventions and Christology

1. On the basic but surprisingly vexed question of whether Akhmim 1 actually can be shown to be (a form of) the *Gospel of Peter*, and whether, indepen-dently of that question, Akhmim 2 can be as well, see the balanced discussion of Nicklas, "Zwei petrinische Apokryphen."

2. Bouriant, "Fragments du texte grec." For the text, see Kraus and Nicklas, *Pe-trusevangelium und die Petrusapokalypse*, pp. 104–17. The best account of the discovery is van Minnen, "Greek *Apocalypse*." For the history of scholarship up to 1988, see Bauckham, "Apocalypse of Peter: An Account."

3. Full discussions of ancient witnesses are in Buchholz, *Your Eyes Will Be Opened*, pp. 20–42, and Kraus and Nicklas, *Petrusevangelium und die Petrus-apokalypse*, pp. 87–99.

4. That is, quotations from church fathers who both cite the text and name the source as the *Apocalypse of Peter*: Clement of Alexandria, the anonymous

pagan anti-Christian polemicist (probably Porphyry, as we will see) cited by way of refutation by Macarius Magnes (Macarius himself does not actually quote the *Apocalypse*), and an anonymous author of a fourth-century Latin homily; see the previous note.

5. "Wir nicht eine selbständige Apokalypse, nicht die Petrusapokalypse vor uns haben, sondern ein Stück eines Evangeliums. . . . aus eben diesem selben Evangelium"; Dieterich, *Nekyia*, p. 16.

6. Zahn, *Grundriss der Geschichte*, p. 25. Zahn provides no evidence or argument for this view but states it simply in one sentence at the end of a long footnote (n. 17), with the claim that it can be supported by comparing the citation of Clement, *Eclogue* 41, with the *Apocalypse of Peter* 26. It is not clear why he thinks this comparison shows the Akhmim *Apocalypse* was inserted into a later Gospel account rather than taken from it.

7. Grébaut, "Littérature éthiopienne pseudo-clémentine"; Grébaut included a French translation with his edition.

8. Published in three parts the following year: M. R. James, "New Text." A second Ethiopic manuscript is now available; see the analysis of Buchholz, *Your Eyes Will Be Opened*, pp. 119–39. The differences between the two have no bearing on my analysis.

9. M. R. James, "New Text," p. 53.

10. Müller, "Apocalypse of Peter," pp. 625–35; Elliott, *Apocryphal New Testament*, pp. 600–612.

11. Bodl. MS Gr. Th. F. 4 [P], described by M. R. James as "measuring three-and-a-quarter inches in height and two in breadth: complete at top and bottom" ("New Text," p. 367). The fragment was classified by E. G. Turner as a "miniature" manuscript (*Typology of the Codex*, pp. 29–30). For paleographic description and text, see Kraus and Nicklas, *Petrusevangelium und die Petrusapokalypse*, pp. 121–25.

12. Wessely, *Plus anciens monuments*, 482–83; Prümm, "Genuine Apocalypsis Petri"; M. R. James, "Rainer Fragment." For an important recent analysis, see Kraus, *P.Vindob.G.*

13. M. R. James, "Rainer Fragment," p. 278; he also notes that R came to Europe in the 1880s and the Bodleian fragment was purchased in 1894.

14. I examine the textual significance of R in Chap. 5.

15. M. R. James, "Rainer Fragment," p. 275.

16. Vaganay, *L'Évangile de Pierre*, pp. 187–92; M. R. James, "Rainer Fragment," pp. 275–78.

17. Additional arguments can be found in Nicklas, "Zwei petrinische Apokryphen," pp. 90–91.

18. He points out, for example, that it was common in antiquity for authors to take previously existing works and combine them (he instances *1 Enoch*, the *Ascension of Isaiah*, and others), whereas "of the converse process, the development of a separate book out of an episode in a larger work, I know of no single instance" (M. R. James, "New Text," p. 581). Still, one would need to

consider whether this could be an exception. And what about, say, the *Acts of Pilate*—the expansion of a brief Gospel narrative into its own account of Jesus's trial?

19. Maurer, "Apocalypse of Peter," pp. 664–665. The argument is mentioned by Bauckham ("Apocalypse of Peter: An Account," p. 4720) in his history of research but again is not developed.

20. Thus, for example: "We twelve disciples" occurs in Akhmim *Apocalypse of Peter* 5 (the parallel: *Gospel of Peter* 59); the same account in Ethiopic instead reads "his disciples" (with the first-person "me" identified in the previous sentence). It is easy to see why an author wanting to establish linguistic continuity between an inserted source and the rest of his style would make the change, but it is much harder to see why an inoffensive phrase would be altered out of conformity with a verbal tic found elsewhere in an author's source. And the pattern repeats itself. The name "Jesus" does occur in the Ethiopic version, in fact in the very same passage, "my Lord Jesus Christ" (Ethiopic 5); but not in the Akhmim version, "the Lord" (v. 4). So too in Ethiopic 16, "God, Jesus Christ," but Akhmim, "the Lord" (v. 12); and a second time in Ethiopic 16, "my Lord and God Jesus Christ," and Akhmim, "The Lord" (v. 20). In one other place also, in the final section not contained in the shorter Akhmim version, the author names "my Lord Jesus Christ" (v. 16).

21. M. R. James ("New Text," p. 579) wrongly claims that the beginning and ending of each text is fragmentary. On the contrary, the Akhmim *Apocalypse* begins with a full sentence and ends with one; the *Gospel* begins with one. On the other hand, they do both presuppose a broader narrative context: the opening words of the *Apocalypse*, "Many of them," for example, presuppose that the author has already said something about "them." If it is understood that both texts are fragments of this larger narrative, or that, with respect to the *Apocalypse*, the scribe was simply copying the portion that he was interested in, the abrupt beginning and ending would make perfect sense: the transitions would have been provided by the verses that preceded and followed.

22. See van Minnen, "Greek *Apocalypse*," pp. 19–22, for the codicological analysis; it will be seen that I disagree with his conclusions.

23. M. R. James, "Rainer Fragment," p. 275.

24. Maurer, "Apocalypse of Peter," p. 667.

25. Nicklas, "Zwei petrinische Apokryphen," pp. 92–93.

26. Nicklas, "Zwei petrinische Apokryphen," pp. 92–93. For another discussion of the relationship of the *Gospel* and the *Apocalypse*, again in light of the developing textual tradition of the latter, see Marcus, "Gospel of Peter."

27. Among the many differences: when the author of Matthew took over Mark, he was producing a new version of the life of Jesus, not combining two previously existing ones. The editor of the *Gospel of Peter* later found in Codex Panopolitanus amalgamated two texts already in circulation, to subsume one into the other.

28. See my discussion in Ehrman, *Orthodox Corruption*, pp. 220–27.

29. As another illustration, dealing now not with a passage or a book, but, by analogy, with an entire corpus, consider what happens when the Pastoral Epistles come to be added to the collection of Pauline Epistles. As Annette Merz has convincingly shown, the forgeries provide "reading instructions" to the rest of the corpus through "reference-oriented" intertexts. See Merz, *Fictive Selbstauslegung;* see also her shorter study, "Fictitious Self-Exposition of Paul."

30. See my discussion and references in Ehrman, *Forgery and Counterforgery*, 324–27.

31. For a concise and informative discussion of all the Greek references and (possible) witnesses, see esp. Kraus and Nicklas, *Petrusevangelium und die Petrusapokalypse*, pp. 11–23, who, despite the generally high-level engagement, do not adequately address the strong arguments in favor of the reference in Justin and, to a lesser extent, in P.Oxy 4009. The person in the Akhmim tomb was apparently identified as a monk simply because he was buried with the book; see van Minnen, "Greek *Apocalypse*," pp. 17–19. On the question of the "other" witnesses to the *Gospel* outside the Akhmim manuscript, see Lührmann, *Fragmente apokryph gewordener Evangelien*, pp. 72–95, and the response in Foster, "Are There Any Early Fragments?" (he answers emphatically, No); and the record of the back and forth (Lührmann's response, Foster's reply) in Foster, *Gospel of Peter*, pp. 57–91.

32. Jouguet and Lefebvre, "Note sur un ostrakon de Thèbes"; Lührmann, "Petrus als Evangelist." See also van Haels, *Catalogue des papyrus littéraires*, p. 268, no. 741. For analysis, see Kraus, "Petrus und das Ostrakon." Foster (*Gospel of Peter*, pp. 83–86) goes out of his way to argue that neither side of the ostracon alludes to Peter as the writer of a Gospel, but he perhaps doth protest too much, as regularly happens in his discussion of all things Lührmann. For a particularly balanced discussion, see Kraus, "Petrus und das Ostrakon," briefly reprised in Kraus and Nicklas, *Petrusevangelium und die Petrusapokalypse*, pp. 20–23.

33. Swete, *Akhmîm Fragment*, pp. xxxvii–lxiii.

34. McCant, "*Gospel of Peter:* Docetism Reconsidered," which is based on McCant, "*Gospel of Peter:* Docetic Question." The anti-docetic view is sometimes advanced on interesting and new grounds, rather than simply reiterated, as, for example, in Combs, "Walking, Talking Cross."

35. Thus Foster, *Gospel of Peter*, pp. 157–65. For a careful analysis of the polymorphic—rather than the docetic—Christology and an intriguing explanation of the personified cross, see Combs, "Walking, Talking Cross."

36. The ὡς in v. 10 is tricky, but to say, as Foster (*Gospel of Peter*, p. 161) does, that a causal understanding makes the passage unremarkable is itself rather remarkable. And to claim that suffering is central to the entire passage (as in McCant, "*Gospel of Peter:* Docetism Reconsidered," p. 261) is precisely the question, so it can scarcely be the answer. Moreover, surely one has to

argue for an interpretation rather than simply assert it to be what the author "intended," as Foster (*Gospel of Peter*, p. 163) does with the modified cry of dereliction.

37. I am assuming, of course, that the form of the text in the sixth-century Codex Panopolitanus was not the one Serapion saw. If by odd chance it was, we still would not know which passages he considered docetic, as I point out just below.

38. See note 29.

39. Foster remains highly skeptical (*Gospel of Peter*, pp. 58–68). He is far more skeptical that the unusually intriguing P.Oxy 4009 with its fascinating conversation between Peter and Jesus about sheep fearing the wolves could be a fragment of the *Gospel of Peter*. I consider D. Lührmann's case for its identity completely plausible; see Lührmann, "POx 4009."

40. Foster (*Gospel of Peter*, p. 64, table 11) argues that the reconstruction leading to that reading is too sanguine and that the only clear word on the papyrus is φιλος, without identifiable letters for πειλατου following. Yet when he provides his own reconstruction and translation, he follows the reading of Πειλατου. In any event, however one reconstructs the line, here we have someone called a "friend" addressing Pilate about a body that is in a tomb. Where else in Christian literature is that found, other than the *Gospel of Peter*? Surely the identification is probable. See further Kraus and Nicklas, *Petrusevangelium und die Petrusapokalypse*, pp. 55–58.

41. Treat, "Two Manuscript Witnesses," p. 398.

42. Treat, "Two Manuscript Witnesses," p. 399.

43. Nicklas, "'Neutestamentliches apokryphon'?"

44. See Ehrman, *Forgery and Counterforgery*, pp. 324–27.

45. For the most useful recent examination, see Dubois, "Docétisme des christologies," along with the bibliography he cites. Dubois argues that the Nag Hammadi tractates call into question the charges against Gnostics in proto-orthodox heresiologists such as Irenaeus and Pseudo-Hippolytus. It is not a particularly surprising claim in se, but Dubois does provide a helpful analysis. See also Verheyden et al., *Docetism in the Early Church*.

46. See my fuller discussion in Ehrman, *Orthodox Corruption*, pp. 140–46, 212–13.

47. For suggestive traces already in the New Testament, e.g., 1 John, see my treatment in Ehrman, *Orthodox Corruption*, pp. 213–15.

48. Translation of Unger, *St. Irenaeus of Lyons*.

49. This is a scholarly path well-trod but worth treading again briefly in the present context. From forty years ago now, e.g., see Pagels, "Gnostic and Orthodox Views." See also Ehrman, *Orthodox Corruption*, pp. 212–30.

50. Thus, e.g., Tertullian, *De resurrectione carnis* 8; or Pseudo-Tertullian, *Adversus omnes haereses* 2: Basilides portrays Jesus as a phantom and rejects the need for martyrdom.

51. The Valentinian treatise affirms that during his life on earth Christ was "in flesh" (σάρξ; 44.16) but argues that the resurrection shows that he

transcended the flesh, as will believers once they pass from the material world (45.14–46.1); Athenagoras insists that bodies must be raised to pay for the sins committed in the body; Tertullian connects Christ's resurrection in the flesh with the Christians' at the end of *De carne Christi*, which he claims was a "preface" to the discussion of the future resurrection of the believer. Augustine's discussion begins with Christ's resurrection in the flesh (*Civ.* 5) as a lead-in to his discussion of believers' eternal life in the flesh (*Civ.* 22).

52.   I am not denying the modern scholarly view of Luke's "passionless passion," but the account was certainly not read that way in antiquity; and however one evaluates the extent of Jesus's internal mental anguish in Luke's narrative, on any reading it stresses that he was abused and crucified and that later his followers were sometimes beaten, stoned, and killed.

53.   Found now as well in Codex Tchacos; see Meyer, *Nag Hammadi Scriptures*, pp. 585–93; I use his translation here. For the Coptic text, see Meyer and Wisse, "NHC VIII."

54.   See my survey of scholarship and discussion in Ehrman, *Forgery and Counterforgery*, pp. 401–4.

55.   See my fuller discussion in Ehrman, *Forgery and Counterforgery*, pp. 407–12, 447–51. There is a third *Apocalypse of Peter* (in Arabic), which does not concern us here. See Buchholz, *Your Eyes Will Be Opened*, pp. 11–16.

56.   The classic study is Perkins, *Gnostic Dialogue*.

Chapter Five. The Justice and Mercy of God in Textual Conflict

1.   Naturally they involve a large range of other theological issues as well, including, for example, what it means to be human, the nature of evil, and ecclesiology.

2.   See, e.g., M. R. James, "Rainer Fragment."

3.   See Ehrman, *Forgery and Counterforgery*, pp. 222–29 (2 Pet) and 239–63 (1 Pet).

4.   See Ehrman, *Forgery and Counterforgery*, pp. 222–29.

5.   See Ehrman, *Forgery and Counterforgery*, pp. 255–59.

6.   In an earlier book I argue even more than that, that scribes were, in a sense, authors of the texts they reproduced; see Ehrman, *Orthodox Corruption*, passim and in particular pp. 336–37.

7.   Even though the number twenty-seven is indeed convenient both for Christian numerologists and mnemonics alike, since it is three to the third power.

8.   It would be equally interesting to explore further the respective canonical fates of the two apocalypses. For that, see Norelli, "Pertinence theologique et canonicite." Norelli seems to assume that the two were in competition for a limited number of spots; his argument is that the Christology and soteriology of John's Apocalypse fit better with orthodox views.

9. Among the other similarities: in both, Peter receives divine notice of his coming martyrdom (2 Pet 1:1–14, *Apoc. Pet.* 14.4). For a brief history of the early research, see Buchholz, *Your Eyes Will Be Opened*, pp. 92–97.

10. For a history of the older scholarship on the question, see Bauckham, "Apocalypse of Peter: An Account," pp. 4721–23. The classic study arguing that 2 Peter used the *Apocalypse* is Spitta, "Petrusapokalypse und der zweite Petrusbrief," even though, as Bauckham points out repeatedly, the article was out of date the moment it was published, since it was based on an analysis of the Akhmim text instead of the then recently discovered Ethiopic version. Still, Bauckham comes to the same basic conclusion in *Fate of the Dead*, pp. 290–303, "Second Peter and the *Apocalypse of Peter.*" For a more recent full discussion, with yet again the same conclusion, see Kraus, "Griechische Petrus-Apokalypse," pp. 78–84. The most recent resurgence of interest has been sparked by the commentary of Frey, *Brief des Judas und der zweite Brief des Petrus*, followed quickly by an English translation, *Letter of Jude and the Second Letter of Peter.* This "new perspective" has led to a set of reflections and reactions, prompted by and including lectures by Frey in 2016, in a volume edited by Frey along with den Dulk and van der Watt, *2 Peter and the Apocalypse of Peter.* For an earlier statement of this perspective, see Grünstäudl, *Petrus Alexandrinus.*

11. A classic discussion is Zahn, *Geschichte des neutestamentlichen Kanons* 1, pp. 310–18; for a full list of possible allusions and direct attestations involving canonicity, see Chaine, *Épitres catholiques*, pp. 1–12. See also Metzger, *Canon of the New Testament*, pp. 138, 151, 203, 212–14, 240–41, 244. These latter two studies have not been surpassed.

12. I continue to consider this traditional dating of the list correct and am not persuaded by the arguments for a fourth-century date by Sundberg, "Canon Muratori," and Hahneman, *Muratorian Fragment;* for critiques of their view, see Ehrman, *Forgery and Counterforgery*, p. 91, n. 70, and Kraus and Nicklas, *Petrusevangelium und die Petrusapokalypse*, p. 88. For a translation of the list, see Metzger, *Canon of the New Testament*, pp. 305–7, with a discussion on pp. 191–201. Also not mentioned in the list are 1 Peter, Hebrews, James, and one of the letters of John (3 John?), whereas, somewhat oddly, the *Wisdom of Solomon* is explicitly accepted. A number of "heretical" writings are explicitly excluded, along with the *Shepherd of Hermas*, though it is recognized as a valuable book. On the *Apocalypse of Peter*, see below.

13. *Non est ignorandum praesentem epistolam esse falsatam quae licet publicetur non tamen in canone est* ("It must not be overlooked that this epistle is false; it may be circulated, but nonetheless it is not in the canon"; *PL* 39, col. 1742).

14. Along with the also-disputed 2 and 3 John. For an older discussion, see Chaine, *Épitres catholiques*, pp. 6–7; more recently, with a helpful appendix laying out the numbering system, see Grenz, "Textual Divisions." My thanks to Dr. Grenz for an email correspondence that helped make sense of the two numbering systems.

15. See Siker, "Canonical Status."
16. See the list in Metzger, *Canon of the New Testament*, p. 314.
17. He mentions Clement's writings on the "Catholic epistles" and then explicates which they are: *id est* (not *per exemplum*) 1 Peter, 1 and 2 John, and James (*De institutione div literarum* 1.8; *PL* 70, col. 1120). Since in the preface of the work, Cassiodorus indicates that Clement commented on "all" the Scriptures, it appears he is here indicating which ones those were.
18. Von Harnack, *Geschichte der altchristlichen Literatur bis Eusebius* 2, p. 84ff; see also Zahn, *Geschichte des neutestamentliche Kanons* 2, pp. 157–72. It is often noted that the four books of the list that did not make it into the canon have a horizontal line placed next to them, and this is often interpreted as meaning that the scribe did not consider them to be canonical. It is a highly problematic assumption. We do not know who drew the lines. Surely not the scribe of the original list, since he then would not have included the books in it (and note: they are not provided simply as an appendix to the list; *Barnabas* occurs in the list *before* the book of Revelation and the Acts of the Apostles). But were they drawn by someone who produced a copy of the list, which then became the exemplar available to the sixth-century scribe of Claramontanus? Did the scribe of Claramontanus draw them? Or did a later scribe who marked up the text of the manuscript after it was produced? Often overlooked in this discussion is the fact that a horizontal line *also* occurs next to 1 Peter. Modern scholars who cannot imagine anyone placing 1 Peter among the noncanonical books sometimes provide extraordinary explanations. Metzger (*Canon of the New Testament*, p. 311) suggests that unlike the other lines, this one is a paragraph marker. At first blush that seems plausible, since the list has been giving Pauline Epistles and has now moved on to other epistles. But it is the same kind of line. Zahn solves the problem by ignoring it, indicating the presence of the line by the other four books but not the one by 1 Peter.
19. Mommsen, "Zur lateinischen Stichometri," p. 146. For the list, see Metzger, *Canon of the New Testament*, pp. 311–12.
20. Metzger, *Canon of the New Testament*, pp. 231–32.
21. Also problematic is the sixth Canon of the Synod of Laodicea (363 CE), which does accept two epistles of Peter, but the canon is not found in most Latin and Syriac manuscripts of the synod and so apparently comes from a later editor. So too Epiphanius mentions the "Catholic Epistles" of James, Peter, John, and Jude but does not say whether there was one by Peter or two.
22. See the list in Metzger, *Canon of the New Testament*, p. 313; discussion on p. 212.
23. See Ehrman, *Forgery and Counterforgery*, pp. 261–63.
24. Thus Libanius, *Oration* 30, 28, and Eusebius, *Life of Constantine*, 4.54.2.
25. So too Kraus and Nicklas, *Petrusevangelium und die Petrusapokalypse*, p. 89.
26. Quotations in Kraus and Nicklas, *Petrusevangelium und die Petrusapokalypse*, pp. 90–92.

27. See esp. Schott and Edwards, *Macarius, Apocriticus*. (I will be using this translation here.) In his discussion of the Hellene's identity (pp. 21–40), Schott sets out the strong case for accepting Porphyry as the author of the polemic, even if in places he remains tentative. The identification is not crucial to my argument; and the exact accuracy of Macarius's quotations of his opponent, as will be evident, are irrelevant to my broader concern.

28. There might be some question of whether he refers to 2 Peter, as he does cite the idea that "a day is as a thousand years" (4.13.10, 15). Unlike with other canonical passages, however, he does not name his source and does not mention Peter. Whether this was a view more widely applied in Christian communities to eschatological issues—based, of course, on Ps 90:4—is difficult to say.

29. See Kraus and Nicklas, *Petrusevangelium und die Petrusapokalypse*, pp. 94–95, who suggest that Methodius's decision not to name his source was either because he recognized that it was seen as dubious and did not want to weaken his point or (directly opposite) because it was so well-known and authoritative that he had no reason to name it. The latter explanation, of course, applies to thousands of biblical quotations and allusions in the patristic writings; the former would be more of an oddity.

30. Famously, but oddly, Eusebius cannot decide about the Apocalypse of John, whether it is one of the homologoumena or also among the spurious. One would think that since, on these terms, there was no consensus, by definition it would be an antilegomenon.

31. Winstanley, "Outlook of Early Christian Apocalypses," p. 161. As he says later, the kind of speculation about the afterlife found in such books "exercised a perennial fascination for the individual reader, especially in the lower strata of society, from which the Christians were mostly drawn" (p. 163).

32. M. R. James, "Recovery of the *Apocalypse of Peter*," pp. 2, 28, 36.

33. M. R. James, "New Text," p. 54. The man was remarkable, and not only for his ghost stories.

34. Text taken from Kraus and Nicklas, *Petrusevangelium und die Petrusapokalypse*, pp. 126–27, accepting without comment the restoration in both text and notes.

35. For prayers of the saints for the dead, see esp. Kraus, "Fürbitte für die Toten." See Trumbower, *Rescue for the Dead*, and the discussion below.

36. See Bauckham, *Fate of the Dead*, pp. 234–35. It is difficult to know whether Rev 6:9–11, or even the *Phaedo* (on which, see below), may have suggested this view (see note 42). One possible reason for thinking that the "called and elect" may be martyrs is a possible characterization of them in ch. 13 as victims of those being tormented. That reading, however, depends on a dubious translation of the Ethiopic by M. R. James, reproduced by Elliott but corrected by Buchholz (see *Your Eyes Will Be Opened*, p. 225, in relation to Elliott, *Apocryphal New Testament*, p. 608). Moreover, nothing indicates the saints above are observing only those guilty of persecution below: all those being tormented are crying for mercy, and the saints are given "whomever

they ask for." We know from ch. 3 that they feel pity for those being tormented in general.

37. Peter van Minnen has proposed that the text of Rainer 14, ὃν ἐὰν αἰτήσωνταί με ἐκ τῆς κολάσεως ("whomever they ask of me out of punishment"), represents a corruption of an original ὃ ἐαν αἰτήσωνταί με ("whatever they ask of me"). He argues that the surviving reading stands at odds with the rest of the text, which stresses that punishments are "eternal." On the basis of his emendation, he suggests that the saints are not asking for the sinners in torment to be saved but possibly that they themselves be avenged against those who had sinned against them, as suggested by *Apoc. Pet.* 13.2. Unfortunately he appears to be basing the suggestion on the translation of this verse by M. R. James and found in Elliott's *Apocryphal New Testament* ("They shall see their desire on those who hated them, when he punishes them"), which was later corrected by Buchholz, *Your Eyes Will Be Opened* ("And they will look at the ones who cursed it [the life from above] while he takes vengeance on them"). Thus, there is no textual basis for supposing the saints are asking for vengeance and, consequently, little support in the text for the emendation. Moreover, van Minnen's point that the text indicates the punishment is "eternal"—and so could not very well end with an ultimate salvation— overlooks the fact that references to "eternal" punishment occur only in the Ethiopic redaction, as I discuss below. It is not the oldest form of the text.

38. As in other texts such as Plato's *Phaedo*, with which it does have other important similarities, but also some fundamental differences.

39. For a compelling exegesis, see Kraus, "Acherousia und Elysion."

40. First by Peterson, "'Taufe' im Acherusischen See," who stressed the Jewish connections of the images, a view that has struck most subsequent investigators as implausible, given the obvious Greek ties. See Copeland, "Sinners and Post-Mortem 'Baptism,'" and most decisively Kraus, "Acherousia und Elysion."

41. See Copeland, "Sinners and Post-Mortem 'Baptism.'"

42. Possibly this text influenced Bauckham's view that the "elect" in the *Apocalypse of Peter* are only the martyrs. See note 36.

43. See van Minnen, "Greek *Apocalypse*," pp. 15–25; and Kraus and Nicklas, *Petrusevangelium und die Petrusapokalypse*, pp. 27–29.

44. Buchholz, *Your Eyes Will Be Opened*, pp. 119–39.

45. For the Ethiopic New Testament, see Zuurmond and Niccum, "Ethiopic Version," p. 235. It is important to stress that we do not know what form of the Greek text of the *Apocalypse* was available to the Ethiopic translator. The scribal alteration of ch. 14 could have occurred any time between the circulation of an original and the date of our Ethiopic manuscripts, in either Greek or Ethiopic.

46. It is odd and not easily explained that the Pseudo-Clementine work that contains the Ethiopic *Apocalypse of Peter* continues after the inserted text concludes with a conversation between Peter and Jesus in which Jesus declares that God,

in the end, will have pity on sinners and all will be saved. Is the conversation based on a form of the *Apocalypse* older than the one the book includes? Buchholz (*Your Eyes Will Be Opened*, pp. 380–81) appears to think so, since he understands the conversation to be a commentary on the narrative itself.

47. M. R. James, "New Text," 36–54. More recently, Kraus, "Griechische Petrus-Apokalypse," pp. 84–89.

48. I use the translation of Collins, "Sibylline Oracles."

49. See further Kraus, "Griechische Petrus-Apokalypse," pp. 84–89.

50. For a helpful discussion of substratum, redaction, and dating, see Collins, "Sibylline Oracles," pp. 330–32.

51. Thus Bauckham, "The *Apocalypse of Peter*: A Jewish Christian Apocalypse from the Time of Bar Kokhba," in *Fate of the Dead*, 210. Bauckham counts eight places of overlap between the two traditions; I count seven. It is important to note that even though he thinks the Ethiopic version added "eternal" on occasion, he maintains that most of the references have been edited out in Akhmim 2.

52. Bauckham, "Apocalypse of Peter: An Account," p. 4717.

53. Buchholz, *Your Eyes Will Be Opened*, p. 342.

54. The main sticking point for later orthodox thinkers was not that humans would all be saved in the end, but that, on the same grounds, so too would the demons and the devil himself.

55. See the two-volume edition, translation, and introduction of Behr, *Origen*, whose translation I use here.

56. There is an extensive literature of course. For an overview, still worth reading is the introduction of Trigg, *Origen*, pp. 108–15; most recently see Behr, *Origen* 1, pp. lxxx–lxxxviii. For a full treatment, see Ramelli, *Christian Doctrine of Apokatastasis*, pp. 137–215.

57. Translation of Behr, *Origen*; see also Origen, *Princ.* 1.2.10, and his exposition of 1 Cor 15:28: "Just as when the Son is said to be subjected to the Father, the perfect restoration of the whole creation is announced, so also when enemies are said to be subjected to the Son of God, the salvation of the subjected and the restoration of the lost is understood in that" (3.5.6), a matter explicated further in 3.6.1–9. For recent discussion, see Behr, *Origen* 1, pp. lvi–lxv and lxxx–lxxviii.

58. Origen tells readers to judge for themselves "whether any of these orders, which live under the rule of the devil and obey his malice, will be able in some future age to be converted to goodness . . . or whether persistent inveterate wickedness might be changed" (1.6.3). He states that he himself thinks so, but then he shows some slight hesitancy in his conclusion; it is not that "every rational being" will necessarily return to the contemplation of God but will be *able* (*posse*) to do so, at the end of a long period of ages (1.6.3).

59. See Trumbower, *Rescue for the Dead*.

60. See the discussion of Bauckham, *Fate of the Dead*, pp. 136–48, "The Conflict of Justice and Mercy."

61. Translation of Bruce Metzger, in Charlesworth, *Old Testament Pseudepigrapha* 1, p. 540.
62. Translation of A. F. J. Klijn, in Charlesworth, *Old Testament Pseudepigrapha* 1, pp. 651–52.
63. Translation of Elliott, *Apocryphal New Testament*, p. 582.
64. Translation of Frankfurter, *Elijah in Upper Egypt*, p. 326; his comment occurs in n. 111.
65. Ramelli, *Christian Doctrine of Apokatastasis.* For a long and devastating review, see McClymond, *"Origenes Vindicatus vel Rufinus Redivivus?"* McClymond points out that for Ramelli, virtually everyone from the authors of the New Testament to the ninth-century Eriugena were "either witting or unwitting followers of Origen" (p. 819). In response, McClymond makes reference to Daley's full and informative study *The Hope of the Early Church*, stressing that "the data that Daley has carefully sifted show 68 authors and texts that clearly affirm the eternal punishment of the wicked, while seven authors are unclear, two teach something like eschatological pantheism, and perhaps four authors appear to be universalists in the Origenian sense" (p. 823). The nonuniversalists are from both East and West, writing in Greek, Latin, Coptic, Syriac, and Armenian. And "there are no unambiguous cases of universalist teaching prior to Origen" (p. 823).
66. Paul does not always lean toward a universalistic salvation; he clearly states, for example, that at the return of Christ, unbelievers will experience "destruction . . . and they will not escape" (1 Thess 5:3).
67. Why are the fires eternal if the torment is not? Possibly because they were created for "the devil and his angels," conceived as immortal beings.
68. There is no need for me to develop at length the fact that neither Jesus nor Paul nor the book of Revelation attests eternal torment for human sinners; I lay out the argument and the evidence in nonscholarly terms in *Heaven and Hell*, esp. pp. 154–66, 225–29. There I also deal with the views of Sheol in the Hebrew Bible, Jesus's teaching about Gehenna, the views of later Gospels (e.g., Luke and John), the transformation of Paul's views over time, and the beginnings of the later Christian adoption of Greek views of the immortality of the soul.
69. Even though the teaching of annihilation may have seemed counterintuitive to Christians of later centuries, it is easily explained by the cultural and religious contexts of Jesus and his earlier followers, all of whom accepted the ancient Israelite and then Jewish commonplace that there was no life after the body died, unless the body were to be reanimated. There was no "soul" that could exist outside the body. The "soul" was more like the breath. God made Adam a living being by breathing the breath of life into him; when the breath left his body, it did not *go* anywhere. It simply disappeared, so that the person no longer existed. Even in the story of Saul and the medium of Endor, Samuel does not return as a disembodied spirit but precisely as a reanimated body, even wearing the same robe (1 Sam 28:14). There is noth-

ing about him residing as a shade in Sheol; and in fact, Sheol in the Hebrew Bible is probably not a "place" that dead souls go at all, a kind of Israelite Hades. The term occurs only some sixty times, and mostly in poetic texts where, strikingly, it is commonly used as a synonymous parallel to truly final destinations: "death" or "the grave" or "the pit" (e.g., Pss 16:10, 49:14). That is why God does not remember or think about anyone in Sheol and why his people cannot worship him there: people don't *exist* "there" (e.g., Pss 6:5; 88:4–5, 11–12; 115:17; Isa 8:18; Sir 17:27–28). The body dies, it is disposed of in some way, and that's where it is—in an individual grave or a mass pit, a decaying corpse, only the remnants of what was once a person.

Only when apocalyptic Judaism developed the notion of a resurrection of the body did the prospect of a postmortem existence develop, and it involved not the life of the soul but of the entire human person, both body and soul, and not in heaven but here on earth. God made paradise for humans and would restore them to it—at least those committed to serving him. The wicked would not be rewarded with life; their punishment was death, forever. An obvious exception is *1 En.* 22, as we have seen. But for most of our texts, including the earliest Christian ones, sinners would never return to life—except to see the error of their ways and be annihilated by the divine wrath. To some extent a shift was made possible, if not inevitable, by the relatively quick introduction of the predominantly (though not exclusively) Greek concept of the immortality of the soul into Christian thinking soon after the New Testament period. This was a natural development, given the realities of the Christian mission: even before the end of the New Testament period the majority of converts came from gentile rather than Jewish backgrounds, and naturally they brought their assumptions about the nature of humans and the world beyond with them. The soul can never die. If it is punished after death, it must consciously experience torment for all time.

70. Traditionally dated, of course, to just after Polycarp's death, probably around 155 CE; for arguments that the work is an early-third-century forgery, see Moss, "On the Dating of Polycarp," and my discussion in Ehrman, *Forgery and Counterforgery*, pp. 493–502, and the bibliography cited there. Translation from Ehrman, *Apostolic Fathers* 1.

71. Translation of Ernest Wallis, in Roberts and Donaldson, eds., *Ante-Nicene Fathers* 5, pp. 404–5.

72. Translation of Ewald, *Homilies of Saint Jerome*, pp. 203–5.

73. Translation from Ehrman, *Apostolic Fathers* 1.

74. Translation of Glover, *Tertullian*.

75. The authoritative account remains E. Clark, *Origenist Controversy*.

76. See E. Clark, *Origenist Controversy*, pp. 11–12.

77. Among Origen's supporters the logic was inexorable. All living creatures have souls; all were created by God; all were created good; all but one had turned bad; and all would necessarily return to the state in which God had created them. The devil therefore must be among them.

78. Jerome, *Comm. Eph. II* (on Eph 4:16; *PL* 26.535); see E. Clark, *Origenist Controversy*, p. 99: "Early in his career Jerome had rehearsed Origen's opinions on the *apokatastasis* in general and on the restoration of the devil in particular without indicating any disapproval of these views." For a fuller exposition, see E. Clark, "Place of Jerome's Commentary."

79. E. Clark, "Place of Jerome's Commentary," passim. On tiers of eternal reward, see, of course, the roughly contemporary *Acts of Paul* (esp. the City of Christ).

80. Four of the seven groups he attacks are not universalists, simply more generous in their inclusionary views than Augustine, claiming in various ways only that some kinds of Christians who begin their postmortem existence in hell will eventually escape its clutches: one group advocated for the ultimate salvation of all baptized Christians; another for those who have sacramentally consumed the body of Christ; a third for those who continued in the Catholic community even while engaged in sin; and the last only for those who have atoned for their sins by giving alms.

81. See, e.g., Brown, *Ransom of the Soul*, pp. 44–45, 83–114.

82. Quotations from *Enchiridion* ch. 110, translation of Harbert, *Augustine Catechism*.

83. Casey, "Apocalypse of Paul," 18–19.

84. See Ehrman, *Orthodox Corruption*, passim. For earlier work on these lines, see *Orthodox Corruption*, p. 49, n. 94; for important subsequent work, see pp. 352–56.

85. See E. Clark, *Origenist Controversy*, pp. 100–101. A rather famous instance of limited self-restraint involves the writings of Origen himself: Rufinus left a good deal of "incriminating" evidence in Origen's *De principiis* even while self-consciously and openly removing other parts offensive to orthodoxy, on the ground that they represented later, non-Origenic, interpolations (*Princ.* Pref. 3). See the discussion of Behr, *Origen* 1, pp. xxi–xxiv.

Chapter Six. The Power of Christ and the Harrowing of Hell

1. I am obviously borrowing the phrase from the classic study of Le Goff, *Birth of Purgatory*. For earlier exceptions to an inescapably eternal damnation for all sinners, see Trumbower, *Rescue for the Dead*, and Merkt, *Das Fegefeuer*, pp. 15–64.

2. There is, of course, a broad literature on the Harrowing of Hell. The most important contribution to date is Rémi Gounelle's magnum opus *La descente du Christ aux enfers*. This study is not, however, focused on the harrowing narratives of my concern but on the theological affirmation "he descended to hell," especially in the fourth to sixth centuries, the period of its most significant growth, development, and reflection. Still, Gounelle's bibliography is full and the analyses unusually helpful, even for the earlier periods, which are covered relatively briefly. See also the following studies: MacCulloch,

Harrowing of Hell; Kroll, *Gott und Hölle;* Bieder, *Die Vorstellung;* Letourneau, "Mythe ou réalité?"; Maas, *Gott und die Hölle;* Roddy, "Politics and Religion" (a refreshing move away from giving the historical development of the theme to considering its originating context in late antique Rome); Wicks, "Christ's Saving Descent"; and Poirier, "Gnostic Sources."

3. See my further explanations of the katabatic features of the narrative below.

4. Or, alternatively, "judged according to human standards in the flesh but live by divine standards in the spirit."

5. The most famous emendation resolves the problem of the text by taking the ἐν ᾧ καί ("in which also") of 3:19 as a corruption of an original Ενωχ (= Enoch): in majuscule script ΕΝΩΚΑΙ and ΕΝΩΧ. See Metzger, *Text of the New Testament,* p. 230, n. 57. Among modern studies of the passage, the most influential has been Dalton, *Christ's Proclamation to the Spirits;* see also the now-classic Reicke, *Disobedient Spirits.* Other studies include Vogels, *Christi Abstieg ins Totenreich;* and more recently Pierce, *Spirits and the Proclamation of Christ,* with a history of research on pp. 1–24.

6. Other biblical passages understandably came into play for the purposes of elucidation and even "proof" of Christ's activities in Hades: e.g., Matt 12:29 (binding the strong man); Matt 12:40 (Jonah in the belly of the fish); Matt 16:18 (the "gates of hell"); Matt 27:51–53 (the dead raised at Jesus's crucifixion); Rom 10:7 ("Who will descend into the abyss?"); Rom 14:9 (Christ as lord of the living and the dead); Phil 2:10 ("Every knee shall bow, in heaven, and earth, and under the earth"); Col 2:15 (Christ disarmed the rulers and authorities when he triumphed over them); Rev 1:18 (Christ having the keys of heaven and hell).

7. For brief commentary, see Vaganay, *L'Évangile de Pierre,* p. 303, and Foster, *Gospel of Peter,* pp. 430–31.

8. See Combs, "Walking, Talking Cross."

9. Justin, *Dialogue* 72, based on the "Jeremiah apocryphon," an otherwise unknown passage allegedly from Jeremiah also quoted by Irenaeus in different forms (*Haer.* 3.20.4; 4.22.1–22; 33.1, 12; *Demonst.* 78). Justin claims that Jews excised the lines from their texts of Jeremiah because of their content: they speak of Christ preaching in Hades, apparently to the righteous of Israel. See also *Epistula Apostolorum* 27: both the Ethiopic and Coptic forms of the text affirm Christ's proclamation to the prophets and righteous of Israel, or at least some of them. A somewhat unexpected alternative view is set forth by Hermas: it was Christ's "apostles and teachers" who preached in Hades to those who had previously died (*Shepherd* 93.5–6).

10. Translation of Knibb, "Martyrdom and Ascension of Isaiah." Other second-century allusions point in the same direction: *Testament of Dan* 5.11 and *Odes of Solomon* 42.11–20.

11. Translation of Steward, *Melito of Sardis,* pp. 81–82.

12. Roberts and Donaldson, eds., *Ante-Nicene Fathers* 6, pp. 72–73.

13. Scheck, *Origen; In Lib. Reg. Hom.* 2 in *PG* 12.1028.

14. So too in his commentary on 1 Cor 15:51, Cyril explicitly states that unlike the saved, at the resurrection "the wicked" will not receive a bodily transformation but "will remain in their dishonorable form" (ἀπομένουσιν ἐν τῷ τῆς ἀτιμίας σχήματι) so that they can undergo physical punishment (*PG* 74.912–14). Elsewhere Cyril indicates that Christ went to Hades and "stripped/despoiled" it (τοῦτον σκυλεύσας; *Epistulae festalis* XXI, 3, *PG* 77.856 A [G]) and he explicitly claims that when Christ rose from the dead, he "emptied out" (κενώσας) Hades (*Homily* 28.4). But then he explains that not everyone taken out of Hades received salvation. On the contrary: "He will come at the proper time to render to each person according to their deeds" (ἀποδώσων ἑκάστῳ κατὰ ἔργα αὐτοῦ; *PG* 77.956 B). That is, Hades is a temporary holding pen before the final judgment.

15. *Alii sunt heretici qui dicunt dominum in inferum descedisse et omnibus post mortem etiam ibidem renuntiasse ut confitentes ibidem salvarentur;* text in Banterle, *San Filastrio de Brescia.* It is important to stress: these "heretics" do not claim that Christ delivered all people from hell; he simply provided them with the *opportunity.* Escaping the infernal realm would require a confession of his lordship. Gounelle (*Descente,* p. 80) is surely correct that in the clause *ut confitentes ibidem salvarentur,* the participle is to be taken as conditional ("if they would confess"): "Christ proclaimed the *possibility* of salvation for all those in hell" ("le Christ a prêché la possibilité d'un salut pour tous aux enfers"); emphasis mine. Like other early Christians, Filaster mentions in particular the great pagan poets and philosophers: surely, *they* would be given another opportunity. Or not? In the end, the Christian answer was decisively "Not."

16. In his refutation Filaster appeals to scripture: Matt 11:22, 24 indicates that some cities will be worse off at the judgment than Sodom and Gomorrah; the book of Proverbs states that the impious and the sinner will be judged; Paul spoke of those who had to appear before the judgment seat; and even Jesus maintained that those who rejected his message would not escape judgment. For Filaster, Scripture settles the issue: Christ did not save all from the torments of hell; on the contrary, various kinds of sins and impieties (*peccatorum atque impiorum*) will lead to corresponding punishments and afflictions (*poenearum atque plagarum*) (*Liber de haresibus* 125.6).

17. Gregory casts aspersions on two clergy from Constantinople, George and Theodore, for claiming that Christ offered salvation in Hades to all who confessed him: "When our Almighty Lord and Savior Jesus Christ descended into Hell, he saved all those who confessed that he was God and freed them from the punishments they deserved" (*Ep.* 7.15; translation of Martyn, *Letters of Gregory the Great* 2). In his response Gregory insists that Christ freed only those who anticipated his advent and lived accordingly and followed his precepts, not sinners who made confession. Otherwise, Gregory insists, "liars without faith or good actions" who lived before Christ would have a better eternity than those who by chance were born after his incarnation.

18. Gounelle (*Descente*, p. 75) argues that "the great majority of texts produced in the Latin world in the period . . . either explicitly uphold the notion condemned by Filaster of Brescia and his successors" ("la grande majorité des textes produits en monde latin au cours de notre période d'étude soit soutient explicitement les theses condamnees par Filastre de Brescia et ses successeurs"), or they do not actually exclude the possibility (Gounelle is careful not to claim too much: "Most writers clearly affirm that all the dead who find themselves in hell have been given the *possibility* to be saved or have been saved"; translation and emphasis mine). For my part, I would emphasize more strongly Gounelle's second option: almost never does a surviving Christian author of the early centuries actually claim that Christ completely harrowed hell, taking out all sinners for eternal salvation (again, contra Ramelli, *Christian Doctrine of Apokatastasis*). Instead, we have such views attributed to others, usually in polemicizing contexts. It is difficult to know whether these charges relate to actual enemies or simply to bugbears. For examples of the polemics, see *Ad Quodvultdeus*, which attacks a group that claimed that when Christ descended to hell, "the unbelievers believed and all were freed from there" (*Ad Quodvultdeus* 79). So too the anonymous author of the *Praedestinatus* mentions as his seventy-ninth heresy an otherwise unknown group called the *Adecerditae*, who, we are told, maintained that when Christ descended to Hades, the "entire multitude of souls ran up to him, came to believe in him, and were set free" (*omnis animarum multitude occurrit, et credidit ei, et liberate est*; *PL* 53, col. 514B). For the name *Adecerditae*, see Gounelle, *Descente*, pp. 69–71.

19. See the discussion in Gounelle, *Descente*, p. 83.

20. Not all the traditions related to the descent narrative in the *Gospel of Nicodemus* matter for our purposes. Thus, for example, we have a Latin version of the *Life of Adam and Eve* that provides an account of Seth's conversation with the archangel Michael and his prediction of the coming of Christ to the underworld (as in *Gos. Nic.* 19.1). The account does not overlap with any of the passages in the *Gospel* involving the extent of the salvation Christ provided at the descent. For fuller discussion of predecessors and possible sources of *Gos. Nic.* 17–27, see Izydorczyk, *Medieval Gospel of Nicodemus*, pp. 48–50; Baudoin et al., "Protean *Evangelium Nicodemi*," p. 22; and esp. Gounelle, *Recensions byzantines*, pp. 38–51. Gounelle argues that of the relevant texts only Pseudo-Augustinian *Sermon* 160 can plausibly be considered a source for the *Gospel's* narrative, but even there, the *Gospel* writer utilized the *source* behind the sermon, not the sermon itself. Again, for my discussion here, that distinction does not matter.

21. Edited in Ozimic, "Pseudoaugustinische Sermo CLX," pp. 19–36.

22. Pseudo-Epiphanius, *Homilia II in Sabbato magno* (as titled in *PG* 43.440–64); for the Greek and old Slavonic versions, see Vaillant, "L'homélie d'Épiphane." For the dating, see Gounelle, *Descente*, p. 408.

23. Presumably "many" refers to the large number of saints, not to a restrictive subgroup among them.

24. The ὅπως is attached to the hortatory subjunctives, not the participle.
25. The most useful introductions and translations are Kaestli and Cherix, *L'évangile de Barthélemy*, pp. 13–142, and Markschies, "Fragen des Bartholomaeus." For an edition of the fullest version of the text, Latin witness C, with a complete collation of the other witnesses, see Moricca, "Nuovo Testo." An edition of the major Greek version H, along with the fragmentary Latin L, can be found in Wilmart and Tisserant, "Fragments grecs et latins." The text has long been thought to have been in circulation since the second century, though Markschies has recently argued that the final product cannot precede the fourth century. Even so, the text is clearly composite, and his reasons for a later dating (e.g., an advanced Mariology) are not persuasive for the portion we are considering here, for which a second-century date continues to be fully plausible.
26. See Kaestli and Cherix, *L'évangile des Barthélemy*, pp. 32–37, and Markschies, "Fragen des Bartholomaeus," pp. 703–8.
27. The different versions disagree on whether Bartholomew's queries began before or after Jesus's death and resurrection. However that is resolved, the question about his disappearance from the cross, naturally, comes afterward.
28. One might try to reconcile the different views by maintaining that those detained "in the same place" as the patriarchs were other righteous people, not sinners; but that would require Hades to have two compartments—a view that is not suggested in this text even though it is in others. More problematic is the fact that those who are delivered have been imprisoned behind the bars and gates of hell by both Hades and the devil, whom Christ comes to defeat. There is no indication that they are in a different place from anyone else.
29. Suggested, e.g., by Markschies, "Fragen des Bartholomaeus," p. 719.
30. This would require a slight alteration to the manuscript stemma drawn by Markschies in "Fragen des Bartholomaeus," p. 704. Greek C is not extant ad loc, but H is shown to stand in linear relationship with the archetype from which derive the respective archetypes of both the Latin and Syriac versions *and* Greek C. Since H lacks the sentence in question altogether (as we will see), the stemma would now require two (not just one) intermediaries descending from it, one leading to C (as already posited) and the other to the shared archetype of the Latin and Slavonic branches.
31. The startling lack of scribal consistency in theologically important textual variations is especially evident among the New Testament manuscripts where, if anywhere, one would expect a fairly standard and regularized process of alteration. See Ehrman, *Orthodox Corruption*.
32. The view that all the dead ascended after worshiping Christ on the cross would not be completely coherent with other parts of the narrative: If the dead ascended before Christ died, as in v. 21, in what sense did Christ harrow hell afterward? But as we have seen throughout our survey of katabasis traditions in antiquity, internal narrative coherence is rarely an overarching

concern. It bears noting that the text presents a number of other cruxes, for example in the further discussion between Jesus and Bartholomew in vv. 29–33, where the textual witnesses provide an even more mind-boggling set of options. See the apparatus of Moricca, "Nuovo Testo," pp. 493–94, and the parallel translations in Markschies "Fragen des Bartholomaeus," pp. 723–36.

33. With two outstanding exceptions: Zbigniew Izydorczyk and Rémi Gounelle, both of whom deserve a call-out for their career-long devotion to the text. Among the most important scholarship and editions for my purposes are the following: Maury, "L'évangile de Nicodème"; Kim, *Gospel of Nicodemus*; Hoffman, "Confluence in Early Christian and Gnostic Literature"; Izydorczyk, "Unfamiliar Evangelium Nicodemi"; Baudy, "Retour d'Adam au paradis"; Gounelle, "Pourquoi?"; Gounelle and Izydorczyk, *L'Évangile de Nicodème*; Izydorczyk, *Medieval Gospel of Nicodemus*; Gounelle, "Évangile de Nicodème ou Actes de Pilate"; Gounelle, "L'enfer selon l'Évangile de Nicodème"; Gounelle, *Recensions byzantines*; Schärtl, "Das Nicodemusevangelium"; Izydorczyk and Bullita, "Troyes Redaction"; Baudoin and Izydorczyk, *Oldest Manuscript*, with these two contributions in particular: Baudoin et al., "Protean *Evangelium Nicodemi*," and Baudoin and Izydorczyk, "*Acts of Pilate*."

34. For all issues of dating of the two major sections of the *Gospel* and of the sundry versions, see esp. Gounelle and Izydorczyk, *L'Évangile de Nicodème*; Gounelle, "Évangile de Nicodème ou Actes de Pilate"; Gounelle, *Recensions byzantines*; and Baudoin and Izydorczyk, "*Acts of Pilate*," and Baudoin et al., "Protean *Evangelium Nicodemi*."

35. Among other pieces of evidence, the added chapters continue the narrative flow from the town of Arimathea to Jerusalem; Simeon and Joseph of Arimathea occur both at the end of the Acts and the beginning of the descent; the robber also reappears; and the resurrection of Lazarus is found in both. See Gounelle and Izydorczyk, *L'Évangile de Nicodème*, pp. 73–75.

36. "Dans presque toutes les langues vernaculaires de l'Occident"; Gounelle, *Recensions byzantines*, p. 7.

37. It might seem, and has often been thought, that the brothers were with the saints and that Hades is portrayed as having two compartments. That is manifestly not so, as we will see: sinners and saints—all the children of Adam who had died down to the time of the crucifixion—are together. Any idea of two separate chambers in Hades must be imported from other sources. It is true that the "saints" are privileged here as the focus of attention, as one might expect from this kind of Christian text. But Christ empties out the entire place of "all" Adam's descendants, explicitly including the unrighteous. For a discussion of Gounelle's change of perspective on the matter, see note 46.

38. For the Latin tradition we especially have Zbigniew Izydorczyk to thank for this labor of love; and for the Greek, Rémi Gounelle. The most recent assessments are in Baudoin et al., "Protean *Evangelium Nicodemi*"; Baudoin and Izydorczyk, "*Acts of Pilate*"; and Gounelle, *Recensions byzantines*.

39. The oldest Greek form of the *Acts of Pilate*, labeled Greek A by Tischendorf (*Evangelia Apocrypha*), does not have the descent narrative. His "Greek B" has been relabeled Greek M (M for "medieval") by Gounelle to avoid the confusion of thinking that Greek A corresponds to Latin A and Greek B to Latin B since, in fact, the descent narrative of Greek B is directly related to Latin A rather than to Latin B; see Gounelle, *Recensions byzantines*, p. 8.

40. See Philippart, "Fragments palimpsestes."

41. For a concise discussion of each form of the Latin tradition, see Baudoin et al., "Protean *Evangelium Nicodemi.*"

42. Kim, *Gospel of Nicodemus.*

43. "La deliverance d'Adam et de tous ses enfants sans exception (soit de toute l'humanité) du monde des morts pour les amener au paradis"; Gounelle and Izydorczyk, *L'Évangile de Nicodème*, p. 84.

44. For his older argument, see Gounelle, "Pourquoi?": "tous les morts sont sauvés" (p. 76); "Tous les mort sont donc sauvés," even the "guilty, impious, and unrighteous." This salvation is not based on Christ's proclamation or the sinners' conversions: "sans predication aux morts ni conversion"; it is not "the recompense for any merit." It is achieved by Christ through his power. Moreover, this salvation comes even to those who will die *afterward*, "qui mourront après sa descent dans le monde infernal" (p. 77). Thus the salvation brought by the descent is not only universal, it is "éternelle" (p. 77). For his later view, see Gounelle, "Enfer vide ou à-demi plein?" His answer is "à-demi plein." For an evaluation, see note 46.

45. Gounelle and Izydorczyk, *L'Évangile de Nicodème*, p. 84.

46. Gounelle's later argument in "Enfer vide ou à-demi plein?" is less convincing. It is true that the text focuses its attention on the pre-Christian saints. Moreover, in just about all the other Harrowing of Hell traditions—including the predecessors and sources of the *Gospel of Nicodemus*—salvation is for the righteous, not the wicked as well. Even so, the text of Latin A is quite explicit that *everyone* in Hades has been taken out. It never suggests, for example, that Hades had two compartments, one for the righteous and the other for the wicked, and that only one was emptied, or that some inhabitants of Hades are taken up to heaven and others thrown into Tartarus. Hades complains that he has been *entirely* emptied, and Satan is the *only* one left there. Tartarus is never mentioned. Gounelle does mount an interesting argument for passages that "seem" to be universalistic by means of a redactional analysis, claiming that chs. 19–20—which are not as obviously universalistic—come from the author of the account, but that the universalistic tendencies of chs. 22–24 are drawn from the author's sources, such as the Pseudo-Augustine *Sermon* 160. There are problems with this view, however. For one thing, as redactional analysis of other Christian texts has long emphasized, an author using sources chooses not only what to change but also what to retain. When an author chooses to incorporate certain passages from a source (but not

others), that is a *decision*. In this particular case, even more problematic is the fact that the passages in chs. 22–24 that are most emphatically universalistic (e.g., 23.1: *totius mundi noxios, impios, et iniustos perdidisti*) are *not* drawn from other known sources. Indeed, Pseudo-Augustine *Sermon* 160, as we have seen, explicitly rejects the idea of a complete Harrowing of Hell. And so, in the end, there seems to be little reason to discount Gounelle's older reading of the text, as narrating "the deliverance of Adam and all his children, without exception (that is, all of humanity) from the world of the dead, to bring them to paradise" (Gounelle and Izydorczyk, *L'Évangile de Nicodème*, p. 84).

47. Again, we lack a critical text, in lieu of which I use the edition in Tischendorf, *Evangelia Apocrypha*. The oldest manuscripts of Latin B date to the eleventh or twelfth century. For an up-to-date assessment of Latin B and its two subgroups (B1 and B2), see Baudoin et al., "Protean *Evangelium Nicodemi*," pp. 24–25.

48. In particular, the subgroups and even the manuscripts within the subgroups of Latin B have variant versions of the descent narrative. Possibly the archetype of the B1 tradition did not have this portion of the *Gospel* at all. The more numerous manuscripts of B2 do have it, however, and it is there that we find attestation of the text I am dealing with here. It appears to be a later recension of this part of the tradition, and if it is, it more or less makes my point: as time went on, the earlier narrative of a complete Harrowing of Hell came to be seen as highly problematic and so was written out of existence. See Baudoin et al., "Protean *Evangelium Nicodemi*," p. 25.

49. Yet another related variant in part of the Latin B2 tradition appears when Leucius and Karinus finish producing their narratives and are dismissed by the Jewish leaders. They then return "to their graves," presumably to await the future resurrection. It is hard to see why they would return to their places of burial if they have already been exalted with Christ up to heaven. The variant is noted by Izydorczyk, *Manuscripts*, Census 44: "*reversi sunt ad sepultura sua*." See also Baudoin et al., "Protean *Evangelium Nicodemi*," p. 25.

50. Gounelle, *Recensions byzantines*.

51. Convincingly argued in Gounelle, *Recensions byzantines*, pp. 38–51.

52. Gounelle, *Recensions byzantines*, p. 70.

53. For my assessment I focus on the tradition shared by M1 and M2; the later M3 is significantly curtailed.

54. As is clear, for example, in 20.2, where Hades expresses wonder at the "power" of Christ, which is greater than the "power" of Satan; no one can resist his "power," and he has planned to come to Hades to seize Satan with his "powerful" hand.

55. This proclamation and demand for repentance, arguably the key to the entire narrative, is missing from M3.

56. I am obviously not covering all the early Harrowing of Hell narratives here, but it is worth noting that others also take a mediating position between universal and restrictive salvation, usually leaning one way or another. One

particularly worth noting is the Coptic *Book of the Resurrection of Jesus Christ*, associated with Bartholomew, variously dated between the fifth and ninth centuries. In this remarkable account, the wicked are indeed delivered from Hades. But not all of them. Like so many other devout Christians, the editor of the account apparently believed in God's unfathomable mercy but also thought there had to be *some* kind of limit. Three humans too wicked for even God to forgive are left in Hades: Judas Iscariot, King Herod, and Cain (7.4; are these three parallel to the famous sinners in Homer's Hades?). For introductions and translations, see Kaestli and Cherix, *L'évangile de Barthélemy*, pp. 143–252, and Schenke, "Koptischen Bartholomaeustexte."

Afterword

1. For the United States see the 2015 poll from the Pew Research Center: roughly seven of ten Americans believe in a literal heaven, and even more remarkably, six of ten believe in a literal hell (Murphy, "Most Americans").

2. See, for example, the discussion among Bible-believing, conservative evangelical Christian scholars about the biblical teaching of hell: Burk, Stackhouse, Parry, and Walls, *Four Views on Hell*. Only one of them believes in eternal conscious torment. See also, as an expression of the popular movement within evangelicalism, Bell, *Love Wins*.

3. Rather than cite the long list of egregious examples, I name only two "favorites," from each side of the heaven and hell divide (both best sellers!): Alexander, *Proof of Heaven*, and Wiese, *23 Minutes in Hell*.

Bibliography

Abbreviations

ANRW   Aufstieg und Niedergang der Römischen Welt
LCL   Loeb Classical Library
PG   *Patrologia Graeca* [= *Patrologiae Cursus Completus:* Series Graeca].
               Edited by Jacques-Paul Migne. 162 vols. Paris, 1857–1886
PL   *Patrologia Latina* [= *Patrologiae Cursus Completus:* Series Latina].
               Edited by Jacques-Paul Migne. 217 vols. Paris, 1844–1864
WUNT   Wissenschaftliche Untersuchungen zum Neuen Testament

Aitken, Ellen Bradshaw. "The Landscape of Promise in the *Apocalypse of Paul.*"
    Pages 153–65 in Shelley Matthews, Melanie Johnson-DeBaufre, and Cynthia
    Briggs Kittredge, eds., *Walk in the Ways of Wisdom: Essays in Honor of Elisabeth
    Schüssler Fiorenza.* New York: Trinity Press International, 2003.

Albinus, Lars. "The Katabasis of Er: Plato's Use of Myths, Exemplified by the
    Myth of Er." Pages 91–105 in Erik Nis Ostenfeld, ed., *Essays on Plato's* Republic.
    Aarhus: Aarhus University Press, 1998.

Alexander, Eben. *Proof of Heaven: A Neurosurgeon's Journey into the Afterlife.* New
    York: Simon and Schuster, 2012.

Allen, Thomas W. *Homeri Opera.* Tomus III. Oxford: Clarendon, 1917.

Anderson, Gary A. *Charity: The Place of the Poor in the Biblical Tradition.* New
    Haven: Yale University Press, 2013.

Annas, Julia. *An Introduction to Plato's* Republic. Oxford: Clarendon, 1981.

———. "Plato's Myths of Judgement." *Phronesis* 27 (1982): 119–43.

Arnold, E. V. *Roman Stoicism.* Cambridge: Cambridge University Press, 1911.

Atkins, Margaret, and Robin Osborne, eds. *Poverty in the Roman World.* Cambridge:
    Cambridge University Press, 2006.

Attridge, H. W., trans. *The Acts of Thomas.* Salem, OR: Polebridge, 2010.

———. "Intertextuality in the *Acts of Thomas.*" *Semeia* 80 (1997): 87–124.

———. "The Original Language of the *Acts of Thomas*." Pages 241–50 in Harold W. Attridge, John J. Collins, and Thomas H. Tobin, eds., *Of Scribes and Scrolls*. New York: University Press of America, 1990.

Austin, R. G. *P. Vergili Maronis Aeneidos Liber Sextus*. Oxford: Clarendon, 1977.

Banterle, Gabriele. *San Filastrio de Brescia: Delle Varie Eresie*. Milan: Biblioteca Ambrossiana, 1991.

Bauckham, Richard. "The *Apocalypse of Peter*: A Jewish Christian Apocalypse from the Time of Bar Kokhba." *Apocrypha* 5 (1994): 7–111.

———. "The Apocalypse of Peter: An Account of Research." *ANRW* 2.25.6 (1988): 4714–50.

———. "Early Jewish Visions of Hell." *Journal of Theological Studies* 41 (1990): 355–85.

———. *The Fate of the Dead: Studies on the Jewish and Christian Apocalypses*. Leiden: Brill, 1998.

Baudoin, Anne-Catherine, Rémi Gounelle, Justin Haynes, and Zbigniew Izydorczyk. "The Protean *Evangelium Nicodemi*." Pages 21–32 in Anne-Catherine Baudoin and Zbigniew Izydorczyk, eds., *The Oldest Manuscript of the Acts of Pilate*. Strasbourg: University of Strasbourg Press, 2019.

Baudoin, Anne-Catherine, and Zbigniew Izydorczyk. "The *Acts of Pilate* and the *Evangelium Nicodemi* in the Age of Manuscripts." Pages 13–23 in Anne-Catherine Baudoin and Zbigniew Izydorczyk, eds., *The Oldest Manuscript of the Acts of Pilate*. Strasbourg: University of Strasbourg Press, 2019.

———, eds. *The Oldest Manuscript of the Acts of Pilate: A Collaborative Commentary on the Vienna Palimpsest*. Proceedings of the International Summer Schools on Christian Apocryphal Literature. Vol. 2. Strasbourg: University of Strasbourg, 2019.

Baudy, G.-H. "Le retour d'Adam au paradis: symbole du salut de l'humanité." *Mélanges de sciences religieuse* 51 (1994): 117–46.

Beard, Mary, John North, and Simon Price, *Religions of Rome*. 2 vols. Cambridge: Cambridge University Press, 1998.

Beck, Eric. *Justice and Mercy in the Apocalypse of Peter*. WUNT 427. Tübingen: Mohr Siebeck, 2019.

Beck, Roger. "On Becoming a Mithraist: New Evidence for the Propagation of the Mysteries." Pages 175–94 in Leif E. Vaage, ed., *Religious Rivalries in the Early Roman Empire and the Rise of Christianity*. Waterloo, ON: Wilfrid Laurier University Press, 2006.

Behr, John. *Origen: On First Principles*. Oxford Early Christian Texts. 2 vols. Oxford: Oxford University Press, 2017.

Bell, Rob. *Love Wins: A Book About Heaven, Hell, and the Fate of Every Person Who Ever Lived*. San Francisco: HarperOne, 2011.

Bieder, Werner. *Die Vorstellung von der Höllenfahrt Jesu Christi*. Zurich: Zwingli, 1949.

Bolkestein, Holken. *Wohltätigkeit und Armenpflege im vorchristlichen Altertum*. Utrecht: A. Oosthoek, 1939.

Bornkamm, Günther. *Mythos und Legende in den apokryphen Thomas-Akten.* Göttingen: Vandenhoeck & Ruprecht, 1933.

Bouriant, U. "Fragments du texte grec du livre d'Énoch et de quelques écrits attribués à saint Pierre." Pages 93–147 in *Memoires publiées par les membres de la Mission Archéologique Française au Caire, IX.1.* Paris: Ernst Leroux, 1892.

Branham, R. Bracht. *Unruly Eloquence: Lucian and the Comedy of Traditions.* Cambridge, MA: Harvard University Press, 1989.

Branham, R. Bracht, and Marie-Odile Goulet-Cazé. *The Cynics: The Cynic Movement in Antiquity and Its Legacy.* Berkeley: University of California Press, 1996.

Bremmer, Jan N. "The Apocalypse of Peter: Greek or Jewish?" Pages 1–14 in Jan N. Bremmer and István Czachesz, eds., *The Apocalypse of Peter.* Leuven: Peeters, 2003; reprint, pages 269–80 in Bremmer, *Maidens, Magic and Martyrs in Early Christianity.* WUNT 379. Tübingen: Mohr Siebeck, 2017.

———. "Christian Hell: From the *Apocalypse of Peter* to the *Apocalypse of Paul.*" *Numen* 56 (2009): 298–325.

———, ed. *The Apocryphal Acts of Thomas.* Leuven: Peeters, 2001.

Bremmer, Jan N., and István Czachesz, eds. *The Apocalypse of Peter.* Leuven: Peeters, 2003.

———. *The Visio Pauli and the Gnostic Apocalypse of Paul.* Leuven: Peeters, 2007.

Brown, Peter. *Ransom of the Soul: Afterlife and Wealth in Early Western Christianity.* Cambridge, MA: Harvard University Press, 2015.

———. *Through the Eye of a Needle: Wealth, the Fall of Rome, and the Making of Christianity in the West, 350–550 AD.* Princeton: Princeton University Press, 2012.

Buchholz, Dennis D. *Your Eyes Will Be Opened: A Study of the Greek (Ethiopic) Apocalypse of Peter.* Atlanta: Scholars Press, 1988.

Burk, Danny, John Stackhouse, Robin Parry, and Jerry Walls. *Four Views on Hell.* 2nd ed. Grand Rapids, MI: Zondervan, 2016.

Callon, Callie. "Sorcery, Wheels, and Mirror Punishment in the *Apocalypse of Peter.*" *Journal of Early Christian Studies* 18 (2010): 29–49.

Carozzi, Claude. *Eschatologie et au-delà: recherches sur l'apocalypse de Paul.* Aix en Provence: Publications de l'Université de Provence, 1994.

Carroll, James. *Constantine's Sword: The Church and the Jews, A History.* Boston: Houghton Mifflin, 2001.

Cartault, A. *L'art de Virgile dans l'Enéide.* Vol. 2. Paris: University of Paris, 1926.

Casey, R. P. "The Apocalypse of Paul." *Journal of Theological Studies* 34 (1933): 1–32.

Chaine, Joseph. *Les épitres catholiques.* Paris: J. Gabalda, 1939.

Charlesworth, James H., ed. *The Old Testament Pseudepigrapha.* 2 vols. Peabody, MA: Hendrickson, 2010.

Chastel, Étienne. *Études historiques sur l'influence de la charité.* Paris: Capelle, 1853.

Clark, Elizabeth A. *The Origenist Controversy: The Cultural Construction of an Early Christian Debate.* Princeton: Princeton University Press, 1992.

———. "The Place of Jerome's Commentary on Ephesians in the Origenist Controversy: The Apokatastasis and Ascetic Ideals." *Vigiliae Christianae* 41 (1987): 154–71.

Clark, Raymond J. *Catabasis: Vergil and the Wisdom-Tradition.* Amsterdam: B. R. Grüner, 1978.

———. "The 'Wheel' and Vergil's Eschatology in *Aeneid* Book 6." *Symbolae Osloenses* 50 (1975): 121–41.

Clausen, Wendell. "An Interpretation of the *Aeneid.*" *Harvard Studies in Classical Philology* 68 (1964): 139–47.

Collins, John. "Sibylline Oracles." Pages 317–472 in Charlesworth, *Old Testament Pseudepigrapha* 1. Peabody, MA: Hendrickson, 2010.

Combs, Jason. "A Walking, Talking Cross: The Polymorphic Christology of the *Gospel of Peter.*" *Early Christianity* 5 (2013): 198–219.

Copeland, Kirsti Barrett. "'The Holy Context': Competition for the Best Afterlife in the *Apocalypse of Paul* and Late Antique Egypt." Pages 369–89 in Tobias Nicklas, Joseph Verheyden, Erik M. M. Eynikel, and Florentino Garcia Martinez, eds., *Other Worlds and Their Relation to This World: Early Jewish and Ancient Christian Traditions.* Leiden: Brill, 2010.

———. "Sinners and Post-Mortem 'Baptism' in the Acherusian Lake." Pages 91–107 in Jan N. Bremmer and István Czachesz, eds., *The Apocalypse of Peter.* Leuven: Peeters, 2003.

Countryman, L. Wm. *The Rich Christian in the Church of the Early Empire: Contradictions and Accommodations.* New York: Edwin Mellen, 1980.

Cullmann, Oscar. *Immortality of the Soul? Or Resurrection of the Dead?* New York: Macmillan, 1964.

Czachesz, István. "The Grotesque Body in the *Apocalypse of Peter.*" Pages 108–26 in Jan N. Bremmer and István Czachesz, eds., *The Apocalypse of Peter.* Leuven: Peeters, 2003.

———. *The Grotesque Body in Early Christian Discourse: Hell, Scatology, and Metamorphosis* London: Routledge, 2014.

———. "Torture in Hell and Reality. The *Visio Pauli.*" Pages 130–43 in Jan N. Bremmer and István Czachesz, *The Visio Pauli and the Gnostic Apocalypse of Paul.* Leuven: Peeters, 2007.

Daley, Brian E. *The Hope of the Early Church: A Handbook of Patristic Eschatology.* Cambridge: Cambridge University Press, 1991.

Dalton, William J. *Christ's Proclamation to the Spirits: A Study of 1 Peter 3:18–4:6.* Analecta Biblica 23. Rome: Pontifical Biblical Institute, 1965.

den Dulk, Matthijs, and Jan G. van der Watt. *2 Peter and the Apocalypse of Peter: Towards a New Perspective.* Leiden: Brill, 2019.

Denis, A.-M. "L'Apocalypse de Sophonie." Pages 793–802 in A.-M. Denis and J.-C. Haelewyck, eds., *Introduction à la littérature religieuse judéo-hellénistique: pseudépigraphes de l'Ancien Testament.* Turnhout: Brepols, 2000.

Desmond, William. *Cynics.* Berkeley: University of California, 2008.

———. *The Greek Praise of Poverty: Origins of Ancient Cynicism.* Notre Dame, IN: University of Notre Dame Press, 2006.

Diebner, Bernd Jörg. *Zephanjas Apokalypsen*. Vol. 5. *Judaische Schriften aus hellenistisch-römerischer Zeit*. Gutersloh: Gutersloher Verlagshaus, 2003.

Dieterich, Albrecht. *Nekyia: Beiträge zur Erklärung der neuentdeckten Petrus-apokalypse*. Leipzig: B. G. Teubner, 1893.

Dillmann, August. *Das Buch Henoch übersetzt und erkärt*. Leipzig: Vogel, 1853.

Dova, Stamatia. *Greek Heroes in and out of Hades*. Lanham, MD: Lexington Books, 2012.

Downs, David. *Alms: Charity, Reward, and Atonement in Early Christianity*. Waco, TX: Baylor University Press, 2016.

Dubois, J.-D. "Le docétisme des christologies gnostiques revisité." *New Testament Studies* 63 (2017): 279–304.

Dudley, D. R. *A History of Cynicism from Diogenes to the Sixth Century A.D.* London: Methuen, 1937.

Dwyer, M. E. "An Unstudied Redaction of the Visio Pauli." *Manuscripta* 32 (1988): 121–38.

Edmonds, Radcliffe G. *Myths of the Underworld Journey: Plato, Aristophanes, and the "Orphic" Gold Tablets*. Cambridge: Cambridge University Press, 2004.

Ehrman, Bart D. *The Apostolic Fathers*. 2 vols. LCL. Cambridge, MA: Harvard University, 2003.

———. *Forgery and Counterforgery: The Use of Literary Deceit in Early Christian Polemics*. Oxford: Oxford University Press, 2013.

———. *Heaven and Hell: A History of the Afterlife*. New York: Simon and Schuster, 2020.

———. *The Orthodox Corruption of Scripture: The Effect of Early Christological Controversies on the Text of the New Testament*. 2nd ed. New York: Oxford University Press, 2011.

———. *The Triumph of Christianity: How a Forbidden Religion Swept the World*. New York: Simon and Schuster, 2018.

Elliott, J. K. *The Apocryphal New Testament*. Oxford: Clarendon, 1993.

Ewald, Marie Leguori. *The Homilies of Saint Jerome*. Vol. 2. Fathers of the Church 57. Washington, DC: Catholic University of America Press, 1966.

Fairclough, H. Rushton, trans. *Virgil: Eclogues, Georgics, Aeneid I–VI*. Revised by G. P. Goold. LCL. Cambridge, MA: Harvard University Press, 1999.

Feeney, D. C. "History and Revelation in Vergil's Underworld." *Proceedings of the Cambridge Philological Society* 32 (1986): 1–24.

Fiensy, David. "Lex Talionis in the '*Apocalypse of Peter*.'" *Harvard Theological Review* 76 (1983): 255–58.

Finn, Richard. *Almsgiving in the Later Roman Empire: Christian Promotion and Practice (313–450)*. Oxford: Oxford University Press, 2006.

Fiori, Emiliano. "Death and Judgment in the *Apocalypse of Paul*: Old Imagery and Monastic Reinvention." *Zeitschrift für Antikes Christentum* 20 (2016): 92–108.

Foster, Paul. "Are There Any Early Fragments of the So-Called *Gospel of Peter*?" *New Testament Studies* 52 (2006): 1–28.

———. *The Gospel of Peter: Introduction, Critical Edition and Commentary*. Leiden: Brill, 2010.

Fox, Robin Lane. *Pagans and Christians*. New York: Knopf, 1987.

Frankfurter, David. *Elijah in Upper Egypt: The Apocalypse of Elijah and Early Egyptian Christianity*. Minneapolis: Fortress, 1993.

Frey, Jörg. *Der Brief des Judas und der zweite Brief des Petrus*. Theologischer Handkommentar zum Neuen Testament 15/11. Leipzig: Evangelische Verlagsanstalt, 2015.

——. *The Letter of Jude and the Second Letter of Peter*. Translated by Kathleen Ess. Waco, TX: Baylor University, 2018.

Friesen, Steven. "Poverty in Pauline Studies: Beyond the So-Called New Consensus." *Journal for the Study of the New Testament* 26 (2004): 323–61.

Garrison, Roman. *Redemptive Almsgiving in Early Christianity*. Journal for the Study of the New Testament Supplement Series 77. Sheffield: JSOT Press, 1993.

Gazis, George Alexander. *Homer and the Poetics of Hades*. Oxford: Oxford University Press, 2018.

Glover, T. R., trans. *Tertullian: Apology, De Spectaculis*. LCL. Cambridge, MA: Harvard University Press, 1931.

Goodman, Martin. *Mission and Conversion: Proselytizing in the Religious History of the Roman Empire*. Oxford: Clarendon, 1994.

Gounelle, Rémi. *La descente du Christ aux enfers: institutionnalisation d'une croyance*. Paris: D'Études Augustiniennes, 2000.

——. "L'enfer selon l'Évangile de Nicodème." *Revue d'histoire et de philosophie religiouses* 86 (2006): 313–33.

——. "Un enfer vide ou à-demi plein?: le salut des 'saints' dans la recension latine A de 'l'Évangile de Nicodème.'" Pages 203–23 in Jean-Daniel Kaestli and Éric Junod, eds., *Poussière de christianisme et de judaïsme antiques*. Prahins: Zèbre, 2007.

——. "Évangile de Nicodème ou Actes de Pilate." Pages 251–59 in Pierre Geoltrain and Jean-Daniel Kaestli, eds., *Écrits apocryphes chrétiens*. Paris: Éditions Gallimard, 2005.

——. "Pourquoi, selon l'Évangile de Nicodème, le Christ est-il descend aux enfers?" Pages 67–84 in J.-D. Kaestli and Daniel Marguerat, eds., *Le mystère apocryphe: introduction à une littérature*. Geneva: Labor et Fides, 1995.

——. *Les recensions byzantines de l'Évangile de Nicodème*. Turnhout: Brepols, 2008.

Gounelle, Rémi, and Zbigniew Izydorczyk, eds. *L'Évangile de Nicodème; ou, Les actes fait sous Ponce Pilate*. Turnhout: Brepols, 1997.

Grébaut, S. "Littérature éthiopienne pseudo-clémentine." *Revue de l'orient chrétien* 15 (1910): 198–214, 307–23, 425–39.

Grenz, Jesse. "Textual Divisions in Codex Vaticanus: A Layered Approach to the Delimiters in B(03)." *TC: Journal of Biblical Textual Criticism* 2 (2018): 1–22.

Grünstäudl, Wolfgang. "Enthüllung im Fragment—Notizen zu Überlieferungsgestalt und Figureninventar in der Apokalypse des Petrus." Pages 109–24 in J. Verheyden, T. Nicklas, and E. Hernitscheck, eds., *Shadowy Characters and Fragmentary Evidence*. WUNT 388. Tübingen: Mohr Siebeck, 2017.

———. *Petrus Alexandrinus*. WUNT 2 353. Tübingen: Mohr Siebeck, 2013.

Hagen, Peter, ed. *Carl-Schmidt-Kolloquium an der Martin-Luther Universität Halle-Wittenberg*. Halle: Universität Halle-Wittenberg 1990.

Hahneman, G. M. *The Muratorian Fragment and the Development of the Canon*. Oxford: Clarendon, 1992.

Halliwell, Stephen. *Greek Laughter: A Study of Cultural Psychology from Homer to Early Christianity*. Cambridge: Cambridge University Press, 2008.

Hands, R. *Charities and Social Aid in Greece and Rome*. London: Thames and Hudson, 1968.

Harbert, Bruce. *The Augustine Catechism: The Enchiridion on Faith, Hope, and Charity*. Hyde Park, NY: New City Press, 1999.

Harris, William V. *Rome's Imperial Economy*. New York: Oxford University Press, 2011.

Hauge, Matthew Ryan. *The Biblical Tour of Hell*. London: Bloomsbury T&T Clark, 2013.

Henning, Meghan. *Educating Early Christians Through the Rhetoric of Hell: "Weeping and Gnashing of Teeth" as Paideia in Matthew and the Early Church*. Tübingen: Mohr Siebeck, 2014.

Heubeck, Alfred, and Arie Hoekstra. *A Commentary on Homer's Odyssey*. Vol. 2: *Books IX–XVI*. Oxford: Oxford University Press, 1989.

Heyne, Christian Gottlob. *P. Virgilii Maronis Opera*. Vol. 2. Leipzig, 1832.

Himmelfarb, Martha. *Ascent to Heaven in Jewish and Christian Apocalypses*. New York: Oxford University Press, 1993.

———. *Tours of Hell: An Apocalyptic Form in Jewish and Christian Literature*. Philadelphia: Fortress, 1983.

Hoffman, R. Joseph. "Confluence in Early Christian and Gnostic Literature: The *Descensus Christi ad Inferos* (*Acta Pilati* XVII–XXVII)." *Journal for the Study of the New Testament* 10 (1981): 42–60.

Holman, Susan R., ed. *Wealth and Poverty in Early Church and Society*. Grand Rapids: Baker Academic, 2008.

Horsfall, Nicholas. *Companion to the Study of Virgil*. Leiden: Brill, 2000.

———. *Virgil, Aeneid 6: A Commentary*. Vol. 2: *Commentary and Appendices*. Berlin: de Gruyter, 2013.

Inwood, Michael. "Plato's Eschatological Myths." Pages 28–50 in Catalin Partenie, ed., *Plato's Myths*. Cambridge: Cambridge University Press, 2009.

Isaac, E. "1 [Ethiopic Apocalypse of] Enoch." Pages 5–89 in Charlesworth, *Old Testament Pseudepigrapha* 1.

Izydorczyk, Zbigniew. *Manuscripts of the "Evangelium Nicodemi": A Census*. Subsidia Mediaevalia 21. Toronto: Pontifical Institute of Mediaeval Studies, 1993.

———. *The Medieval Gospel of Nicodemus: Texts, Intertexts, and Contexts in Western Europe*. Medieval and Renaissance Texts and Studies 158. Tempe: Arizona State University Press, 1997.

———. "The Unfamiliar Evangelium Nicodemi." *Manuscripta* 33 (1989): 169–91.

Izydorczyk, Zbigniew, and Dario Bullita. "The Troyes Redaction of the *Evangelium Nicodemi* and Its Vernacular Legacy." Pages 571–617 in Luciana G. Soares

Santoprete and Anna Van den Kerchove, eds., *Gnose et manichéisme: entre les oasis d'Egypte et les route de la soie.* Turnhout: Brepols, 2017.

James, M. R. "A New Text of the *Apocalypse of Peter.*" *Journal of Theological Studies* 12 (1911): 36–54, 362–83, 573–83.

———. "The Rainer Fragment of the *Apocalypse of Peter.*" *Journal of Theological Studies* 32 (1931): 270–79.

———. "The Recovery of the *Apocalypse of Peter.*" *Church Quarterly Review* 159 (1915): 1–36.

James, William. *The Varieties of Religious Experience.* New York: Longmans, Green, 1902.

Jirouskova, Lenka. *Die Visio Pauli: Wege und Wandlungen einer orientalischen Apokryphe im lateinischen Mittelalter unter Einschluß der alttschechischen und deutschsprachigen Testzeugen.* Leiden: Brill, 2009.

Johnson, Ronald R. "Does Plato's Myth of Er Contribute to the Argument of the *Republic?*" *Philosophy & Rhetoric* 32 (1999): 1–13.

Johnson, W. R. *Darkness Visible: A Study of Vergil's Aeneid.* Chicago: University of Chicago Press, 1976.

Johnston, Sarah Iles. "Delphi and the Dead." Pages 283–306 in Sarah Iles Johnston and Peter T. Struck, eds., *Mantikē: Studies in Ancient Divination.* Leiden: Brill, 2005.

———. *Restless Dead: Encounters Between the Living and the Dead in Ancient Greece.* Berkeley: University of California Press, 1999.

Jones, C. P. *Culture and Society in Lucian.* Cambridge, MA: Harvard University Press, 1986.

Jouguet, P., and G. Lefebvre. "Note sur un ostrakon de Thèbes." *Bulletin de correspondance hellénique* 29 (1905): 104.

Kaestli, Jean-Daniel, and Pierre Cherix, eds. *L'évangile de Barthélemy: d'apres deux écrits apocryphes.* Turnhout: Brepols, 1993.

Kim, H. C., ed. *The Gospel of Nicodemus, Gesta Salvatoris.* Toronto: Pontifical Institute of Mediaeval Studies, 1973.

Klijn, A. F. J. *The Acts of Thomas: Introduction, Text, and Commentary.* 2nd ed. Leiden: Brill, 2003.

Knibb, M. A. "Martyrdom and Ascension of Isaiah." Pages 143–76 in Charlesworth, *Old Testament Pseudepigrapha 2.*

Knibb, Michael A., and Edward Ullendorff. *The Ethiopic Book of Enoch: A New Edition in the Light of the Aramaic Dead Sea Fragments.* Vol. 1: *Text and Apparatus;* Vol. 2: *Introduction, Translation and Commentary.* Oxford: Clarendon, 1978.

Koschorke, Klaus. *Die Polemik der Gnostiker gegen das kirchliche Christentum.* Leiden: Brill, 1978.

Kraus, T. J. "Acherousia und Elysion: Anmerkungen im Hinblick auf deren Verwendung auch im christlichen Kontext." *Mnemosyne* 56 (2003): 145–63.

———. "Fürbitte für die Toten im frühen Christentum: 'Ich werde . . . den gewahren, den sie aus der Strafe erbitten.'" Pages 355–96 in Hans Klein, V. Mihoc, and K. W. Niebuhr, eds., *Das Gebet im Neuen Testament.* WUNT 249. Tübingen: Mohr Siebeck, 2009.

————. "Die griechische Petrus-Apokalypse und ihre Relation zu ausgewählten Überlieferunsträgern apokalyptischer Stoffe." *Apocrypha* 14 (2003): 73–98.

————. "Petrus und das Ostrakon *van Haelst 741.*" *Zeitschrift für Antikes Christentum* 7 (2003): 203–11.

————. "*P.Vindob.G* 39756 + *Bodl. S Gr. Th. F.* 4 [P]: Fragmente eines Codex der griechischen Petrus-Apokalypse." *Bulletin of the American Society of Papyrologists* 40 (2003): 45–61.

Kraus, Thomas J., and Tobias Nicklas, eds. *Das Petrusevangelium und die Petrusapokalypse: Die griechischen Fragmente mit deutscher und englischer Übersetzung.* Berlin: de Gruyter, 2004.

Kroll, Josef. *Gott un Hölle: Der Mythos von Descensuskampfe.* Darmstadt: Wissenschaftliche Buchgesellschaft, 1963; reprint of 1932 original.

Lampe, Peter. "Social Welfare in the Greco-Roman World as a Background for Early Christian Practice." *Acta Theologica* 23 (2016): 1–28.

Lauwers, Jeroen. *Philosophy, Rhetoric, and Sophistry in the High Roman Empire: Maximus of Tyre and Twelve Other Intellectuals.* Leiden: Brill, 2015.

Le Goff, Jacques. *The Birth of Purgatory.* Translated by Arthur Goldhammer. Chicago: University of Chicago Press, 1984; French original 1981.

Lehtipuu, Outi. *The Afterlife Imagery in Luke's Story of the Rich Man and Lazarus.* Leiden: Brill, 2007.

Letourneau, Laval. "Mythe ou réalité? La descente du Christ aux enfers aux 2e et 3e siècles." *Studies in Religion* 3 (1974): 249–59.

Lieberman, Saul. "On Sins and Their Punishments." Pages 29–56 in Saul Lieberman, ed., *Text and Studies.* New York: Ktav, 1974; Hebrew original 1945.

Lin, Yii-Jan. *The Erotic Life of Manuscripts: New Testament Textual Criticism and the Biological Sciences.* New York: Oxford University, 2016.

Lipsius, R. A., and M. Bonnet. *Acta apostolorum apocrypha.* Vol. 2. Hildesheim: Olms, 1959.

Long, A. A., ed. *The Cambridge Companion to Early Greek Philosophy.* Cambridge: Cambridge University Press, 1999.

Long, A. A., and D. N. Sedley. *The Hellenistic Philosophers.* 2 vols. Cambridge: Cambridge University Press, 1987.

Lührmann, Dieter. *Fragmente apokryph gewordener Evangelien.* Marburg: N. G. Elwert, 2000.

————. "Petrus als Evangelist—ein bemerkenswertes Ostrakon." *Novum Testamentum* 43 (2001): 348–67.

————. "POx 4009: Ein neues Fragment des Petrusevangeliums" *Novum Testamentum* 35 (1993): 390–410.

Maas, Wilhelm. *Gott und die Hölle: Studien zum descensus Christi.* Einsiedeln: Johannes Verlag, 1979.

MacCulloch, J. A. *The Harrowing of Hell: A Comparative Study of an Early Christian Doctrine.* Edinburgh: T&T Clark, 1930.

MacMullen, Ramsay. *Christianizing the Roman Empire.* New Haven: Yale University Press, 1984.

————. *Paganism in the Roman Empire*. New Haven: Yale University Press, 1981.

Marcus, Joel. "The Gospel of Peter as a Jewish-Christian Document." *New Testament Studies* 64 (2018): 473–94.

Markschies, Cristoph. "Die Fragen des Bartholomaeus," Pages 702–850 in Christoph Markschies and Jens Schröter, eds., *Antike christliche Apokryphen in deutscher Übersetzung*. 1. Band: *Evangelien und Verwandtes*. Tübingen: Mohr Siebeck, 2012.

Marrassini, Paolo. "L'apocalisse di Pietro." Pages 171–232 in Yaqob Beyene, ed., *Etiopia e oltre: studio in onore di Lanfranco Ricci*. Naples: Istituto universitario orientale, 1994.

Martyn, John. *The Letters of Gregory the Great*. Vol. 2. Toronto: Pontifical Institute of Mediaeval Studies, 2004.

Matijević, Krešimer. *Ursprung und Charakter der homerischen Jenseitsvorstellungen*. Paderborn: Ferdinand Schöningh, 2015.

Maurer, C. "Apocalypse of Peter." Pages 663–83 in Wilhelm Schneemelcher, ed. *New Testament Apocrypha*. Vol. 2: *Writings Related to the Apostles, Apocalypses and Related Subjects*. Translated by R. McL. Wilson. Philadelphia: Westminster, 1965.

Maury, Alfred. "De l'évangile de Nicodème." *Revue de philologie de littérature et d'histoire anciennes* 2 (1847): 428–49.

McCant, Jerry. "The *Gospel of Peter:* The Docetic Question Re-examined." PhD diss., Emory University, 1978.

————. "The *Gospel of Peter:* Docetism Reconsidered." *New Testament Studies* 30 (1984): 258–73.

McClymond, Michael. "*Origenes Vindicatus vel Rufinus Redivivus? A Review of Ilaria Ramelli's The Christian Doctrine of Apokatastasis*." *Theological Studies* 76 (2015): 813–26.

Merkt, Andreas. *Das Fegefeuer: Entstehung und Funktion einer Idee*. Darmstadt: Wissenschaftliche Buchgesellschaft, 2005.

Merz, Annette. "The Fictitious Self-Exposition of Paul: How Might Intertextual Theory Suggest a Reformulation of the Hermeneutics of Pseudepigraphy." Pages 113–32 in Thomas L. Brodie, Dennis R. MacDonald, and Stanley E. Porter, eds., *The Intertextuality of the Epistles: Explorations of Theory and Practice*. Sheffield: Sheffield Phoenix, 2006.

————. *Die fictive Selbstauslegung des Paulus: Intertextuelle Studien zur Intention und Rezeption der Pastoralbriefe*. Göttingen: Vandenhoeck & Ruprecht; Fribourg: Academic Press, 2004.

Mestre, Francesca. "Lucien, les philosophes et les philosophies." *Itaca: Quaderns Catalans de Cultura Classica* 28–29 (2012–2013): 63–82.

Metzger, Bruce. *The Canon of the New Testament: Its Origin, Development, and Significance*. Oxford: Clarendon, 1987.

————. *The Text of the New Testament: Its Transmission, Corruption, and Restoration*. 4th ed. New York: Oxford University Press, 2005.

Meyer, M., and Frederik Wisse. "NHC VIII, 2: 'Letter of Peter to Philip.' Pages 234–51 in John Sieber, ed., *Nag Hammadi Codex VIII*. Coptic Gnostic Library. Leiden: Brill, 1991.

Meyer, Marvin, ed. *The Nag Hammadi Scriptures*. San Francisco: HarperOne, 2007.

Michels, Agness Kirsopp. "Lucretius and the Sixth Book of the *Aeneid*." *American Journal of Philology* 65 (1944): 135–48.

Mitchell, Stephen, and Peter Nuffelen. *One God: Pagan Monotheism in the Roman Empire*. Cambridge: Cambridge University Press, 2010.

Mommsen, Theodore. "Zur lateinischen Stichometri." *Hermes* 21 (1886): 142–56.

Moricca, Umberto. "Un Nuovo Testo dell' 'Evangelo di Bartolomeo.'" *Revue biblique* 30 (1921): 481–516.

Moss, Candida. "On the Dating of Polycarp: Rethinking the Place of the *Martyrdom of Polycarp* in the History of Christianity." *Early Christianity* 1 (2010): 539–74.

Müller, C. Detlef G. "Apocalypse of Peter." Pages 620–38 in Wilhelm Schneemelcher, ed., *New Testament Apocrypha*. Vol. 2: *Writings Related to the Apostles, Apocalypses and Related Subjects*. Louisville: Westminster/John Knox, 1992.

Murphy, Caryle. "Most Americans Believe in Heaven . . . and Hell." Pew Research Center. November 10, 2015. http://www.pewresearch.org/fact-tank/2015/11/10/most-americans-believe-in-heaven-and-hell/.

Mynors, R. A. B. *P. Vergili Maronis Opera*. Oxford: Oxford University Press, 1969.

Nesselrath, Heinz-Günther. "Lucien et le Cynisme." *L'Antiquité Classique* 67 (1998): 121–35.

———. "Skeletons, Shades, and Feasting Heroes: The Manifold Underworlds of Lucian of Samosata." Pages 45–60 in Ilinca Tanaseanu-Döbler, Gabriela Ryser, Anna Lefteratou, and Konstantinos Stamatopoulos, eds., *Reading the Way to the Netherworld: Education and the Representations of the Beyond in Later Antiquity*. Göttingen: Vandenhoeck & Ruprecht, 2017.

Nickelsburg, George *1 Enoch 1: A Commentary on the Book of 1 Enoch, Chapters 1–36; 81–108*. Hermeneia. Minneapolis: Fortress, 2001.

Nickelsburg, George, and James C. VanderKam. *1 Enoch: A New Translation Based on the Hermeneia Commentary*. Minneapolis: Fortress, 2004.

Nicklas, Tobias. "'Insider' und 'Outsider': Überlegungen zum historischen Kontext der Darstellung 'Jenseitiger Orte' in der *Offenbarung des Petrus*." Pages 35–49 in Walter Ameling, ed., *Topographie des Jenseits: Studien zur Geschichte des Todes in Kaiserzeit und Spätantike*. Stuttgart: Franz Steiner Verlag, 2011.

———. "Ein 'neutestamentliches apokryphon'? Zum Umstrittenen Kanonbezug des sog. 'Petrusevangeliums." *Vigiliae Christianae* 56 (2002): 260–72.

———. "Zwei petrinische Apokryphen im Akhmim-Codex oder Eines? Kritische Anmerkungen und Gedanken." *Apocrypha* 16 (2005): 75–96; reprinted and expanded, pages 32–50, in T. Nicklas, ed., *Studien zym Petrusevangelum*. WUNT 453. Tübingen: Mohr Siebeck, 2020.

Niebuhr, Reinhold. *The Nature and Destiny of Man*. Vol. 2. New York: Charles Scribner's Sons, 1943.

Nixon, Paul. *Plautus.* Vol. 5. LCL. Cambridge, MA: Harvard University Press, 1938.

Nock, Arthur Darby. *Conversion: The Old and the New in Religion from Alexander the Great to Augustine of Hippo.* London: Oxford University Press, 1933.

Nongbri, Brent. *Before Religion: A History of a Modern Concept.* New Haven: Yale University Press, 2015.

Norden, Eduard. *P. Vergilius Maro, Aeneis Buch VI.* Leipzig: Teubner, 1903.

———. "Die Petrus-Apokalypse und ihre antiken Vorbilder." Pages 218–33 in *Kleine Schriften zum klassischen Altertum.* Berlin: de Gruyter, 1966; original article 1893.

———. "Vergilstudien." *Hermes* 28 (1893): 360–406.

Norelli, Enrico. "Pertinence theologique et canonicite: les premières apocalypses Chretiennes." *Apocrypha* 8 (1997): 147–64.

Norwood, Frances. "The Tripartite Eschatology of *Aeneid* 6." *Classical Philology* 49 (1954): 15–26.

Ogden, Daniel. *Greek and Roman Necromancy.* Princeton: Princeton University Press, 2001.

O'Hara, James J. *Inconsistency in Roman Epic: Studies in Catullus, Lucretius, Vergil, Ovid, and Lucan.* Cambridge: Cambridge University Press, 2007.

Oikonomopoulou, Katerina. "Journeying the Underworld of Lucian's *Cataplus.* Pages 61–74 in Ilinca Tanaseanu-Döbler, Gabriela Ryser, Anna Lefteratou, and Konstantinos Stamatopoulos eds., *Reading the Way to the Netherworld: Education and the Representations of the Beyond in Later Antiquity.* Göttingen: Vandenhoeck & Ruprecht, 2017.

Otis, Brooks. "Three Problems of *Aeneid* 6." *Transactions and Proceedings of the American Philological Association* 90 (1959): 165–79.

Ozimic, D. "Der pseudoaugustinische Sermo CLX." PhD diss., University of Graz, 1979.

Pagels, Elaine H. "Gnostic and Orthodox Views of Christ's Passion: Paradigms for the Christian's Response to Persecution?" Pages 262–88 in Bentley Layton, ed., *The Rediscovery of Gnosticism.* 2 vols. Leiden: Brill, 1981.

Parkin, Anneliese. "'You Do Him No Service': An Exploration of Pagan Almsgiving." Pages 60–82 in Margaret Atkins and Robin Osborne, eds., *Poverty in the Roman World.* Cambridge: Cambridge University Press, 2009.

Parry, Adam. "The Two Voices of Virgil's *Aeneid.*" *Arion: A Journal of Humanities and the Classics* 2 (1963): 66–80.

Partenie, Catalin, ed. *Plato's Myths.* Cambridge: Cambridge University Press, 2009.

Perkins, Pheme. *The Gnostic Dialogue: The Early Church and the Crisis of Gnosticism.* New York: Paulist, 1980.

Peterson, Erik. "Die 'Taufe' im Acherusischen See." *Vigiliae Christianae* 9 (1955): 1–20.

Philippart, Guy. "Les fragments palimpsestes de l'Évangile de Nicodème dans le *Vindobonensis 563.*" *Analecta Bollandiana* 107 (1989): 171–88.

Pierce, Chad T. *Spirits and the Proclamation of Christ: 1 Peter 3:18–22 in Light of Sin and Punishment Traditions in Early Jewish and Christian Literature*. Tübingen: Mohr Siebeck, 2011.

Piovanelli, Pierluigi. "Katabáseis orphico-pythagoriciennes ou *Tours of Hell* apocalyptiques juifs?: la fausse alternative posée par la typologie des péchés et des châtiments dans l'Apocalypse de Pierre." Pages 397–414 in P. Bonnechère and G. Cursaru, eds., *Katabasis dans la tradition littéraire et religieuse de la Grèce ancienne*. Namur: Société des Études Classiques, 2015.

———. "The Miraculous Discovery of the Hidden Manuscript, or the Paratextual Function of the Prologue to the *Apocalypse of Paul*." Pages 23–49 in in Jan N. Bremmer and István Czachesz, eds., *The Visio Pauli and the Gnostic Apocalypse of Paul*. Leuven: Peeters, 2007.

———. "Les origines de l'Apocalypse de Paul reconsidérées." *Apocrypha* 4 (1993): 25–37.

Poirier, Paul-Hubert. "Gnostic Sources and the Prehistory of the *Descensus ad Inferos*." *Apocrypha* 21 (2010): 73–81.

Prümm, K. "De genuine Apocalypsis Petri textu: Examen testium iam notorum et novi fragmenti Raineriani." *Biblica* 10 (1929): 62–80.

Rambo, Lewis R., and Charles E. Farhadian, eds. *The Oxford Handbook of Religious Conversion*. New York: Oxford University Press, 2014.

Ramelli, Ilaria L. E. *The Christian Doctrine of Apokatastasis: A Critical Assessment from the New Testament to Eriugena*. Supplements to Vigiliae Christianae 120. Leiden: Brill, 2013.

Reardon, B. P. *Courants littéraires grecs des IIe et IIIe siècles après J.-C.* Paris: Belle Lettres, 1971.

Reece, Steve. "Homer's Asphodel Meadow." *Greek, Roman, and Byzantine Studies* 47 (2007): 389–400.

———. "The Miraculous Discovery of the Hidden Manuscript, or the Paratextual Function of the Prologue of the *Apocalypse of Paul*. Pages 23–49 in Jan N. Bremmer and István Czachesz, eds., *The Visio Pauli and the Gnostic Apocalypse of Paul*. Leuven: Peeters, 2007.

Reicke, Bo. *The Disobedient Spirits and Christian Baptism: A Study of 1 Peter III.19 and Its Context*. Eugene, OR: Wipf & Stock, 2005; originally published 1946.

Rettig, John, trans. *Augustine: Tractates on John 1–10*. Washington, DC: Catholic University of America Press, 1988.

Rhee, Helen. *Wealth and Poverty in Early Christianity*. Minneapolis: Fortress, 2017.

Rives, James. *Religion in the Roman Empire*. Oxford: Blackwell, 2017.

———. "Religious Choice and Religious Change in Classical and Late Antiquity: Models and Questions." *Antigüedad, religiones y sociedades* 9 (2011): 265–80.

Roberts, Alexander, and James Donaldson, eds. *The Ante-Nicene Fathers*. Vol. 5: *Hippolytus, Cyprian, Caius, Novatian, Appendix*. New York: Christian Literature Publishing, 1886.

Roddy, Kevin. "Politics and Religion in Late Antiquity: The Roman Imperial *Adventus* Ceremony and the Christian Myth of the Harrowing of Hell." *Apocrypha* 11 (2000): 147–79.

Rohde, Erwin. *Psyche: The Cult of Souls and Belief in Immortality Among the Greeks.* 8th ed. Translated by W. B. Hillis. Eugene, OR: Wipf & Stock, 2006; German original of 8th ed. 1925.

Rosenstiehl, Jean-Marc. "L'itineraire de Paul dans l'au-delà: contribution à l'étude de l'Apocalypse apocryphe de Paul." Pages 197–212 in Peter Hagen, ed., *Carl-Schmidt-Kolloqium an der Martin-Luther Universität Halle-Wittenberg.* Halle: Universität Halle-Wittenberg 1990.

Roukema, Riemer. "Paul's Rapture to Paradise in Early Christian Literature." Pages 267–83 in Anthony Hilhorst and George H. van Kooten, eds., *The Wisdom of Egypt: Jewish, Early Christian, and Gnostic Essays in Honour of Gerard P. Luttikhuizen.* Leiden: Brill, 2005.

Schärtl, Monika. "Das Nicodemusevangelium, die Pilatusakten und die 'Höllenfahrt Christi.'" Pages 231–61 in Chrisoph Markschies and Jen Schröter, eds., *Antike christliche Apokryphen in deutscher Übersetzung.* Tübingen: Mohr/Siebeck, 2012.

Scheck, Thomas P. *Origen: Commentary on the Epistle to the Romans, Books 1–5.* Washington, DC: Catholic University of America Press, 2009.

Schenke, Hans-Martin. "Die koptischen Bartholomaeustexte: 'Das Buch der Auferstehung Jesu Christi, unseres Herrn.'" Pages 581–85 in Christoph Markschies and Jens Schröter, eds., *Antike christliche Apokryphen in deutscher Übersetzung.* 1. Band: *Evangelien und Verwandtes.* Tübingen: Mohr Siebeck, 2012

Schmiel, Robert. "Achilles in Hades." *Classical Philology* 82 (1987): 35–37.

Schneemelcher, Wilhelm, ed. *New Testament Apocrypha.* Vol. 2: *Writings Related to the Apostles, Apocalypses and Related Subjects.* Translated by R. McL. Wilson. Louisville: Westminster/John Knox, 1992.

Schott, Jeremy M., and Mark J. Edwards. *Macarius, Apocriticus: Translated with Introduction and Commentary.* Liverpool: Liverpool University Press, 2015.

Sedley, D. N., ed. *The Cambridge Companion to Greek and Roman Philosophy.* Cambridge: Cambridge University Press, 2003.

Siker, Jeffrey. "The Canonical Status of the Catholic Epistles in the Syriac New Testament." *Journal of Theological Studies* 38 (1987): 311–40.

Silverstein, T., and A. Hilhorst. *Apocalypse of Paul: A New Critical Edition of Three Long Latin Versions.* Geneva: Patrick Cramer, 1997.

Silverstein, Theodore. "The Date of the *Apocalypse of Paul.*" *Mediaeval Studies* 24 (1962): 335–48.

Sock-Hesketh, Jonathan. "Circles and Mirrors: Understanding 1 Enoch 21–32." *Journal for the Study of the Pseudepigrapha* 21 (2000): 27–58.

Solmsen, Friedrich. "Greek Ideas of the Hereafter in Virgil's Roman Epic." *Proceedings of the American Philosophical Society* 112 (1968): 8–14.

———. "The World of the Dead in Book 6 of the *Aeneid.*" *Classical Philology* 67 (1972): 31–41.

Sommer, Michael. "Between Jewish and Egyptian Thinking: The Apocalypse of Sophonias as a Bridge Between Two Worlds?" Pages 319–42 in Jens Schröter, Tobias Nicklas, and Armand Puig i Tàrrech, eds., *Dreams, Visions, Imaginations:*

Jewish, Christian, and Gnostic Views of the World to Come. Beihefte zur Zeitschrift für die neutestamentliche Wissenschaft 247. Berlin: de Gruyter, 2021.

———. "Von Monstern und Männern. Eine Auseinandersetzung mit E. Reinmuths 'Parodien der Macht.'" Pages 353–76 in Stefan Alkier and C. Böttrich, eds., *Neutestamentliche Wissenschaft in gesellschaftlicher Verantwortung. Studien im Anschluss an Eckart Reinmuth.* Leipzig: EVA, 2017.

Sourvinou-Inwood, Christiane. *"Reading" Greek Death to the End of the Classical Period.* Oxford: Clarendon, 1996.

Spitta, Friedrich. "Die Petrusapokalypse und der zweite Petrusbrief." *Zeitschrift für die neutestamentliche Wissenschaft und die Kunde der älteren Kirche* 12 (1911): 237–42.

Stanford, W. B. *Homer: Odyssey I–XII.* London: Bristol Classical Press, 2003; reprint of 1959 2nd ed.

Stark, Rodney. *The Rise of Christianity: How the Obscure, Marginal Jesus Movement Became the Dominant Religious Force in the Western World in a Few Centuries.* San Francisco: HarperSanFrancisco, 1996.

Steindorff, R. F. *Die Apokalypse des Elias: eine unbekannte Apokalypse und Bruchstücke der Sophonias-Apokalypse: koptische Texte, Übersetzung, Glossar.* Leipzig: Hinrichs, 1899.

Steward, Alistair. *Melito of Sardis: On Pascha.* Yonkers, NY: St. Vladimir's Seminary Press, 2016.

Stuckenbruck, Loren. "The 'Otherworld' and the *Epistle of Enoch.*" Pages 79–93 in Tobias Nicklas, Joseph Verheyden, Erik M. M. Eynikel, and Florentino Garcia Martinez, eds., *Other Worlds and Their Relation to This World: Early Jewish and Ancient Christian Traditions.* Leiden: Brill, 2010.

Sundberg, A. "Canon Muratori: A Fourth Century List." *Harvard Theological Review* 66 (1973): 1–41.

Swete, H. D. *The Akhmîm Fragment of the Apocryphal Gospel of St. Peter.* London: Macmillan, 1893.

Tarrant, H. A. S. "Literal and Deeper Meanings in Platonic Myths." Pages 47–65 in Catherine Collobert, Pierre Destrée, and Francisco J. Gonzalez, eds., *Plato and Myth: Studies on the Use and Status of Platonic Myths.* Leiden: Brill, 2012.

———. "Myth as a Tool of Persuasion in Plato." *Antichthon* 24 (1990): 19–31.

Tarrant, R. J. "Aeneas and the Gates of Sleep." *Classical Philology* 77 (1982): 51–55.

Tigchelaar, Eibert. "Is the Liar Bar Kokhba? Considering the Date and the Provenance of the Greek (Ethiopic) *Apocalypse of Peter.*" Pages 63–77 in Jan N. Bremmer and István Czachesz, eds., *The Apocalypse of Peter.* Leuven: Peeters, 2003.

Tischendorf, Constantine. *Evangelia Apocrypha.* 2nd ed. Hildesheim: George Olms, 1966; original Leipzig, 1866.

Tissot, Yves. "Les Actes apocryphes de Thomas: exemple de recueil composite." Pages 223–32 in François Bovon, Michel van Esbroeck, Richard Goulet, Eric Junod, and Jean-Daniel Kaestli, eds., *Les Actes apocryphes des Apôtres: christianisme et monde païen.* Geneva: Labor et Fides, 1981.

———. "L'encratisme des Actes de Thomas." *ANRW* 2.25.6 (1988): 4415–30.

Treat, Jay. "Two Manuscript Witnesses to the *Gospel of Peter*." Pages 391–99 in David J. Lull, ed., *Society of Biblical Literature 1990 Seminar Papers*. Society of Biblical Literature Seminar Papers 29. Atlanta: Scholars Press, 1990.

Trigg, Joseph. *Origen*. Atlanta: John Knox, 1983.

Trumbower, Jeffrey A. *Rescue for the Dead: The Posthumous Salvation of Non-Christians in Early Christianity*. New York: Oxford University Press, 2001.

Tsagarakis, Odysseus. *Studies in Odyssey 11*. Stuttgart: Franz Steiner, 2000.

Turner, E. G. *The Typology of the Codex*. Philadelphia: University of Pennsylvania, 1977.

Unger, Dominic J. *St. Irenaeus of Lyons Against the Heresies*. Book 1. Ancient Christian Writers 55. New York: Paulist, 1992.

Vaganay, Léon. *L'Évangile de Pierre*. Paris: J. Gabalda, 1930.

Vaillant, A. "L'homélie d'Épiphane sur l'ensevelissement du Christ: texte vieux-slave, texte grec et traduction française." *Radovi staroslavenskog instituta* 3 (1958): 6–100.

van Haelst, J. *Catalogue des papyrus littéraires juifs et chrétiens*. Paris: Publication de la Sorbonne, 1976.

van Minnen, Peter. "The Greek *Apocalypse of Peter*." Pages 15–39 in Jan N. Bremmer and István Czachesz, eds., *The Apocalypse of Peter*. Leuven: Peeters, 2003.

Verheyden, Joseph, Reimund Bieringer, Jens Schröter, and Ines Jäger, eds. *Docetism in the Early Church: The Quest for an Elusive Phenomenon*. WUNT 402. Tübingen: Mohr Siebeck, 2018.

Veyne, Paul. *Bread and Circuses: Historical Sociology and Political Pluralism*. London: Allen Lane, 1990; French original 1976.

Vogels, Heinz-Jürgen. *Christi Abstieg ins Totenreich und das Läuterungsgericht an den Toten: Eine bibeltheologish-dogmatische Untersuchung zum Glaubensartikel "descendit ad inferos."* Freiburg: Herder, 1976.

von Harnack, Adolf. "Bruchstücker des Evangeliums und der Apokalypse des Petrus." Pages 949–65 in *Sitzungsberichte der Königlich Preussischen Akademie der Wissenschaften zu Berlin*. Berlin, 1892.

———. *Geschichte der altchristlichen Literatur bis Eusebius*, Vol. 2: *Die Chronologie*. Leipzig: Hinrichs, 1904.

Vorwerk, Matthias. "Mythos und Kosmos: Zur Topographie des Jenseits in Er-Mythos des platonischen 'Staates.'" *Philologus* 146 (2002): 46–64.

Wacker, Marie-Theres. *Weltordnung und Gericht: Studien zu 1 Henoch 22*. Würzburg: Echter, 1982.

Weinel, Heinrich. "Offenbarung des Petrus." Pages 285–90 in Edgar Hennecke, ed., *Handbuch zu den neutestamentliche Apokryphen*. Tübingen: Mohr, 1904.

Wessely, C. *Les plus anciens monuments du christianisme: écrits sur papyrus II*. Patrologia Orientalis 18/3. Paris: Firmin-Didot, 1924.

West, Martin L., ed. *Homerus: Odyssea*. Bibleotheca Teubneriana 2026. Berlin: de Gruyter, 2017.

Whitmarsh, Tim. "The Invention of Atheism and the Invention of Religion in Classical Athens." Pages 37–52 in Babett Edelmann-Singer, Tobias Nicklas, Janet E. Spittler, and Luigi Walt, eds., *Sceptic and Believer in Ancient Mediterranean Religions*. WUNT 443. Tübingen: Mohr Siebeck, 2019.

Wicks, Jare. "Christ's Saving Descent to the Dead: Early Witnesses from Ignatius of Antioch to Origen." *Pro Ecclesia* 17 (2008): 281–309.

Wiese, Bill. *23 Minutes in Hell: One Man's Story About What He Saw, Heard, and Felt in That Place of Torment*. Lake Mary, FL: Charisma House, 2006.

Williams, R. D. "The Sixth Book of the *Aeneid*." *Greece and Rome* 11 (1964): 48–63.

Wilmart, A., and E. Tisserant. "Fragments grecs et latins: de l'Évangile de Barthélemy." *Revue biblique* 10 (1913): 161–90, 321–68.

Winstanley, E. W. "The Outlook of Early Christian Apocalypses." *Expositor* 19 (1920): 161–84.

Wintermute, O. S. "Apocalypse of Zephaniah: A New Translation and Introduction." Pages 497–516 in Charlesworth, *Old Testament Pseudepigrapha* 1.

Witakowsky, Witold. "Apocalypse of Zephaniah." Pages 2:528–29 in Roger S. Bagnall, Kai Brodersen, Craige B. Champion, Andrew Erskine, and Sabine R. Huebner, eds., *Encyclopedia of Ancient History*. 13 vols. Malden, MA: Wiley-Blackwell, 2012.

Wortley, John. "The Spirit of Rivalry in Early Christian Monachism." *Greek, Roman, and Byzantine Studies* 33 (1992): 383–404.

Zahn, Theodore. *Geschichte des neutestamentlichen Kanons*. 2 vols. Erlangen: Andreas Deichert, 1888.

———. *Grundriss der Geschichte des neutestamentlichen Kanons: Eine Ergänzung zu der Einleitung in das Neue Testament*. 2nd ed. Leipzig: Deichert, 1904; 1st ed., 1901.

Zetzel, James E. G. "Romane Memento: Justice and Judgment in *Aeneid* 6." *Transactions of the American Philological Association* 119 (1989:) 263–84.

Zuurmond, Rocus, and Curt Niccum. "The Ethiopic Version of the New Testament." Pages 231–52 in Bart D. Ehrman and Michael W. Holmes, eds., *The Text of the New Testament in Contemporary Research: Essays on the Status Quaestionis*. Studies and Documents 46. 2nd ed. Leiden: Brill, 2012.

Index

Abel, 58, 250n15

abortion, 75, 76, 99, 159t.1, 195

abstinence, 97, 114

Acheron river, 193

Acherusian Lake, 80, 93, 95, 163, 190, 192, 193, 194

Achilles, 15; arrival narrative, 242n21; *kleos* of, 13, 17, 18–20; on life as preferred to death, 18, 20–21, 63, 243n29; Neoptolemus, son of, 20–21, 242n25; as ruler of Hades, 19–20, 243n29

Acts, 67, 81, 121, 213, 218

Acts of Paul, 183, 187, 274n18

Acts of Peter, 147

Acts of Pilate, 224–26, 268n18, 285n35, 286n39

Acts of Thomas, 1, 7, 100, 102, 113–15, 125, 139–41, 235, 263n29

Adam: Christ's blessing of, 231; deliverance of, 226, 227; descendants of, 221, 226, 227, 228, 285n37; Eve, 219, 258n88; in Hades, 224, 232; his responsibility for all peoples' deaths, 200–201; paradise of, 93, 258n88; salvation of, 219, 221, 226, 227, 266n46; Seth, son of, 226, 229, 283n20; sin of, 215, 216, 227; soul of, 278n69; tree of the knowledge

of good and evil, 227, 230; work of Christ compared to work of, 201–2

adultery, 34, 75, 83, 87, 90, 140–41, 159t.1, 195

Aelius Theon, 78

Aeneas: Anchises, reunion with, 27–28, 35–36, 41–43; Dido's encounter with, 31–32; encounters with the dead, 28–31; exit through ivory gate, 46; future descendants of, 42, 43; katabasis of, 2, 23–24, 26, 27–28, 68–69; pity for the unburied, 29–30, 32; refrain of "how did you get here," 30; return to false dream world, 47; Sibyl as guide for, 27–31; toil of, 24

Aeneid (Virgil): Aeneas and Sibyl leave the underworld, 45–46; Aeneas's visit to Hades, 6; authorship of, 23–24, 26, 243nn37,38; entrance to the underworld, 28–29; inconsistencies in, 26–27, 35–36, 39, 41, 244n46, 245n53, 246n62; katabasis, 2, 23–24, 26, 68–69; murder victims, 58; *Odyssey* compared with, 11, 24, 248n85; postmortem experience in, 81; redaction of, 26; shades in, 45, 46, 47, 239n10; structure of, 24; textual transpositions in, 39, 246n62